THE ARAB WORLD TODAY

MORROE BERGER is professor of sociology and director of the Program in Near Eastern Studies at Princeton University and a consultant to the Ford Foundation's program of training on foreign areas. He has been a visiting professor at Columbia and the University of California at Berkeley and consultant on special projects to the U.S. National Security Resources Board, the Twentieth Century Fund, and the Fund for the Republic. Born in New York City in 1917, he attended the City College and did his graduate work at Columbia under Robert M. MacIver. In recent years he has also been active in international scholarship. In 1960 he organized and directed an international conference, held in Cairo, on "The New Metropolis in the Arab World." He is corresponding member of the Institute for the Study of Economic and Social Development of the University of Paris and honorary member of the Peruvian Institute of Higher Islamic Studies. In addition to three previous books, he has been widely published in the scholarly journals, general magazines, and newspapers, and is the translator and editor of *Madame de Staël on Politics, Literature, and National Character*.

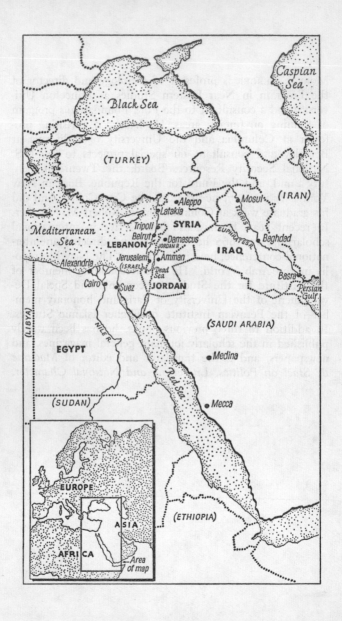

THE ARAB WORLD TODAY

Morroe Berger

ANCHOR BOOKS
Doubleday & Company, Inc.
Garden City, New York
1964

The Arab World Today was originally published by
Doubleday & Company, Inc., in 1962.

For PAULA

Contents

List of Tables

Chapter 7

Preface

In 1902 James Bryce, using language that our more equalitarian and scientific generation carefully avoids, remarked in a lecture on "The Relations of the Advanced and the Backward Nations of Mankind": ". . . our own time stands eminent and peculiar in this, that it marks the completion of a process by which all the races of the world have been affected, and all the backward ones placed in a more or less complete dependence upon the more advanced." Just sixty years later virtually all these "backward nations" are at least politically "more or less" completely independent of the "advanced" ones.

It took Europe four hundred years to reach that apogee of its remarkable expansion to other continents. Now the burst of energy that propelled Europe seems to be stirring the new nations and states created out of Europe's overseas domains. Intensely nationalistic, they at once claim to be seeking to express their own nature and in fact seek to become more and more like their former rulers. Their histories are rather diverse but they all strive for the same future: national strength through "modernization."

There has been a quickening in the process of subjection and liberation. When the British were defeated by the thirteen American colonies they had been there for nearly two hundred years. When Spain lost its colonies in South America it marked the end of an empire three hundred years old. But Europe went into Africa on a grand scale only in the latter half of the nineteenth century, and less than one hundred years later its empire is fast slipping away. The Arab world from Egypt to Iraq, the subject of this book, was under Western political control for an even shorter period. It was only sixty or sixty-five years from the British occupation of Egypt in 1882 (followed by the British-French mandates under the League of Nations after World War I) down to the end of substantial British influence in Jordan and Iraq somewhere in the 1950s. Yet so profound has this Western influence been that no facet of Arab life today can be considered apart from it, even though the impulse toward change among Arabs is now largely self-generated.

On the surface, much of what can be said about the Arabs can also be said about other peoples of Asia, Africa, and Latin America. Nationalism, industrialization, secularization and so on, are goals that absorb them all. But each deserves its own treatment, for the differences in the development of these new nations and states are far more significant (and interesting) than the fact that they have much in common. The Arab world is worth our attention not merely because it produces oil and headlines but because it is the center of a great historic civilization very close to our own. We ought to know more about these people whose history and culture are so meshed with ours and who are stirring again.

Ignorance of the Arab world in the West is often appalling. A Palestinian Arab friend of mine was asked, by a lady interested in exotic Christians, to address her congregation on the "mission" that converted his people. He had to explain patiently that his ancestors were converted by Jesus Christ and the Apostles. Lack of knowledge about Arabs is equaled by lack of sympathy for them. People who melt at the plight of Asians and Africans are unaffected by that of Arabs and Moslems. One reason is the Arab-Israeli conflict. Another is the common but mistaken impression that all Arab lands have great oil resources that they waste. A third is Arab opposition to Western political influence, which puts the Arabs in headlines that spell trouble for the West.

I have tried in this book to get away from the Arabs of the newspaper headlines and to see how they live, work, marry, bear and rear children—how what they do makes

them what they are. This is not easy, because what I have
personally been able to observe is, of course, limited, and
there are few objective studies to draw on. The journalists
are concerned with the news of war and diplomacy. The
Orientalists have been absorbed in detailed philological
and literary analysis. The historians of the Near East are
few and have produced surprisingly little that is relevant
to the Arabs of today. And the Arabs themselves have only
recently begun to study their past and present institutions
in a way that can help the Westerner to understand them.
I have drawn on such studies as I have found useful, as
well as upon what I have seen of Arab life. I am indebted
to the Arabs for their hospitality and for their willingness
to suffer—and to satisfy—my curiosity about them over
many years. I do not delude myself by thinking that I
have described them adequately in all their variety. But I
hope that my considerable effort to understand them and
to help others to do so will justify the faith many Arabs
have placed in me.

I think I may have drawn too sharp a distinction between "the Arab" and "the Westerner" and perhaps identified "the Westerner" with "the American." So this book
undoubtedly tells not only about the Arabs but also, in
what it includes and omits and in its comparisons, about
the author as an American and a social scientist. "Comparison," said George Santayana forty years ago in *Character and Opinion in the United States,* "is the expedient
of those who cannot reach the heart of the things compared. . . ." Though this may be true, I have been unable
to avoid comparison, just as I have been unable to avoid
the abstraction of "the Arab" and "the Westerner." Santayana had to admit his own guilt on the latter point. "I
speak of the American in the singular," he wrote, "as if
there were not millions of them, north and south, east and
west, of both sexes, of all ages, and of various races, professions, and religions. Of course the one American I speak
of is mythical; but to speak in parables is inevitable in
such a subject, and it is perhaps as well to do so frankly."
Even if he had spoken of classes of Americans or of indi-

viduals, he added, he would still be speaking in symbols and abstractions. And so it is exactly in this book on "the Arab."

I must add a word of acknowledgement. I am very grateful to two scholars for their helpful comments on the first draft of this book. They are Mr. Albert Hourani, Director of the Centre of Middle Eastern Studies, St. Antony's College, Oxford, and Mr. Bernard Lewis, Professor of Near Eastern History in the School of Oriental and African Studies of the University of London. I have been helped, also, by Mr. Elie Kedourie, Reader in Political Science and Public Administration at the London School of Economics. Mr. William Michelson and Mr. Nadim Khalaf assisted me in research. The Program in Near Eastern Studies at Princeton University has provided several occasions and the means for me to study and visit the area.

Several publishers have kindly permitted me to use material which first appeared in their pages: Congress for Cultural Freedom, publisher of *Encounter;* Center of International Studies at Princeton University, publisher of *World Politics* and the author's monograph, *Military Elite and Social Change* (1960); and Frederick Praeger, publisher of *The Middle East in Transition* (New York, 1958, edited by Walter Z. Laqueur).

Part One

ARABS AND MOSLEMS:
HISTORY AND PERSONALITY

Section One

MARX AND ENGELS:
HISTORY AND PERSONALITY

CHAPTER 1

The Arab World

The Arab Moslem countries occupy a special place in the relations between the Western world and the emerging nations of Asia and Africa. Most of these peoples the West simply ignored until it conquered them. Only with the world of Islam has Western Europe ever had intimate relations, peaceful or warlike, on a level of equality. Whereas the West became involved with most of Asia and Africa only after its own expansion in the modern era, its involvement with the Arabs and Moslems began at the birth and first deployment of the Islamic community more than thirteen hundred years ago. Western Europe has spread toward Asia and Africa, but the Arab Moslem world expanded into Europe centuries before the Crusades and later invasions reversed the process. Geographical proximity between Europe and the Near East has been matched by cultural and religious affinity. Although the world of Arabs and Moslems is a "foreign" one to us, it has never been an unknown, "exotic" civilization to be "discovered" in the manner of Japan, China, and inner Africa. True to its name, the Near or Middle East has been only slightly more remote from the West than, say, southeastern Europe, and much closer to the West in all respects than the Far East and Africa.

Relations between the Arab and Western worlds have assumed a new significance in this century after a long period during which the Near East lay on the periphery of Western oversea interests. It has moved closer to the center not only because the new means of communication have reduced distances and the Soviet Union has by its world-wide challenge given added importance to all areas in dispute. The Near East now has a special importance to the West because of its geographical position: it is a water, land, and air route to the East, and it lies close to the U.S.S.R. To this importance has been added the fact that it contains about three quarters of the world's oil reserves and produces a quarter of the world's crude oil, including most of that used by Western Europe. As the place where Judaism, Christianity, and Islam arose, the area is also a focus of religious interest and political complications flowing from it, the most acute of which are the problems of the relations between the Arab states and the West in Palestine and their relations with Israel since the establishment of that state in 1948.

The importance of their land to the West has combined with the Arabs' military weakness to spell out their fate in the modern era: domination by the West. Three current influences, however, have considerably weakened the Western position since World War II. First, the West itself has become weaker economically and militarily and less able to sustain empires; at the same time the British and French people have been less willing to support imperialist policies. Second, the United States and the Soviet Union have risen to world power, and neither of these two dominant states has a history of control over Arab countries. Both have pressed Western Europe to reduce its influence in the Arab world—of course, from different motives and with different goals. Finally, new standards of international relations, the spread of industrialization and communications, and the training of native elite groups by the West itself, have made it more and more difficult to justify one nation's control over another's destiny.

I have used several terms to refer to the people we are discussing: Near East, Moslem, Arab. The Near East is a modern geographical term. Moslem refers, of course, to a religious group whose history is closely related to that of the Arabs. The term Arab itself is the most complicated of all. Before and during the time of Muhammad, the Prophet of Islam, it was used to mean the nomadic bedouin population of the Arabian peninsula, a usage that remains widespread. As Arab conquerors spread Islam, they absorbed other cultures, and Arab came to mean a certain kind of Moslem in a society that classified people chiefly by religion. Nowadays, with the growth of nationalism under Western influences, Arab increasingly refers, as the British historian of the Near East, Bernard Lewis, says, to the "Arabic-speaking peoples as a nation or group of sister nations in the European sense, united by a common territory, language and culture. . . ." They also have certain political aspirations, but beyond "independence" and "unity" these are still not so widely shared among them.[1]

Our concern will be chiefly with five of these countries: Egypt and Syria (which formed the United Arab Republic in 1958), Lebanon, Jordan, and Iraq. Lodged in a greater Arab Moslem world that extends eastward from Morocco to the southern region of the Soviet Union and from the Sudan to Pakistan, these five countries are at once the core and the most advanced societies of Arabdom. They have more in common with one another than each has with the rest of the Islamic world of several hundred million adherents. In this nearly contiguous area about a fifth the size of the United States live more than 40 million people, almost all of them both Arab and Moslem.

The Arab countries with which we are concerned in this book took their present political form between the two world wars. Lebanon, Syria, Iraq, and Jordan were all detached from Turkish rule by the Western Allies and placed under French and British direction in 1920. Iraq achieved formal independence in 1932, Syria and Lebanon during World War II, and Jordan in 1947. Egypt, the most important of the Arab countries, has had a somewhat different political history, having been occupied by the British as early as 1882. It was granted formal independence in 1922.

These countries have taken their present socio-economic and ideological character only since World War II. They are the product of three major trends: the reduction of

[1] Lewis, *The Arabs in History*, Introduction, esp. pp. 16–17. (Sources are cited briefly in the footnotes. Full citations appear in the list of sources following the last chapter.)

British imperial power, the rise of the United States and the Soviet Union to world power and the cold war that has since ensued between them, and the advent of what we may call the United Nations ideology of the creation and protection of small states and the industrialization of "underdeveloped areas." These developments have provided a protective covering under which the Arabs have intensified earlier nationalistic feelings, moved to greater unity, adopted "positive neutralism" or a pro-Russian policy in international affairs, identified themselves with the newly independent states in Asia and Africa, and sought internal reforms and economic growth.

The Near East as a whole does not tidily mark itself off from the rest of the world. Although its main language is Arabic, it includes Israel, Turkey, Iran, and Afghanistan, where other languages are spoken and which, therefore, are impervious to the slogans of Arab unity. Although it includes mainly recently created states, it also includes Turkey, with a very long tradition of independence, as well as Aden and several Persian Gulf "shaikhdoms" not yet entirely independent. Although most of the Near East was once part of the Ottoman Empire and shared the unity of subordination to it, part of Iran, the center of the Arabian peninsula, and the Sudan were never subdued by the Turks (though an independent Egyptian empire, under Turkish suzerainty, did conquer the Sudan in the early nineteenth century). Nor is the Arab area really contiguous, since Egypt is separated from the lands to the east by Israel and the Red Sea. In the strategic thinking of the West the entire Near East is viewed as a unity, but that conception is based not upon cultural but upon geopolitical and military grounds.

It is religion that is the Near East's most important common trait, for the entire area, except Israel (and Lebanon in a sense) and small minorities here and there, is Moslem. This fact has even greater significance than it would have elsewhere because Islam has traditionally imposed not merely a religious doctrine but a legal and moral code, a social system, and a culture as well. Recently, these broad claims of Islam and its hold upon the population have become reduced but its legacy remains one that we shall have to consider from many sides.

The five Arab countries that are the subject of this book constitute the most homogeneous group within the larger world of the Arabs, Islam or the Near East. There are of course many differences among and within them in style of life and the level of economic and political development. But there is similarity even in these differences; if village life in Lebanon is different from city life, each is similar in many ways to the corresponding mode of life in Syria or Iraq. Jordan does not fit into this group of countries so well as the others but even it is moving in their direction and may indeed be absorbed politically by one or more of them before long.

Arabs share certain characteristics which I shall later describe in greater detail. Here I shall summarize them at the risk of failing, through brevity, to distinguish them sufficiently from the characteristics of other Asian, African, or Latin American societies at a similar stage of development. In doing so I shall be making implicit or explicit comparisons between Arab society and others because it is only by seeing such differences and similarities that we can place the Arabs among the cultures we know. In the statements that follow, the reader should take care to remember two general points. First, if I say, for example, that in Arab families the father exercises great authority over his children I should add that this is true compared to societies like our own where he exercises less authority. Second, the reader must be aware that the degree of authority an Arab father exercises over his children will differ in a desert community, a village, and a large city, and that everywhere the relations among members of the family are changing. To avoid repetition I shall take for granted the reader's understanding of these two qualifications and shall make them explicit only where it seems to be especially warranted to do so. Later chapters will in fact deal specifically with such differences within Arab society and with the changes now taking place in it.

The Arabs live in three broad kinds of community, each with its own social and economic foundations. A small and declining number are still desert nomads, wresting a living from a niggardly environment by raising livestock and wandering according to well-established patterns. Having no specialized political institutions, they live wholly within a tribal structure which is governed by tradition rather than written law. The vast majority of Arabs live in villages and earn their living by cultivating the land around them. They too are bound by tradition but increasingly feel the influence of the city and the central government. The family rather than the tribe is their most important social unit, though an intermediary unit between these two, the clan, is also important. A substantial and powerful minority of Arabs live in large cities, which are the centers of economic, political, and cultural life as well as the medium through which Western and native modernism enters the society. Social differences are more marked in the cities, which display a patchwork of "quarters," that is, homogeneous districts of commerce, the crafts, and residences.

In all three types of community the family is the basic social group, but it is in the village that the family is strongest. Among the nomads, the tribe exerts much influence and among the city dwellers other associations, voluntary and state-controlled, have assumed many functions still carried out by the family in villages. Although the family is a major source of security for the individual, it is also rent by faction and rivalry between father and sons, between brothers, and between brothers and half-brothers. Women are severely restricted by their families and have only recently begun, in the cities, to emerge from their double seclusion within the household and, out of it, behind the veil.

The emphasis on traditional values in a familial, agricultural society has given the Arabs a very high birth rate which, increasingly combined with a declining death rate resulting from more modern measures to guard public health, has produced a high rate of population growth. In earlier eras disease and famine took a heavy toll of life. Now more people survive but a large proportion of them only at a very low standard of living and with diseases which maim and enervate without killing.

Poverty as well as disease pervades the Arab countries. Centuries of isolation from the centers of scientific learning, technological progress, and economic development have left them at the mercy of their stark geographical position. Their cultivable land is only a small portion of the entire area, most of which is desert, arid steppes, and mountains. The regions with enough rainfall are northern Iraq and the fertile coast of Lebanon and Syria extending inland to the mountains and plateaus until very quickly the arid steppe and desert lands are reached. On either side of the north-south belt lie the great river valleys, the Nile in Egypt and the Tigris-Euphrates in Iraq, which are highly fertile. In these three strips of land, roughly forming an inverted "u," live the vast majority of the population. Ironically, these advanced Arab countries are not so blessed with lucrative oil resources as are the less advanced ones to the south. In Iraq alone have rich oil deposits been found. Other mineral resources exist but thus far have not been exploited because of the lack of capital and low level of technology. Manufacturing accounts for a very small part of the national income. All the Arab countries have recently adopted plans to make their agriculture more productive, to exploit their mineral resources more intensively and to increase industrial production, but these plans have been thwarted by lack of experience, capital and political stability. Foreign capital and *expertise* have not seriously affected the economy except, of course, in Iraq's oil industry. The two leading regions, Egypt and Iraq, derive their foreign exchange mainly from a single product, cotton in the case of Egypt, oil in the case of Iraq. Syria and Lebanon have a more diversified economy, while Jordan lives mainly on foreign subsidies and loans rather than the yield of its own economy.

Politically, the Arabs have lived for centuries under some form of authoritarian regime, foreign or native. By

Western example or direction, parliamentary systems were introduced first in Egypt and then in the other countries, but power lay in the hands of the British or French rulers, the landowners who dominated the legislature and administration, and the royal family in Egypt, Iraq, and Jordan. Authoritarianism has remained, even become intensified, but the wielders of power have changed. In Egypt and Iraq the royal families and the British have been ejected and the influence of the large landowners curtailed; power has been seized by groups of army officers owing no allegiance to any of these repudiated elements. The move toward military republicanism has encompassed Syria (and Lebanon, too, to a mild degree), while Jordan, for the present, preserves the older pattern under the protection of the West and the United Nations. In all these countries there is greater passion for equality than for democracy: equality of nations, and equality of opportunity for the educated and articulate elite within the framework of the military regimes.

Nationalism is the overriding sentiment among the Arabs. It is the mood that impels them to expel any trace of foreign influence and to seek military and economic growth. Arab leaders are as much the victims as the beneficiaries of nationalism, for they must constantly appease its appetite for self-glorification and acquiesce in its suspicion of other countries, even at the cost of political stability and economic betterment. President Gamal Abdel Nasser of Egypt has fired the imagination of large numbers of Arabs who had not figured in the plans of previous leaders. He represents rejection of Western control and hope for a renaissance of Arab strength. This is his nationalist appeal: he can humiliate those who have humiliated the Arabs. As the leader of an Arab country that does not enjoy a large income from oil resources and as the conqueror of the old coalition of royalty and landownership, he is a symbol of the masses who want a better life and a more equable, rational use of the great wealth from oil which thus far has enriched only a few Arab rulers and left the remainder without even hope for improvement.

The intimate relationship between the West and the Arabs has had paradoxical results. The Arabs resent the West politically but reflect Western social and ideological influences. "Modernization," a process that combines Western influences with native impulses toward change, has produced serious social strains. Education has been expanded but the economy has not been able to absorb the secondary school and university graduates in the positions to which they aspire. Girls and women, especially, have been going to modern schools in rapidly increasing numbers, yet they find upon graduation less freedom than they had been led to expect in family life, economic opportunities, and social life. The Arabs' growing familiarity with countries enjoying a high standard of living and the promises of improvement their leaders have freely made have aroused expectations that are not only far from realized but, even more serious, have little prospect of realization. The Arabs want change but they disagree to some extent on the kind of change and to a greater extent on the method by which change is to be introduced.

These internal dislocations have had repercussions upon the international relations of the Arab states. Eager to strengthen themselves economically and militarily, some of them have looked to the Soviet Union not only as a model of economic development but also for aid in removing such Western political and economic influences as remain. The result has been increasing repression of domestic opposition and "positive neutralism" on the side of the Soviet Union. A tangled skein has emerged from the shifting lines of domestic and international policy, replete with sudden changes of direction and apparent contradictions. The Lebanese crisis in 1958 displayed this confusion in abundance. The commander in chief of the army was able to resist the government's pressure to put down a revolt. At one point the government threatened to boycott the impending election unless its own army chief took resolute action against rebels who had tried nothing less than to murder the prime minister. The army chief, meanwhile, hesitated to take such action because it might make the rebels too angry. He later became president of the republic, and the rebel leader, prime minister; together they gave Lebanon a "neutralist" position. Meanwhile, this change from a pro-Western government was protected by American troops and supervised by American diplomats: the United States had thus intervened to help get rid of a government that was too pro-American.

The explanation of these events involves some of the leading themes in Arab society: the interplay of Islam and Christendom (especially in modern Lebanon), the relation between being Arab and being Moslem, and the claims of Islam in what the West looks upon as secular life. These subjects will occupy us in later chapters but here we must deal, in our summary, with two sets of interrelationships: between Arab and Moslem, and between religion and state in Islam.

Although several of the world's religions make claims to universality, they are historically linked with certain national groups. Christianity, for example, appeals to all men everywhere, irrespective of race, nationality or culture, but as a community it has been chiefly identified with later Roman society and its colonies, that is, in our day with Europe and the New World. Similarly, the message of Islam is proclaimed for all men but it was directed by its founder, Muhammad, toward Arabs. Although Islam quickly expanded far beyond the Arab milieu in which it arose and now embraces far more non-Arabs than Arabs, its essential qualities developed out of the interplay of the urban and desert Arab values of the seventh century A.D. Arabic is the holy language of Moslems, and their holy places are in Arabia. The early conquests of Islam, which carried them eastward through Persia and Central Asia all the way to India, and northward to Syria, westward to Egypt and North Africa, then to Spain, and (briefly) to France, were largely Arab conquests. Islam's greatness was coincident with Arab greatness. Very soon the Arabs, having spread their language and religion to many peoples with highly developed civilizations of their own, intermarried with them. Anyone who spoke Arabic and accepted Islam became an equal. The contributions of these Arabs to the arts, sciences, and philosophy were thus made by thinkers who wrote in Arabic but who were of various national origins; many were even unconverted Christians and Jews rather than Moslems.

Because of the intimate relationship between Arabism and Islam, the Arab Christian of today owes much of the basis of his culture, which is exclusively Arabic, to a religious-linguistic complex, Moslem Arab civilization, the first part of which he rejects. The ordinary Moslem, on the other hand, tends to identify all things Arabic with his own religion. Until the recent development of secular Arab nationalism (which even now touches only a small proportion, the educated classes) Arab Moslems could hardly conceive of Christians as genuine Arabs, and Arab Christians themselves looked to Europe for their cultural and religious sustenance as well as for political leadership and physical protection. The Christian Arabs have consequently had a contradictory relationship to Arab nationalism: some embraced it wholeheartedly and indeed put themselves in the ranks of its leading theoreticians, and others abhorred it. The first group felt that Christians in the Arab countries must become part of the reviving nationalism and keep it in a secular track to safeguard the Christian community; the others saw this policy as an illusion and the first step to rapid absorption or elimination of Arab Christianity. Echoes of this tactical difference were heard in the Lebanese crisis of 1958, although all groups among the Christians publicly avowed their loyalty to Arab nationalism.

Arab nationalism itself is not a unitary thing. For many Moslems it means Islamic revival, for they cannot separate their Arab from their Islamic loyalty. The educated Moslem elites can better separate these two loyalties and, indeed, often do so in their writings. Political leaders likewise make these reassuring distinctions but some of them pander to (and use) purer Islamic nationalism by overlooking anti-Christian sentiment and action. The Islamic fervor in the Arab countries, moreoever, is itself divided.

Among the religious leaders and traditionalist thinkers, this feeling extends to Islam the world over. Among the masses, however, it includes only Arabs, for "Moslem" and "Arab" are inseparable qualities in them.

The special conditions under which Islam arose has left another legacy to the Arab world: a religion that recognized no separate spheres for "church" and "state" but unified religious doctrine, morality, and legality into one inclusive system of the Islamic community. This community (the *ummah*) was at once a religious brotherhood, a political association, and a social order. Religious law, the *shari'ah*,[2] regulated all aspects of social life. The holy book, the Koran, dealt with all life, not merely an identifiable domain called religious or spiritual. Because it was accepted as the word of God heard by his messenger, Muhammad, the Koran was considered infallible in all its prescriptions and prohibitions, which covered not only matters of belief and worship and ritual but social and political life as well. The Koran tells Moslems what names they may and may not give themselves, musical instruments they may not play, and deals also with such matters as clothing, sports, sexual intercourse, and the suckling of children. Religious and secular law become one in Islamic doctrine, for all the rules have the same divine quality. These rules were given effect after A.D. 622 by Muhammad's organization of the Moslem religious community into a political order at Medina, where prospects for the new faith seemed better than at Mecca, its place of origin. In Medina Muhammad ruled as political leader, religious leader, judge, and military commander. Shifting the basis of Arab unity from tribe and kinship to that of religious faith, he at once created a religion and a state.

This unity broke down not long after Islam, following

2 In transliterating Arabic words into English I have adopted a common-sense approach that some specialists will regard as inconsistent. Arabic words and names that have become familiar in English are given their usual English spellings. Others are transliterated to the closest English sound without, however, resort to diacritical marks.

Muhammad's death in 632, spread to Central Asia and North Africa. To this day, nevertheless, the old sweeping claims are still made by certain religious leaders and are still effective among many Moslems little touched by modern movements and doctrines.

Two important consequences of this Islamic background are conservatism and quietism. Since the Koran was the word of God, it could not be changed; indeed, the Islamic community developed several institutions to prevent the acceptance of new interpretations of it. The role of tradition had been important in pre-Islamic Arabia and it continued to be influential in making it difficult to introduce innovations in Islamic society. Islamic beliefs have been few and simple, placing no great burden of doctrine upon the faithful; but Islamic prescriptions for conduct have been many and detailed, giving Islam a heavier emphasis upon right deeds than upon right beliefs.

Such a combination of conservatism and practicality induced political quietism. Most religions have such an effect because they generally encourage other-worldly attitudes. Although Islam is not especially of this character, it has nevertheless, on other grounds, discouraged political responsibility in the community. First, the leader of the faithful has been not only a secular but also a religious guide, a role that imparted a certain degree of sanctity to his person, at least in theory. Second, the very experience of political instability, with its threat to the unity of Moslems in the face of an ever alert enemy beyond the border, induced them to accept any kind of government in preference to the confusion which might result from attempts to overturn it. As a well-known proverb, supported by jurists down the centuries, puts it, "An ignorant sultan is better than perpetual civil war or sedition."[3]

The briefest summary of the social life of the Arabs shows a deeper interpenetration of the various elements which in the West are conventionally separated into more

[3] Burckhardt, no. 334, p. 105.

autonomous groupings such as family or social class, or into distinct categories such as political, economic, and religious. Less secularized and less economically developed, the Arab world has not evolved to the point where different areas of social behavior may be so easily distinguished. The family, for example, bears much more heavily on the nature of politics and economic life in the Arab countries than in the West, where the evolution of various institutions has relegated the family to a more restricted and self-contained place in the society. To analyze the effects of the oil industry in the Near East brings one to many facets of life there. Thus one can discuss oil and international politics, oil and domestic politics, oil and economic development. Similarly a discussion of the recent trend toward military republicanism in the Arab states brings one to the problems of domestic politics, foreign occupation, Westernization, and socio-economic reform.

Social Science and History

The difference between the degree to which institutions interpenetrate in Arab and in Western society does not destroy the usefulness of a social science developed mainly in the West. It merely means that the concepts and methods of social science must be applied only where they help to explain Arab social life. This book is not filled with methodological discussions; but social scientists, and especially sociologists, will recognize its implicit dependence upon Western social science as a fund of knowledge about human behavior and as a body of concepts and methods for the study of it. The study of a "foreign area" is thus different only in degree from the study of a "Western" society. If, as I believe, our social science helps us to understand our own society it should help us, with appropriate adjustments, to understand another as well. Indeed, the sociological approach that I find most congenial turns out, I believe, to be especially appropriate for the understanding of a society, like the Arab, in which various institutions and groupings permeate one another. This is a

kind of sociology that has found its place as the discipline
that studies precisely the vaguely defined but very important border areas between older social sciences, that is,
the human behavior that is not so "purely" economic, or
political, or religious.

It is true that historians have long tried to chart these
border areas, but their work differs significantly from that
of the sociologists. The historians have, of course, studied
the past, while sociologists have much more often studied
the present, with consequent differences in method. And
historians have less often sought to generalize about the
human record they have reconstructed or to relate such
generalizations, as sociologists do, to a larger body of theory
about social behavior. As I have already tried to show, history and the present are intimately related in the Arab
world. It shall be my task, in succeeding chapters, to show
what this relationship is, rather than merely to assert this
pious faith and leave it at that. For we may take it as a
general rule that the origin of a social practice is not an
adequate explanation of its continuation into the present.
Consider, for example, the Koranic injunction that proof
of adultery by a wife requires four witnesses. The historians tell us[4] that it originated in a revelation which came
to Muhammad when a young wife of his was accused of
adultery upon being seen in the company of a young man
after she had been accidentally left behind during a journey. What has that incident and the revelation to do with
the subsequent acceptance of this injunction and its continuation down to the present in some places? Its preva-
lence both then and now are better explained by the place
that the rule of four witnesses occupied in social relations
among Moslems. Adultery by a wife disgraced not only
herself but also her husband and his as well as her family.
As a very serious crime, it had very serious consequences
for the guilty woman and for the status of all with whom
she was related. An accusation of this kind must therefore
not be made lightly, especially in a society in which sexual

[4] E.g., article on "Aisha," *E.I.*, Vol. I, p. 217b.

power was highly regarded in the male. If the charge were lightly made and easily sustained, the stability of the family would be in constant jeopardy. Hence it was congenial and useful to make proof of it difficult and, moreover, to order, as the Koran does, a lashing for the accuser who fails to produce four witnesses. In our own society, and indeed in much of the urban Arab world today, where adultery does not entail such serious consequences, it is easier to prove in court. Moreover, in our society adultery is one of the chief bases for divorce; if there is to be divorce, which the community now seems to insist upon, adultery must not be impossible to prove. But in Islamic communities divorce has not depended so much (indeed, at all) upon proof of adultery; hence it has not prevented easy divorce, which the men in Moslem communities have long enjoyed.

Unfortunately most of the explanations we have of Arab social life are of the type that falls back on origins. This is because historians and philologists rather than social scientists have put them forward. It is a truism that to understand the present we need to know something of the past. But it is also true that knowing something of the present can help us to understand the past. First, the study of contemporary societies has yielded a great amount of information about human behavior—family organization and roles, social classes, political forms, the nature and role of public opinion. What we have learned about our own times can suggest new approaches to the study of earlier times. It would be foolish to study past human behavior without taking into account what we know of present human behavior. Moreover, the "perspective" which the historians insist upon is really a constant process of the unfolding of the past into the present. In studying the eighteenth century, why should one stop at the vantage point of the nineteenth? Why not see also what the "perspective" of the twentieth will yield? If it is true that we cannot understand Soviet Russia today without understanding Marxism of a hundred years ago, it is equally true that we cannot understand Marxism without seeing what it has become today. If to understand "Nasserism" it is helpful to understand traditional Islam and Egyptian and Arab history, it is equally true that a proper assessment of "Nasserism" will help us to understand the history that was capable of producing it.

CHAPTER 2

Islamic Background of Arab Society

Two pairs of concepts are essential to an understanding of the Near East: the relationship between Islam and the Arabs, and the joining of the secular and the religious realms in Islam. In Western terms, the first is a little like the early relationship between the religion of Christianity and the nation of Romans who spread it; the second resembles the medieval Christian world before the sharpening of the difference between religious and secular power and obligations.

The intimate connection between Islam and Arabdom begins with the Muhammad's religious mission in the seventh century A.D., in a society that by that time must have become accustomed to the propagation of revealed religions. Semitic peoples, that is, the speakers of Semitic languages such as Aramaic, Hebrew, and Arabic, created Judaism, Christianity, and Islam, a fact which prompted T. E. Lawrence to call them "monopolists of revealed religions" whose "largest manufacture is of creeds."[1] From the very beginning, Muhammad preached to Arabs, seeking to replace their paganism with loyalty to the god of Abraham. In his first years as a religious teacher he borrowed much from Judaism and Christianity and preached to the followers of both those religions. His message was accepted, however, chiefly by the pagan Arabs. Although Islam retained some of these borrowings, it soon developed its own traditions and rituals. Recognizing the divine origin of the Old and New Testaments, Islam nevertheless held that Jews and Christians had falsified their holy books and that God's final revelations were made to Muhammad as the

[1] Introduction to Doughty, p. 22.

last and greatest (the "seal") of the prophets. Muhammad had much the same character as other religious teachers; he lived simply, taught justice tempered by love and kindness; and words and deeds attributed to him have been taken as parables and given interpretations ranging far beyond the immediate circumstances of their origin. As one who worked miracles and delivered oracles, Muhammad was in later generations portrayed as even more humble and artless than he was. Thus the tradition that he was illiterate has been exaggerated as if to give greater credence to his pronouncements and his deeds.

The doctrines and rites of Islam embodied not only features of the older revealed religions but carried over and modified certain of their elements. It is these elements that gave Islam its Arab character. Thus Muhammad retained the notion of looking toward the geographical center of the religion in prayer but he early changed that center, for Moslems, from Jerusalem to Mecca, already an important center of Arab pagan worship. He retained the idea of a holy day but made it Friday, the day on which he reached Kuba, near Medina, the scene of his first successes; and he did not make the entire day a holy one, as with the Jewish Saturday and the Christian Sunday, but only that part of it spent in prayer. He retained the custom of fasting but enlarged the period to a full month (from sunrise to sunset), the month of Ramadan, in which the Koran was revealed to him. In this way Muhammad brought monotheism to the Arabs and created a new religion for them which, despite its spread to distant places and other peoples, has been identified with the national community that first adopted it. At the same time he transferred the basis of loyalty in the Arab community.

Muhammad was born into a society in which kinship was the chief tie among men and in which the family, the basic kinship unit, embraced and exercised the rights as well as the duties of the individual. Without changing the kinship system itself, Islam took the place of kinship as the social bond. Arabs changed in Muhammad's lifetime from a group of tribes in changing alliances, each held

together by family and tribal loyalty, to a broad community unified by a religious faith. This broader unity permitted Muhammad to establish a political community as
well, a state. Thus from its inception the Islamic community had no separate secular loyalty but a religious one
that did not distinguish what Greece and Rome had
known as civic loyalty and what Western Europe was later
to know as national and political loyalty.

As a religious system Islam requires of its communicants
five acts known as the "pillars of Islam." The first is bearing *witness* to the oneness of God and to the belief in
Muhammad as his prophet (or messenger). The second
requires *prayer* in prescribed ways at prescribed times. The
third enjoins the giving of *alms*. The fourth calls for *fasting*
and abstentions of other kinds during the month of Ramadan. The last pillar requires all believers to make the
pilgrimage to Mecca at least once during their lifetimes.
The sources of these and other rules in Islam are the Koran
and the traditions concerning the actions of Muhammad
(which are known as the *hadith*).

The Koran, the definitive, sacred book of the Moslems
which contains Muhammad's revelations, means recital or
discourse, the words Muhammad heard and then recited
to others. How he heard these words is not explained in
detail in the Koran itself, although the traditions do tell
about his emotional state when he heard them. Muhammad believed that these revelations came to him from a
hidden book in heaven, not directly from God but through
the angel Gabriel. During Muhammad's lifetime this discourse was written down, but it did not receive final form
until after his death, when his revelations, of course,
ceased. The traditions or *hadith* are incidents in the life
(or path, *sunna*) of the Prophet as described by his companions and helpers. These stories were passed orally from
generation to generation, their degree of authenticity
measured by the character of the first one who told it and
the reliability of the chain (*isnad*) of persons who transmitted it. The several collections of traditions which are
now accepted by the "orthodox" wing of Islam (the *Sunni*)

were written down beginning a century after Muhammad's death and then codified during the ninth century A.D. (the third century of Islam). "Purified" of forgeries and fabrications, the traditions became an important source of Islamic law and custom, for pious Moslems undertook to act as the Prophet had acted.

As a religious system, Islam is direct and uncomplicated. It was adopted quickly in the Arab world in which Muhammad preached, and it expanded as Arab military power expanded in the seventh and eighth centuries A.D. Its early unity under the caliphate (from *khalifa*, meaning successor, that is, to Muhammad as leader of the Moslems) were destroyed by the ninth century, after which local sources of power became autonomous throughout the Arab Moslem world. Even under the Ottoman Turks, who imposed a greater degree of unity during the sixteenth to the nineteenth centuries, Arab society comprised merely a large number of small, virtually self-sufficient local groupings. Yet there has always been an urge toward unity whether expressed in religious or political terms or a combination of both. The Arab provinces of the Ottoman Empire were in turn detached from it by the Western powers in the nineteenth and twentieth centuries. At first these territories were Western dependencies but in the wake of the two world wars they became independent Arab states. Immediately the urge toward unity expressed itself in many proposals for integration or federation and in the loose structure of League of Arab States created in 1945. The most powerful impetus of this kind comes now from Egypt's assumption, under President Gamal Abdel Nasser, of Arab leadership despite a traditional reluctance of that nation's previous governors to identify Egypt with Arab causes and culture. Syria and Egypt were joined in the United Arab Republic, and in the summer of 1958 it looked as though Iraq, Lebanon, and Jordan could easily have been brought into the same framework or into some looser relationship. This tendency remains a strong one and has had the power of a leader, Nasser, who has stirred the Arabs everywhere, and of a strong protector, Russia, which has supported the Arab goals of unity and military strength. These two goals are secondary to Russia's interests or even in ultimate conflict with them, but Russia must support them in order to help the Arabs achieve a goal that is primary to Russia's interests: the removal of all Western power and influence in the Arab world. The West has refused to help unify the Arab states as quickly as the nationalists have wanted, and Russia, only a recent arrival on the scene, cannot do so itself. But Arab unity is again being furthered by a new combination: a popular Arab leader under the protection of a major power.

Historically, Islamic influence spread with Arab power. This process may be taking place today too, for Islam is making gains in Africa among the colored peoples not yet or only recently Christianized. This growing Islamic influence, however, has nothing to do with a central Islamic power expressed in religious terms. Rather it is a recurrence of the attraction Islam has exerted among pagan masses by virtue of its simplicity, flexibility, and its continuous identification as a religion of Asians and Africans, and not, like Christianity, of Europeans who have dominated those two continents. Islam's strong but simple monotheism, its clear prescriptions for daily life uncomplicated by speculation and doubt, and its straightforward promises for a pleasurable afterlife in reward for piety on earth have so great an appeal in Africa and Asia that it now looks as though Islam, and not Christianity, will be the monotheistic faith of those areas. Like other religions, Islam has among its less educated followers large numbers who are superstitious, believing in magic, sorcery, and animistic practices at the same time that they are sincere Moslems. One experienced observer of "popular Islam" insists that such beliefs and practices antedate Islam but are recognized in the Koran and the traditions.[2] Certainly, according to a field study of one case of pagan adoption of Islam,[3] the religion easily accommodates primitive no-

[2] Zwemer, *Studies in Popular Islam*, pp. ix, 70–73.
[3] Greenberg, pp. 55–63, 69–70.

tions. A Hausa-speaking Negro community in Northern Nigeria was won over to Islam largely through the efforts of native Moslem teachers rather than through direct contacts with Moslem missionaries of other cultures. These native teachers reconciled pagan belief in godly spirits with the ancient Arab Moslem belief in evil *jinns* (or "genies"); indeed Satan himself is referred to in the Koran (ch. 18, verse 48)[4] as a *jinn* who disobeyed his Lord. In this way the belief in spirits was not disturbed but the converts now believed them to be evil instead of godly.

Persistent Features of Islam

The close relationship between Islam and Arab society arose, as we have seen, when Muhammad created a state to embody the religious ideas and practices he taught to Arabs. As an ethical system, Islam has always covered all areas of social life, yet has never succeeded in imposing uniform legal practice in human relations upon the varying Moslem communities. Joseph Schacht, the foremost Western authority on Islamic law, points out that Muhammad sought not to change the customary law of the Arabs but "to teach men how to act . . . in order to pass the reckoning on the Day of Judgment and to enter Paradise." This meant that the Koranic prescriptions, even those relating to contracts and legal testimony, for example, were moral norms; punishment for violating them was secondary, an action of the Islamic state (which was created only later) or, according to ancient Arab custom, to be imposed by the victim himself or by his family. Concerned mainly with ethical norms and indifferent to law, early Islam relied upon Arab customary law and was quick to adopt the legal and administrative institutions of the peoples it conquered. It was during the first great caliphate, beginning in the middle of the seventh century A.D., a generation after Muhammad's death, that the foundation of the Is-

[4] *The Koran*, tr. by J. M. Rodwell, Everyman's Library edition. All quotations from the Koran are from this edition.

lamic legal system was laid. This task was accomplished not by legal scholars, according to Schacht, but by religious men who applied Koranic moral norms to the customary law they found. They judged existing practices by Islamic precepts and on this basis they endorsed, modified, or rejected what they examined. Thus Islamic law was created as a moral code directly out of religious precepts which later were to be put into practice by secular authorities. As Schacht says, Islamic law "developed not in close connection with practice, but as the expression of a religious ideal in opposition to practice."[5] The original gap in Islam between moral precept and legal regulation was not fully bridged at any time, for no governmental power ever enforced the ethical system or the legal code constructed upon it over a large area of a materially advanced civilization. The ensuing divorce between ideal and fact has pervaded Moslem thought from earliest times down to the present. There is resistance among religious thinkers to accommodating the ideal to the reality of social life, and social life cannot be raised to the level of the ideal. So the Islamic moral code is not revised; it is merely ignored. Islamic communities are now governed by secular legal codes borrowed largely from Europe.

Three characteristic balances or tensions may be found in traditional Islam which still affect Arab Moslem society —the balances between religious and secular elements, between the individual and the group, and between desert and urban ideals.

RELIGIOUS-SECULAR BALANCE

To the Western observer Islam appears as a paradox: a religion that penetrates all aspects of social life yet seems to be "secular" in the very fact of this close connection with worldly affairs and its acceptance of the world as it is. This appearance results from Islam's claim to regulate all details of social life and its acquiescence in the failure to do so.

[5] Schacht, "Pre-Islamic Background . . . ," pp. 31–40.

The secular-religious balance is displayed in Islam's position on free will and determinism, a perennial problem of religious systems. In the Koran there are elements on both sides of this issue but the sense of it is clearly that all-powerful Allah has ordained every man's life and that he can do nothing to change his fate. "Nothing can befall us," according to one verse (ch. 9, verse 51), "but what God hath destined." Another (ch. 54, verse 49) proclaims that Allah has decreed everything that happens: "All things have we created after a fixed decree." Men therefore have no control over their own destinies. "No people," the Koran says (ch. 15, verse 5), "can forestall or retard its destiny." Nor can men choose where Allah has chosen (ch. 33, verse 36): "And it is not for a believer, man or woman, to have any choice in their affairs, when God and His Apostle have decreed a matter . . ." Even those who disobey Allah do so by His will: "God will mislead whom He pleaseth, and whom He pleaseth He will place upon the straight path" (ch. 6, verse 39; see also ch. 16, verse 95); and again, of those who worship other gods: "Had God pleased, they had not joined other gods with Him" (ch. 6, verse 107). Yet other verses in the Koran suggest that Allah has left men free to do good or evil but that the good they do comes from Him and the evil from themselves. One verse (ch. 18, verse 28) sums up this spirit: "And say: the truth is from your Lord: let him then who will, believe; and let him who will, be an infidel."

In the traditions, however, which were accumulated after the Koran was written down, there is even more emphasis upon the element of predestination. As a student of this subject puts it, "A survey of even a small part of the field of the traditions soon reveals that they contain much material and many conceptions which are foreign" to the Koran. There is, he adds, one difference between the determinism of the Koran and of the traditions. In the Koran it is Allah who predestines and ordains, but in the traditions that power is left unidentified, or is portrayed as impersonal and mysterious without being at all divine. Thus pre-Islamic Arab non-religious ideas found their way into the religious structure of Islam.[6]

Although Islam, like most religions, enjoins forbearance and turns believers away from worldly pleasures, it lacks the ascetic quality of the more austere and other-worldly religions. Especially towards sexual pleasure is Islam more indulgent than either Christianity or Judaism. In requiring abstention during daylight for the whole month of Ramadan, the Koran assures believers that they may "approach" their wives each night: "Now, therefore, go in unto them with full desire for that which God hath ordained for you . . ." (ch. 2, verse 183). As to sexual abstention and fasting, the Koran shows Allah almost apologetic for in the same verse (ch. 2, verse 181) in which He imposes this strict regime, the believers are assured: "God wisheth you ease, but wisheth not your discomfort . . ."

Islam does not hesitate to encourage a reasonable consumption of goods. The Koran counsels (ch. 7, verses 29–30): "O children of Adam! wear your goodly apparel when ye repair to any mosque, and eat ye and drink; but exceed not, for He loveth not those who exceed. Say: Who hath prohibited God's goodly raiment, and the healthful viands which He hath provided for his servants? Say: These are for the faithful in this present life, but above all on the day of the resurrection." As for life in the next world, infidels are of course promised (ch. 18, verse 28) fire, scalding water and an "unhappy couch" (or place of rest) but for believers material comfort is in store (ch. 18, verses 29–30): "For them, the gardens of Eden, under whose shades shall rivers flow: decked they shall be therein with bracelets of gold, and green robes of silk and rich brocade shall they wear, reclining them therein on thrones. Blissful the reward! and a pleasant couch!"

There is much in Islam that requires self-denial. For a long time Western writers described it as a "sensual" re-

[6] Watt, *Free Will and Predestination in Early Islam*, pp. 19, 20, 28, 172.

ligion, chiefly because the Koran permits a man to take as many as four wives. It was against this kind of misunderstanding that Richard Burton, the great nineteenth-century traveler and Orientalist who knew Arab Moslem life intimately, protested when he demanded: . . . *can we call that faith sensual which forbids a man to look upon a statue or a picture? Which condemns even the most moderate use of inebrients, and indeed is not certain upon the subject of coffee and tobacco? Which will not allow even the most harmless game of chance or skill? Which vigorously prohibits music, dancing, and even poetry and works of fiction upon any but strictly religious subjects? Above all things, which debars man from the charms of female society, making sinful a glance at a strange woman's unveiled face? A religion whose votaries must pray five times a day at all seasons . . . Whose yearly fast often becomes one of the severest trials to which the human frame can be exposed? To whom distant pilgrimage with all its trials and hardships is obligatory at least once in life?*[7]

Burton was right to protest the unfavorable stereotype, which stressed only "sensual" elements and the violations of those requiring forbearance. The point is that in Islam both forbearance and indulgence are found in greater balance than in other religions familiar in the West. This is not necessarily "bad" or harmful even by common Western standards today, when extreme self-denial is widely considered an encouragement to excessive repression and guilt-feelings. Moslems used to reply to the charge of "sensuousness" by denial. Nowadays, some of them, familiar with modern Western psychoanalytic theory, have begun to defend the traditional Moslem approach as liberal and wholesome. One such writer deplores the avoidance of discussion of sex as leading to "psychological complexes" difficult to correct. "The strange thing is," he points out, "that our Arab ancestors were not like us. Their stand on sex was one of utter freedom."[8]

[7] Burton, pp. 327–28.
[8] al-Munajjid, p. 6.

In comparison with Christianity, classical Islam has a
secular look in its lack of a priesthood. As the late British
historian of the caliphate, T. W. Arnold, has said, "Islam
knows of no priesthood, of no body of men set apart for
the performance of religious duties which the general body
of the faithful are not authorized to perform."[9] There is
no hierarchy such as in the various forms of Christianity.
Anyone may lead the faithful in prayer; I have seen servants and factory hands doing so. There are, however, the
adepts of religion in Islam, the "learned men" (*'ulama*),
that is, religious teachers, scholars, and judges, who may
interpret doctrine and law rather than create or change it.
But the *'ulama* are given recognition and power by virtue
of their knowledge rather than their piety (though the two
often go together), and do not perform rituals. The requirements of Islam being individual ones, no man may
stand between another and God. This was true even during the glorious era of the caliphate in early Islam. The
caliph himself was not a spiritual leader nor a mediator
between believer and God. He was the leader of the faithful, the protector of the Islamic community and their religion, not a priest or a leader of priests. This is not to say
that there is no class with exclusively religious functions,
for in this sense Islam has a "priesthood" of leaders in
prayer, officials of the mosques, preachers at prayer services, judges, and theologians.[10]

To Western observers Islam appears secular, also, in its
greater emphasis upon action than upon doctrine, upon
conduct rather than belief once its few and simple articles
of faith are accepted. As we saw earlier in this chapter,
Muhammad taught Arabs how to become and act as true
believers in the one God, how to conduct themselves in
such a way as to enter Paradise. Indeed, according to a
leading Orientalist, G. E. von Grunebaum, Islam shows
this path in "a purely rational, almost technical manner."[11]
The difference between Christianity and Islam in this re-

[9] Arnold, p. 15.
[10] See, for example, Zwemer, *Heirs of the Prophets, passim.*
[11] von Grunebaum, *Islam,* p. 3.

spect is displayed in a story told in the New Testament (Acts 16:30) to which there is a parallel in the collected traditions of Islam, mentioned by the Dutch Orientalist, A. J. Wensinck.[12] The keeper of the prison in Macedonia where Paul and Silas are detained asks them: "What must I do to be saved?" The answer is: "Believe on the Lord Jesus Christ, and thou shalt be saved, and thy house." In the Moslem tradition a bedouin comes to Muhammad and asks: "O Muhammad, tell me, what can bring me to Paradise and keep me far from Hell?" Muhammad answers: "Thou shalt serve Allah, without associating anything with Him; thou shalt perform the *salat* [prayer], hand over the *zakat* [alms] and keep sacred the bonds of relationship." In the Christian story, the answer commands belief. In the Moslem story the question asks not directly about salvation but about the path to Paradise, and the answer clearly commands action and implies belief only in service and prayer to God.

With regard to unbelievers, the early emphasis was more upon the need to defeat them in *jihad* (literally, an effort or a striving, commonly "holy war") than to convert them to Islam. Ignaz Goldziher, one of the greatest pioneer scholars of Islam, went so far as to say, "That which Mohammad leaves behind as a legacy for the future conduct of his community is embodied in what he enacted in his Arabian environment: i.e. to fight unbelievers and to spread the kingdom of Allah's power, rather than of faith."[13]

Traditionally, too, one became a Moslem at once, as an act of submission to Allah, rather than after a period of study and preparation and innovation into the mysteries of the new faith. The British Orientalist D. S. Margoliuth has pointed out that Islam does not encourage examination of its system by unbelievers—the Koran is to be kept away from them and they are to be kept away from the mosque, and the pilgrimage rites in Mecca may not be seen by unbelievers. Islam, he says, admonishes: ". . . let people pay

[12] Wensinck, pp. 20ff., 283.
[13] Goldziher, p. 26.

homage to it first, recognize that it is the divine revelation, and then they may, or indeed must, study it."[14]

There is, lastly, evidence of Islam's emphasis upon conduct in the very words that are prominent in the religious system. *Sunna* means custom or manner of living, referring both to the Prophet and to any community. It comes from a root having to do with creating a path or way. Moslems are enjoined to follow the *sunna* or path of Muhammad, but the *sunna* of the entire Islamic community and even of the pre-Islamic era have also been held up as ideals. *Shari'ah*, likewise derived from a root having to do with opening a path or way, means the canon law of Islam based upon the Koran and the traditions, governing all aspects of the Moslem's conduct and of the community's affairs.

The word *islam* itself is significant. Used to indicate the whole religion and the civilization built on its foundation, it is derived from a verb which means to be whole, unbroken, and by extension to be safe, sound. Literally, the verb form of *islam* means to deliver over in a sound condition; and Islam, itself, means the act of giving one's self over, that is, to Allah. In this way, the common definition of *islam*, submission, is derived. Another word is used almost synonymously with *islam*; this is *iman*, meaning an act of belief, faith, or trust. Scholars[15] have drawn attention to the difference in spirit between these two words. Islam is an act of submission of one's self which, at least in the early era of the religion, seems to have been distinguished from belief or trust: an overt yielding to the religious system by doing certain things required by it, as distinct from belief or trust in God as a matter of conviction. The distinction between these two ideas appears in the Koran (ch. 49, verse 14) where it is clearly implied that Muhammad's followers were to regard themselves as merely *professing* Islam until faith "found its way into your hearts," whereupon they could call themselves *believers*. To this day there are two words to denote the

[14] Margoliuth, pp. 1–4.
[15] See, for example Ringgren, pp. 31, 33, and article on "Iman," *E.I.*, Vol. 2, p. 474.

members of the community of Islam, each emphasizing one of these two stages: *mu'min*, one who trusts in Allah, and *muslim*, one who has submitted himself to Allah.

Because Islam carries such emphasis upon conduct, ritual, and order, it has been one of the most important means by which people in the Near East have been able to achieve some degree of psychological security, for it has been the nearest approach to the rule of law that they have experienced.

INDIVIDUAL-GROUP BALANCE

Arab Moslem society strikes the Western observer as paradoxical not only in the tension between its religious and secular elements but also in the way it combines a submergence of the individual within the group with a fierce equalitarianism.

Through most of their history, despite the recent introduction of Western political forms, Arab communities have been collections of groups rather than of individuals. The family and the tribe have been the social units through which the individual has related himself to others and to governments. His status and his rights have been expressed through the medium of three kinds of groups. First there has been his kinship group—family, clan, or tribe. Next came his occupational group if he lived in an urban area—this was the guild until the guild system virtually disappeared under the impact of Western penetration of Near Eastern markets and the development of local modern industry. In Egypt and Syria, some form of occupational grouping is now reappearing in the urban trade unions and the rural co-operatives organized and directed by the central government. Beyond these two there has been the ethnic-religious group, for until recently the European communities had their own civil courts and even now the various religious groups in some Arab countries have their own legal systems which govern their personal, as distinct from their civil, status. This exercise of individual rights through one's group, however identified in

various concepts, was retained by Islam from the previous
Arab social organization.

It is precisely this group basis of individual rights that
permits Arab society also to stress equality among individuals. Since social differences are expressed as between
groups, equality can be urged as between individuals. The
first Arab Moslems had a fierce sense of brotherhood, for
they were rebels against the dominant Arab tribes with
their pagan creeds and against established Jewish and
Christian faiths as well. Substituting faith for kinship, Muhammad nevertheless retained the emphasis upon brotherhood but expanded it to include all Moslems together
against all others—in belief and in battle. As the Koran
warns believers (ch. 8, verse 74), "The infidels lend one
another mutual help. Unless ye do the same there will be
discord in the land and great corruption." The principle
of equality lies at the heart of the Arab Moslem conception of the leader as the first among equals, to be elected
informally by the group as the need arose. The later obsequiousness toward hereditary "Oriental" monarchy represents the accretion of Persian or Byzantine influences
following the Arabs' absorption of features of these civilizations which they had subjugated. Equalitarian rather
than democratic, the social principle has not precluded
autocracy and despotism so long as all have been equal under the master.

In its views on the nature of justice, Islam has stretched
to the limit of practicability, and perhaps beyond it, the
early Judaeo-Christian conception that its essence is reciprocity, that is, equality between the parties. Islamic law
tries to redress a wrong by removing its effects upon the
victim or by inflicting the same or an equal situation upon
the guilty one. This goes beyond the Biblical injunction
of an eye for an eye and a tooth for a tooth.[16] In Moslem
law punishment is viewed as the right of God or the right
of man.[17] Where it is the right of man, it is conceived
primarily as the injured party's right to retaliation, rather

[16] See De Santillana, p. 309.
[17] See article on " 'Adhab," E.I., Vol. I, p. 132b.

than the community's judgment upon the culprit. Retaliation (and blood money where retaliation is renounced, impossible, or prohibited) is the life of justice.

A vivid example of this conception of justice was the response of the late King Abdel Aziz Ibn Saud of Saudi Arabia to President Franklin D. Roosevelt's request for a suggestion as to how to help the Jewish victims of Nazism. Displaying the Arab and Moslem tendency to hold the whole group responsible for the acts of its members and to insist on absolute reciprocity, he said simply: "Give them and their descendents the choicest lands and homes of the Germans who had oppressed them."[18]

The Koranic prohibition against the taking of interest (not merely usury) is likewise an example of this devotion to the principle of equality, for it involves an increase (or *riba*, meaning increase, the technical term for interest) in one's possessions at the expense of another. The exigencies of economic life have, of course, overcome this extreme attitude, but only through the creation of convenient legal fictions which have enlarged the gap between ideal and practice. Indeed, the spirit of several other admonitions is directed against risk and speculation of almost any kind as a prelude to inequality due to chance (and perhaps as a certain challenge to one's fate).[19]

The fierce sense of individual equality has been largely confined to status and esteem, the conception of the individual's worth as a Moslem on a par with all others and equal before Allah. It has, of course, not prevented or even mitigated sharp differences among the various classes, or authoritarian government, which have characterized Islamic societies beyond the desert. There has been a rapid circulation of rulers and elite groups of various kinds, military, administrative, religious, and admission to them has generally been open to all classes. Although the make-up of the classes has been fluid, the class structure itself has been solid; anyone could aspire to high status and wealth but the distance between the layers has been great and

18 Eddy, p. 34.
19 On risk see Levy, p. 204, and De Santillana, p. 309.

constant, with few limitations upon the prerogatives of wealth, political power, or religious leadership.

Islam as a religion has lent support to authoritarian tendencies in Arab society. Its emphasis upon a mode of conduct based upon the "path" (*sunna*) of Muhammad suggests a rigidity that has only recently been seriously challenged. Although there are mechanisms for innovation, these have served equally as means of enforcing authoritarian and traditional practices, according to a leading Orientalist, Professor H. A. R. Gibb. One such principle is *ijtihad* (literally, exerting one's self, striving), the process of discovering the way in which the Koran and the traditions govern a particular situation. Traditionalists seek to limit the right to *ijtihad* because it can lead to free interpretation which may change accepted doctrines and practices, while modernists appeal to it for precisely that reason. But the resort to this mechanism remains the private viewpoint of isolated individuals unless the community accepts a given interpretation. The process by which the community does this is called *ijma'* (literally, agreement), and it has seemed to embody a liberal principle, for if the Moslems accept a belief or practice it becomes justified even if not contained in the Koran and the traditions. But *ijma'* can be authoritarian too, because, as Gibb points out, the group's determination may not be denied; one may not follow a path not acceptable to all. Although *ijma'* is relied on by modernists to facilitate innovation, the principle originated as a conservative one which permitted the early Moslem community to accept pre-Islamic practices so deeply embedded in Arab society that they survived prohibition or indifference in the Koran and the traditions. Indeed, Gibb asserts that *ijma'* has supported only those new interpretations which have meant a return to primitive Islam rather than an advance to a modernist conception of it.[20]

These Islamic doctrinal influences have operated throughout the history of Arab Moslem society but have

[20] Gibb, *Modern Trends in Islam*, pp. 11–13; see also articles on "Idjma'" and "Idjtihad" in *E.I.*, Vol. 2.

been recently attenuated by many social changes. They are in no way "inherent" in Islam, which is a religious system like most others in that varying interpretations can be placed upon its holy scriptures. In the past, the interpretations of Islam that held sway have been of the character just described, but in the last generation or two new ideas have been put forward which, given the secularizing trend in the Near East, are very likely to find wide acceptance in the future.

DESERT-URBAN BALANCE

Islam is an urban religion that emerged from urban needs and desires. But it was intimately connected with the desert society around Mecca, its place of origin in west central Arabia, in several ways. First, the desert nomad society supplied social and cultural values. Second, it possessed the manpower to spread the religion far beyond Mecca in a series of rapid campaigns which in less than a decade brought Arab Moslem rule over Arabia, Syria, Iraq, and Egypt, formerly provinces of the Byzantine and Persian empires. Third, Muhammad's own tribe, the Quraysh, had only recently emerged from nomadism to leadership of Mecca.

Monotheism was an urban belief which the Arabs in pre-Islamic times knew from the scattered Jewish and Christian settlements in the Arabian towns. Muhammad himself was born in Mecca, a leading urban center at that time. His message was first heard and heeded by the lowly and the dispossessed of the town. The peoples whom the Moslems conquered and whose civilizations they absorbed and extended were likewise urban in spirit. So, too, were the finest expressions of Arab Moslem civilization itself in various centers of Asia, Africa, and Europe from the seventh to the twelfth century A.D.

The desert, nevertheless, played its part. Mecca and Medina were really not much more than large oases in a vast desert, rather than urban centers like Damascus, Jerusalem, or Alexandria, or like the cities, notably Baghdad and Cairo, that the Moslems themselves later established.

As Lewis observes,[21] Mecca was ruled by an oligarchy, the tribe of Quraysh (into which Muhammad was born), which was not far removed from its recent nomadic origin. The ideals of the desert nomads found their way into these oases and ultimately into the message that Muhammad preached as well as the community he created. These are the ideals of bravery, courage, and defiance; generosity, hospitality, and chivalry; fierce loyalty to one's own and hostility to all others. The spirit of much of the Koran breathes this desert air. It teaches "submission," but only to Allah. It calls for war against unbelievers. It promises spoils in this world and regulates their distribution.

The preaching of war itself is a desert trait, for it was the nomadic bedouin who engaged in war and raids rather than the downtrodden urban groups or their commercially minded masters, who were usually the victims. Although religious sentiment undoubtedly impelled the Moslem armies, their advances were also new outbreaks of warrior tribes from the desert into the richer urban centers around it—outbreaks that began well before the rise of Islam. Muhammad's word had little effect upon the bedouins so long as he was only a preacher of religion; they had their own paganism with which they seemed perfectly satisfied. It was the growing strength of the Moslems, under Muhammad's leadership, that impressed them, especially after he led the believers to victory in a raid upon a large Meccan caravan at Badr in A.D. 624. The Moslems looked upon this victory as a sign that God was on their side (Koran, ch. 3, verse 11)—a sign not only to the believers but also to the infidels. Muhammad and his followers now felt more confident and acted more like a victorious movement. He was able to win the allegiance of the nomadic tribes around Medina, or at least their neutrality in his struggle against the townspeople not yet converted, especially the Quraysh in Mecca. Indeed, the revelations Muhammad received after this battle are those in which the

---

[21] Lewis, *The Arabs in History*, pp. 31, 35; see also, Watt, *Muhammad at Mecca*, pp. 1, 72–77. On the urban characteristics of classical Islam, see also Marçais.

believers are urged to spread the new religion by force of arms; there is thus some reason to believe that he had already made some headway among the desert tribes and was appealing to them further in a skilful blend of their traditional interests, values and practices with the mission of the believers.

The incorporation of the nomadic tribes within Islam has always been something of a problem to the urban Moslem leadership. Muhammad appears to have solved it by turning their aggressive ways outward, by shifting them for a time from intertribal warfare and raiding to warfare against other societies and other religions—in brief, to an outside enemy. Gibb suggests[22] that when a new nomadism from Central Asia threatened Islam with disintegration late in the tenth century A.D., mysticism in the form of *sufism* helped the urban society to absorb the tribal social structure and values. *Sufism* began in urban centers as a reaction against Islam's worldly successes and failures. Emphasizing certain aspects of the Koran, the *sufis* preached on extreme form of abstinence, asceticism, self-immolation, mystical interpretations of Islamic doctrine, and withdrawal from the affairs of this world in preparation for life in the next. It was a form of political quietism that enabled Islamic society to hold together in the face of several divisive tendencies based on socio-economic interest as well as religious sentiment.

Bedouin religious tendencies continued to create difficulties but after the fragmentation of Islam such impulses were seldom more than a local desert phenomenon. The main such movement has been *Wahhabism*, named for its eighteenth-century originator, who rose to leadership in Central Arabia teaching a fundamentalism that was puritanical and austere and opposed to the subtleties and symbolism of the *sufis*. Since that time the movement, whose leaders took control of the Arabian peninsula, has enjoyed several revivals but these have not shaken the Moslem Near East as a whole, largely because of the secu-

[22] Gibb, *Mohammedanism*, pp. 11–13.

larizing impact of the European powers at the same time. The present dynasty in Saudi Arabia is descended from one of the first *Wahhabi* converts but the doctrine no longer governs conduct in this oil-rich kingdom.

In its origin and early form Arab Moslem society was at once an urban and a desert creation. Both the townsmen and the nomads despised the sedentary tillers of the soil, the peasants who now comprise the great majority of the population in the Near East. As the French geographer, Jacques Weulersse, put it, nomadic Arabdom and urban Islam both have been hostile to rural values. "From whatever side one examines it," he concludes, "secular or religious, Moslem Arab civilization thus appears profoundly foreign to the life and things of the land; there is here the unusual case, perhaps unique, of a great civilization without a land base."[23] Of course Islamic society acquired such a land base with the conquest of the surrounding area, but the observation is nevertheless an apt one in regard to the predominant values and the spirit of Islam.

The cultural achievements of Arab Moslem society have been urban ones, for the early nomads who rode to triumph across deserts and towns were themselves conquered in two ways. First, they were urbanized (or civilized in the precise sense of the word, that is, made into city people); their culture became part of the urban religion but did not dominate it. Second, the entire Arab Moslem community itself was culturally "conquered" in varying degrees by those civilizations it subjected or came into contact with—the Persian, Byzantine, and European Christian. There is no need to enter here into the old dispute as to how original the Arabs were in the golden era when they transmitted Hellenistic science and philosophy to Western Europe. In borrowing, they did as all societies do. Nor was their contribution therefore not "creative." According to the historian of science, George Sarton, the Arabs "increased the Greek heritage and bequeathed a richer one

[23] Weulersse, pp. 68–70.

to their Latin successors."[24] The situation is probably best summarized by Lewis: "Despite this diversity of its origins Islamic civilization was no mere mechanical juxtaposition of previous cultures, but rather a new creation in which all these elements were fused into a new and original civilization by the transposition into Arabic and Islamic forms, recognizable and characteristic in every phase of its achievement."[25]

[24] Sarton, *The Incubation*, p. 41.
[25] Lewis, *The Arabs in History*, p. 135. See also Hitti, pp. 174-75.

CHAPTER 3

Patterns of Living:
The Desert, Village, and Urban Communities

It is easy to overlook the fact that the Arab world contains more than political harangues, street demonstrations, nationalist tracts, and economic plans. There is a whole world outside these urban manifestations of social turmoil, the world of desert and village life. To be sure, these two kinds of communities are themselves changing rapidly, perhaps even more rapidly than are the cities which, as the dynamos of change, are much more accustomed to it. In considering both tradition and change, then, we must look at the non-urban patterns of life: the communities in the desert, not numerous and declining, and in the village, which comprehends the vast majority of Arabs and is likely to do so for a long time to come, despite the push toward urbanization inherent in the efforts to industrialize and modernize.

Desert, village, and city are intimately related to each other in Arab society. Many Islamic and purely Arab values derive from the desert, as we have already seen. The village is home for most Arabs. The city sets the pace for change. Traditionally the desert made the villages and towns its prey but now it is coming under the firm control of modern national governments ruled from the cities. The deserts used to seethe with raids. As the central governments acquired the more advanced means of violence and transport, they pacified the desert and began to settle its tribes on the land. At the same time, the cities themselves increasingly seethed with ideologies, demonstrations, violence, and revolution. While imposing tranquility upon the desert, the city has sown discord within itself.

The Desert Communities

Our interest in the nomads is neither romantic nor folklorish, our purpose neither to extol the past and deplore the present nor to welcome the creation of peasants and oil workers out of bedouins. (The word bedouin comes from the Arabic *badawiyin*, meaning originally people who appear in open country or in a vast expanse such as a desert.) Though they constitute only a small and declining proportion of the Arab population, the bedouins are important for their role in creating the values of Arab civilization and for their economic functions as well.

Nomadism does not mean aimless or whimsical wandering through desert and steppe. It is, rather, a highly rational adaptation of human life to a severe environment. In pastoral nomadism, the form which prevails in the Arab world, a tribe keeping herds of camels, sheep, or goats follows a regular pattern of movement between desert oases and the edges of established agricultural communities or towns. Far from being entirely self-sufficient in their austerity, bedouins have always depended for many things upon the settled communities. Some they have taken by force in raids which are nowadays infrequent. Others they obtain by barter and, increasingly today, by cash. The milk and meat they obtain from their animals is supplemented by grain foods, dates, and fruits from farms and groves. From the towns and cities they obtain utensils, cloth, and coffee, tea and sugar. Traditionally and at present the bedouins are the stock-breeders for Near Eastern agricultural regions which, needing every bit of land for cultivation, cannot afford to devote much to pasturage. The bedouins provide beasts of burden, wool and other animal products, and manure for fertilizing. They have largely lost one of their oldest and most lucrative functions, that of guiding, protecting and raiding the caravans of merchants and religious pilgrims who now use motor vehicles and airplanes without benefit of bedouin hosts. Historically the relationship between desert and agricultural settlement was intimate, for nomads often settled on land they conquered, and regularly dealt with these virtually defenseless communities by trading and raiding. The towns and cities were less vulnerable and contacts between them and the desert communities were traditionally less frequent. Today, however, with the advent of the oil industry and others, and the improvement of communication, bedouins have an increasing number of direct relations with urban areas; many nomads, moreover, in the process of becoming sedentary, are bypassing agricultural life and going more directly from nomadic to urban industrial communities.

Despite these new amenities, nomadic life remains what T. E. Lawrence called it: "that most deeply biting of all social disciplines." And the great traveler Charles Doughty aptly described the bedouins, in the townsman's view, as "the demons of this wild waste earth."[1] How, indeed, are we to comprehend a type of society whose "level of living" cannot be measured in national income per capita, where there is little cash, no police force, no written literature, none of the many specialized devices of settled life such as schools, shops, courtrooms, post offices? This harsh, spare mode of life is no longer important for its few useful or irksome dealings with village and town. It is worth our attention chiefly because it is still followed by perhaps half a million persons in Egypt, Syria, Iraq, and Jordan (and practically none in Lebanon),[2] and because bedouin values still persist in Arab society through their early influence upon Islam and upon tribal loyalties. It is not uncommon for a deposed politician in Jordan or Iraq to obtain protection from his tribe (usually sedentary but with a strong memory of recent nomadism). Even in Lebanon, virtually devoid of nomads, tribal vestiges color the loyalties of village, clan and religion which remain so important to this day.

[1] Doughty, p. 21, and Vol. 1, p. 46.
[2] There is no dependable figure on the nomadic population. The one given here is based on conflicting estimates by governments, the U.N. and individual observers.

NOMADIC INSTITUTIONS

Their harsh nomadic life, their innocence of hygiene, and their considerable sexual activity combine to make the bedouin mature and grow old early. A woman ages at thirty, a man is considered venerable at forty. The bedouin family resembles that of the village more than it does the urban family. The requirements of nomadic life make the family dependent upon clan and tribe; these larger units are the family's outer limit in its social relations and they also determine the family's welfare, its movements from place to place, and indeed are its entire ken.[3]

Traditionally, the bedouin man has fought and looked after the camels, leaving to his women the care of the other animals, provision of water, and the management of the household including the children, the tent, and such mobile property as coins and jewelry. Though the bedouin is no longer a warrior, this sexual division of labor still prevails. The functions of the nomadic woman, which take her outside the tent and involve her in the periodic travels of the tribe, have given her greater freedom of movement than women enjoy in the villages. Her subordinate status, however, remains unaffected, except that a divorced woman in the desert is not disgraced, and easily finds another husband. Child rearing is the same as in the village, except for the somewhat different environment and tasks. The infant is allowed considerable freedom from adult control or guidance. An abrupt transition begins at about age seven, when boys are initiated into the company of men and their ways, while girls begin to help in the tent and with the animals. At twelve, they reach adolescence, during which the strict guidance by the parents continues as the boys and girls are prepared for adulthood. The boys now join the men more often at the *majlis* (meeting place) or reception-tent of the *shaikh* (tribal leader), where they learn the lore of the tribe and how to behave

[3] Bedouin life and social institutions in several parts of the Near East are described well in Musil, Dickson, Murray, and Jarvis.

as men. Between sixteen and twenty the young men and women marry, preferably their first cousins, and assume full adult responsibilities. Even more so than in the village, the family in the desert seeks merely to reproduce the mode and cycle of life bequeathed to it.

Strong individualists and believers in equality, the Arabs of the desert do not take easily to the restraints of government. More than five hundred years ago Ibn Khaldun described them as the least capable, among all peoples, of governing or being governed.[4] Proud and unwilling to acknowledge another's superiority, he asserted, bedouins are difficult to lead except when they follow a prophet or saint, for religion alone can diminish their "haughtiness" and restrain their "jealousy and competition." Though their chiefs must be "able to use force in order to check disobedience," these leaders must at the same time "humor" them and avoid a show of force, which might cause so much rebellion as to destroy the power of the leaders and the unity of the group itself.

Despite this equalitarianism, bedouin society hardly recognizes the individual but subordinates him to the family, clan and tribe. He sees no coercion in following their ways. He begins to balk and to display his recalcitrance only at those efforts to control him which come from beyond the tribe, from states and empires. The family is the bedouin's training ground for social life, as it is in other societies, but it is also a political unit in the sense that it is responsible for the individual's conduct. Families related to one another form clans, which are the permanent, effective unit of social organization among bedouins. The clan is the smallest unit in which social distinctions occur, for it is led by nobles who carefully protect their status and power by intermarriage among themselves or by allowing their sons to take wives from lesser families but seeing to it that their own daughters stay within the fold of nobility. The tribe is the next

---

[4] Ibn Khaldun, Rosenthal's translation, Vol. I, pp. 305–6; Issawi's translation, pp. 58–59 (Book One, Ch. II).

larger unit, made up of clans but not always the same ones. The tribe is the nearest thing to the state among bedouins, for the tribe fixes the wanderings in the desert, makes treaties with other tribes, and exercises some degree of social control.

This form of government is accomplished through the tribal leader and the council of elders from the various clans. The tribal *shaikh* is not an autocrat, though within the bounds of tribal custom he has considerable power. He must use it, however, in accordance with the tribe's traditional interpretation of its interests, so that he is bound by well-remembered precedents as well as by tribal opinion expressed through the elders whom he must consult before embarking upon any course of action. Leadership is passed on to the *shaikh's* son or, if he is not acceptable, to someone else in the *shaikh's* family. The qualities sought in a tribal leader are courage, tempered by caution and wisdom; wealth, to enable him to be generous; a fatherly attitude toward his people: firm but just and kind.

The absence of specialized political institutions among the bedouins, such as parties, government offices, courts, and police, places upon other more general agencies the task of carrying out such political functions as desert communities require. The family and tribe are the agencies which educate the child, train youth for their economic roles, and exercise over the individual the broad social controls which in more evolved societies are relegated to specialized agencies. Moreover, these arrangements are not, as in evolved societies, codified and written down. Social controls are nevertheless definite and well understood despite the absence of written laws and courts and police.

One of the basic features of bedouin society is the assumption by family and tribe of responsibility for the conduct of its individual members. Crimes, insults, and wrongs in general place a heavy burden upon the groups to which the offender belongs. Because his behavior involves these groups so seriously, the individual is subject to the close supervision and discipline of the group. If a man steals from another, he lays his own group open to revenge by the victim's. In such a situation no group can ensure stability and continuity if it allows its members to embroil it in endless disputes and warfare with others. To a considerable extent this system, as described below, now is being superseded by control from the central governments but enough of the traditional practice remains to justify a review of it.

Punishment for wrongs is imposed by a tribe itself upon its own members. Punishment is retributive and equalitarian, that is, it aims to inflict upon the offender the same damage he inflicted upon his victim: it aims at a literal interpretation of the biblical injunction, an eye for an eye and a tooth for a tooth. Though it is imposed as a deterrent to further crime, its chief function seems to be to "compensate" the victim through satisfying his desire for revenge or through awarding him "blood money," at the cost of the offender's family or tribe, to the extent of his injury.

Such an approach to punishment is in part merely the result of bedouin society's isolation from the application of scientific psychology and humanitarian ideas to problems of social control. It is also, however, a continuing accommodation to the conditions of nomadic life. Punishment is harsh because there are virtually no institutional means to treat offenders—no jails, specialized courts, and so on. The desert community deals severely with offenders because they break the bonds which enable such a social order to maintain the balance necessary for survival. Where there are no specialized guardians of the rules, it is easy to break them. Where pride and honor, moreover, are so important to the group as among the bedouins, the victim of a wrong must be satisfied. Hence the society cannot develop or afford humanitarian ideals of punishment which are concerned as much with the offender as with the victim. In the stark life of the desert the offender who breaks the social bond cannot be given consideration over his victim. In more evolved legal systems the community as a whole punishes the offender because he has likewise broken the social bond, but they can do so from the point of view of the offender too. In the desert community where revenge, honor, and status are matters of immediate common knowledge to all, the community is concerned largely with the feelings of the victim and his kin. He must be satisfied before any consideration may be shown the culprit who wronged him.

The shaping of this system of control by the character of bedouin society is revealed in the Sinai peninsula, where in cases of assault upon women the evidence given by the victim is accepted without corroboration. Such crimes must be discouraged at any cost because interference with women who tend flocks and draw water would prevent their free movement in the desert and thereby upset the traditional sexual division of labor. A woman's testimony is therefore not contestable; too much is at stake for the community to admit the slightest threat to the arrangement that enables men to confine their duties to war, the chase, camels, and leisure.

Though bedouin society plays a declining role in the modernizing Arab world, certain bedouin values have so permeated Arab life and Islam that these values persist through the changes. They persist as personality traits, such as I shall describe in Chapter 5, and as ideals: bravery, pride, generosity, cunning. These qualities are both fact and legend in all types of Arab community but the factual element is greatest in the nomadic.

Generosity and courtesy are typically bedouin qualities. They are related to the strong pride of the individual nomad, for each man's self-esteem must be respected by proper formality in address. Formal, stereotyped greetings and inquiries are almost inexhaustible, and each has its own stereotyped response. Bedouins may engage in this sort of dialogue for a long time without reaching intimacy and without breaking off a seemingly casual encounter. It may very well provide a useful means for each to size up the other or, more often perhaps, it may indicate peaceful intentions and avoid arousing easily ruffled tempers and pride. In any case it is a form of avoidance rather than of intimacy, which is reserved exclusively for a very few members of one's own family.

Generosity breeds proverbial desert hospitality to a friend. The occasion to entertain a visitor is eagerly seized to exhibit great generosity, which is a sign of a man's status and personal quality. A guest is considered almost a sacred trust, to be treated, if he is friendly or from one's own tribe, as well as or better than one's own immediate family. Institutionalized limits are placed upon such expensive displays, however, for a guest is not supposed to stay with his host for more than three days, after which he departs as he and the host exchange gifts for all the persons in each party.

But hospitality of this sort is not merely an exercise of the ego. In desert society it is connected with personal safety. The man who dwells in the desert cannot ignore others in it. He is either allied to them by blood or treaty, or they are strangers to be attacked, entertained, or propitiated in accordance with their intentions and their capabilities. Anonymity in the desert environment is not possible—those who occupy its space must know each other's identity. Indifference to neighbors is possible in towns and even villages, but is an inappropriate attitude in the desert. Hospitality in part grows out of human helplessness in the desert, the utter dependence of man upon other men. Another aspect to this treatment of strangers is the widespread superstition about their mysterious powers. A stranger may have an evil eye, be capable of magic, or bring evil as well as good. So he must be propitiated and special care must be taken to avoid making the stranger-guest angry: he can easily bring a curse down upon the tent.

Hospitality of the tent is granted not only to travelers but also to those in need of protection from an avenger or an oppressor. None may refuse such a request for protection but must admit the pursued man and offer him food and a place to sleep; sometimes the pursued man may pitch his own tent alongside his protector's. A whole clan may seek refuge with another clan. So strong is the right of a bedouin to protection by another that it is respected even by the pursuer. The tent becomes a sanctuary. During the three days he offers protection, the bedouin is bound to visit the pursuer and to try to settle the dispute. After that time the pursued man must leave and seek protection elsewhere or forfeit his right to the protection of his host. In the absence of specialized agencies to protect the rights of accused persons and in view of the ease with which revenge may be carried out, this practice of protection softens the rigor of an excessively individualistic approach to law enforcement. It provides an accused man both a refuge and an advocate in his host. It permits third parties to come between disputants and to seek an honorable settlement.

Bedouins do not have a specifically religious organization though religion is important among them. The desert is believed to be the natural home of religion. In George Santayana's novel, *The Last Puritan*,[5] someone tells the hero: "The sea was never Christian and never will be. Your religions can spring up only on dry land, very dry land, all rocks and pits and sand deserts and burning sun, except for an occasional terrific thunderstorm from nowhere. That's what that blasted Palestine is like—I've seen it— and that infernal blighted Arabia. People discover God only where he has cursed them."

Ibn Khaldun insisted that the bedouins, because of their simple, uncorrupted ways, are the "quickest of peoples to follow the call to truth and righteousness."[6] Yet many observers have noted that the bedouins are even now hardly affected by Islam's purely religious precepts. Islam as a religion, says one, "has flown over their heads."[7] Another observer writes of a different area that the uncertainty of desert life leads the bedouin to "put his trust in

5 Santayana, p. 201.
6 Ibn Khaldun, Rosenthal's translation, Vol. I, p. 306; Issawi's translation, p. 58 (Book I, Ch. II).
7 Murray, p. 149.

the one God who alone can protect him from enemy, hunger, sickness and death, who can order the seasons, who can grant him water and rain. Hence his deep religious feeling . . ."[8]

There are two aspects of religion that must be distinguished in the bedouin. First, he believes deeply that the world is ordered by the one God whose Prophet was Muhammad. Since his mode of life is so difficult, so directly dependent upon his environment, the bedouin believes in supernatural powers beyond his own control. But he does not allow this religion to come to rest on earth, upon the shoulders of other men. Relying on himself and on God, living from day to day with little thought of the future, the bedouin does not take to rules of religion proclaimed by other men. He is not a faithful practitioner of religion as prescribed by formal religious agencies. In the Koran itself skepticism is shown concerning the "Arabs'" (bedouins') fidelity. "The Arabs of the desert," according to one verse (9:98) "are most stout in unbelief and dissimulation . . ." The very next one (9:99) says: "Of the Arabs of the desert there are some who reckon what they expend in the cause of God as tribute . . ." The Czech Orientalist-explorer Alois Musil put the matter most accurately for bedouin society in general: "The Bedouin does not think deeply on religious matters and follows no rules in his religious observances. Nevertheless, he guides himself in all his social and private undertakings by certain fixed customs, observes the various natural phenomena, and pays heed to internal impulses and dreams which he holds to be signs or warnings sent to him by spiritual beings who wish him either good or ill."[9]

Religion among bedouins has a stronger element of superstition than among villagers and townsmen, who have absorbed Islam more fully. As Ibn Khaldun observed centuries ago, the desert becomes a very powerful community when religion unites the nomads and gives them a spiritual

8 Dickson, p. 45.
9 Musil, p. 389.

cause to buttress their material interests and ambitions. This happened when Muhammad preached and, in the first century or so after his death, when Islam triumphed over large areas. It has happened since then from time to time as religious purity has excited the bedouins to social protest, fundamentalism, and conquest. The present ruling house of Saudi Arabia arose in such an outburst in the eighteenth century A.D., and reached new heights under the fundamentalist leadership of its late monarch, Abdel Aziz Ibn Saud, who died in 1953. It is not merely the bedouins' simple faith that has attracted religious reformers to the desert. As Gibb has pointed out,[10] they have sought the desert as a "region which was out of reach of an organized political authority, where there was, therefore, an open field" for the spread of religious ideas and where reformers could build among the hardy and warlike tribes a powerful, conquering, theocratic organization— that is, precisely the force which Ibn Khaldun described as so powerful: bedouins disciplined by a prophet or a saint.

The values we have been discussing developed in a bedouin society which was seldom subjected to a state powerful enough to impose centralized decisions upon it. But this is precisely the situation modernization has created in the desert: bedouins are now brought under increasing control of the governments which, unlike even the recent past, are determined to exercise dominion over all who live within their more precisely defined borders.

The nomad was traditionally able to avoid control by the established governments in cities because he was isolated, highly mobile, had few wants, and was a good fighter. But with the growing application of modern Western technology, he lost these advantages. Motorization has made the governments more mobile than the bedouin and has therefore reduced his isolation and his capacity to escape. New weapons monopolized by governments have further weakened bedouin tribes. Finally, the increase in

[10] Gibb, *Modern Trends in Islam*, p. 26.

communication has induced the bedouin to adopt tastes and habits that can be satisfied only by or in towns, and governments have been able to control unruly tribes by forbidding them entry to the towns. Moreover, the new technology in the Near East has weakened the old nomadic society by depriving it of its functions. The auto, truck, bus and airplane, as well as improved public security, have practically eliminated the bedouins' policing function in the desert and destroyed the camel market at the same time.

The bedouin has reacted to these changes in three ways. Some individuals and tribes have striven to retain their traditional life with some modifications—they have turned to herding animals for which a market still exists, or have adopted a mode of life on the margin of legality and subsistence which has only pathetic traces of its former nobility. Thousands of other bedouins have taken jobs in the oil industry (especially in Iraq and Saudi Arabia), or have become soldiers in national armies, or have joined special police forces. A large number, remaining with their tribes, have settled on the land.

T. E. Lawrence testified to the bedouins' receptivity to change. "Their few vested interests," he wrote, "make it simple for them to change their ways; but even so it is astonishing to find how whole-heartedly they adopt an invention fitted to their life. Coffee, gunpowder, Manchester cotton are all new things, and yet appear so native that without them one can hardly imagine their desert life." But now they face changes not "fitted to their life,"[11] for to become a job holder or a peasant means a decline in self-esteem and in their conception of the regard in which others hold them. Yet in the oil and other industries they seem to have adjusted at least as well as other social groups new to the industrial discipline.

Governments in the Near East have adopted programs to help settle the bedouin on the land, including the provision of water and of education for literacy and agri-

[11] Introduction to Doughty, p. 25.

culture.[12] But even when sedentary, the tribes still complicate matters for the governments, though in varying degree, of course. In Lebanon there are virtually no bedouin tribes. In Jordan the tribes, far from being a burden to the government, have been the most steadfast and the strongest bulwark of this last Hashimite kingdom. In Egypt the bedouins, in the desert or on the land, do not constitute a political problem. In Syria the planned policy of sedentarization has combined with other developments to reduce the problem of tribal power considerably. Only in Iraq, among the five countries we are considering, has the political influence of the tribes been a serious matter to the central government.

As the tribes settled on the land in Iraq during recent generations, the power of the *shaikhs* increased enormously because they became the largest landowners while retaining their leadership. Meanwhile, the central government could deal with the tribes only through the leaders, many of whom were members of parliament, where they were generally reactionary. During his reign from 1921 to 1933, King Faisal I, according to one scholar with experience in Iraq,[13] skilfully mediated between the tribes and the urban groups. But after his death Iraq had no such leader who could go directly to the tribes. Later difficulties are illustrated by the events of 1936–37, when an Iraqi reform cabinet had to give up a program of tribal land reform because the *shaikhs* simply rejected it. The cabinet wanted to allay the resentment of the poverty-stricken tribes of the middle Euphrates area and thus reduce their hostility to the government and make them less susceptible to propaganda against the regime. The new land policy sought to benefit the ordinary tribesmen but the *shaikhs* were able to rally them against the proposals and to threaten a revolt if the program was carried out. Eventually the government simply dropped the plan. The regime had no way of reaching the tribesmen directly; contact

[12] On the "direct" and "indirect" methods by which bedouins become sedentary, see Awad, pp. 35–38.
[13] Khadduri, *Independent Iraq*, pp. 116–18.

with them was possible only through the *shaikhs*, who, though they had political power, really lay outside the formal lines of authority in the state. More recently the tribal leaders have opposed the leftist policies of the military regime which took power in 1958, and the regime early adopted several measures to break the economic basis as well as the political power of the tribal *shaikhs*.

The difference between this tribal policy and that of the regimes in more traditional Arab states, such as Saudi Arabia, is illuminating. In Iraq the true nomads are only about a tenth of the population but the sedentary tribes of relatively recent origin constitute perhaps a quarter more. The present regime seeks to break their power. In Saudi Arabia tribal society includes about three quarters of the population, so its regime has merely brought the tribes under royal domination without otherwise changing them seriously. Iraq seeks to modernize quickly and to become a secular, industrial society. The Saudi royal house merely wanted hegemony within the tribal system and only recently moved toward the creation of the rudiments of a modern state. In Iraq the tribes have been marginal to the society, especially to the one the dominant urban elite has wanted to construct. In Saudi Arabia the tribes have been the very elements of the social structure itself, and they could not be destroyed without destroying the society.

Throughout the Near East bedouin society is changing and disappearing, though undoubtedly thousands of people will continue to live the rugged life of the desert for generations to come. But bedouin functions and power are gone—perhaps even the impetus they have given to the values of all Arabs is exhausted. As one writer says of this traditional mode of adaptation to the desert: "The freedom it conferred has been seriously curtailed; the nomad can no longer raid a neighboring or distant camp or attack a caravan . . . He sometimes protests that the desert is his own land to do with what he likes; but he does not dare to persist in such a claim. His Bedouin code is no longer allowed to govern the affairs of the nomads, either among themselves or with their neighbors. Any case of murder, theft or crime of any kind is dealt with by the competent state authorities, which apply laws specially enacted to meet desert conditions. In some countries they may still allow tribal committees to judge special minor cases, but a member of the state administration is always present at such committees. Little wonder then that the number of nomads has been drastically reduced in the last fifty or sixty years . . ."[14]

Village Communities

Though its sedentary character makes the Arab village more like the city in social and economic organization, the rural community has been rather like the desert in its alienation from the urban concerns of politics and administration. In 1856 an influential former adviser to Muhammad Ali, the ruler of Egypt, told a British visitor to Cairo: "The Fellah [peasant] is an animal—kind, docile, laborious: a higher sort of dog. The Bedouin, too, is kind and laborious after his fashion . . . but he is not docile. . . . When we are talking of political life on a great scale, the Fellah and the Bedouin must be left out of the question."[15]

Even this judgment of the village community must be modified in the light of recent changes, however slow they may be. When, in 1960, President Nasser announced the nationalization of the press, he incidentally drew attention at home and abroad to the Egyptian village. Complaining that newspapers gave too much space to sensational trivialities, he pointed to a village near Alexandria, Kafr el Battikh, as the place where the "true" Egypt might be found. This remark was the occasion for solemn comment in the press and some cynical observations in clubs, cafés, and hotel lobbies. A New York *Times* reporter took Nasser

14 Awad, p. 39.
15 Senior, Vol. I, p. 273.

at his word, visited Kafr el Battikh, "Watermelon Village," and wrote a story about it.[16]

The reporter found a simple, poor community like thousands of others in Egypt in most aspects and different from those in the rest of the Arab world only in its greater poverty. Kafr el Battikh, the reporter found, covers 30,000 acres, of which 14,000 are cultivated. The 20,000 villagers live in brick houses and mud huts. There is a mosque, a kindergarten attended by 30 girls and 156 boys, a primary school with 230 girls, and another with 350 boys. "The village," he reported, "has no movie theater, no electricity, no piped water." The peasants wear the traditional gown, the *galabiya*, worn and patched. "The average family has seven children. The poorer the man, the bigger his family. The village has one grocer and one government medical unit for internal diseases. The doctor lives . . . nearly four miles away, and is unavailable at night. There is one barber, who also performs minor operations. There are no paved roads and no public transport."

Public order is maintained simply. "A constable is in charge of the police station. He has thirty ghaffirs (watchmen) armed with rifles . . . Their task is easy, for no major crime has been committed in ten years, and even minor crimes have been committed by strangers, the villagers say." Personal affairs are tied closely to the land. "Marriages are contracted in October and November, for by then the harvest has been sold and a village youth can pay a modest dowry ranging from $12.00 to $50.00."

World affairs do not yet touch Kafr el Battikh intimately. "Summit crises do not bother the villagers. Apart from the *omda* (mayor) and the constable, none read newspapers. . . . Abdul Masoud Kusba, an agricultural worker who has ten children and earns 33 cents a day, said he had heard of the atomic bomb but did not care about it, because Allah had not taken the trouble to create the world only to let wicked men destroy it." But the new media of communication have wrought some changes

[16] The New York *Times*, June 4, 1960, p. 4.

and give promise of even greater ones to come. "A loud-speaker is installed in the middle of the village. Any villager, grown-up or child, who loses or finds something announces the fact on the loudspeaker, which may also be used for seeking help." The radio plays a more significant role in relating the villagers to the world outside. Through the radio they hear Nasser's speeches. The mayor has grand ideas now that his village has been singled out by the President. He told the reporter that he wanted government aid first to enlarge the canal, on which the village utterly depends, and then to provide a "resident doctor and veterinary, and electricity and running water in every house."

About three quarters of the Arabs live in villages and derive their income from agriculture. In the economy of each country, agriculture provides a large proportion of the total income. The village ties of most Arabs are, therefore, still strong even when they live in cities. In Lebanon, especially, the villages are in close contact with the large towns, partly because of the country's small size but also because so many villages are in the mountains and are summer resorts. In Egypt the villages are strung along the banks of the Nile and form an almost continuous chain. In Jordan the villages have recently been little more than semipermanent nomadic encampments but true agricultural villages are now increasing and forming a numerous type of settlement between the desert camp and the town. In Syria and Iraq the village is still rather more isolated from the towns than elsewhere in the Arab world. Whatever its ecological pattern, the village has for centuries been economically and politically exploited or ignored by the urban centers of power. A French observer, having mainly Syria in mind, has offered this historical "balance sheet" of the village: ". . . material devastation by the nomads and internal dispersion of rural society by the virus of nomadism; double exclusion by Islam and Arabism cast upon the man of the plough and sedentary labor; uprooting by religions; a supra-territorial conception of the state, condemning the men of the land to political nothingness; parasitic oppression by the cities, economic and spiritual."[17]

SOCIAL STRUCTURE AND VALUES

In its social organization the village lies between the desert and urban community. The desert encampment has virtually no occupational specialization geared to a market, and the town has a refined devision of labor producing for a market far beyond its own confines. The village has some division of labor within agriculture, largely between owners of land and men who work on the land owned by others; and it has a small number of crafts and services which seldom serve a market beyond the village itself. The village is thus little more than a group of houses made of stone, adobe, or mud and thatch, depending on its location and degree of prosperity, with a few shops and services, all surrounded by the fields which sustain it.

There are few or no social classes in the urban sense. The sharpest difference is between the absentee owners of large estates (a dwindling group) and the wage-workers on them. The depth of feeling against these "feudal" masters is revealed in a story, perhaps apocryphal, which a British police officer relates about Egypt. He had remarked to a rich pasha that upper-class Egyptians read very little, though life on country estates seemed conducive to reading in the evening on a cool verandah. The pasha answered: "You don't really think that a landlord in the districts could sit out on the verandah after dinner, with a bright light over his head, do you, and not get shot."[18] But in Egypt, Syria and Iraq absentee land-ownership of this "feudal" sort has been almost entirely eradicated by land reform. The wage-workers and the poor tenant-farmers remain but now their sporadic, uncoordinated yet deep-rooted hatred of the absentee "pashas" is muted.

Among those who live in the village, life is so simple

17 Weulersse, pp. 88–89.
18 Russell Pasha, p. 33.

as to offer few opportunities to establish differences in class. Most villages have homogeneous populations in which there are differences in the degree of prestige enjoyed by various families, but these are not so uniformly related to income and occupation as to be associated with differences in social class. One source of prestige is piety. Another is education, especially if a family is able to send one or two sons to the metropolis—Cairo, Baghdad, Damascus, or Beirut—to attend a secondary school or university. The Arab village has not produced a large class of prosperous owners of medium-sized holdings, no "yeomanry" or solid peasantry such as developed in England and Europe. Until recently, however, there was at least a small group of this type in some Arab countries. Egypt, notably, according to Father Ayrout, who has known its countryside intimately, had such a group of medium landholders who made an important contribution to political and cultural life. Conservative, unpretentious, prudent, these relatively prosperous but not wealthy peasants filled the primary and secondary schools with their children who, in the first half of the twentieth century, became prominent in the nationalist movement, in politics under independence, and in literary and religious life as well. For two reasons, this group began to decline towards the middle of this century. First, the youth who went to the large cities tended to stay there, with the result that this prosperous peasantry did not replace itself. Second, the endless division of estates through inheritance laws caused an increasing number of medium landholders to sink into the ranks of the small holders.[19] Current land reforms in the Arab world are not likely to reconstitute such a group because the size of the holdings distributed to the landless is small, and those peasants who receive it become tied to the state through indebtedness and the compulsory co-operatives.

Political life in the village is likewise simple. Most are governed by an elected headman, who is advised by an elected or informally chosen council of elders. The head-

[19] Ayrout, p. 43.

man's main function is to maintain public security, for which he may have a small police force or may call upon such a force in a nearby town. The mayor and elders are generally unpaid, though they are granted certain minor privileges; this fact, in addition to the prestige which wealth brings, usually means that they are members of the most prosperous families in the village. The mayor is the only link—a weak one—to the central government. During the phase of parliamentary regimes and political parties, the villages were the objects of campaigns at election time. Now, with only one party or none permitted in most of the area we are discussing, the central governments themselves, through the mass organizations they have set up, try to penetrate the villages and arouse a sense of national loyalty among its indifferent inhabitants.

As in other agrarian societies, land is held to be the greatest value in the Arab village. To own the land one works is to have the highest prestige. The Arab peasant and his family live on, from, and for the land. They incessantly hope for more land and their savings often go for the purchase of additional plots, however small. Land and water for it are the cause of most of the dissension within the village and among members of a family, especially at the death of its head when the land must be distributed according to the complicated laws of inheritance laid down in the Koran. An Egyptian anthropologist, Hamed Ammar, investigating the little village in which he was born and reared, has reported that the peasants have elevated farming to the level of a divinely approved calling, though Islamic law does not itself contain anything to support this notion. They look upon the income from the land as *halal*, legitimate, hence sanctioned by God. Such income is the result of one's own labor applied to nature and does not involve contact with other human beings "whom one might oppress or be oppressed by." Ammar points out that this attitude is a justification of the "most secure source of livelihood" in an agrarian society and at once reveals the peasants' religious orientation and their sense of insecurity where dealings with other human be-

ings are involved.[20] So profound a place has the land
among Arab peasants that some of them reckon the ages of
boys partly in terms of the kind of work they are able to do
on the farm. At one stage a boy is called one who "chases
the animals," that is, can prevent them from running
away. Later he may be called a goatherd or shepherd and
in adolescence a "ploughman."[21]

Though—perhaps *because*—the land is so important,
ownership is not always very clear and there are several
forms that overlap and others that have little more than a
legal existence. Land ownership in the Arab world was
based until recent times on an Ottoman codification of
1858, which further confused the various systems then
prevailing. There are at present two major forms of tenure.
One is *mulk* land (from the Arabic root *malaka*, to own),
which is absolute ownership in fee simple, giving the individual owner title to the land and the right to use and
dispose of it as he chooses. The other is *miri* land from
the Arabic word *amiri*, princely or governmental), to which
the government holds title but which is rented to tenants
for a stated period or, in effect, forever. The "tenant"
has the right to use the land as he chooses and even pays
taxes as an owner (rather than rent as a tenant), and
may bequeath such land upon his death. *Miri* land is
still the most widespread form of ownership in the Arab
world. Another form of ownership is *waqf* land (from the
Arabic root *waqafa*, to stand, to stop or to remain im-
mobile) which is land permanently endowed for a religious
or charitable use. This form was abused considerably and
became a means of perserving a family's right to the
product of the land. That particular type of *waqf* has
now been abolished in most of the area we are considering.
A fourth kind of ownership is *musha'* land (from the
Arabic root, *sha'a*, to be diffused, to share or spread), a
kind of collective ownership of a certain amount of land
the parcels of which are rotated regularly among those

[20] H. Ammar, p. 21.
[21] Granqvist, *Marriage Conditions in a Palestinian Village*,
p. 36.

families that traditionally have a share. This type of ownership has been found largely in Syria and Jordan but has been declining there too. Most of these categories of ownership failed to establish title clearly, did not encourage care and improvement of the land, and could not halt the fragmentation of holdings.

Though the significant distinction among families is between those who own land and those who do not, there are three types of non-owning peasants we must distinguish: the tenant, the sharecropper, and the day laborer. The tenant rents land from an owner at a very high rate. He bears the expense of exploiting the land, except for the taxes the owner pays, and is entitled to all that he produces. The sharecropper works the land of an owner, who pays taxes and other expenses, and provides the implements, animals, and other requirements. In exchange for his labor and management of a usually small plot, the sharecropper receives the proceeds from about a fifth or a quarter of the land's yield. The day laborer is a wage-worker hired regularly or for specific tasks, usually on larger estates. He is generally the poorest of these three non-owners, all of whom are the poorest people in the countryside. In Egypt, many live even below a minimum subsistence level; in other Arab countries they live just at that level or not much above it. Indeed, owners of small plots, who comprise the vast majority of owners in the Arab world, themselves enjoy a standard of living only slightly higher than that of the landless tenant, sharecropper, and day laborer.

Absorbed for ages in its intimate concerns and by the task of squeezing a livelihood out of the soil, the village community has evolved a group of values that reflect this existence, and justify and honor it as well. These values are at the opposite remove from those loyalties to nation, state, and various forms of voluntary associations that have developed in the West, even in the rural communities. They pertain, rather, to religion, family, and personal relations. We have already mentioned the importance of the land not merely as the basis of sustenance but also as a value in itself. Religion has been the great emotional and

spiritual cement of the Arab rural community. Religion
has been mixed with pagan vestiges among the nomads
and with secular tendencies among the city dwellers, but it
has been unchallenged in the villages. There animism and
superstition have even strengthened the hold of traditional religion. The family has been another center of attachment in the village—the extended family including
several generations. Its functions are still important not
only in marriage, birth, and death, but also in work, ownership of land, and material aid.

In interpersonal relations rural values show a historic
affinity to the desert values we have earlier discussed, and
hence are not easily distinguished from them. With the
increasing urbanization of the Arab world and the growth
of modern industry, however, it is becoming clearer that
traditional Arab values are chiefly maintained in the villages.

Hospitality and display go together in the village as
they do in the desert. The guest is shown great honor.
Each village has a guest house for visitors who do not
stay with families. The mayor, like the tribal *shaikh*, en-
tertains considerably and as lavishly as his means permit;
indeed, one of the qualifications for the post is the possession of the means to entertain in a manner pleasing
to the villagers who enjoy the hospitality themselves and
who like to see their leader able to extend proper treatment to visitors. Reverence for leaders and for age are
both more pronounced in the village than in either the
desert or the city. In the love of leisure, gregariousness,
and sociability, the men of the village are like those of
the desert and city. They also share the sentimentality
and excitability of other Arabs in their reaction to immediate and personal questions. Proverbs and aphorisms
are probably resorted to most in the villages, where religion is strongest. Bravery is valued not so much in the
form of personal strength in combat but in the form of
courage and cunning to defy a traditional foe, largely the
constituted authorities. The cultivation of skill in this
sort of deception is well advanced in the village. A popular

story illustrates not only this guile but also the official defenses against it. The mayor tells a boy: "Go to your father, my lad, and tell him that the Bey [his creditor] is waiting here for him. If your father isn't there, tell him to come all the same, for the Bey knows that he is there."[22]

The physical structure of Arab villages differs somewhat from country to country and from the mountains to the plains, as well as from areas where they are built close together, to the oases and to settlements on the edge of the desert. Their chief common feature is the concentration of dwellings, shops and public buildings in the center, and the radiation of small plots of cultivated land from that center to the periphery. Rather than attempt to describe "the" village in its variety, we shall briefly give some of the main characteristics of Egyptian villages, which include a majority of the total population of the region we are considering.[23] The most striking aspect of Egyptian villages is their density of population, which approaches that of urban areas. Indeed, these villages make a string of small towns along the Nile, built on hills (where possible) within a few hundred yards of the river and along the numerous canals which bring the river's water to the parched land. The village is divided into several districts both at its center, where the homes are located, and at the periphery, where the cultivated plots of land are maintained. Generally, a group of families occupies a certain residential district toward the center of the village and cultivates contiguous plots of ground out towards the periphery. There is, however, a different tendency among the older families which occupy the very center of the residential district; instead of being contiguous, their holdings tend to be dispersed around the farther points of the cultivated periphery. Despite the fact that the villages are so close to one another and that there

[22] Ayrout, p. 134.
[23] See the helpful discussions of this point in the writings of Jacques Berque: (1) "Dans le Delta du Nil," (2) "Sur la Structure Sociale de Quelques Villages Egyptiens," (3) Histoire Sociale.

are many pairs of villages with almost no space between them, it is common for each village to live entirely within itself except for the sale of its crop to the city. Villages, indeed, appear to be unrelated to each other directly and only through their bilateral relation, so to speak, with a large city nearby. Villages are not oriented toward one another; rather, several villages in a region are all oriented toward the large city in it and toward Cairo as the seat of government.

TRADITION AND CHANGE

The conservatism of the Arab village has been affirmed so often that it need not be insisted upon here. Yet there have been changes in the relationship among what the French sociologist Jacques Berque has called the "five heroes of this rural drama"—water, land, man, animal, and plant.[24] These elements are again in a period of rapid change after centuries of stagnation. In the past half century or more there have been changes in agricultural methods and products. Now, with the introduction of modern means of communication and the growth of nationalism and independence, changes are occurring in social and political life which affect even the insulated villages. Many of the changes are taking place in and through a great transformation, now only beginning, in the relations between the village and the central government, that is, in the villagers' conception of themselves as members of a national state and a supranational Arab society. Though it is easy to exaggerate the change in this direction, it is even easier to overlook it in the apparent stability of village life as it appears to the casual observer. Just after World War II, a French geographer could say that to the Arab peasant the state was an arbitrary thing unrelated to his life, and that he completely lacked the patriotism of the European peasant. This divorce between the peasant and the state led to the following paradox: ". . . on one side, states without national territories, without a nation

[24] Berque, *Histoire Sociale*, p. 9.

or patriotism; on the other, peasant masses, amorphous and undifferentiated. To states without a national territory correspond peasants without a fatherland." He contrasted the rapid change in the cities with the "aggressive conservatism," stagnation, and even retrogression of the countryside, and he speculated how long such a difference could continue under national independence.[25] Undoubtedly the same thing cannot be said of the Arab world today.

Now the village hears echoes of the rumble of great political struggles between Arabs and Europeans, among the Arab states themselves and among the world powers. Each new crisis—such as the nationalization of the Suez Canal and the ensuing attack by Israel, France and England; the struggle in Lebanon and the landing of United States Marines; the creation and dissolution of the United Arab Republic; the revolution in Iraq and the subsequent dispute with the U.A.R.; the Arab interest in the Algerian nationalist war—brings new awareness to the countryside of the world outside through the radio and newspapers. The traditional reverence for age is reduced as younger leaders become prominent in the central governments and as village youth increasingly aspire to work or study in the great cities. Even in the villages themselves, authority and prestige are flowing—though sluggishly—to the literate young, who through reading or even experience understand better what is happening in the cities whence come the radio programs, newspaper reports and governmental actions that have a growing impact upon daily life in the village. This does not mean the village is about to rise up for or against anything. Grievances and complaints, awareness of new things, and alertness to the world outside are waxing, but there seems to be as yet little questioning of the fundamental rightness of things as they are.

Several recent studies offer evidence of these changes. One[26] sought to discover the degree of political awareness in a random sample of people in five villages in Lower

25 Weulersse, pp. 85, 313-14.
26 Hirabayashi and El Khatib.

Egypt, almost fifty miles northwest of Cairo, with populations ranging from 700 to 5000. About a fifth of those interviewed read newspapers and more than half listened to the radio. The favorite topic of the readers was political news, while the listeners preferred the recitations from the Koran, music and then news. With the increase in literacy among the youth from six to fourteen years of age (not included in this study), it may be expected that newspaper readers will increase rapidly in the coming years. Moreover, a considerable proportion of leisure-time talk, especially among men, was devoted to local and national affairs, news of which was communicated by those who had read newspapers and listened to the radio. How much awareness and knowledge did these villagers have? Not much by the standards of highly educated urban groups in the West, but certainly more than one would expect judging by the impressions reported by observers of peasant life for many decades. For example, 20 per cent of the men in the study were able to distinguish between a plebiscite (one was held in Egypt in June 1956, two months before the villagers were interviewed) and an election; the authors report that in an "informal poll" only 50 per cent of university graduates were able to make that distinction, indicating a surprisingly high degree of awareness, for Egyptian society, among the villagers. In addition, 80 per cent of the males and half of the females knew that Nasser was president of the republic. As the authors say: "It is striking that the majority of villagers knew of the changes that had occurred in Cairo, that the monarchy was terminated and a republic had been established." That this comment is warranted indicates both the recent increase in political awareness and the profound unconcern of the village in earlier times with what went on in the capital among their rulers.

A second study[27] sought to discover the degree to which inhabitants of thirteen villages in central Lebanon expressed "modern" values, such as specialization in oc-

[27] Armstrong and Bashshur.

cupation, expectation that education will be more important than religion in solving social problems, confidence in technology and education, and belief in the need for innovation. With one minor exception, more than half of the villagers—Moslem and Christian, peasants and others —favored these modern values.

Though there are no studies of an earlier era to which we can compare these, the results just reviewed certainly suggest that the village is undergoing change from its traditional isolation and conservatism. One of the surest indications of change is the emergence of several social groups in the village beyond the obvious two traditional ones of large landowners and all others. A recent study[28] of eleven villages in Lebanon found five occupational groups which differ significantly from one another in socioeconomic status (income, occupation, possessions, housing, education). It is not yet established just how much these differences measured by the social scientist are reflected in the attitudes of the villagers. They may still look upon themselves in terms of how much land they own. Yet these statistical differences indicate the effects of certain social and economic changes by which the outside world increasingly impinges upon the village. Very likely these changes are occurring earlier in Lebanon than elsewhere in the Arab world, but they are undoubtedly an indication of that society's future.

The village in the Arab world is like its Western counterpart in one respect: it is both idealized and satirized. The city pays lip service to rural values and goes on ignoring them. National leaders point to the village as the eternal source of all that is good, true, and beautiful—and they continue to initiate and execute programs which are changing the village down to its roots. The greatest praise of village life comes from pundits who live in cities. The village ideal is now widely portrayed in Arab films, made chiefly in Cairo. In these films, which are seen by city

[28] Armstrong and Hirabayashi.

audiences whose rural ties are still strong, the village is the place where one can find peace, understanding, and unquestioning acceptance. When someone in a film story is depressed and disappointed, he is often shown returning to the village; there he finds surcease from the confusion, hustle, and impersonality of urban life. Greeted by simple people in village dress, he finds solace in their unspoken affection. Typically, however, he never remains long in the village but soon returns to the life he has just fled in despair.

Few writers in any medium of expression seem willing to say openly or implicitly what is clearly intended in the satirical treatment of village characters and the superficial idealization of rural values that are being abandoned in the rush toward modernism. Some may genuinely mourn this trend, others may be indifferent to or welcome it, but few are willing to speak of the village in the way most people seem to think of it. An exception is the great Egyptian novelist and playwright Tewfik el-Hakim, who has the narrator in a popular novel write in his diary: "My poor assistant needed something to cure him of his boredom. But there is no cure for village life except marriage or riotous living, or reading, or writing a diary, as I do whenever I can."[29]

Urban Communities

The glamour of the desert lies in the struggle for survival, a heroic contest between man and the elements, and between man and man. It appeals to those who endure its hardships and stirs the imagination of many who —from afar—admire the qualities of independence and tenacity which the desert has both demanded and fostered. Arab literature, even after the advent of Islam, paid literary tribute to the desert. As von Grunebaum puts it, "The real centers of pre-Islamic civilization were urban settlements, but its literature was dedicated to the glorification

[29] el-Hakim, p. 40.

of Bedouin ideals. The authority accorded it kept an incongruous note of desert lyrics in Islamic poetry."[30] The Arab village, too, commands loyalty and stirs sentimentality but it casts no halo of glamour. Its tedious dependability of work, poverty, and disputation over things big and small does not arouse feelings of greatness either in those who still remain in it or in those who contemplate it, usually with fondness but with no intention to return permanently, from the city. The city is the one kind of Arab community that arouses no loyalty but is merely the preferred mode of life. No one writes poems in its praise but all know that social power emanates from it. Everyone feels the city's power as it radiates and shapes life everywhere, and everyone also feels the city's power to attract and concentrate people within itself.

The desert and village communities send people, values, and products to the urban communities but are relatively self-contained and can endure even more isolation than has prevailed until now. The city which absorbs these desert and village contributions cannot maintain itself without them, or without a lively interchange among its energetic population, or without some contact with other cities near and far. More powerful than the desert and village community, the city is also more fragile. It is a relatively delicate structure of finely meshed specializations, a minute division of labor which gives it power but makes it vulnerable. Through this power derived from concentration and specialization, the Arab city has a commanding position over a vast, far less specialized agricultural and pastoral civilization. Through its concentration of governmental power, the Arab city dominates politically. Through its trade connections internally and with the outside world, the city dominates the economic life of the hinterland. Through its concentration of the media of communication the city dominates—indeed, *is*—the cultural life of the Arab world. It is the center of traditional and modern culture, high and low art. Even today literacy

[30] von Grunebaum, *Islam*, p. 18.

and education are hardly to be found anywhere else. There are few secondary schools outside large cities and no universities. The Arab world has no provincial press, no local radio—all cultural creativity flows to the big cities, where it is absorbed and rechanneled outward in all directions.

The City and Its Institutions

The Arab city, like others, has its characteristic structure and institutions, its sights, sounds, and smells. One thing has been missing from the urban atmosphere: the sight and smell of factory smoke. For Arab cities are only now becoming somewhat industrial, having been built rather out of considerations of military strategy, commerce, dynastic or national pride, and administrative convenience. The Arab city has also been a conglomeration of enclaves whose inhabitants have felt themselves to be a part not of some great urban center but only of the particular quarter they belonged to on the basis of occupation, religion, nationality, village of origin, or family. Yet there has been enough interaction among the enclaves and enough loosening of personal ties within them to create the classic urban impersonality and segmented relationships among people, the kind of pathology of urban life so familiar in the modern industrial cities of Europe and America. While the Arab city is highly specialized compared to other Arab communities, it is much less specialized in occupation and its use of land than is the Western industrialized city.

Some Arab cities have been created by conquerors seeking to perpetuate and protect their domains. The cities of today, too, owe much of their appearance as well as their amenities to European rulers, Europeans, and the Europeanized minorities who have especially given their stamp to the new sections. The physical and social separation between the "new" and the "old" city is characteristic of the area and has continued into the period of independence. But change is taking place in the cities even faster than in the village and the desert; with increasing population and industry, the cities are growing outward, creating new patterns of city streets, new kinds of buildings and new patterns of social life. The cities, moreover, not only are themselves changing but are the vehicles through which change is introduced into all of Arab society.

Created by conquerors and perpetuated through dynasties, Arab cities have remained the wards of central governments. They have not developed specifically municipal institutions outside of those imposed by distant seats of empires. Their characteristic form is not, as in Europe, the independent municipality with a certain heritage of autonomy which survived incorporation within a national state. Rather, the most striking aspect of the Arab city is its separation into "quarters," each with its homogeneous population, its law and its custom. The quarters were related to each other chiefly through a common subordination to a central regime and through commerce. In other respects, each quarter was until recently a city unto itself. The European city, as the late historian, Henri Pirenne, has shown,[31] was transformed in medieval times by the arrival and growth of a new class of merchants who achieved for themselves—and then for their cities—a privileged position within a larger domain. Finding themselves in the tangled midst of an overgrowth of feudal restrictions, these new men of the middle class needed freedom of action and of status to thrive in their chosen way of life. By both peaceful pressure and violence where necessary, they won new kinds of freedom: freedom of personal status to end all traces of serfdom; freedom to hold, sell, and mortgage land in the city; freedom from old restraints upon trade and the easy movement of goods; and lastly, freedom of contract. The European city also won the right to maintain public order and so formed a legal community. These municipal institutions protected the individual in the city, providing a stark contrast to the dangers which beset the city dweller when he ventured

[31] Pirenne, *Economic and Social History of Medieval Europe*, Ch. II; *A History of Europe*, pp. 215–26; *Medieval Cities*, pp. 121–51.

outside its bounds. Accompanying them, in consequence, was a civic spirit which marked a man's devotion to his community—his interest in seeing it prosper, in improving its appearance, and his concern to defend it.

The Arab city passed through no such stage on the road to incorporation within the modern national state. Perhaps its closest parallel to the medieval European experience was the regime of capitulations instituted by the Ottoman Empire in which Europeans, engaged mainly in trade, were permitted to live and work under the legal system of their own countries. But the capitulations anchored the privileged status of the Europeans to their own capitals and so could not encourage autonomy in the Arab cities, which were objects not of loyalty but of exploitation. The present municipal institutions of the Arab world are essentially the product of administrative arrangements adopted by the Ottoman Empire in an attempt to provide adequate services chiefly in Istanbul (Constantinople), which was developing in European style.[32] A municipal commission made many recommendations borrowed from European practice and in 1857 they were accepted but applied for the time being only to one district in the capital city, and later to others. A municipal council was provided for and granted certain functions and powers, but on the whole the reform created only a new administrative agency to conduct urban affairs; it did not change the character and status of the city itself.

This Ottoman municipal code of 1864–77 was applied in the Arab provinces of the Empire, except Egypt. It was maintained for a time by the British and French after they assumed control under the mandate system after World War I. In Egypt municipal institutions developed along similar lines, though not imposed by the Ottomans. Urban

[32] On these reforms and their effect in the Arab world, see the article "Baladiyya," E.I. (New), Vol. I, pp. 972–76 and Bernard Lewis, "Municipal Reform in the Ottoman Empire: The Legacy to the Independent Arab States," paper presented to seminar on "The New Metropolis in the Arab World" (see note 46 below).

services were generally provided through concessions to private foreign companies which are now being nationalized, or through commissions established and controlled by the central governments. Local government in the Arab world thus remained subordinate to the central government. In recent years, however, with the further rapid growth of the large cities, their autonomy is increasing. The obvious need to put urban services on a firm footing has been realized, and it has been possible to find more and more capable Arab engineers to whom the task can be delegated.

In the summer of 1960 the United Arab Republic revised municipal administration in its Egyptian region. For many decades attempts had been made to develop limited local autonomy but the functions assigned to village and city councils exceeded their resources and authority. The Constitution of 1956 provided for local "administrative units," headed by a council of elected and appointed members, and "empowered to establish the institutions capable of coordinating social, economic, cultural and health activities" (Articles 157–59). In 1959 few towns and villages had councils,[33] but the following year new regulations were issued prescribing the exact method by which they were to be established and conducted.[34] There are three "administrative units": governorates, large geographical units, each headed by a governor appointed by the president of the republic; towns (or cities), headed by a chairman, appointed by the president of the republic; and villages, whose affairs are conducted by a council appointed by the governor.

Local government will be tied closely to the National Union which, according to the Constitution of 1956 (Article 192) was established for the duration of the period

[33] Institute of Public Administration, Cairo, "Developments of Local Government in the U.A.R. (S.R.)," 1959 (mimeographed memorandum).

[34] Law No. 124 of 1960, U.A.R., *Official Gazette* (in Arabic), No. 76, April 4, 1960, pp. 475ff. See also newspaper summary in *The Egyptian Gazette*, June 27, 1960, p. 2, and June 28, 1960, p. 2.

in which political parties were suspended. The purpose of the National Union is stated to be the "realization of the aims of the Revolution" and the mobilization of "all efforts for the sound building of the nation in political, social and economic matters." The National Union, in accordance with the Constitution, nominated the candidates elected to the National Assembly, a limited parliament, in 1960.

Each city council is composed of elected and appointed members. The elected members, who are the majority, must come from the executive committee of the town's National Union branch. The appointed members include several persons active in the National Union, and one representative each from six central government ministries concerned with local affairs. The city council meetings are open to the public except when it decides to meet in private or is ordered by higher authority to do so. The council's function is to (1) carry out the plans for urban services as set down by the next larger unit, the governorate (or province), (2) establish and perform certain services such as traffic control, fire fighting, markets, and others in the field of education, health, and welfare. Finally, any council may be dissolved by the president of the republic with the consent of the National Union.

By these regulations Egypt is seeking to decentralize some administrative functions without reducing the central government's control over policy. At the same time, by tying local administration to the National Union, it seems to be seeking to strengthen the latter while making it a public forum with characteristics of both a political party and a governmental agency. Thus the city council must refer to the local branch of the National Union any proposal of general interest made at a public session. The Union branch then holds open meetings to ascertain public opinion, and issues a report which the council must consider before taking action. The National Union is thus the link between the public and the administration in the village, city, province, and the country as a whole. This innovation is apparently intended to induce some feeling of local public participation in government, decentralize certain administrative tasks, and to give the National Union a commanding position at all levels of politics and administration. In general, it is an attempt to mobilize the masses to help achieve the aims of the leaders, to concentrate their attention upon specific governmental functions rather than divisive and hence dangerous party activities—in a word, to substitute administration for politics from the grass roots upward.

SOCIAL AND ECONOMIC CHARACTERISTICS

The Arab world, as was shown in Chapter 2, has had from the start a strong urban character. Evidence of the persistence of this trait may be found in the present demographic situation, for a rather high proportion of the Arab population live in large cities.[35] In Egypt, Iraq, and Jordan about one sixth of the total population live in cities of 100,000 or more; in Lebanon and Syria the proportion appears to be even higher, about a quarter. Such high proportions in major cities are found only in the more industrialized countries of Europe rather than in the mainly agricultural economies of Asia with which the Arab world presumably has more in common. The urban tradition of Arab and Islamic civilization seems to be still alive; aside from religious and cultural impulses which favor urban life, economic considerations, such as the high density of the settled areas in a largely desert-steppe region, must also play a part.

Arab countries, moreover, are dominated by a few large cities, next to which the secondary ones pale in comparison. Cairo with three and a third million people, and Alexandria with a million and a half, are the two real metropolises in Egypt, and other sizable cities such as Port Said, with fewer than a tenth the number of people in

[35] The demographic data are so variable and unreliable that the writer has based a reconciliation of several official and unofficial estimates upon his own familiarity with the area. On the general subject of the "overurbanization" of the Near East, see articles by Davis, and Foley, *passim*, esp. Table 3, p. 16.

Cairo, are never mentioned in the same breath. In Iraq, Baghdad has more than half a million people, and Mosul, with less than a quarter of that number, is hardly a rival in any sense despite its oil wealth. In Jordan, Amman has been growing more rapidly than was thought possible, until now with a population of about 200,000 it overshadows Arab Jerusalem except in religious significance. In Lebanon, Beirut has a population of almost half a million, and Tripoli, the next largest city, has only a fifth to a third that number; after these two cities, others come far behind in size and importance. In Syria, Damascus and Aleppo dominate, each with a population of 350,000 to 400,000, although the difference between them and Homs and Hama, each with well over 100,000, is less than that between the major and secondary cities elsewhere in the Arab world; this is so because Syria has relatively large, productive agricultural regions which have supported big cities of their own.

It appears, too, that the larger cities are growing at a faster rate than the smaller ones, probably because they offer the most of whatever urban advantages migrants may be seeking. Such industrialization as is taking place in the Arab world is located in the existing metropolitan centers, which increases their population at a still more rapid rate. This trend is especially clear in Egypt, where the cities of 100,000 and more have been growing about twice as rapidly as those between 30,000 and 100,000. Urban population in Egypt is growing more rapidly than rural. Between 1937 and 1947, for example, total population increased about a fifth but the village population grew by only a tenth while the towns increased by more than two fifths. In all provinces the towns increased their population more than did the villages, and in two provinces the village population actually declined.[36] The same, how-

[36] "Observations on the Urbanization and Distribution of Agricultural Population in Egypt," National Bank of Egypt, *Economic Bulletin* (1955), 8:171–81, and U.A.R. (Egypt), Statistical Dept., *Statistical Pocket Year-book, 1957*, Cairo, 1958, Table 2 (a), p. 2, and Table 2 (b), p. 5.

ever, is probably not true of Syria and Lebanon, where agriculture is more prosperous and the pressure of population on the land less serious.

The attractive power of the large Arab city is not merely its capacity to provide jobs, for it does not offer so many purely economic advantages. The metropolises grow most rapidly when job opportunities are greatest, of course; the usual influx into Cairo, for example, was augmented considerably during World Wars I and II when the presence of large military forces created many jobs and other sources of wealth. But the "pull" of the large city is felt even independently of business conditions because for the rural poor and the underemployed it can provide a more tolerable setting for their poverty. Charity and the leavings of the rich are more abundant and accessible in the large city than in the countryside. The government must for political reasons alleviate urban poverty even when it ignores rural poverty. The glitter of the one or two metropolitan centers in each Arab county is so great that it blinds people to the smaller and middle-sized cities; these have so few more amenities than the countryside that a dissatisfied villager is hardly attracted to them but wants to go right to the fabled metropolis he has heard so much about. And for those families who want good secondary education and any kind of higher education the big city is the only place to send their children.

The Arab city has with little modern industry supported a population proportionately as large as that which Western cities have sustained upon a broad base of manufacturing. There is an interesting parallel between highly advanced, wealthy urban conglomerations in the West and such cities as Cairo, Alexandria, and Beirut. In the "Megalopolis" formed by the urban area encompassing Boston, New York, Philadelphia, and Washington, D.C., there is a high and increasing proportion of people employed in myriad services demanded and made possible by that area's advanced technology, wealth, and refined division of labor.[37] As manufacturing leaves the central business districts of such urban concentrations, the economic base shifts to specialized services such as finance, management, communications, and research. On a preindustrial basis, the same refined division of labor may be seen in many Arab cities (and some on the other side of the Mediterranean). By the standards of industrial cities, these Arab cities have far more people than their economic-technological base warrants. How do they live? In the first place, many live only at the edge of subsistence. Secondly, there is a proliferation of services in connection with the commerce, handicraft, tourism, and government administration which provides most of the employment. It almost seems as if these services expand merely to provide some sort of earning opportunity for the masses who come to the city, rather than in response to the needs of the industries already there. Every source of income, however meager, is stretched a long way to cover several persons who perform services that may or may not be wanted. Shops and offices have several messengers for different kinds of errands. Apartment and office buildings have several kinds of doormen, messengers, cleaners, some of whom are not actually employed but simply are around for whatever task comes up and for whatever they can earn. In the streets there are men who help drivers find and squeeze into parking places, and there are others who help the helpers. In many barber and beauty shops there is so refined a division of labor that the operator commands a small crew of aides. Labor is so cheap to hire that it encourages a constant division of tasks to provide one for the latest addition to the force.

In the postmanufacturing urban center of the West this proliferation of services is based upon technology and wealth and is stimulated by competition. In the premanufacturing Arab city it is based upon cheap labor and poverty and is encouraged by a relatively "irrational" market

[37] This parallel was suggested to me by Dr. Jean Gottmann, the French geographer, who develops the Western urban side of it in his study of "Megalopolis," Ch. 11.

in which costs are not reckoned to so fine a point. In the West the proliferation of services demands a high education on the part of those who perform them and it creates a large middle class of employed professionals and semi-professionals. In the Arab city the phenomenon is connected with jobs which pay little even by local standards and which require no education or training. In the West it is profit that governs the expansion of such services, while in the Arab city it appears to be rather the desire to increase the employer's status or ease his task, or merely to provide a pittance for a poor relative or someone from one's own village or town.

The existence of such employments has not altered the sharp difference between the few main social classes in the Arab city. These jobs do not depend upon the modernization of the economy but are rather associated with traditional (and still prevailing) institutions which have only recently been undergoing change. Urbanization and industrialization, however, are creating new employments which are beginning to make occupation a more important determinant of one's social class. As this process continues, the number of discernible social classes will tend to increase and the gap between them to narrow somewhat. Another important determinant of social-class position is the advent of the military regimes and their augmentation of the role of the state in the economy through regulation, government investments in private firms, and outright nationalization of property. The effect has been to raise the power and prestige of the military elite and the upper levels of the civilian bureaucracy while reducing the influence and status of the large landowners, industrialists, and bankers, who are declining in number, and of the deposed professional political "class" which is today extinct in Egypt and Iraq, and weakened in Syria.

A picture of this changing social hierarchy would look about as follows. At the top are still the absentee owners of large agricultural holdings, joined in the last three or four decades by purely urban wealthy groups such as industrialists, important merchants and bankers—all known by family as well as by economic interest. Second are the independent professionals (engineers, doctors, lawyers), other professionals such as journalists and writers, and the upper reaches of the army officers (as a group they fall here, though the individual officers who have become national leaders are, of course, in the top level). Third are the mass of white-collar workers in government and other offices, teachers, and other employed persons with only moderate incomes and higher education than most people. Fourth are the skilled artisans, small merchants, and the more skilled workers. Fifth are the vast urban mass, some clearly defined, some nondescript—the porters, messengers, laborers, and those large numbers who earn little money and only desultorily and who seem to constitute an undifferentiated mass on the edge of subsistence. (This listing omits the influences of religious, national, and ethnic affiliation, which are discussed in Chapter 7.)

"Membership" in a given social class has not provided the urban Arab with a sense of community. That feeling of unity is still largely provided by the family, religious affiliation, and the neighborhood to some extent. As the older urban forms are steadily eroded by increasing migration, industrialization, and secularization, this integrating function is less and less fulfilled by traditional agencies and is not fully assumed by new ones appropriate to the new conditions. The result is an increasing tendency to rootlessness. This is not an invariable concomitant of urban life, nor is it unknown in other types of community; yet it accompanies rapid change and afflicts people who have lost certain human ties which help to adjust to such change.

The traditional Arab city down to the late nineteenth century had two types of associations which integrated its masses into a strong unit beyond family and religious groups. The first was the neighborhood or "quarter," itself homogeneous in respect to religion, national origin, even occupation and income to some extent. Here the individual had intimate, lasting bonds of kinship and

creed and calling. Here, too, was a thriving refuge for the
newcomer, who needed only to seek out the appropriate
"quarter" to find acceptance and sustenance. The second
institution was the guild, vestiges of which still had some
vigor in the nineteenth century. These guilds, different
from those in the West, were a means of social protest as
well as agencies for the regulation and protection of the
crafts.[38] Though the guilds had political influence in the
cities, they did not have municipal functions and did not
become part of the machinery of municipal government. Indeed, they were generally hostile to the established order. But they did provide solidarity and security
and were not so exclusive as the European guilds. The
distinction between masters and journeymen in the guilds
in Arab cities did not harden into a distinction of social
class, nor did the guilds habitually exclude non-Moslems.

The Western impact in the nineteenth century weakened both associations, the quarters and the guilds,
through the introduction of industry and the expansion of
commerce and banking. The great influx of Europeans led
to the creation of new quarters and the modernization of
some old ones. Roads and public transport were put
through traditional centers and broke them up. The
growth of the indigenous population, too, combined with
new job opportunities, diluted the homogeneity of old
quarters of the cities. At the same time the introduction
of the products of Western manufacturing gave the final
blow to the already weak guilds by destroying many crafts
on which they were based. The quarters still exist in attenuated form but the guilds have not survived.

City dwellers have, of course, adjusted somewhat to
these changes. It must not be assumed that the Arab city
has become a crucible of wandering unrelated particles
of humanity. Religious brotherhoods, ethnic societies, and
trade unions—formal and informal groupings—still provide
the social bonds beyond the immediate family that are

[38] See *Encyclopedia of the Social Sciences*, Macmillan, New
York, 1933, "Guilds, Islamic," Vol. 7; also Lewis, "The Islamic
Guilds."

necessary for the spiritual and emotional nourishment of the individual. There are, however, few studies of how satisfactorily these groups carry out this function and the consequences of failure to do so. One study of Alexandria[39] shows that the greatest degree of individual participation is still in the traditional formal groups based on religion and kinship and in unorganized or informal ones such as the "café group." Ethnic groups were found to be very numerous among both the Europeans and others. The 60,000 Greeks, for example, had forty-seven associations. The Nubians, Sudanese, and even Egyptians from certain provinces had their own organizations. Thirty-one associations served 105,000 Upper Egyptians. The lowest degree of participation was found in those organizations established specifically to promote certain common interests such as occupational, economic, and cultural, and to provide some service to the community—that is, the sort of "voluntary" societies characteristic of the West. Nevertheless, this is certainly not a picture of "atomized" individuals without ties to others or without roots in tradition.

The trade union is one of the most appropriate agencies for the integration of urban masses whose old bonds have been disrupted with the removal of the workplace from the home, a phenomenon of the city that is in sharp contrast to agricultural and village life. The new discipline of industrial labor and the fleeting contacts of urban life are unsettling conditions which trade unions can meliorate in addition to dealing with wages and hours. But this has not yet developed much in the Arab world. First, the unions are few, weak, inexperienced, and have not attracted large proportions of workers. Second, they were at first frowned upon by the old regimes and more recently have been smothered in the eager embrace of the new ones. Between the insecurities of industrial life and direction of trade unions by the state, the urban working class has been unable to find the spontaneous organizational ties it needs for protection and self-respect. In their restlessness, work-

[39] Sedky, *passim*. On Cairo see the paper by Janet Abulughod (note 46 below).

ers are easily aroused to dissatisfaction and then easily manipulated by the leaders of their unions and the governments whose permission they need merely to exist. Like European workers fifty and a hundred years ago, the Arab workers are susceptible to extremist appeals, some relevant to their interests and some not. The unions also fall quickly into the hands of a few leaders, themselves easily managed by others in the government, leftist parties, or clandestine groups. In such a situation Arab trade unions have not succeeded in finding a way to express the sense of protest and the demands of the workers while keeping them independent of employers and governments (though the ideal is not such a perpetual state of hostility toward them that accommodation becomes impossible). It is through trade unions, however, and other occupational and professional associations, as well as through traditional kinship and religious ties, that the integration of urban dweller with urban group will take place. Despite the many rural survivals, such as village and even tribal loyalties, Arab cities are really cities and will attain a viable, satisfactory social life not through vestigial bonds but through those—not yet fully developed—appropriate to modern urban society.

PHYSICAL CHARACTERISTICS

During the last century or so Europe has altered the traditional structure of Arab cities not so much by tearing down the old sections and replacing them with new ones but chiefly by building a "new city" alongside the *medina* or old city. Under independence, the Arab countries have continued this process although they have also revamped the old cities to some extent out of pride and the desire to be modern. With increasing industrialization, new functions are added to the cities' traditional ones pertaining to religion, commerce and administration. Expansion of function and the growth of transport facilities has encouraged and made possible the creation of suburb after suburb around the major cities until now they are the centers of large metropolitan complexes. Around Cairo, for example, industrial suburbs are growing up to a distance of ten or fifteen miles, with the distinct possibility that the lines between Cairo and these suburbs will one day constitute continuous ribbons of urbanism. On a smaller scale, two adjacent cities in Iraq, nearly a hundred miles south of Baghdad, have been expanding towards each other. They are Nejef and Kufa, now chiefly of religious significance but destined for industrial expansion. Blocked in other directions, the two cities have been expanding along the road that joins them. A city-planning consultant has proposed that, rather than have the "backs" of the two cities connect ultimately, they should be planned now as a unit with a single central area somewhere along the path of their growth and then allow to develop around this center.[40] Though such a situation is not found frequently as yet, it will arise increasingly around some of the Arab metropolises and perhaps along new axes of growth such as, in Syria, the line between the port of Latakia, recently enlarged, and the important city of Aleppo.

The traditional Arab town took its shape from two main considerations: religion and protection. Religion required that the mosque should be at the center and related structures close by. Strategy dictated that, as Ibn Khaldun wrote six centuries ago, a town should be located in an "inaccessible place, either upon a rugged hill or surrounded by the sea or by a river," and protected by a wall. He also pointed out, not altogether accurately because of his usual pique (mixed with admiration) at the bedouins, that towns were established by rulers who had to force the people to build them. Under bedouin influence, early Islam did not have the capacity or the inclination to build cities but used what they had conquered. Indigenous urban Arab civilization had only a short period in which to express itself in architecture and city planning, Ibn Khaldun asserted. That period lay between the Islamic conquest of Persia, when Arabs acquired the peace and luxury necessary for the construction of great cities, and

[40] Doxiadis Associates, *Nejef and Kufa*, esp. pp. 76–78.

the destruction of the great Abbasid dynasty only several hundred years later in the middle of the thirteenth century A.D. Other nations, he remarked, had thousands of years to leave a legacy of buildings and towns. The Arab city, he wrote in an era of Islamic disunity and weakness, is born with a dynasty and dies with it: ". . . the life of the dynasty is the life of the town."[41]

The weakness of the tradition of urban construction and the absence of a municipal autonomy perhaps account for the confusion of styles and patterns in the old Arab city. The gridiron (or checkerboard, or rectangular) pattern was the dominant one, but even within towns so constructed, numerous winding little streets and evidences of a circular or radial pattern, more common further east, are found. The center of the town is the mosque, which served not only religious functions but was also the main gathering-place for all purposes. Probably because of this character of the mosque, open squares were not favored, as they were in Europe; indeed, the mosque (like the traditional Arab house), is an open space enclosed within its own walls, rather than, as in classical and later European squares, within a group of buildings. It was not until the advent of European notions of city planning, late in the nineteenth century, that open squares were regularly built in Arab cities, for example in Cairo and Alexandria. In the latter a substantial number of open squares was not envisaged until just after World War I.[42]

Around the mosque in the traditional town are the bazaars, arranged usually in the order in which the products are related to the functions of the mosque.[43] Then came

41 Ibn Khaldun, Rosenthal's translation, Vol. II, pp. 235, 244, 267–69. On the traditional Moslem town, see the brief but comprehensive treatment by von Grunebaum, *Islam*, Ch. VIII.

42 McLean, pp. 62–63.

43 There appears to be some parallel between the proximity of the crafts to the central mosque and the degree of prestige of each craft as measured in the rule of *kafa'ah* (or equality), discussed in Chapter 4, according to which a woman was not supposed to marry a man whose family was socially beneath her own.

the inns, warehouses, public baths, and the trades which required more room, followed by the residential district with its well-defined quarters, and finally the cemeteries on the outskirts. The main government building was near or even connected to the mosque but where there were several buildings, as in a capital city, they were usually near the outermost area of the town.

Though the gridiron is the most common type of traditional Arab town, one of the earliest and most illustrious ones, Baghdad, was built in the eighth century on the circular or radial plan.[44] Called the "Round City," it was located by the second Abbasid Caliph, al-Mansur, on the west bank of the Tigris River. From the outside, first came a large ditch, then a quay of bricks, a first wall, a space, the main wall with numerous towers between the gates, officers' homes, a third wall, and finally an inner space with the caliph's palace, the mosque, and government offices. The city was divided into four equal parts by two roads between the four main gates. This city, built with religion and strategy in mind, its founder called "the city of peace."[45]

A hierarchy of trades and occupations was elaborated by the jurists in this connection which conforms somewhat to their allotted place in relation to the central mosque. Thus the crafts which were not closely related to religious functions and which involved noise and dirt and chiefly manual operations were placed farthest from the mosque. And these are the crafts which were held in lowest esteem for purposes of marriage as well. Convenience and propriety seems to have dictated the place of the crafts in relation to the mosque and then this spatial progression may have been converted into a hierarchy of prestige, as well, in the popular mind.

[44] "Baghdad," *E.I.* (*New*), Vol. I, p. 894ff., and Creswell, pp. 170–73.

[45] Not only was this pattern followed in other cities (and even villages not concerned with defense), but a prominent economic historian went so far as to claim that it was the model for many medieval cities in Europe which were likewise built on high ground near a river and then expanded by reclamation of land in a concentric pattern. This method of construction required certain engineering techniques, such as canalization and embankment, which were spread from Mesopotamia to the Levant and by the

The present Arab city, especially if it has become large enough to be called a metropolis, is considerably different from the traditional one yet shows signs of its heritage. Most cities retain a vestige, called the *medina* or old city, of their earlier structure. Often this is the city's origin as well, once at the center but now, after centuries of growth, just outside it. The old city is the area with both the worst slums and the greatest historical treasures. Originally composed of the various "quarters," it is now most often only an undifferentiated area of poverty and ill-health, and of narrow, winding streets. The traditional bazaar, with its concentration of trades and crafts, is still located in or near this district. As in former times, the old city is a mixture of homes and shops.

Adjacent to the old city is the present center of the city, at its edges rather slum-ridden but at its own center a place of modern residential and commercial buildings. This is usually built in European style, with broad streets and avenues lined by fine shops. It is the commercial center of the city, the entertainment district, the tourist center with the largest and newest hotels. The government buildings are usually in or near this area. Beyond this central business-residential district is the mass residential district still close to the center of the city (before the nearest suburbs are reached). Here are the homes and shops for the middle and lower-middle classes, with some light manufacturing beginning to appear. The newer and more elegant suburbs lie beyond, with fine, modern apartment buildings and villas for the upper middle class and

Christian traders of Syria to Europe. The evidence offered for this assertion of Moslem influence on the European cities of Christendom is the presence on the reclaimed land of these medieval cities of churches and shrines dedicated to St. Nicholas. This cult, the author argues, originated among the Christians of the Syrian cities, Antioch and Alexander, and then spread to Europe partly through the Crusades. St. Nicholas became the patron saint of merchants and sailors. Thus the cult and the method of town building were both spread, so the claim was made, by the merchant-sailors of the Near East. See Unwin, "Eastern Factors . . . ," and *Studies*, pp. 67–70.

the wealthy and the foreign groups as well. Though no city may be built in exactly this way, most of them are close enough to it to let this pattern stand as the modal type.

Even this pattern, however, is already undergoing considerable change under the impact of the growth of urban populations and areas and as a result of the development of a modern professional city-planning movement in the Arab world.[46] Though this movement is only in its infancy, it is already beginning to have an impact as more and more Arabs become urban experts. Until recently city planning was done exclusively by Europeans both under foreign rule in the Arab countries and after they had achieved independence. They introduced a systematic approach to the building of modern cities in the first half of this century in Alexandria, Cairo, Damascus and lesser cities. At first, planning was confined to the built-up areas, then it was extended to anticipate the creation of additions to them. In 1909 Alexandria became the first city to have building regulations adequate from the point of view of planning and zoning, and in 1921 it acquired a plan of growth which guided further building.[47] Until that time, it suffered the familiar consequences of unplanned growth: congestion, slums, high land values, and disorder.[48] Cairo has a master plan worked out by Egyptian planners but it is not yet in effect.[49]

The idea of comprehensive planning, with its requirement for controls as well as building, has not yet been widely accepted, according to one European planner with experience in several Arab countries. Arab ideas of plan-

[46] See, for example, the collection of papers presented at an international seminar on city planning and urban social problems, "The New Metropolis in the Arab World," held in 1960 in Cairo under the auspices of the Congress for Cultural Freedom and the Egyptian Society of Engineers.

[47] McLean, pp. 60, 115, 125–28.

[48] Abdel Hakim, pp. 326–28. On Cairo, see Niazi, pp. 20–21, and Clerget, Vol. I, pp. 255–56, 290–93.

[49] Municipality of Cairo, *Master Plan*.

ning, too, are thus far chiefly concerned with the development of resources rather than the needs of the ordinary man.[50] An Arab planner trained in the West and with considerable experience throughout the Near East has pointed to these limitations on the efficacy of city planning there: unregulated land policy, Arab individualism, governmental preoccupation with national economic planning and politics, lack of trained planners, and lack of appreciation of the nature of planning on the part of municipal authorities.[51]

In building the new cities on top of the old, the Arabs have constructed many roads, monuments, and impressive buildings but have done little comprehensive planning for the mass of the population. Under the old regimes planning was hindered because private interests could prevent the adoption of the restrictions required to put a stop to wild speculation in land and absolutely free construction irrespective of the consequences. Under the new regimes it is possible to obtain the necessary regulations but the danger is that these may go to the other extreme and permit bigness and waste inspired and executed by the state. One of the greatest needs, for example, is better housing for people who simply cannot pay the high rents of new housing built by private interests. Though a beginning has been made in government-subsidized housing, a dent has hardly been made in the problem, and all major Arab cities have high proportions of people living in substandard dwellings whose collapse seems to be prevented only by a continuous miracle. Thousands of migrants from the villages flock to the cities, in some of which, notably Baghdad, they live in vacant lots. Yet, according to one European planner familiar with the Near East, the scanty building codes already do not permit a traditional housing design which would be both cheap and satisfactory.[52]

[50] Lock, pp. 2–5.

[51] Saba George Shiber, "Structure and Planning of Arab Cities: Needs and Obstacles," paper presented to seminar on "The New Metropolis in the Arab World," see note 46 above.

[52] Doxiadis, p. 55.

Accompanying this lack of feeling for human needs in the rush to be as modern as possible has been a disregard for the treasures in most of the old cities in the Arab world. Both under European control and under independent regimes, streets have been bulldozed through areas that could have been preserved, not to mention the failure to restore rapidly deteriorating buildings of great distinction. In Cairo, for example, Europeanization destroyed antiquities in every part of the city, though the intervention of a Commission for the Preservation of the Monuments of Arab Art, created in 1881, managed to save some. A great many others—mosques, houses, and monuments—were privately owned and could not be touched. "The Government," a historian of Cairo remarked at the turn of the century, "apparently has no power either to compel owners to maintain or preserve the historical buildings which they inhabit or let, or to force them to sell."[53] This was not the first complaint, and there have been many since that one. Thirty years ago the architectural consultant to the Commission found it necessary to make a forceful plea to accompany his precise statement of what should be done in the old city of Cairo—but he was skeptical, justifiably, as to the efficacy of his protests after the failure of so many earlier ones.[54] He made two points which still touch the very heart of the problem. First, that the Egyptians do not recognize the treasures they possess: "For them a poor but new building is preferable to an old palace."[55] Second, a plan for the preservation of a city's artistic treasures must accompany the plans for the extension of the city—the two must go together.[56] The lesson seems at last to have been learned, for in planning the high dam at Aswan in Upper Egypt the authorities have enlisted international assistance to remove or protect famous antiquities threatened by the new construction.

[53] Lane-Poole, p. 308.
[54] Pauty, p. 135n.
[55] *Ibid.*, p. 136.
[56] *Ibid.*, p. 142.

The same problem of preservation faces other cities—preservation not only of antiquities but also of some of the comfortable character and beauty built up slowly through centuries and now threatened by the headlong rush to adopt anything modern. Europeans in the nineteenth century destroyed needlessly out of a desire for convenience, familiarity, and economy. Arabs are now destroying their heritage out of a pride that is satisfied with nothing less than the ultimate in modernity and scale. E. M. Forster wrote a guide to Alexandria just after World War I. When he returned for a visit a few years later he was shocked by the ugliness modernism had wrought.[57] And today one hears by word of mouth that Mecca, the holiest Moslem city and the place of pilgrimage for Moslems the world over, has been converted, in part, into a mélange of new structures. Convenience has been achieved at the cost of harmony, and the modernizers destroy not only antiquities already exposed to view but also the possibility of excavation for others still undiscovered.

Some of the complaints of this kind, it is true, hardly conceal a lack of concern for present human needs in the concern for ancient treasures. But that does not vitiate the point that a maximum of destruction of the old accompanies a minimum of accomplishment in building the new.

Arab cities may seem alike in their broad outlines: the inevitable winding streets of the old city and the open character of the new districts. Yet each has a special flavor, though it may not be the same one for all palates.

Cairo has majesty and excitement. It has more dirt and poverty than most other Arab cities but it also has a metropolitan style and grandeur rivaled only by Alexandria. Though Old Cairo has its charms, the modern districts also excel. There the city has size and people, broad avenues and open spaces, and its combination of Oriental and Mediterranean architecture is not ashamed to reach

[57] Forster, p. iii.

and strain for effect. Some cities have the Mediterranean Sea, an undoubted advantage. Cairo has only the Nile, yet it seems less cramped than several cities which can look out over the Mediterranean. It has used the river to give the city range. Cairo has its problems, of course: housing, traffic, too many cars seeking to negotiate too narrow streets and too few places to park, haphazard industrial location, too few open spaces. It is, however, in a favorable position to solve them, for it has a modern planning tradition, some well-trained planners and urbanists in several ministries, and a good municipal authority. Today its public services (always the butt of good and ill humor in the old days) are efficiently maintained and the city is cleaner. A campaign to beautify Cairo led to furious activity from 1954 to 1956, much of it successful. New roads, open spaces, and buildings have, under full independence and a highly nationalist regime, ironically made the city even more European in appearance. The city remains as Flaubert described it more than a century ago, when he saw it after Alexandria: "It is at Cairo that the Orient begins." Now a master plan has been prepared which even envisages a subway system to replace the surface tracks between Cairo and the industrial (formerly tourist) suburb of Helwan fifteen miles south and passing through the fashionable residential suburb of Maadi. The plan also proposes to:

> divide the city of Cairo into eight units distributed round the central business area. Each of these units will approximately accommodate half a million inhabitants completely self-contained with its schools of different types, secondary business centers, hospitals, police, branches of local authorities and Government departments, etc. The open spaces in between these units will contain the main large neighborhood parks, the large sports club and playing fields, the stadium and other recreational, playing activities.[58]

[58] Municipality of Cairo, *Master Plan*, pp. 112, 138.

Ambitious and redolent of a thesis for a degree in a Western city-planning institute, the plan is nevertheless imaginative.

If such a plan were to be realized in fifty years, Cairo would probably still have an electric atmosphere. Its air seems as charged with energy as its streets are filled with people. At once more European *and* more Oriental, Cairo's size and scope permit it to have more than one aspect. Damascus, by contrast, is tranquil. Except for the bazaar district, it is solemn and subdued, almost a cross between a little French and a Dutch city without obvious extremes of wealth and poverty. Cairenes are explosive, Damascenes phlegmatic. The Damascenes seem like nothing so much as mountain people on a plain that is not quite comfortable. A higher proportion of Damascenes wear Western clothing but the men don't look at ease in it and the women wear fine and colored veils over their faces even when they dress in chic style.

Beirut is unique, neither Oriental nor European. Its traffic congestion and building density are justly famous. It is the perfect example of a city that has managed to make itself look cramped despite the Mediterranean on one side and the mountains on the other. To get a sense of space the Beiruti must flee to the mountains, for the city itself lacks scope. It is liberal and tolerant to the point of anarchy. Almost completely Western in appearance, except for a few districts, Beirut is a fledgling—flashy and brash—but somehow not able to soar. The Beiruti knows the ways of the West, but it is the small-time West although he likes to think of his style as sophisticated and cosmopolitan. After ten minutes the most sophisticated among them will tell you, "But you must let me take you to my village. It's in the mountains, less than an hour away." Beirut lives in close relationship with the villages and small towns in the mountains, which double as summer resorts. Unlike Damascus, where the people of the mountains are not the people of the city, Beirut has unending traffic with the mountains. Damascus stands by itself; Beirut is unthinkable without its appended mountain villages.

Beirut's beautiful setting is in a continuous state of decline as unrestricted and unplanned buildings spring up along the coast and inland. It has some fine buildings but they are so badly placed that they go unappreciated. Streets are considered only an unfortunate obstruction in the way of tall buildings. Only the big streets in various districts have widely known names. Sometimes a name seems to refer to a street but turns out to be a small quarter instead. Maps have street names, and recently the government has put up street signs with numbers. No one heeds them in the slightest and few even know them. Streets are known by the buildings in them and the buildings are known not by numbers but by the names of the builders or owners or occupants. It is the Beiruti's genius to get along without the kind of order others seem to need. His government is an obstacle to overcome by acting as if it were not there at all. Yet the government is ubiquitous notwithstanding its impotence. Government buildings are located in several parts of the city but are concentrated in the highly congested central commercial district, where they are considered unproductive users of good and expensive space. For years it has been felt it would be better to collect them all in some out of the way place so that the energetic Beirutis can get on better with their private commerce that is the country's lifeblood. Such a suggestion has been made with a formidable array of facts and arguments by a group of planning consultants engaged by the government itself.[59]

[59] Doxiadis Associates, *La Cité Gouvernementale*, pp. 6, 10, 15, 25.

CHAPTER 4

Men, Women, and Families

Recently I attended a variety show produced by students of the Faculty of Commerce of the University of Cairo. The curtain rose on a replica of the outdoor tea garden adjoining the students' lunchroom on the campus. Several young men seated at the tables were discussing—women, of course. Presently a few pretty girls drifted onstage and took seats at other tables. For a few moments the two groups talked towards rather than to one another. Then a couple of the boys went over to the girls, stood alongside their tables, and the two streams of dialogue became one as they began to discuss whether it was right for boys to approach unchaperoned girls and how they might do so with the greatest chance of success. Beneath the surface of comedy there were undertones of a serious problem seriously considered.

Only on the well-insulated university campuses of the Arab world can one regularly see respectable unmarried young men and women talking freely with one another with implied consent of their absent elders. In the last few years I have seen boys and girls on afternoon dates in quite respectable places, but such meetings are still very rare. Even the university students who mingle freely on the campus do not make dates away from it. So, although the relations between men and women in the Arab world are changing every day, they are still governed, especially in the less sophisticated social classes and places, by old and strict codes of meeting, mating, and the creation of new families.

Because the Arab family has not yet lost so many functions to other agencies as have the European and Ameri-

can family, its influence even upon political and economic
behavior, for example, is still formidable. But considering
the variety of Arab life, how can we speak of *the* Arab
family? To do so is, to be sure, to ignore certain differences
in family life as between, say, Egypt and Jordan, urban
and rural areas, businessmen and laborers, university graduates and illiterates, and, of course, Moslems and Christians. Yet one can profitably discuss the Moslem family
in general, despite these differences, because it displays
certain patterns. This is a result of the strength of tradition in the Arab world, the confinement thus far of profound social change to the wealthier and more educated
classes in the cities, and the pervading influence of Islam
and its prescription for family life. In his perceptive treatment of the Moslem family in Syria, Dr. Kazem Daghestani, a Syrian social scientist and lawyer, points out that
husband-wife relations vary with educational level, wealth,
and social status. "It would certainly be dangerous to generalize," he warns. "We have known, in the large cities,
some Syrian wives who are freer than European women.
We have known some others who still submit to the most
archaic traditions of an oppressive, fanatic and egotistical
husband."[1] Yet he has managed convincingly to describe
a pattern of family life in Syria despite the differences
even within that single region.

Love, Marriage, and Divorce

The most pervading feature of the Arab family is the
strong code governing relations between the sexes. The
highest value is placed upon premarital chastity in women
and upon their marital fidelity. Young men and women
are not free to meet one another as they please or to choose
whom they will marry. Arrangements by which they come
together are made largely by the parents, who take into
account not only family needs and position but also the
wishes of their sons and daughters. But marriage is chiefly

[1] Daghestani, *Etude*, p. 84.

a joining of two families rather than of two individuals. Family life is shaped by the older generation for the younger, and by the desires and values of the men imposed upon those of the women. The Arab Moslem family is rather like the Western family in that both are based upon similar attitudes towards sex, but the Arab attitudes are more rigid and more effective in practice. There are also important differences, which stem from male dominance among Moslems, such as polygamy and the greater ease with which men may divorce their wives.

The high value placed upon female chastity before marriage and fidelity in it is enforced by largely confining women, after puberty, to their own company. Loss of chastity in a girl is still viewed, in all classes and communities, as the gravest kind of misbehavior, to be punished by her father and brothers; the penalty varies from severe disgrace to banishment and even to death in some traditional communities. As for infidelity in a woman, this is considered an affront not merely to her husband but also, since marriage is a joining of families, to her own family; it is her father and brothers who administer the punishment, which, again, ranges from serious censure to isolation, banishment, or death. It is not surprising, therefore, to find that, according to the testimony of young men, few Arab women have sexual intercourse before marriage. Two psychologists asked 113 male students at the American University of Beirut, half of them Moslem and half Christian, to estimate the number of women in their home communities who had such experience. The average of their estimates was four to ten per cent, compared with an estimate of forty-four per cent given, in a corresponding survey, by a group of American college men. In Kinsey's sample of American women, nearly fifty per cent reported that they had had sexual intercourse before marriage.[2]

The strict code forbids discussion of sex between men and women, even between husbands and wives, but it is a

[2] Melikian and Prothro, "Sexual Behavior . . . ," p. 64, and Kinsey, p. 286.

common topic of conversation among men and among women when the other sex is not present. Because so many village families live in one or two rooms, children inevitably see and hear much of sex, yet they must restrain the curiosity and interest which such familiarity arouses. Observers who have lived in the villages report that children hear much sexual talk from the women especially. Winifred Blackman, a woman who spent some time among the Upper Egyptians, says, "Sexual matters form the chief topic of their conversation . . ." Even before children adults "discuss the most private matters without the slightest reserve," so that from their "very early years" children hear sexual matters "spoken of and joked about."[3] But when they reach puberty boys and girls are placed under severe sexual restrictions.

Sexual relationships are dominated by male impulses, of which jealousy is one of the strongest. What Daghestani says of the Syrian husband may be extended to other Arabs as well. "His jealousy," he points out, "derives from his pride and familial honor, rather than from love. His wife is his 'ird, his honor. It is his honor which would be injured if his wife misbehaved."[4] Precisely because the honor of a husband, a father and brothers is tied up with a woman's sexual conduct, men are highly suspicious of women in this respect. They believe (or at least they act as though they believed) that women have strong sexual desires which they are too weak to control. For this reason, they must be carefully guarded; if they were not, the combination of their impulses and their weaknesses would soon disgrace their fathers and brothers and husbands. Hence they are justifiably secluded and confined to their own company. Perhaps the most effective way of preventing such conduct and of ensuring a marriage that would not reflect poorly on the family has been child betrothal and marriage. A girl who is early promised to a man is under the surveillance of two families. Moreover, by selecting her husband when she is young, the family reduces

[3] Blackman, p. 43.
[4] Daghestani, *Etude*, p. 58.

the likelihood that she will be able or even want to exercise her own judgment or preference. The older the girl is when her marriage is arranged, the more likely she is to have her own views.

All this may be only a rationalization for the subjection in which men hold women in the Near East. It may also express their own sense of guilt because they are concerned mainly with their own gratification in sexual relations. Indeed, it may well be that married women, especially, are willing to have extramarital sex experience, and if this is so the inclination may be the result of sexual disappointment. This view is of course only an inference from certain observed practices and attitudes, for there are no reliable data on Arab women's sexual pleasure and it would be virtually impossible to obtain such information among even the most sophisticated classes.

Male suspicion of female sexuality is probably the counterpart of the great value men place upon their own sexual prowess. Though men boast of their virility, they must be careful not to become victims, through their wives and unmarried daughters and sisters, of the virility of other men. The emphasis upon male potency is consonant with early marriage, the practice of taking more than one wife, and easy divorce by the husband. But in recent years, and especially in the cities and among the more educated classes, marriage occurs later, polygamy has almost disappeared, and divorce is hedged about with customary restrictions which make women more nearly the equal of men and legitimately available to men under more restrictive conditions. In such circumstances, the continued consecration of male sexual vigor has increased unsatisfied male desires to the point where sex may be called an obsession with many young men. Dr. Hamady, a woman social scientist of Arab birth, goes so far as to say, "The code of sexual behavior is so strict and restraining that whenever an Arab man finds himself in solitude with a woman, he makes sexual approaches to her."[5] Though

[5] Hamady, p. 58.

this may be an exaggeration, it indicates the extent of male preoccupation with sex.

Potency is so highly valued that resort to special devices to increase it is proverbial in the East. Very recently, the Egyptian anthropologist Hamed Ammar has noted their use in a village in Upper Egypt.[6] The study of Arab students at the American University of Beirut, already referred to, shows that they have had more heterosexual and homosexual experience than a comparable group of college students in the United States.[7] More of the Arab students' heterosexual experience than the Americans' was with prostitutes. Male homosexuality does not seem to be so widespread today as Arab medieval poetry suggests it might have been in earlier eras. The decline of desert-warrior society, the advance of urbanization and the rising status of women reduce the conditions favorable to it. Close friendship among Arab men and boys is often mistaken for homosexuality. The greater resort of Arab students to prostitutes, close friendship among men, and such male homosexuality as remains are all related to the fact that women are still confined to the home and are available to men only under comparatively strict and guarded conditions.

The high value simultaneously placed upon premarital chastity in young women and sexual prowess in men puts a strain upon still another value—fidelity in married women. The strain is eased, as in other societies, by prostitution, which provides a sexual outlet for men that diverts them somewhat from threatening the chastity of unmarried women and the fidelity of the married. Plural marriage and easy divorce (or successive monogamy) among Moslems likewise provide sexual opportunities within accepted, legitimate relationships. But the strain upon fidelity in married women, as in other societies, can become too great. In Western Europe and America premarital chastity and postmarital fidelity in women are valued about equally and therefore, probably, violated about

[6] H. Ammar, p. 97.
[7] Melikian and Prothro, "Sexual Behavior . . . ," p. 64.

equally. But in the Near East, it appears that chastity is more highly valued than fidelity, for married women seem to be freer than unmarried girls. Students, for example, have told me that when they seek sexual relations with women other than prostitutes, they look for prospects among married women rather than among unmarried girls. In part, they do so because married women in the Arab world enjoy greater freedom and mobility. But there is another reason: the consequences of such a liaison are less drastic for both parties. The infidelity of a married woman is serious, but male responsibility for her actions is divided between her father and brothers, on one side, and her husband on the other. Though her ties to her original family are still close, they are weaker than the ties of an unmarried girl to her father and brothers. The wrath of a husband is less feared, by both the woman and the man, than the wrath of an unmarried girl's father and brothers, for her disgrace falls only—and therefore more heavily—upon her family. Moreover, an unchaste girl is a greater burden than an unfaithful wife. The latter's marriage may even survive her conduct, or if it does not she has some small chance of marrying again; even if she is repudiated by her husband and goes back to her own family, she still retains certain rights as a divorced woman and (if such is the case) as the mother of her children. An unchaste girl's chances of respectable marriage are nil, and she has no rights at all because she has no formal status such as even the divorced woman has. So the sanctions against unchastity are greater than those against infidelity, serious as the latter undoubtedly are. Because there appears to be more infidelity than unchastity, common jokes and popular sayings refer more to the supposedly strong sexual appetites of married women than of unmarried girls; unchastity is too serious, apparently, to joke about. One popular saying illustrates the men's belief in the incontinence of women and characteristically involves a married woman: a man is asked which of his children he loves most; he answers, the one

of whose mother's fidelity he has no doubt because he
most strictly guards it.[8]

Free mixing of young men and women, dating and
courting as we know these patterns of behavior in the
West are still largely foreign to Arab society, although
something resembling them has begun to appear among
urban, educated, upper-income families with Western ties.
Western-style romantic love is, of course, known in the
Near East. In fact, some scholars believe that Islamic
poetry was the source of that sentiment, which the trou-
badours spread throughout medieval Europe in the age
of chivalry. In the West, romantic love leads to marriage
but in the Arab world these two institutions have thus
far remained largely unconnected. In Arabic literature
there is much courtship and romantic love but not between men and women who marry one another. Just as
in the literature of European chivalry the main concern
is what the knight does to win the favor of his lady and
not the development of love between them, so in much
traditional Arabic literature the main concern is the writer's ability to express himself beautifully about love and
his lady's attractive features rather than his creation of a
love *story* involving her emotions as well as the man's.
In literature romantic love has not been connected with
marriage because in Arab life marriage has been the consequence not of love between a man and woman but of
a social and economic agreement between the heads of
two families. And because of women's low status in the
Near East, Arabic romantic literature has traditionally
dealt almost exclusively with the emotions of men about
women and hardly at all with the feelings of women (except their physical desires). Women have been merely the
occasion for the creativity of men, for the expression of
their sentiments and the description of their exploits.

Daghestani's observation about Syrian Moslems may be
applied generally to the Arab world. Even in the cities,
he says, marriage is rarely the result of love. Although

[8] Literally, by having his hand upon her sexual organ. Burckhardt, no. 633, p. 224.

love sometimes grows between a man and wife who had not been acquainted before their marriage, even more frequent is the opposite case, in which husband and wife go on living together without loving or even understanding one another. Among the lower classes, he adds, the infrequent marriages based upon love rarely succeed.[9]

Marriage as a union of two families is demonstrated in the betrothal and wedding ceremonies. These vary somewhat as between Arab countries, types of community, and social classes, but they have a common core. When a boy or girl reaches the age at which marriage becomes feasible (usually sixteen to twenty years for daughters and eighteen to twenty-five for sons), the parents look among their relatives and acquaintances for a proper match. Very often two pairs of parents have agreed years before that their children will marry at the appropriate time. Usually, a girl is expected to become the wife of her paternal first cousin, who expects to have the option of choosing her or another girl (although this custom is declining so rapidly, even in traditional communities, as to warrant special mention of this change). In the cities, at least, the girl is always consulted by her parents, as Daghestani points out.[10] Though she may reject her parents' choice, he adds, she may not declare her love for someone not selected by her parents; the well-bred girl, when asked her opinion on this matter, is expected to defer to her father's or brothers' wish. There are still some communities in which marriages are contracted at birth and consummated when the girl has just reached puberty, and where girls are given in marriage to much older men; but such arrangements are becoming less frequent and are certainly not the usual ones.

When parents agree on a match, the bridegroom or his father pays the "bride-price" or a part of it to the wife, and the amount of her dowry is pledged by her own parents. In the presence of a Moslem official authorized by religious and civil law, the marriage contract is signed.

[9] Daghestani, *Etude*, pp. 62–63.
[10] *Ibid.*, p. 13.

This is a secular ceremony by Western standards, for the only religious elements in it are that the contract itself begins with the traditional *bismillah* (the phrase, "In the name of God, the compassionate, the merciful") and the contractors recite the opening verse of the Koran. The groom signs, but the bride's consent is given by her father, brother or some other male relative or guardian. This contract is virtually binding although the marriage is not yet consummated. A few days to a few months later, the wedding ceremony takes place. Separate feasts and entertainments are enjoyed at the home of the bride's parents and at that of the groom's. Then the bride, her parents, relatives and friends go to the groom's house in as elaborate a procession as they can afford, carrying along the goods they are contributing to the union. There another celebration takes place, after which the couple occupy the part of the house reserved for them. Throughout the process, from mate selection to the contract and the consummation of the marriage, the family functions on both sides are much more important and much more in evidence than in the West; the transition is slower to an independent life for the Arab bride and groom.

Who may a Moslem marry? This is governed by the Koran, which forbids a man to marry an idolatress until she becomes a Moslem (ch. 2, verse 220) but permits him to marry "virtuous women of those who have received the Scriptures before you" (ch. 5, verse 7)—that is, Christian and Jewish women who do not become Moslems. Because of certain contemporary practices, or those still within the memory of persons living at the time, the Koran also forbids a man to marry women to whom he is intimately related by birth or by other marriages (ch. 4, verses 26–27). As to the number of wives a man may marry, the Koran says he may take two, three or four but that if he cannot treat them equally then he should marry only one (ch. 4, verse 3). A woman is less free, for she may marry only a Moslem man and may not be married to more than one man at a time.

Though still permitted, polygamy is declining, especially in the cities but even in the villages and among desert tribes. The rising level of education of both men and women, economic changes, and new moral and religious ideas are bringing forth a society in which polygamy becomes increasingly anachronistic. Moreover, most polygamy today is accounted for by men with two wives only. In urban areas the disrepute into which polygamy has fallen is indicated by Daghestani's comment on the circumstances in which a Syrian takes a second wife. The event is accomplished unobtrusively, with no celebration, and the second wife is generally a stranger to the families of both the husband and his first wife. Since a well-to-do or middle-class family will rarely permit a daughter to be taken in marriage by a man who already has one wife, the woman who becomes a second wife is usually from a poor family. The husband, Daghestani continues, tries to conceal the fact from his first wife and to present her with a *fait accompli*. "If the first wife knows in advance that her husband is going to marry again, she leaves their home to spend a few days or weeks with her family and does not return until after the mediation of the two families and at the insistence of her husband, who usually gives her a present when she does."[11]

A traditional restriction upon Moslem women is worth mentioning. This is the doctrine of equality in marriage (*kafa'ah*), that is, that a woman must marry a man equal to her in social position. Professor F. J. Ziadeh, a student of Near Eastern legal institutions, points out[12] that the doctrine has also permitted the guardian of a woman to dissolve her marriage to a man not her social equal if he, the guardian, had not consented to it or had been deceived in granting his consent. What was meant by social equality? Ziadeh mentions six elements: lineage, or degree of relationship to the family of Muhammad the Prophet; Islam, or how long a family has been among the ranks of the believers; freedom, or the number of

[11] Daghestani, *Etude*, pp. 76–77.
[12] F. J. Ziadeh, pp. 503, 510.

generations during which the family has enjoyed free, as opposed to slave, status; piety, including moral conduct; wealth; and trade or calling—here the lowest status was usually reserved for manual labor and work involving dirt.[13]

Ziadeh indicates two points of significance about this doctrine which interest us. First, he says, the doctrine shows the importance of the family in marriage. A proposed groom must be the social equal of the proposed bride so as to maintain the status of her family. Her father and brothers place this limitation upon her because her marriage concerns them as much as (if not more than) it does her, for she is their *'ird,* their honor and responsibility. Second, Ziadeh asserts, the doctrine reveals again the male's distrust of female sexuality and weakness; it was "one of the ways to protect the men of the Islamic society against the shame of a woman's supposed predilection to do wrong."[14]

How far has the doctrine been put into practice? Judging from several of the six criteria just listed, the doctrine is more relevant to the conditions of early Islam than to our own day. Indeed, it is believed that it was one of the later Persian influences upon Islam and that it is actually opposed to the whole spirit of the society, although the formal traditions contain some elements in its defense.[15] As to its practice, the evidence is scanty, though court cases involving the doctrine are found as early as the second century of Islam and as late as 1904.[16] Yet its formal existence must have exerted some effect, for Daghestani asserted in the early 1930s: "Among city-dwellers, the custom which requires the husband to be the equal of his wife in lineage and which prohibits a *mésalliance* only for the woman is disappearing more and more, especially in the large cities, although it is still sanctioned by law."[17]

---

[13] *Ibid.,* pp. 510–14.
[14] *Ibid.,* p. 510.
[15] *Ibid.,* p. 508.
[16] *Ibid.,* pp. 504, 515.
[17] Daghestani, *Étude,* p. 17.

The rules of divorce in Arab Moslem society have emanated from the nature of the relations between the sexes before and in marriage. Until recently, divorce too was governed exclusively by the Koran (ch. 2, verses 226–38) which, like the Old Testament, gives only men the right to dissolve a marriage. The Koran simply says that a man may divorce his wife but that he should wait three months to see if she is to bear a child by him; if so, it would be "more just" if he took her back but he is not required to do so. In any case, the Koran enjoins the husband to be just in the process of divorcing his wife, probably because men, as the Koran puts it (ch. 2, verse 228), are "a step above" women and must therefore protect the weaker partner. The husband, in much of the Arab Moslem world until recently, dissolved the marriage merely by saying to his wife three times, in the presence of two witnesses, "I divorce you." In doing so, he must pay her that part of the bride-price he did not pay at the time of marriage; a divorced wife returns to her father's family and usually finds little difficulty in marrying again if her reputation is good. Her children go with their father if they are seven years old or more and those who are younger remain with her (supported by the father) only until that age, when they join their father; if she has mature children in their own households, a divorced wife may go to live with one of them. Traditionally a woman could obtain a divorce only if her husband concealed his impotence from her before marriage. In such a case she could go to a religious court and demand that the judge require the husband to divorce her.

The Arab Moslem countries have since World War I adopted secular legislation to give further protection to women. The Ottoman codification of family law in 1917, applied in Syria, Jordan, and Lebanon, was an important step. Egyptian laws of 1920 and 1929 went so far as to enlarge the grounds upon which a wife could divorce her husband. A Syrian law of 1953 gives a court the right to refuse a married man permission to take another wife where it is shown that he cannot support both. And in the

United Arab Republic it was proposed to make it grounds for divorce by a wife if her husband takes a second one, and to require a man to go to court in order to divorce his wife, and then only for desertion or adultery.[18] Such legal changes, though based on new public attitudes, usually take a long time to reach the traditional communities, where older customs prevail despite the new laws.

The ease with which a man may divorce his wife is consonant with the general male superiority in Arab Moslem society and with the limitations upon what, in the West, are considered normal social relations between the sexes before marriage. If men and women marry without knowing one another well (indeed often without having seen one another), and in response chiefly to the wishes of their families, it seems natural to expect that some means of adjustment to individual tastes will be found. In the West, it is found in the dating and courtship period in which young men and women get to know one another in relatively unrestricted social intercourse. In the Arab Moslem world the adjustment takes place after marriage rather than before it. And because it is a world dominated by men, the freedom to adjust is almost exclusively granted to the husband; he may divorce his wife easily and take other women as wives. Though there are as yet no statistics to show it, wherever in the Arab Moslem world the relations between young men and women are becoming freer and their own sentiments taken more into consideration in the planning of marriages, there also polygamy and divorce are becoming less frequent because less necessary.

Family Roles

The structure of the Arab family, Moslem or Christian, is basically the same as that of the Western family but the former has changed less and is therefore closer to the

[18] Anderson, pp. 49, 53–54; Daghestani, "The Evolution of the Moslem Family . . ."; The New York Times, Feb. 23, 1960, p. 11, and Jan. 15, 1961, Sec. 1, p. 19.

common basis. As in the West, descent is reckoned through the males, and the father is the head of the family; the Arab father, however, exercises greater authority. When an Arab couple are married they generally go to live in the establishment of the husband's father, a custom which used to prevail but is now rare in Western society. The Arab family is thus still an "extended" one— that is, a household generally consists of a man, his wife, his unmarried sons and daughters, and his married sons and their wives and children. Among the urban educated classes, however, the married couple usually set up their own household, forming the "conjugal" or "nuclear" family, including only husband and wife and their children, which is the prevailing kind in the West.

In the Arab world the extended family is tied to the ownership and inheritance of land. As Ammar points out,[19] a married man can own no land while his father lives, so he remains part of his father's household. If his brothers work together on land left to them by their father, they and their families are likely to live together; if they divide the land, the families live apart. If a widow transfers her land to her brother or lets him till it, she goes to live with him and his family. Inheritance of all forms of property among Moslems is governed by the detailed rules set forth in the Koran (ch. 4, verses 12ff.), in the traditions of the Prophet and in intricate tables of family relationship based upon these sources. A Moslem may in his will freely dispose of only about a third of his property; the remainder must be distributed in accordance with the Koranic prescriptions, which, like the Old Testament, do not give any advantage to the oldest son. Sons inherit equally, and each one twice as much as a daughter. A daughter who is an only child inherits half the property. A wife inherits a quarter of the property if there are no children but only an eighth if there are children to share the legacy.

[19] H. Ammar, pp. 42–43.

The extended family is not, however, an economic unit unless its members live in the same household. There is, as Ammar further remarks,[20] no regular means of economic cooperation among members of an extended family who live in different households, although their unity is nevertheless demonstrated in public and on formal occasions, such as births and marriages. The members are also still held responsible for one another's conduct and for the punishment of those who do wrong. The proper roles of the members of a family are more minutely laid out than in the West. Formal respect is due to the father in the way in which others in the household speak to him and in the way they act in his presence both in the house and in public. As the family's main contact with the world outside the home, he is expected to be a forceful person and generous to the point of ostentation. The Arab mother is formally more subordinate to her husband than a mother or wife in the West, but also wields considerable power through her almost sole responsibility in rearing the young children and in her function as exclusive guardian of the household's finances. As such, she is expected to be frugal and industrious, unlike her husband.

The relationship between man and wife, especially in public, is somewhat more formal than in the West. The division of functions between them is more precise and less often ignored. The Arab husband has fewer tasks in the home itself. In public, the wife must maintain about the same respectful distance from the head of the family as the children are expected to maintain. Little initiative is permitted to children, especially daughters. Sons are expected to be tender toward their mothers, who generally favor them over daughters. Sons are also expected to be less intimate with their fathers than with their mothers. The relationship between sons and fathers is indeed clouded by two features of their proper roles: first, the expectation that the father shall be generous to the point of ostentation outside the home; second, that the son

[20] *Ibid.*, p. 44.

shall at an early age relieve his father of the burden of work. As the son approaches adolescence, he may resent the position into which he is placed by such expectations and by his dependence upon his father's largess.

The Arab extended family has traditionally engendered feuds among wives and generations and sons. A hundred years ago the Frenchman Clot-Bey, who established the first medical school in Egypt, told a visitor to Alexandria concerning the Moslem family of the middle and upper class: "Every hareem [women's apartment in a Moslem home] is a little despotism in which the vices of a despotism—its lawlessness, its cruelty, its intrigues, the pride and selfishness of its master, and the degradation of its subjects —are reproduced on a smaller scale, but not with less intensity. Each wife is, of course, the enemy of all the others. The children take part with their mothers, and hate their half brothers and sisters. They are trained up in the evil passions of a family war—its stratagems, its falsehood, its spite and its revenge."[21] And in our own time Hamady has described the effects of even the monogamous family in similar terms: "Serious conflicts inevitably arise from the communal life of an extended or tribal family in which a large number of people from various generational and collateral relationships live together. This is a fertile source of jealousy, hatred, and defiance among the married brothers and their wives; the mothers transmit these feelings to their children. In general it is a life full of pain, bitterness, and insecurity."[22]

All this is not to say that the Near Eastern family does not satisfy the emotional needs of its members; but in doing so it generates hostility as it provides security, stimulates rivalry as it enforces cooperation. And as the changing outer world impinges more and more upon traditional familial values, the younger members feel increasingly smothered even as the parental grip upon them loosens.

21 Senior, Vol. 2, p. 198.
22 Hamady, p. 39.

The Rearing of Children

In emphasizing Arab modes of child rearing, I do not insist that they alone fix adult character. Undoubtedly the experiences of infancy and childhood, those physical, emotional, and intellectual habits of which both parents and children are often unaware, have great influence upon the kind of adults a society will develop. But even if it were possible to measure precisely the extent of such influences compared to others which go to determine personality, and even if it were reliably established that from its mode of child rearing one could fully describe a group's values and sentiments, there would still be uncertainty because it is not easy to discover and describe just what these modes are and what they mean to the infants being reared in accordance with them. Since this is so in the relatively well-studied, self-conscious cultures of the West, it is much more so in the Near East, about which there are very few good reports either on modes of child rearing or on the social values they are presumed to produce and reflect.[23]

Most Arabs raise their children according to fixed notions accumulated over many centuries. Unlike the educated middle class of the West, their ideal is to bring up children in exactly the same way that they themselves were brought up. Although the educated urban Arabs are moving away from this pattern, the vast majority cannot imagine themselves questioning the rightness of these traditional ways; they would think it funny, if not insane, for example, to go to doctors or to books to learn how to handle children. They want to do as their own parents did, rather than, as so often is the case in the West, deliberately to adopt a different way.

The birth of a baby to an Arab family is the occasion for much more joyous celebration and ritual than in West-

[23] One of the best of such studies concerning the Arab world is H. Ammar's *Growing Up in an Egyptian Village*.

ern societies, even though it is a more common one in the Near East with its high birth rate. This is especially true if the baby is a boy, for boys are highly valued as carriers of the family tradition, the embodiment of the culture's ideals and economic assets in an agricultural society. Infants live in close proximity to adults, but mainly to the women of the household; men and older boys have little to do with infants. Babies are, of course, fed at the mother's breast and are given it whenever they cry rather than according to a schedule. Most infants are weaned after a year but many are not weaned until two years old and some even later. Toilet training is highly permissive; parents seldom try to teach infants to control excretory functions. When the child indicates adequate muscular control, casual efforts are made to instruct it as to the proper place and time for excretion.

Parents pay less attention to children between the ages of three and about six, when they are able to get around by themselves but as yet have no household or economic functions to perform. In this period children learn from their brothers and sisters and begin to participate in groups of their own age outside the home. In later childhood parents begin to train boys and girls for the roles expected of them. In the cities this function is assumed to an increasing extent by modern secular schools, but in the villages and among the depressed urban population it is still the mother who initiates the girl into the routine of household work and the father who takes the boy to the field or to the shop or into the streets.

In the villages, too, the boy goes to the local school in which he learns about his religion and the rudiments of reading and writing.

As boys and girls approach adolescence they prepare to assume adult roles. It is only in the educated urban class that adolescence has become the kind of "problem" period between childhood and adulthood that it is in the West. In the desert, in the villages and among the uneducated urban masses adolescence is hardly long enough to be considered a special interval. In these communities, when the girl approaches twelve or thirteen and the boy fourteen or fifteen they must begin to carry a full adult share of the family's burdens and to think about their own marriage as well. For the girl, adolescence means increasing restriction of the way she dresses and acts and the places she may go to alone or with her friends; the families into which she may marry are already observing her conduct to see if she is suitably chaste and modest. Above all, she must not, by her dress or her actions, display her sexual attractiveness. For a boy, however, this is a period of growing freedom. Almost at man's estate, he now has adult responsibilities in and out of the home but he also has the freedom to move about as he pleases and is less likely to be restricted or punished by his parents. The physical change adolescents undergo are sources of embarrassment, for expressions of sexual interest are severely controlled, especially among girls. There is no such thing as the Western kind of dating among teen-agers. Girls may try to learn from one another how to become sexually attractive, and boys may enjoy horseplay involving talk and daydreams about sex and may even visit prostitutes, but there is no direct discussion of sex between adolescents and adults.

There is thus a serious break between infancy and early childhood on the one hand, which is highly permissive and only casually directed, and later childhood and adolescence on the other, which is restricted and carefully guided. Many observers have noted that Arab children are self-assertive and alert, whereas youths are more timid, retiring, and even apprehensive. Clot-Bey remarked: "During childhood the Arab is cheerful, lively, even clever; but on arriving at manhood, he takes on . . . [a] dull and grave disposition . . ."[24] He attributed this change to the influence of religion upon the youth who becomes an adult, but Ammar sees it, more reasonably, as the cumulative effect of the years of severe discipline beginning in later childhood. Children and the aged are the freest to act as

[24] Clot-Bey, Vol. 1, p. 282.

they please with least regard to conventions. At adolescence boys are less restrained and enjoy increasing freedom as they reach manhood. But girls are even more restricted as they reach adolescence and do not gain in freedom until they are married and become mothers and managers of households.

Child rearing in the Arab world, as elsewhere, is a process of teaching the young to become like the mature. But children in the Near East are made to get over their childhood as early as possible. Parents make their children conform to the ideal: well-mannered, modest, respectful of elders, helpful and obedient. In a word, the child must be *mu'addab*. The common derived meaning of this word when used about children is "well-behaved" (what the French call *sage*) but its original sense is also relevant; this meaning carries the notion of education, training, improvement by careful disciplining. Dr. Sarhan, an Egyptian psychologist, has shown that Egyptian children are more interested than American children in self-improvement and in acquiring social graces, and less interested in material things.[25] These findings attest the effectiveness of parental and religious training, which emphasize acceptance of one's material lot in life and encourage propriety as well as obedience to and respect for elders. More than 150 years ago a British observer of Arab life noticed this type of child rearing and aptly indicated that its effectiveness was linked to the absence of influences other than those of home. "The children of the Arabs," he wrote, "early attain the character of manhood. A grave demeanor, fortitude in suffering, respect for age, filial affection, contempt for frivolous amusements, frugality, temperance, hospitality, are taught in the earliest and most effectual manner—by example; and where there is least probability of counter-instruction—in the house of the father."[26]

This process of cultivation still takes place largely in the home; most Arab children see little if anything of

25 Sarhan, pp. 34, 37–38, 83–84, 91.
26 Browne, p. 427.

formal schools. Most schools, moreover, from those in villages with one teacher to the large modern ones in the cities, emphasize obedience and memorization. With political independence achieved, Arab governments have recently begun to build schools that encourage spontaneity and freedom in learning but this movement has not yet gone very far, for freedom and recreation are looked upon as unbecoming. Play, for example, is tolerated among children only outside the home or school and is expected to end at adolescence. These new schools, nevertheless, along with the media of mass communication, are now beginning to compete with parental influence.

Though Arab parents discourage idle play, they at the same time indulge children's desires and whims. Children find it easy to manipulate their parents, who readily "spoil" them by yielding with little sense of that discipline which they exercise regarding the children's proper conduct and demeanor. This is true especially with boys; they are allowed to dominate all the women in a household, including the mother, sisters, grandmother, aunts, and cousins. Such a privileged position in youth often has harmful effects in adulthood, when men cannot always bend others to their will as they could the women at home. And recently, with changing conceptions of family and sex roles, young men raised in such a way also develop guilt feelings toward their mothers, who bear the brunt of male self-indulgence and egotism.

The overwhelming feature of socialization in the Near East is the requirement that the individual subordinate himself to his family, tribe, or any other group with which he is identified. This is true to a certain extent everywhere in human society but it is certainly more characteristic of Arab than of Western group life. Traditional Islam deals mainly with the community of the faithful and is less concerned with the individual believer. Arab social order in desert and village has likewise treated family, clan, and tribe as more fundamental than the individual. But individual self-assertion is not lacking in Arab Moslem life; it takes the form of a fierce equalitarian sense, as we saw in

Chapter 2. This perennial personal revolt against the smothering influence of the group waxes and wanes in the life cycle of the individual as well as in the history of the entire society.

The frustrations of group domination are most strongly felt by males when, upon reaching adolescence and young manhood, they find that they are expected to make life easier for their fathers and to bend their own desires, regarding education, job, marriage, and so on, to family needs. Among females, the greatest resentment comes, for those who have been to school, when they find in later adolescence that family and other group traditions do not permit them the degree of personal freedom they enjoyed at school and for which their education seemed to prepare them. As for the uneducated majority, from a Western viewpoint we would assume it comes with adolescence, when parents select a daughter's husband and determine much of her future for her. They do this, to be sure, with an eye to her welfare and happiness, but they permit her little freedom to decide how that goal is to be pursued. There is, however, little evidence of much resentment at this stage. From Arab traditional literature, current cinema and discussion and observation, it appears that it is after marriage that the uneducated women express, indirectly, some resentment of group control; they use their small degree of freedom to adopt various subterfuges to acquire more.

Precisely because he is seeking greater individual freedom, the burden of group discipline lies heavily upon the Arab today. Hamady points out that it is the fear of shame that impels the Arab to abide by group standards rather than the prospect of being conscience-stricken.[27] The Arab's morality, she says, "depends on the pressure of an audience. . . . 'What would people say' is the main criterion for his choice." The immediate group, family and neighbors, is ready to blame and punish severely any tendency to assert individuality. Although this bond between

[27] Hamady, pp. 34–35.

individual and group has its beneficial effects, it encourages acts that are approved merely because they are traditional and not because they are good or useful from another or changing standpoint. The individual sees society, therefore, as his "worst enemy": "Rarely does he receive credit for his good deeds, but if he errs, the whip of society" is always in readiness. The educated urban Arab is in a better position to protest with impunity. No longer ashamed of his modern ways, he flaunts them and finds himself considered "shameless"; but such judgments, in the relative anonymity and liberality of urban life, do not exert the control they do in the villages. It is there in the villages, where the great majority of Arabs live, that the individual feels the constraint of the group. "Arab society," according to Hamady, "is ruthless, stern, and pitiless. It worships strength and has no compassion for weakness. . . . Judgment is severe. It is rarely that a bad deed is forgotten; and the heedlessness of a moment may annul the merit of a lifetime."[28]

Changes in the Family

Traditional family life becomes increasingly burdensome to the Arab son or daughter brought up in a changing society that emphasizes education, nationalism and industrial development. The personal initiative implied and evoked by these new values is not compatible with the older kind of family loyalty and the subordination of the individual to parents and a large group of brothers, sisters, cousins, aunts, and uncles. Dormant resentment against the extended family finds greater expression among young Arabs as social change reduces its function but not its claims. Hamady[29] points to the discrepancy between what the family expects of the individual and what it can do for him. In earlier times the family not only commanded loyalty but also gave economic security and protection. In

[28] *Ibid.*, pp. 34, 38–39.
[29] *Ibid.*, p. 33.

a society in which population is rapidly increasing and communication has reduced the isolation of group from group and place from place, the individual finds the large family less and less able to provide the things he wants. As Hamady says, "He questions the right of his relatives to control his life when they neither support him nor help him when he needs them." In his study of a village in the Nile Delta, an American anthropologist, John Adams, found[30] that the extended family performs very few functions; most of the work even in such a village is performed by the smaller conjugal family, non-family peer groups, and specialized governmental or voluntary agencies. The extended family depends upon the land but the pressure of population growth and the attractions of the city induce younger people to live away from the main family home or to leave villages altogether. The ideal of the extended family, Adams asserts, nevertheless retains its hold upon the men. "A man cannot achieve full adult status until he is married, has sons, finds wives for them, and exercises absolute control over them, their wives, and their children." Yet it becomes increasingly difficult to achieve this ideal as fragmentation of landholdings makes it improbable that a man will be able to support his wife and children on what he can expect to inherit, let alone take on the traditional role of head of an extended family household. If the extended family is losing its functions to other agencies, if sons cannot confidently look forward to taking on the role of head of a traditional establishment because they cannot hope to inherit enough land, then the influence of the authoritarian extended family is declining. For sons, as Adams remarks, need not accept their subordinate status in a family system that makes many demands but offers few advantages, especially when opportunities in the cities beckon.

Traditional family functions are declining in the city too. Trade unions, social security, and factory legislation, for example, mean that the state is beginning to do what

[30] Adams, pp. 16–17.

the working-class family may be still willing but is increasingly unable to do in a way that satisfies modern demands. As the state performs more of these functions, including that of education and regulation of marriage, the traditional family will perform them to a decreasing extent.

The individual's growing desire for emancipation from the constraints of the traditional family is shown, I believe, in the results of a study comparing the responses of American and Arab college students to a question asking them to state their three greatest wishes. Among the American students a quarter of the men and a third of the women mentioned family welfare but among the Arabs less than a tenth mentioned it. The authors of the Arab study explain this difference as a reflection of the "strength rather than . . . weakness of family ties in Near Eastern culture"; the desire for family welfare is so great as not to require explicit statement. I should explain the result rather as an indication that these articulate young Arabs, attending the American University of Beirut, seek to get out from under their families' control, however much they may profess loyalty to it in other ways. Long restrained by the family, they now want to express their individuality. This interpretation is supported by the finding that among the Americans less than a third of the men and only an eighth of the women mentioned some sort of personal achievement or self-improvement, whereas among the Arabs this type of wish was given by nearly three quarters of the men and three fifths of the women. Arab concern with self-improvement (as against family welfare) is further shown in the responses to another hypothetical situation, this one asking the students to state three things they were incapable of doing. More than half the Arab students mentioned their inability to change their own personality or character, indicating again their absorption in their individuality; among the Americans, none at all gave this type of response. It is equally interesting that about two fifths of the Americans but less than a sixth of the Arabs mentioned that they were incapable of controlling some feature of their environment rather than their own selves.[31]

The declining social and geographical isolation has, as we have seen, reduced the functions of the traditional large family and the authority of the father. It is also weakening the position of the older generation. As the American sociologist Daniel Lerner points out concerning Lebanon,[32] young men can emigrate from the village and earn money in the cities or abroad. Literate and with some formal education, they acquire prestige through their knowledge of the world outside the village, a world that is increasingly shaping life in the hinterland because of growing economic interdependence, nationalist sentiment, and political unity imposed by central governments. It is to these political and economic changes, indeed, that Berque in part attributes the weakening of old family rites; new sentiments inspired by the wider community, the nation, diminish the intensity of the traditional concerns built around the family and village in Egypt.[33]

One of the most important consequences of these changing relationships within the family is that young men and women are undoubtedly exercising greater personal choice in the selection of those whom they marry. This development and increasing formal education for both boys and girls as well as the growing opportunities for women to follow careers in commerce, industry, and the professions, are all postponing the age of first marriage. This change is reflected in the declining proportion of marriages each year in Egypt, for example; in 1942 there were 15 marriages per 1000 of the total population, in 1952 only 11 and in 1955 only 9.[34] It may be significant that the number of divorces has likewise steadily declined from about 4 per 1000 of population in 1942 to about 2 in 1955.[35]

[31] Melikian and Prothro, "Goals Chosen by Arab Students . . . ," pp. 5–6.

[32] Lerner, pp. 186–87.

[33] Berque, *Histoire Sociale*, p. 42.

[34] U.A.R. (Egypt), Statistical Dept., *Statistical Pocket Yearbook*, 1957, Table 12, p. 16.

[35] *Idem.*

A study of age at marriage of Egyptian men, their wives, and their parents reveals this trend more plainly. Of 658 *fathers* of respondents in this study, about half had been married before the age of 20, but of the 267 married respondents themselves, only a quarter were married so early. Of the 658 *mothers* of the respondents, two fifths had been married before the age of 15, but of the 267 *wives* of the respondents, only a sixth were married so early.[36] Similar evidence has been compiled for Lebanon, where a sample of 1665 men in Beirut were studied in 1952–53. Among them, only an eighth were married before they reached 20 years of age, but among their fathers, in the previous generation, a third married so early. Among their wives only 18 per cent were married before the age of 15 but among their mothers, in the older generation, 29 per cent married that young.[37]

Changing Status of Women

The most profound changes in the Arab family are the result of the emancipation of women through education and their growing freedom to move outside the home. Though it would be premature to speak of equalization of status between the sexes, there is no doubt that Arab women are moving toward equality. There is resistance, especially among men, to the more obvious concomitants of equal status for women, such as freedom to move about in public, adoption of European dress and manners, and employment outside the home. The basic processes leading to the emancipation of women, however, are not opposed but are enthusiastically embraced in the strong desire for national strength. These are education and industrialization, through which the role of women is changing rapidly in and outside the home.

The traditionally degraded status of Oriental women is associated with Islam but does not necessarily flow from

[36] Marouf, pp. 3–6.
[37] Churchill, pp. 32–33.

it. Islamic doctrine does not require such a relationship between the sexes; but what matters is what one argues from Islamic doctrine. In recent years Moslem advocates of emancipation have turned to Islamic doctrine to buttress their position just as the defenders of female seclusion have appealed to doctrine to prevent changes. One traditionalist thus quotes Koranic verses to demonstrate man's superiority over women and goes so far as to claim that a woman in the world of business cannot retain her chastity.[38] At the same time a progressive Moslem woman educated in American schools in Egypt (and the wife of a former Egyptian ambassador to the United States) argues that Islam, so far from enforcing female subordination, actually raised the status of women from its pre-Islamic pagan level. She asserts that (1) the veiling of women antedates Islam; (2) Islam permits women to retain their own names after marriage, to dispose of property without the mediation of husband or guardian, to be themselves guardians over minor children, and to follow any trade or profession without the husband's approval; (3) Islam gave women inheritance rights they had not earlier enjoyed; (4) Islam did not introduce polygamy but limited it, and protects women to some extent from abuse of the man's right to divorce.[39] Granted that all this is true, it is also true that women in traditional Islamic society have been prevented from assuming full individuality by their seclusion and by the practice of polygamy. Though both, especially the latter, are declining, they still retain enough force to keep women in greater subjection to men than is the case in Western society, where the reinterpretation of religion and tradition (which has only recently begun in Islam) has permitted a greater degree of equality between the sexes. There is nothing in Islamic doctrine which cannot be reasonably interpreted today to support the trend toward emancipation of women.

There is, however, much in the Near Eastern social tra-

[38] Kotb, pp. 49–54.
[39] A. Hussein, pp. 442–44.

dition and in the psychology of men that stands in the
way of this trend. Men little touched by the modern world
insist upon maintaining ancient custom with respect to
women as with respect to other aspects of social life. They
cannot, for example, abide the "exposure" of women in
Western dress. It is inconceivable to them that a decent
woman would dress in such a way as to make herself sexually attractive in public. Why should she exhibit her
charms if she does not mean to sell or give them away? It
is indeed a question relevant to any society, including our
own, in which intimate sexual relations are supposed to be
enjoyed only in wedlock. It is only recently that some
classes of men in the Near East have been able to accept
such display without putting that interpretation upon it.

Among highly educated and sophisticated men one
sometimes hears the complaint that equalization of the
sexes will "defeminize" women. It seems true, as these
critics maintain, that Near Eastern women are more "feminine" than Western women. That is because Oriental
women have been trained for centuries to take a place
subordinate to men; they have been bred to please men
and they have done so by cultivating their femininity, by
emphasizing the differences between themselves and the
men upon whom they have depended so utterly. An Egyptian man of letters, Mahmoud Taymur, has deplored this
separation especially because it limits the participation of
women in social life.[40] Girls begin to cultivate their
charms at a very early age under the guidance of their
elders; the Near East does not encourage tomboys. Secluded in their own world, girls and women have not competed in the world of boys and men, so that no masculine
qualities have rubbed off on them, as in the West. A pre-
mium has been put on their femininity and they have
guarded it, nourished it, and developed it to a fine point
which men are reluctant to see abandoned now. But the
women themselves, I believe, take a rather different view
as to the value of their femininity to themselves: they

[40] Taymur, p. 70.

seem to be willing to run the risk of sacrificing it if they can gain greater freedom.

Though it is the educated and middle-class women who most ardently seek emancipation, there is some evidence that their enthusiasm is shared to some extent by the less educated working-class women as well. A study[41] made in the Sudan in 1953 is relevant here, for it was made among Arab-oriented Moslems and probably reflects opinion in the Near East as a whole. In planning new housing, the government asked men and women in two working-class suburbs of Khartoum to rate the importance to them of five features only a few of which could be incorporated. These features were (1) a wall between houses which would give the women seclusion in the yard, (2) a bathroom, (3) a store room, (4) a verandah, (5) a shelter for earthenware water jugs. The men gave the highest priority to the dividing-wall but women gave it the lowest. As the author of the study points out, the men attached the greatest importance to the wall, which would permit the women to be secluded, because they were "conscious of themselves as the guardians and protectors of women . . ." But the women apparently were perfectly willing to do without this form of protection in return for a small household convenience of another kind.

Other evidence of Arab women's aspiration for greater freedom is equally striking. In the study already mentioned calling for Arab students to state their three greatest wishes, the women turned out to be no more interested in marriage than the men; among both sexes about two fifths mentioned it. The study compared the responses of Arab women to the same questions in 1952 and in 1956. In this brief period of four years the proportion of women who mentioned marriage among their three greatest wishes declined from 57 per cent to 41 per cent. Moreover, this proportion, 41 per cent, is actually lower than the proportion of American college women, 48 per cent, who mentioned marriage in exactly the same type of study.

[41] Fawzy, p. 36, and *passim*.

Finally, it is significant that in 1952 only 28 per cent of the Arab women mentioned a personal achievement among their three wishes but in 1956, 58 per cent did so.[42]

There is a wide gulf between what educated Arab women want and what Arab men want for them. This difference is clearly brought out in a study of attitudes of college students in ten countries, including Egypt. It was found, for example, that the Egyptian men *expected* to have an average of 4.3 children each whereas the woman expected only 3.16. This male expectation was the next to the highest in all ten countries; the Egyptian female expectation was far from the highest and indeed was slightly lower than that of American college women. Asked how many children they *wanted* to have, the Egyptian men's responses yielded an average of 3.53, compared with only 2.74 for the women. Again, the Egyptian women said they wanted fewer children than the American women, whose average was 3.76. Moreover, the difference between the *expectation* of the Egyptian men and women is the greatest in all the ten countries, while the difference in the number they *want* is the second largest.[43] An equally revealing response was given to the question regarding the propriety of a woman working after marriage. Three quarters of the Egyptian men disapproved but only 38 per cent of the women did so. Again, the difference between the Egyptian men and women was the largest one between the sexes in all ten countries.[44] The ideological emancipation of Egyptian women students is further revealed in the proportion who expressed a need for religious faith. Among the men 68 per cent did so, compared with only 59 per cent among the women. These results placed the Egyptian men among the male groups most favorably disposed toward religion and the Egyptian women among the female groups least disposed in that direction. It is in-

[42] Melikian and Prothro, "Goals Chosen by Arab Students . . . ," Table 1, p. 5.
[43] Gillespie and Allport, Table 2, p. 54.
[44] *Ibid.*, Table 13, p. 60.

teresting to note, furthermore, that the proportion of Egyptian women expressing a need for religion, 59 per cent, is lower than that of American women, 77 per cent.[45]

A study of two generations of women in Amman, Jordan, confirms these reports from other Arab countries. A higher proportion of the younger women were found to be literate and their average number of years of schooling was greater. Among them, also, a higher proportion are employed outside the home, have abandoned the veil, and participate in community activities. As to the manner in which their husbands were selected, almost half of the younger women, as compared with only an eighth of the older, reported that they were consulted by their parents in this decision. This result may partly reflect only their greater desire to be consulted; but there is no uncertainty regarding the fact the average age at marriage was higher for the younger women. In attitudes, too, these younger, more educated women display modern expectations, for the average number of children they say they want is smaller than that given by the older women. It is significant, moreover, that the older women, too, place a limit on the number they want rather than acquiescing in having as many as God grants them.[46]

These studies show chiefly the aspirations of Arab women for greater freedom. Similar evidence that they actually enjoy greater freedom is unfortunately not so abundant as that given for Amman. Yet, anyone who has visited the Arab countries from time to time can testify to the easily visible differences in the role of women, their increasing freedom of movement, larger numbers working in factories and shops, and their progressive discarding of the veil and the traditional Oriental gown and shawl for Western dress as a sign of their changing status. Formal public education for girls has become much more common not only in the cities but in villages as well. The following table shows that enrollment of girls in public primary

45 Gillespie and Allport, Table 8, p. 57.
46 Hirabayashi and Ishaq, pp. 38–39.

schools increased nearly five times in the last generation (while total population increased only by about a half).

TABLE 1. *Enrollment of Girls in Public Primary Schools*

	1931	1954
Egypt	109,932	588,689
Iraq	7,046	62,530
Jordan	—	62,327
Lebanon	27,256	63,302
Syria	19,173	90,555
Total	163,407	867,403

SOURCE: *Compulsory Education in the Arab States*, Unesco, Paris, 1956, p. 67.

Although most parents remain more reluctant to place or maintain their daughters than their sons in school, even this old prejudice is becoming weaker. In Egypt, for example, the discrepancy is lowest for the Arab world; yet even there about a quarter of the girls (but half of the boys) of school age are actually attending public school. Girls, however, form a rather high proportion of the total enrollment in public primary and secondary schools, as the following table shows:

TABLE 2. *Proportion of Girls to Total Enrollment in Public Schools, 1954*

	PRIMARY SCHOOLS	SECONDARY SCHOOLS
Egypt	40 per cent	38 per cent
Iraq	25	26
Jordan	30	25
Lebanon	39	41
Syria	29	31

SOURCE: Constructed from data in *ibid.*, p. 68.

A higher proportion of girls attend schools in the cities, of course. Although, as we have just seen, only a quarter of all Egyptian girls of school age were enrolled in public schools, a study of a foreign-owned firm in Cairo reveals that fully half of the daughters of manual laborers were in attendance.[47]

The effect of education and employment is to give Arab girls a wider perspective and to create desires which traditional seclusion cannot satisfy. Emancipation has led to the organization of hundreds of women's clubs and societies. Some of these are feminist, seeking to expand women's rights and to promote their welfare in modern terms. Others have charitable and educational functions. Many are affiliated with international women's groups.[48]

Emancipation of women in the Arab world has proceeded indirectly largely as a consequence of their greater education and freedom to work outside the home, rather than as the result of direct legislation aimed at revolutionizing their status. The distinction between the pace and means of emancipation of Turkish and Egyptian women, made in 1940 by a prominent Egyptian feminist, is still valid and for the entire Arab world as well. "In Turkey," she asserts, "it was done in a sudden and planned way. It was the work of Kemal Ataturk who, enjoying absolute power, could disregard the weight of tradition and realize his reforms as he intended them. It was not the same in Egypt. If women . . . dedicated themselves to the cause of feminism, they found before them many obstacles erected by conservative minds."[49]

Some interesting evidence of the growing freedom of women in Egypt is revealed in a study by an Egyptian social scientist.[50] He interviewed 500 girls in the secondary schools of Alexandria, of whom three quarters were between sixteen and eighteen years of age, and their mothers, three quarters of whom were thirty-nine to forty-eight. Of the girls, none, of course, were illiterate and all

[47] Socony-Vacuum Co., unpublished study.

[48] A list of these Arab women's organizations and a brief description of them is given in *The Arab World* (The Arab Information Center, New York) May–June 1958, Vol. 4, Nos. 5–6, pp. 2–6.

[49] Shafik, p. 164.

[50] Mito.

had graduated from a primary school. But among the mothers, two fifths were illiterate and only another two fifths had completed primary school. In the generation before that, among the girls' grandmothers, nearly three quarters were illiterate and only a tenth had completed primary school. The study confirms other impressions too. This present generation of middle-class girls enjoy more personal freedom to move about, to leave the house alone and to stay out later, and to choose their own clothing. Their amusements, too, are less sedentary and secluded than were those of their mothers, and no longer include such pastimes as playing cards and breeding birds.

The attitude of Arab men towards all these changes is ambivalent. I believe that most men are very sentimental about their mothers, whose subjection and seclusion they resent. This attitude is favorable for the emancipation of succeeding generations of women, but the conditions of family life and the values implanted by it and the society at large dispose men toward keeping their own wives in traditional subordination to themselves and in relative seclusion as well. When it comes to their daughters, however, they are more easily convinced of the advantages of female emancipation and independence, especially from their husbands. Men who don't mind their own wives' lack of education, for example, want very much to have their daughters educated. This is not only a reflection of changing times and a realization that education is valuable; it also reflects men's perhaps subconscious feeling that what they regard as the mixed blessing of education for girls will bring only advantages to the fathers and the disadvantages to the husbands. They are more willing to accept change that does not ultimately touch their own family life, for their daughters will marry and become the responsibility mainly of someone else. Men are increasingly aware of the repressive character of traditional family life for women but they find it easier to insist upon female self-direction where their daughters, rather than their wives, are the ones to achieve this goal. Young men, themselves more highly educated than the previous generation, have become more imbued with ideals of sexual equality and usually seek wives on at least their own educational level. This means that now proportionally more marriages begin with a greater measure of independence for the wife.

The rising status of women and their emergence into the world of affairs is one of the most powerful forces for change not only in the Arab family but in Arab society in general. If forces already set in train are permitted to work out their potentialities or, as is likely, even to become more pronounced, there is no doubt that women's aspirations, demands, and successes will transform Arab society profoundly and permanently.

CHAPTER 5

Personality and Values

People interested in the Arab world today want to know simply: what kind of person is the Arab? To the social scientist such a plain question is exasperating and forbidding. He begins to think of the statements he can make about Arabs in general, and the more he thinks the more qualifications he feels he must put upon any answer he might give. Arabs, he says, differ from country to country, and certainly the Arab of a hundred years ago—or even twenty—is different from the Arab today. Yet the simple question has a nagging relevance; is it really unwarranted? Unanswerable, perhaps, in a definitive way, but not unwarranted. For that is what anyone, social scientist or not, wants to know about any social group: what kind of people are they?

Having examined some socio-historical forces in the Arab world and certain leading current institutions, we are now in a position to see how these two sets of influences combine to produce the Arab personality or general outlook. The idea of an "Arab personality" is a formidable abstraction to which I must resort in order to say what "kind of person" the Arab is. I shall take it for granted that no one expects such a summary statement to describe all Arabs in all their individuality—old and young, male and female, Moslem and Christian, Westernized and traditional, peasant and worker, educated and uneducated. What I shall attempt is to delineate a group of traits encompassing the Arabs in their variety, a kind of modal point which they approximate in varying degrees. To be sure, Arab values, attitudes, and ways of doing things are changing under the impact of the events and ideas examined in the previous and succeeding chapters. Conditioned by the past, personality also changes with and in turn helps to change social institutions. The Arab personality I shall describe has many sources: the nomadic bedouin values that permeated Arab society and Islam, the claims of the religious system itself, the long history of subordination, crushing poverty, and patterns of child rearing which stem in part from these sources and reinforce them in generation after generation.

Egotism and Hospitality-Hostility Pattern

Discontented with the centuries of stagnation, humiliated at having to adopt the ways of their conquerors, frustrated in their efforts to wrest more power to direct their own affairs, the Arabs display the double effect of wounded pride—self-exaltation and self-condemnation. If it is the former side that the West sees most often, it is because that is the side the Arabs present to others and because the West knows little of the Arabs' relations among themselves.

The self-exaltation so prominent in Arab nationalism has characterized most other nationalisms that have had to struggle for self-expression against materially superior rule from the outside. But the same exaggerated self-esteem may be seen in the conduct of the individual Arab in his day-to-day relations with others, entirely apart from political and nationalist affairs. The Arab seems to harbor two major contradictory impulses: egotism and conformity. The first takes the forms of extreme self-assertion before others, pride, and sensitivity to criticism. The second is reflected in obedience to certain group norms which are resented, and an inability to assert independence as an individual with confidence or finality.

The paradox has two explanations. The individual rivalry that is manifest in bombast and sensitivity is itself engendered by the values of the group, that is by the family,

clan, tribe, religious, or national group to which the individual owes allegiance and his very being. Each of these
groups has a fierce sense of self-identity and of difference
from others, but as yet no one of them has been able to
command enough of the Arab's loyalty for long enough
to preclude the hostility between the smaller groups within
it. It was only for a brief time that Islam was able to encompass the conflicts, always latent and often demonstrated, between families or tribes, the desert and the
settled areas, or even between ethnic groups or different
nations in the Moslem fold. More recently, pan-Arabism
has seemed to be destined for the role of internal pacifi-
cation, but it has not yet succeeded in overcoming even
broad national differences and is certainly far from creating the kind of unity that would materially reduce conflict and rivalry on less exalted levels of the society. So
group loyalties have themselves produced the easily injured pride of the Arab.

Moreover, in recent generations the individual Arab's
self-assertiveness has been directed not only against other
groups but also against his own. This is particularly true
of the family, the group that presses most heavily upon
the individual, and, in the villages, of the neighborhood
as well.[1] For a long time Arab society has revealed a
tension between individual claims and the claims of the
group. Incompletely emancipated, the Arab's resentment
has exploded in the same direction as before: boastful-
ness, exaggeration of his capabilities, and a tendency to
see the slightest skepticism in another as a grave insult.
But now his resentment toward his own groups has intensified his inner discomfort. The rivalry the family has
nurtured is being directed against it as well as other groups
and individuals. And the tempest of change that has bat-
tered the Arab world has scattered and confused loyalties
that were once firmly grounded, if only in the immobility

[1] In many cases the locale and the family are identical, owing
to the frequency of marriage among cousins, the broad definition
of family to include distant relations, and the extreme care with
which family connections are reckoned and preserved.

of the society. The result is that the Arab's self-assertiveness can no longer be controlled in the old ways and
spills out in any direction the individual is inclined to
take, either through deliberation or unconsciously, without
knowing what moves him.

As a result of historical influences and contemporary
patterns of child rearing and family relationships, the Arab
displays what might be called a negative individualism
which is less an affirmation of his own worth than a revolt
against the groups that hold him in thrall. It is an excessive reaction stemming from frustration and the impulse to cast off restraint, but as yet only a subconscious
and inchoate effort to realize and extend his capacities.
As Hamady summarizes it,[2] the Arab manifests his individualism "in a unique sense of self-esteem, in his wish
to assert differences, in lack of social consciousness and
civic responsibility, in an unruly spirit and disobedience
to authority, and in the absence of cooperation with and
trust in others." Dr. Jamil Saliba, a leading educator from
Damascus, points to some interesting aspects of Arab individualism as it relates to civic order. Though the Syrians
and Lebanese are extreme individualists, he says, they
want the government to do everything for them. "They
ask their governments to plant their deserts with figs and
olives, to make their wells gush forth, to revive the land
for them, and to guarantee their livelihood. But whenever
they are called upon to work in cooperation, they object
and each one prefers to do the work individually."[3] The
Arab cannot conceive that various interests can be har-
monized in such a way as to make a general rule work
in his own interest. As Saliba puts it, "he does not like
any system imposed from outside and he will not be bound
by it. His main concern is with his private welfare, and
he is egocentric in his family, trade union or political
party, as though any system imposed from outside must
be inherently chaotic because it must be composed of the

2 Hamady, p. 87.
3 Saliba, p. 29.

incompatible inclinations, desires and interests of individuals."[4]

The Arab's incomplete emancipation from the groups that dominate him intensifies the lack of personal security resulting from casual child rearing, family instability, arbitrary rule, and poverty. His insecurity shows itself in a considerable amount of oral activity, in the relation between hospitality and hostility, in suspicion, and in a certain kind of extremism.

The Arab's virtual obsession with oral functions can hardly escape notice; it strikes the observer in Arab reverence for language and oral arts as well as in the Arab attitude toward food. The richness of Arabic has had an almost bewitching effect upon those for whom it is the native language. Gibb remarks,[5] "The medium in which the esthetic feeling of the Arabs is mainly (though not exclusively) expressed is that of words and language—upon the Arab mind the impact of artistic speech is immediate; the words, passing through no filter or logic or reflection, which might weaken or deaden their effect, go straight to the head." The spoken word has entranced Arab society before and after Islam, in poetry (which is chiefly oral rather than written), in sermons, in song, and now even in political speeches.

Oral communication, of course, assumes great importance in a society with a high proportion of illiteracy, but the infatuation with "artistic speech" and song extends to the literate Arab as well. Education does not seem to reduce the Arab's susceptibility to the charms of a good sermon, a political harangue, or the songs of popular male and female entertainers. Great value is put upon the ability to chant the Koran and to memorize it completely, and upon recitation or verbal dexterity in every conceivable form. The Arabic root *qara'a* (from which "Koran" is derived), means to read but more specifically to recite or read aloud. The word *shahid* means a witness but more

[4] *Ibid.*, p. 30.
[5] Gibb, *Modern Trends in Islam*, p. 5.

specifically one who testifies orally. Oral testimony in Islamic law is superior to circumstantial evidence. An Arab political scientist, perhaps exaggerating out of dissatisfaction with Arab politics, has gone so far as to claim that esthetic appreciation of the language has hindered its use as a means of conveying ideas clearly. "Unless one is in full command of an idea," he writes, "and unless he has it precisely articulated in his head, he should not attempt to publish it in Arabic—for somewhere on the way he will eventually lose it and find himself, to his surprise, writing thoughts he never dreamed of."[6]

Jacques Berque, the French student of Arab and Moslem affairs, has remarked with good reason that the Oriental prefers words to things and speech to action because he has not mastered the world of things. To the Westerner, nature rules but can be mastered if understood; to the Oriental nature simply rules.[7]

The preoccupation with food in Arab society begins in infancy and extends through childhood. The essence of hospitality is the offering of food. In Islam, as in other Semitic religions, food is sacred. But the Islamic attitude toward it that prevails today comes from other influences as well—from endemic poverty and constant hunger, and from an unconscious seeking for the emotional security social life fails to provide in adequate measure. Ammar[8] notes Arab children's continual concern with food; they are nearly always eating or chewing something, and their stories and teasing games usually deal with food. Adults, too, seem always to be chewing, smoking, and drinking, whether in company or not. I remember a Christmas broadcast over the Cairo radio in 1953 in which the listeners were told not what messages were preached or ceremonies performed around the world but what foods were eaten.[9]

[6] Salem, "Form and Substance . . . ," pp. 19, 17.

[7] Berque, Leçon Inaugurale, pp. 14–15.

[8] H. Ammar, p. 115.

[9] This may attest, also, the interest in food among the people who observed the holiday, but it is significant that for the Arab radio audience it was the only feature thought worthy of mention.

The famous Egyptian writer, Taha Hussein, describes a revealing incident in his autobiographical story[10] about a blind boy. He gives more attention to the boy's shame and embarrassment at his clumsiness while eating than to his inadequacy, for example, in running and playing with other children. He describes how the blind boy tried one day to eat a morsel of food with two hands instead of one "as was customary." His brothers laughed at him and his parents were critical. This incident of failure in eating etiquette deeply affected him: it "curbed his curiosity, and filled his heart with a shyness which lingers even yet." It is hard to imagine such a situation in a comparable Western home.

What happens when two exaggerated egos meet? They either clash or find some mode of accommodation. These are the extremes of Arab interpersonal relations: excessive hostility alternating with excessive politeness.

Politeness and hospitality are virtues Arabs extolled before the rise of Islam. As one writer puts it, "The pagan Arab's idea of morality is expressed by the word *muruwwa*, that is, manliness, *virtus*. This consists mainly in courage and generosity. His courage is shown by the number of enemies he kills, by his defending his own clan, but also by chivalrous treatment of his foes very much akin to that of the mediaeval knight. His generosity appears in his being always more ready to join in the fray than to share in the spoil, in his readiness to slaughter his camels for behoof of the guest and of the poor and helpless, and in his being generally more willing to give than to receive."[11]

There are special reasons why such a pattern should develop among desert nomads but, like so many other of their values, it has permeated the rest of Arab life. In the desert, hospitality comes about as a means of overcoming the individual's helplessness in so harsh an environment. In the villages and cities, it has a different function; it

10 T. Hussein, pp. 17–18.
11 Article on "Djahiliya," *E.I.*, Vol. 1, p. 999b.

reduces the tendency of the ever-present hostility to burst into violence at every moment. Exaggerated hospitality and politeness are reactions to exaggerated hostility, at least in part.

Arab life is filled with interpersonal rivalry—tribal feuds in the desert, family and village feuds in the settled areas, and intergroup hostility (more controlled, however) in the towns. Arab political writers never tire of stressing not only Arab brotherhood but also Arab contentiousness which they blame, together with imperialism, for the Arab failure to achieve total unity. Poverty and frustration— sexual as well as economic and political—are so pervasive that there is a great deal of what we may call "free-floating" hostility. Politeness is a means of maintaining enough distance to prevent aggressive tendencies from becoming actual. Hospitality and generosity are means of demonstrating friendliness; they ward off expected aggression. One has the feeling, indeed, that the hostility that becomes overt aggression is so uncontrollable that such measures as excessive politeness (a form of avoidance) or hospitality (a form of ingratiation in a situation where intimacy cannot be avoided) are at times absolutely necessary if social life is to be maintained at all.

Conflict is so much on the verge of breaking out that interpersonal relations seem to be largely directed at avoiding or covering up the slightest tendency toward the expression of difference. There are few informal mechanisms for the serious discussion of opposing beliefs without a display of intense animosity; except among a few highly educated members of one elite group or another, people do not discuss differences, or they do so with a bitterness that is constantly at or over the edge of violence. People seem to sense that the slightest tendency to verbal disagreement may easily lead to unmanageable discord, and must therefore be suppressed or channeled through a mediator. Most visiting in homes is the occasion for a display of hospitality, rather than for an animated exchange of views on any subject, serious or trivial; people sit around and exchange pleasantries, family news and gossip but avoid subjects that may evoke the expression of difference. An Egyptian social scientist has said that Arab society as a whole has an "excess in personal feelings which makes the individual avoid a difference in opinion and consider it a personal insult . . ."[12] Saliba makes a similar comment on the Syrian and Lebanese: "He holds fiercely to his own opinion and would like to impose it upon everyone; and if people disagree with him, he will intrigue against them and consider them inimical."[13]

An Arab historian[14] says of Syrians and Lebanese: "Suspicion, fear, restlessness, lack of confidence in the future, lack of social balance and stability are characteristics which the people display." A study previously cited reveals that a sample of Arab Moslem students at the American University of Beirut made a significantly higher average score than a sample of American college students on a scale designed to measure feelings of hostility toward others.[15] Suspicion is not only the outcome of the experiences of the individual in his own childhood and later years but also a heritage of Arab history. Centuries of arbitrary rule by native or foreign predators have created a fear of revealing personal facts that may be useful in setting tax rates or conscripting youth for military service. The whole tenor of Arab society is to encourage self-esteem and egotistical claims of personal worth while discouraging the public display of possessions that in private becomes the essence of hospitality. Openness and friendliness are valued, but suspicion is never dissipated. A popular saying[16] tells of one who says, in reply to an offer of something for nothing, that his sack is not big enough to hold it. The advice is precisely the opposite of that given in the maxim popular in the West, "Don't look a gift-horse in the mouth." The Arab feels that a gift is just

12 Rizk, "The Individual and Society," p. 93.
13 Saliba, p. 22.
14 N. Ziadeh, p. 237.
15 Melikian, pp. 48–50.
16 Burckhardt, no. 254, p. 80.

what one ought to question, and the terse parable implies that an apparently selfless donor is not to be trusted.

A comparative study of attitudes among college students of ten countries in different regions showed the Egyptians to be especially suspicious. In listing three influential events in their lives, Egyptians mentioned more often than any others disagreeable experiences that engender distrust of people. The reply to another question showed Egyptians leading all other respondents in the proportion agreeing with the statement that the "world is a hazardous place, in which men are basically evil and dangerous."[17]

The Egyptian anthropologist Hamed Ammar tells of the suspicion and mistrust he found when he studied the town in which he was born and raised and where his family still lived. He remarks[18] that he could not obtain usable life histories of individuals because of resistance on the part of those he approached. "They were ill at ease," he says, "at doing things for research, reluctant to engage in any activity which might be considered as dangerous gossip, especially when recorded on paper, and might reach official circles. Their attitude is that personal problems should be 'covered' and not 'exposed' to others." This is the universal attitude, of course, about facts one is ashamed to reveal. Hamady points out that secrecy comes from "fear of negative judgments" by family and neighbors, who are so quick to find fault. She quotes[19] two Arabic popular sayings enjoining this resort to secrecy: "He who has done a shameful deed must conceal it for revealing one disgrace is another disgrace"; and "A concealed sin is two-thirds forgiven."

But Arab secretiveness also extends to facts that one is not necessarily ashamed to reveal. I learned this in a vivid way in 1953 when I was preparing a questionnaire to be answered by higher civil servants in Egypt, a rather well-educated and sophisticated group, certainly more familiar than peasants with social research. In a draft of a letter

[17] Gillespie and Allport, p. 23.
[18] H. Ammar, p. 10.
[19] Hamady, p. 37.

explaining the nature and object of the research, I followed the usual procedure in the West of encouraging the prospective respondents to reply by pointing out that their answers would be kept confidential and that I was not so much interested in eliciting their "opinions" as I was in obtaining "some facts" about themselves. I showed the draft to a group of Egyptians who were helping me, and when we came to this part of the letter several of them could not understand it at all. After much explanation back and forth, it became clear that they and I had perfectly opposite notions of what the Egyptian civil servant would consider an encouragement to respond to the questionnaire. I had assumed he would find it reassuring to learn that I was not seeking his "opinions" but only "some facts" about himself, whereas my Egyptian advisers felt that to ask for facts would be disastrous, but that the civil servants would find it relatively harmless to express their opinions.

Arabs do not like to give information about themselves to strangers and officials. Place of birth, age, occupation, parents, wives, and children, all are felt to be private matters in an original meaning of that word, that is, to inhere in themselves in almost a physical sense. Such facts are part of one's person, and to display them is not only to invite gossip or to facilitate taxation and military conscription but also to expose oneself to the evil eye, to the hostile spirits infesting the very atmosphere. This is a fear found among many preliterate peoples. Among Arabs there is interesting linguistic usage to illustrate the same trait. The word for "reveal" is *kashafa*, which also means to remove the veil, a woman's proper face covering. A *makshufa* (the past participle of the same root) is an immoral woman, that is, one who is "revealed" or "displayed" because she does not wear the veil. The opposite conception, to "cover" or "conceal," is *satara*, which means also to "take care of," or to "protect." If one is asked how things are, one answers, *mastur al-hal*—we're fine, getting along well—literally "the condition is covered," not revealed, not open to others.

This reluctance to reveal more than is absolutely necessary takes an amusing form that I have witnessed. On
entering a taxicab, a Near Easterner, non-Arab as well as
Arab, very often will not tell the driver the exact destination but will give piecemeal directions as the trip pro-
gresses. Near the end, he will point to the place where he
wants the driver to stop. Now there are two simple and
perhaps sufficient explanations. First, precise addresses
have not been used regularly and so are frequently not
known. Second, a passenger often fears that the driver,
deliberately or through ignorance, will take a circuitous
route and so run up the charges. But I always sense other
impulses at work too. The passenger, I feel, hesitates to
announce his destination because to do so would give the
driver too much knowledge—hence power?—over him.
Why should the driver, a stranger, be told any more than
he needs to know at any moment? Moreover, is it not
challenging fate to announce a destination? How can the
passenger be so confident as to say where he is going when
so many things may prevent his getting there? And might
not such arrogance tempt disaster? From his side, the
driver too is wary of challenging fate. When a passenger
enters his taxi, he asks, "Where to—if God wills?"

As we saw in Chapter 4, Arab parents do not regularly
attend to children in a predictable, routine way; the general practice is to give only such attention as cannot be
avoided because of the child's insistent demands. An infant is called a *jahil*, an ignorant one; as such he need
not be noticed much. The parents simply wait until he is
old enough, perhaps six or seven, to be formed properly
into an adult as quickly as possible. From the casualness
of infant care there is an abrupt transition to rigidity in
training the older child. In both cases the approval, indeed
even the attention, of parents is bestowed seldom and without predictability. The arbitrariness of parental control
induces children to learn ways of getting attention and
approval, to ingratiate themselves in order to qualify for
the rewards and avoid the punishments Arab parents consciously confer as a calculated method of getting children

out of the period of "ignorance" and into one of usefulness. Centuries of arbitrary government by overwhelmingly
superior forces, native or foreign, have further supported
this pattern of ingratiation. Such power could be placated
only in day-to-day relationships, and though there was
plenty of hostility it could not often take the form of
revolt. Subordination induced obsequiousness. Nor has the
development of nationalism and the achievement of political independence changed this pattern as yet. Today the
Arab must seek to ingratiate himself with the arbitrary
native ruler just as he formerly did with the foreign one.
George Young, the British historian and diplomat, has
shrewdly observed[20] of Egypt that its typical stories show
the nation in a feminine role conquering by ingratiation
and wiles the male representatives of a succession of
foreign rulers—Greeks, Romans, Arabs, Mameluks, Turks,
Albanians, and British. Egypt is the "designing minx" and
its history may be read "as the story of a captive Cleopatra
and of a conquering Antony or Caesar."

A proverb expresses the value placed upon ingratiation:
"Humility in need is manliness."[21] The Arab's ability to
carry out this advice is described by Hamady: "The Arab
changes his identity with little reluctance. With the
Asiatics he is an oriental, with people from the West he
is an occidental, with the old societies he is a traditional man, with the new a modern. The Arab is ready
and able to form an in-group on relatively meagre bases
for identification. He always manages to find some common ground and hastens to create the atmosphere of an
in-group necessary for the success of conducting a business, carrying out a plan or obtaining a favor."[22] Although
this characterization best fits the "Levantine" Arab traders
in the big commercial centers, it also applies, with appropriate adjustments, to the Arab population as a whole.

[20] Young, pp. xi–xiv.
[21] Burckhardt, no. 248, p. 78.
[22] Hamady, pp. 67–68.

Hamady refers to the two modes of obtaining the favor of others—*tadlis*, or deluding, and *tamliq*, or wheedling.[23]

In a society in which interpersonal relations are so marked by tender egos, hostility, display, and suspicion, it is not surprising to find a great deal of personal and group rivalry. Individuals strive to emulate others comparably situated; families and tribes and clans in all circumstances and styles of life make great efforts to display their equality with others, or their superiority. Much of the Arab's nationalist passion is, indeed, a desire to see his people respected in a world of nation-states, to know that Arab countries separately and together count for something and are abreast of the latest accomplishments in technology and statecraft.

On the interpersonal level, it is so important for Arabs to display a capacity to entertain that they go deeply into debt to arrange elaborate wedding celebrations and funerals, especially in the villages. In the cities they spend large proportions of their incomes in the cafés, where they find the opportunity to display hospitality before a big audience. Since everyone understands this impulse on the part of everyone else, each person is constrained not only to offer but to accept hospitality. To refuse another's hospitality is to insult him by denying him the opportunity to display his valued qualities of character: generosity, good-fellowship, and a certain ability to spend. Even if it is overwhelming and inconvenient, one is under compulsion to accept another's hospitality; a refusal to do so may lead to counterrefusal by another to accept one's own hospitality when it is offered. In this way an elaborate and orderly set of conventions has been accumulated to regulate the offer and display of hospitality and its acceptance.

Rivalry is used by parents deliberately and regularly to spur children to improvement and greater responsibility. This sense of competition extends into the school years and up to the university as well. For most families it is

[23] Hamady, p. 66.

a great sacrifice to send a son or daughter to school, especially to a secondary school and university. Students are therefore under great pressure, from home and from their own sense of obligation and their ambition, to succeed.

More than a century ago Clot-Bey, the French physician who directed medical education in Egypt, recognized this zeal and channeled it in his administration. "The Arabs," he wrote, "are highly susceptible to emulation, are proud and become easily enthused. I have taken advantage of these inclinations and have stirred these feelings among them by establishing, in the [medical] school, ranks, grades, and insignia. The result has fully met my expectation. In examinations and competitions the students make incredible efforts to win promotion. One day a student who had not been able to obtain the post of assistant for which he had just competed, cried out before the gathering that death was preferable to such a disgrace and that he would leave the school. Those who, on the contrary, were successful, displayed the greatest joy and were kissed, congratulated, and feted by their families."[24] The same scene may be observed in Arab schools at all levels to this day.

More recent evidence of an experimental kind reveals the interpersonal hostility, competitiveness, and ingratiation I have been discussing. An Egyptian psychologist, Sarhan, several years ago studied the attitudes and interests of 700 Egyptian school children in grades corresponding to the fifth to eighth in American schools. His sample included boys and girls in all types of secular schools in Cairo and certain rural areas. He compared the results of his investigation with those of comparable surveys of American school children. A third of the Egyptian children expressed "negative feelings toward people," a proportion three to six times higher than that of American white children who expressed a similar attitude. Among a sample of Negro children in the United States, however,

[24] Clot-Bey, Vol. 2, pp. 415–16.

nearly half expressed the degree of hostility revealed in the Egyptian responses.[25] As to competitiveness in school, two fifths of the Egyptian children as against less than one per cent of the American said their favorite activity after school was to prepare their school homework and to study for examinations.[26] This Egyptian response may indicate not only a competitive spirit but also, to some extent, an inclination to give the answers the children thought would be most approved. If so, it is another indication of the next characteristic Sarhan found, a greater desire among Egyptian children to develop the social graces, to adopt the behavior the society rewards, to learn politeness and good manners—that is to say, to master the means of ingratiation and manipulation. None of the American children displayed such an interest; among the Egyptian children a decreasing proportion did so going from the lower to the higher grades. Among fifth graders a quarter showed this interest, among the sixth and seventh graders only a tenth did, and in the eighth grade only 4 per cent. Sarhan explains this on the ground that as children reach adolescence (1) their interests widen, (2) they probably have acquired the social graces and may therefore express less interest in them, and (3) they tend more to question or reject the received norms.[27] Sarhan gives no data on this point, but it is very likely that the children in the conservative rural areas do not show so great a decline in interest in the social graces as the children in Cairo, where there are many more stimulants to doubt.

Rivalry is a form of intimacy; it cannot survive indifference of people toward one another. Among Arabs intimacy and rivalry nourish each other. Saliba remarks that the Syrian or the Lebanese "tends to interfere in the affairs of others. He likes to know their private lives and to criticize their conduct, and he tries to correct the error of their ways. . . . This interference, which ostensibly aims at correcting evil, is in many people actually the result

[25] Sarhan, pp. 101–3.
[26] Ibid., p. 111.
[27] Ibid., pp. 34, 37–38, 91–92, and Table XV, p. 85.

of jealousy and hatred. The Syrian or Lebanese would like to see his neighbor happy but he would not like to see him successful. That is why he will try to cause the downfall of a successful neighbor and denigrate his worth, in order to step into his place. You rarely find in present society the successful man encouraging the beginner and helping him to advance and to succeed, or the beginner exalting the successful man and acknowledging indebtedness to him."[28]

Hostility and suspicion directed toward those outside the large family group give a special character to co-operation among Arabs. In the West we have become familiar, in the last century or so, with conscious, institutionalized co-operation among individuals and groups entirely unrelated to one another. We find such co-operation in economic life, among farmers or among consumers, as well as in political and religious life. But co-operation in the Near East is still largely a family affair and little of it is found outside the blood group or village. The long tradition of separate enclaves based on religion, ethnic group, nationality, and occupation, reinforced by separate residential and business quarters, has largely confined co-operative endeavor within each of these units, rather than between them (except in finance and commerce, to a small extent). Even in religion one mosque has little to do with another. Co-operation in the Near East is not a conscious effort of distinct groups to come together for mutual benefit but simply the result of each individual playing his part as a member of his family or other group. There is not sufficient trust to extend co-operation beyond these "in-groups" of long standing. Father Ayrout has vividly described the Egyptian village as just such a collection of discrete units, "not an organism, but a mass." The peasants have little genuine individuality but neither do they act co-operatively, he says. "This absence of co-ordination among elements in themselves homogeneous has kept the Egyptian village, the typical peasant group, in the primi-

[28] Saliba, p. 24.

tive state of a conglomeration lacking either material or
intellectual system. Through fifty centuries Government
after Government has maintained this formlessness, as
it greatly strengthens the central authority."[29]

Within the co-operating units, however, there is a well-
established exchange of help and favors in which the obligation to extend assistance is matched by an equally strong
and articulated expectation to receive it. As Hamady puts
it, " 'Please don't be grateful, you will repay me,' is uttered
whenever a favor is granted. . . . the giver deliberately
lets his act be registered and makes it known that he
expects reciprocal treatment . . . when the debt of grati-
tude has been repaid, the former recipient of a favor makes
it plain that he is now free of any obligation. Any one
who fails to repay a good deed or procrastinates in doing
so becomes subject to *ma' yara* (shaming) . . ."[30] Mutual
aid among various groups, from immediate family to village, is highly developed despite the harsh judgments people make of one another. Great value is placed, too, on
generosity to the needy. But this generosity is usually extended only to those who display their dependence upon
the benefactor. One is seldom generous to an equal, but
one is more often willing to help the weak even while
contemptuous of them, for contempt soon gives way to
pity.

The pattern of hostility and hospitality, suspicion and
ingratiation, intimacy and formality, suggests the rapid
alternation of extremes in Arab interpersonal relations.
Though secretive about facts, the Arab is quick to express his feelings. He knows few bounds in revealing his
emotional state, especially in pain or sorrow, and this
inclination has resulted in a sharp demarcation line between formality and informality. Yet, as Hamady points
out, the very rigidity of the distinction sends the individual to the other extreme when the bar is let down.
Permitted a certain degree of familiarity, the individual,

[29] Ayrout, p. 110.
[30] Hamady, p. 30.

it is feared, "would trespass on any privacy, he would ask the most personal impertinent questions, he would lay bare his opinions and feelings, and would expect many services from and strong ties with the other."[31]

Even the casual observer of groups in city streets and villages will notice extremes of friendship and enmity expressed in words and gestures; the frequent disputes break out suddenly and then end as suddenly, with a strong tendency to physical violence and loud argument. Friendships become profound, with the exchange of complete confidence and allowance of little personal privacy, and then, out of jealousy or misunderstanding, quickly turn to absolute hatred and enmity. There is frequent divorce owing to the ease with which it is achieved and the scant regard paid to individual predilection in the parents' choice for their children. As a consequence children are frequently shifted from home to home and from mother to stepmother, since boys at age seven and girls at nine may be taken away from the mother and brought to the father's house. Polygamy, though becoming rare, still produces great rivalry among children of different mothers but the same father; and where polygamy is not actually practiced, its possibility breeds insecurity in the mother which probably is communicated to children in some form. Friendship is consequently highly valued among Arab youths and men but their volatility, pride, and envy lead to the frequent transformation of friendship into enmity, love into hatred.

Such influences combine with the effects of socio-economic tradition. Economic insecurity in desert, village and urban communities has been endemic among the mass of the people. In the desert and villages, especially, there has been little respect for the man-made law imposed by the alien central governments from afar. Moslem law-abidingness has recognized the law of Islam, not so much of governments. So peasants, for example, take considerable measures to protect themselves by various means, includ-

[31] *Ibid.*, p. 71; see also pp. 45–46, 55.

ing indifference, against the whims of their superiors; especially in Egypt, they shut their houses tight after dark in complete withdrawal from everything strange and hostile outside.[32] In the cities, too, until recently houses were built only behind walls. The houses afforded little privacy within (except for the separation of the women's chambers) but complete isolation from without.

Personal security in such a society, to the degree that it is achieved at all, comes from three sources: parental approval, the routine of daily life, and the dependable ritual and doctrine of Islam. We have just seen that the great need for parental approval encourages ingratiation, and that the family itself is not much of a haven from rivalry and envy. The rhythm of daily life, though one of poverty, is a more predictable source of personal security, especially in the village and the desert. Here the Arab can depend at least upon the certainty of work and rest according to the changes of the seasons, dry and wet, hot and cool.

But the most important source of security is Islam. The historical characteristics of Islam described in Chapter 2 may now be seen in their effect upon the individual Moslem's personality. The force and simplicity of its doctrinal side make Islam easy to grasp, while its prescriptions for behavior provide a guide for almost every aspect of social life. It gives the believer confidence in an attractive life in the next world without requiring him to deny himself the pleasures he can afford in this one. It supplies routine and regularity in daily life with the frequent rituals of washing and praying, which are prescribed in detail. The emphasis upon behavior, doing, living—a way of life, a path to follow—gives the believer a certain framework for his life day by day. And finally Islam also provides what most religions do: a satisfying interpretation of man's place in the world, a means of explaining things not otherwise explainable, a code by which the individual can re-

[32] See the description based on much observation in Ayrout, p. 109.

late himself to other human beings. Because it is the "cement" of the society, Islam itself is strong and can resist change. Islamic countries undergo changes, but Islam changes least because its great value to the individual is precisely its firmness, the security it offers in the midst of suspicion, uncertainty and poverty.

There are two important consequences of this strength. First, there is great resistance to changing any feature of a system of thought and ritual that plays so great a part in the security of the individual. Second, Islamic countries have fiercely resisted the influence of those features of Western society that touch directly on their religion.

Formality and Rigidity

Arabs know their own attachment to tradition. To the four "natures" into which Arab physiologists used to divide human character (the choleric, bilious, melancholy, and phlegmatic), a popular saying adds another: "Custom," it is said, "is a fifth nature."[33] Arab speech is filled with such prefabricated wisdom: from the Koran, in old proverbs and folk sayings, and in the formalities of courteous discourse. The Koran is known to the least educated people and even to illiterates because it has for centuries been the main text in the village schools, and in weekly "sermons" in the mosque. Ordinary conversation includes many references to God, the Prophet, and Koranic verse; suggestions, plans, and advice appeal to Koranic and other proverbs for justification. Two Arabs can exchange greetings and courtesies in stereotyped phrases for an inordinately long time by Western standards. Such conventional speech has several functions, as the anthropologist Edward Westermarck observed[34] in his study of Moroccan Arabs. By providing ready-made phrases, it obviates the need for thought and originality, and encourages the treatment of every situation in a traditional, familiar manner.

[33] Burckhardt, no. 133, p. 42.
[34] Westermarck, *Wit and Wisdom in Morocco*, pp. 57–59.

It also, therefore, emphasizes the authority of the tradition and custom that impel people to speak that way in the first place. Finally, it is useful, in a society that values overt politeness and ceremonial forms, to have an impersonal means by which to disagree, oppose, and criticize. By using proverbs, stereotyped phrases, and Koranic references one avoids a show of hostility and can express denials or refusals with a minimum of personal offense.

Arabs are also devoted to these mannered relationships because they keep affairs within the bounds of the known and the predictable. The society resists forays into the unknown. I referred briefly to this trait in Chapter 2 in discussing the Koranic rejection of various forms of risk; there I related it to the strong equalitarian strain in Islam which is offended by the unequal returns resulting from risk in the form of interest on loans, for example. Now we can look at risk in a different context. Risk, uncertainty, free forms in art and literature, scientific exploration, philosophic speculation, the questioning of systems of government and of authority, all are leaps into the unknown and hence challenges to fate, to what has been laid down by religious and secular authority, to the perfection of Islam and to its completeness. This attitude shows itself in fatalism, authoritarianism, and the Arab view of the external world of nature.

Many observers have reported the Arab's acceptance of his fate or lot in life. Ammar, for example, says that the villager's apparent happiness comes from his sense of resignation regarding things as they are.[35] This contentment (perhaps a more appropriate word than happiness) derives from his acquiescence in what has been ordained by God and cemented by tradition. Until quite recently there was no questioning of this prescribed order of things. Popular belief has held, as the Finnish anthropologist Hilma Granqvist shows,[36] in many expressions current among Palestinian Arabs, that heredity fixes human character in

[35] H. Ammar, pp. 36, 231.
[36] Granqvist, *Birth and Childhood among the Arabs*, pp. 166, 177.

such a way as to make it useless to try to change it; one's nature is fully determined before birth and merely plays out its appointed roles in life. Fatalism is a way of defeating the fear of the unknown. If one expects something, one is not surprised. But if something unexpected happens, a fatalistic attitude immediately encompasses it as one's apportioned, predetermined share or lot,[37] so that, in the end, nothing is really unexpected: one already has explained the unexplainable, foreseen the unforeseeable. Even the hazards of those pagan, relatively uncontrolled forces—the spirits, the evil eye, the *jinn* (or genie) —can be managed if one follows certain prescriptions, such as avoiding physical exposure, staying out of the dark, using certain substances, or uttering the holy words of the Koran.[38]

Political quietism has been another facet of behavior through which Arab society has expressed its tenacious refusal to confront the unknown, to challenge fate or the predetermined order of things. Nowadays we call this tendency authoritarianism. We saw in Chapter 2 the authoritarian influence in religious doctrine. Politically, too, the Near East has been authoritarian, whether under native or foreign rule. When Britain and France became dominant, in the late nineteenth century and after World War I, in Egypt, Iraq, Syria, Lebanon and what is now Jordan, they continued earlier tendencies toward a parliamentary system or introduced one. But the parliamentary regimes never replaced the old authoritarianism, and with the departure of the Western powers since World War II, they have one by one fallen as the area has reverted to government by military or civilian bureaucracies without benefit of Western democratic forms.

There is a high degree of authoritarianism in the personal make-up of Arabs, doubtless the result of centuries of life under authoritarian political and family life. Two

[37] The Turkish word *kismet*, meaning fate or destiny, is from the Arabic *qisma*, meaning a share of something that is divided and meted out.

[38] E.g., Westermarck, *Pagan Survivals*, pp. 5–10, 21–26.

related studies have recently shown this facet of Arab personality as compared with the American. A widely used set of questions, developed in America, has been designated a "scale" indicating, according to one's responses, the degree to which the respondent is authoritarian in personality, that is, in outlook on life and on relations with others. In one study,[39] this scale of 33 items was administered to 130 Arab students at the American University of Beirut, in Lebanon, of whom 70 were Christian and 60 Moslem. On 22 items in the scale, these Arab students responded in a more authoritarian way than Americans did, and in all but one item the differences were so large as to make it unlikely that they were due merely to chance. It is interesting, also, that among the Arabs, the Moslems revealed a higher degree of authoritarian predilection than the Christians. In another study,[40] a similar scale was administered to 90 Moslem Arabs at the American University of Beirut and to 97 white Protestant students at Cornell and Colgate universities in the United States. The Near Easterners revealed a higher average score than the Americans, and again the difference was of such a magnitude as to make it unlikely that chance could explain it. Apparently authoritarian institutions in political life, religion, the family, and education and authoritarian tendencies in personality have reinforced one another.

Arab views of the external world of nature and of the arts display a similar rigidity, formalism, and disinclination to look into the unknown. The late historian of science, George Sarton, refers[41] to a "genuine hunger for knowledge which possessed the Arab leaders" in medieval times. A prominent contemporary Moslem philosopher, Muhammad El-Bahay, argues[42] that Islam can be shown to encourage the scientific attitude. So it is not "inherent"

[39] Prothro and Melikian, "The California Public Opinion Scale . . ."

[40] Melikian, pp. 38–40, 48–50.

[41] Sarton, "Islamic Science," p. 88.

[42] El-Bahay, *passim.*

or inevitable in Islam that it should for long periods have failed to encourage the quest for knowledge of this world. But there is little doubt that the dominant interpretations of Islam have had this effect. In the early period of expansion and progress Arab Moslem society was interested in science as a method, as a key to the understanding of this world, and as a humanistic pursuit valuable in itself. Today its interest is reviving, but it takes the form, thus far, of a purely instrumental interest in technology as a means of developing the national economy and military power. What happened in the centuries between these eras? Gibb points out[43] that Islam looked upon knowledge as a mechanical process of gathering in the known, the given and eternal, rather than a creative reaching out for the unknown. Fundamentalist ideas resulted, which crushed independent intellectual activity and destroyed the scientific curiosity displayed in early Islam. Traditionalism insisted that nothing accumulated and accepted could be discarded as outmoded or invalidated; nothing new could be incorporated unless it was in harmony with what was already known. This tendency, Gibb concludes, led to the enthronement of deductive reasoning, moving from the known to the implications contained within what is known. Even in their science the Arabs were wary of abstract ideas, Gibb says;[44] the atomism, discreteness, and concreteness of their thought, however, enabled them to develop the experimental method. But the bold, imaginative questioning of the nature of things which leads to the fundamental theories at the basis of experimental and technological advances remained foreign to them.

In Arab philosophy and the arts the same formalism may be seen, accompanied by an inability to take a complete, organic view of human experience. Except for a short period in its early history, Arab Moslem civilization has emphasized structure, repetition, and perfection in detail at the expense of meaning, originality, and the join-

[43] Gibb, *Modern Trends in Islam*, pp. 64–65.
[44] *Ibid.*, pp. 7–8.

ing of parts into a related unity. As language is the chief bond among Arabs, so language is the basis of their greatest cultural achievements—the Koran, medieval poetry, parables, legends, philosophy, and biography. Their arts began in a rich combination of borrowed and original contributions but soon displayed that rigidity and incapacity for development that made their literary forms intellectual strait jackets, static vehicles for a show of geometric virtuosity rather than plastic means for conveying emotions, ideas, or a rounded interpretation of human life. Veneration of the Koran and of the Arabic in which it came to the Moslems led to an obsession with structure from which the society has only recently begun to emerge; in the late nineteenth century younger Arab poets, writers, artists, and scholars began to experiment with and adopt the new forms and ideas they saw in Europe.[45]

The Ideal and the Real

One aspect of the cultural outlook we have been discussing is the Arab's infatuation with ideal forms; he clings to them emotionally even while he knows they are contradicted by reality. The distinction between ideal and real exists in other societies too, but there is more awareness of the gap between the two, and the ideal is more consciously held up as basis upon which to *judge* the real. Arabs confuse the two, professing to believe against reality that the ideal is carried out in conduct and is identical with practice rather than merely constituting the criterion by which practice is to be judged. A Christian missionary has told a revealing story of how he placed before an Arab audience the question as to which son in the New Testament parable (Matthew, 21:28) is the better: the one who, when asked by his father to do something, replies that he will and then does not, or the son who replies that he will not and then does what his father asks. Virtually all

[45] For broad, convincing interpretations of Arab Moslem culture see Lewis, *The Arabs in History*, Chapter 8, and von Grunebaum, *Medieval Islam*, pp. 221–33.

the Arabs said the son who answered that he would was the better because, even though he did not carry out his father's wish, he showed proper respect in his reply. Respect, for the Arab, consists in conforming to an ideal form of verbal acquiescence rather than in a real act of obedience ("real" by Western standards). The confusion of ideal and real is attested by Saliba, who says that the Syrian and the Lebanese "often imagines things and believes that they really exist because they fit his feelings and dreams whereas actually they remain confined to the world of the imagination. . . . Feelings are to him the criterion of existence."[46]

Perhaps the modern form this addiction takes is the Arabs' predilection for adopting plans—for economic development, domestic reform, and so on—that are often not closely related to their capacity for carrying them out or, for that matter, to their most pressing needs. But a plan has a seductive quality they can hardly resist. Unlike reality, a plan can be a perfect thing, like a work of Arab calligraphic art: complete, structurally neat, self-contained, with the emphasis upon appearance and not meaning. There is also the feeling that one need not go beyond the plan, for the ideal picture is sufficient and is in any case esthetically far more pleasing than the uncertainty and disorderliness of reality. One can sense here the influence of religious fatalism too; it is all very well for mortals to make plans but they ought not to challenge fate by trying to realize them—that is someone else's affair, perhaps God's. According to a world-wide proverb that seems to be especially popular in the Arab world, man proposes but God disposes.

Historically, the great confusion between ideal and reality may be traced in three spheres: the caliphate, the relation between law and custom, and more recently the efforts to modernize Islamic doctrine.

In early Islam the caliph, the successor to Muhammad, was theoretically and in fact the leader of the faithful.

[46] Saliba, p. 22.

But by the middle of the third century of Islam (tenth century A.D.), the holders of this post had lost virtually all their authority to secular rulers who acquired and retained their authority by force. But the orthodox theologians continued to teach the old view that the caliph was the commander of the Moslem community, for it was painful to see such a powerful office, dating back to the infancy of the Moslem state, reduced to nothingness. Moreover, theologians held that if the caliphate were admitted to have ceased to exist, then the entire Moslem community would be living in sin, for a correct life required the existence of the successor to the Prophet. Although, as Arnold puts it,[47] the caliph "could not give an order outside his own palace," the fiction was adopted whereby a diploma that he granted the temporal ruler became the source of the latter's real authority in the realm. Later the classical theory of the caliphate was modified, but not discarded, by acceptance of the notion that the community must obey even a usurper who exercises power. Yet the original doctrine was never entirely revised.

In the larger area of Islamic law and custom (of which the caliphate is but one phase) the same gap may be seen. In no society does practice always correspond to formal law, but in Islamic communities the difference seems to be institutionalized to the extent that each sphere is cultivated by itself on the implicit assumption that the ideal form should be preserved even if it is related only slightly or not at all to the reality of conduct. Custom and law each has its own kind of sanctity. Custom is revered because it is the way of the folk, the *sunna* of the Arabs before and after they became Moslems. Even Muhammad, for all his innovations, had to respect many of the customary regulations of his time; after his death some tribes had to be reconquered by the Moslems and again converted to Islam because they assumed that their

[47] Arnold, pp. 77, 89; see also Gibb and Bowen, Part I, pp. 27–35.

previous adherence was only in accordance with a contract with the Prophet which expired upon his death. Custom was also powerful because it assimilated the acts of the first Moslem community; these acts came to be regarded as obligatory upon the faithful apart from any formal legal regulation. Law is revered because it is in the Koran, the commands of Allah to the Moslems through the angel Gabriel and the Prophet Muhammad. The ideal Islamic community is thus truly a theocracy (as it has often been called) not in the sense that Allah is the immediate ruler but in the sense that his *law*, as enshrined in the Koran, governs all conduct.

The exigencies of daily life led to some change in the formal law as administered by governments but the divine law remained virtually intact despite social and governmental development. As Schacht says,[48] "The antinomy between a religious ideal and the changing demands of everyday life was indeed inherent in Muhammadan law from its very beginnings." He also shows (as we saw briefly in Chapter 2) that although many existing customs ultimately found their way into Islamic law, on the whole custom was not formally looked upon as a source of law. The source was the revelations to Muhammad from Allah. Such custom as was incorporated by the early jurists was first reconciled with these divine commands. The growing gap between the law in the Koran and the law actually obeyed by the people and enforced by governments in Islamic society was simply ignored most of the time. Schacht refers to a truce between the authorities on religious law and the authorities who ruled the people. "The sacred law," he adds, "could not abandon its claim to absolute theoretical validity, but, as long as it received formal recognition from the Muslims as a religious ideal, it did not insist on being carried out in practice." This truce produced some advantage for Islam despite the weakness it revealed. At the beginning, Islamic law assimilated custom. When the doctrine had later hardened to such an

[48] Schacht, "The Law," p. 78.

extent that changing practice could no longer penetrate its crust, the truce came into play. What did Islam gain by it? Nothing less than the continued adherence of the faithful to the religion as distinct from the political community. Though doctrine did not admit this distinction, practice did. Schacht says that the "sacred law of Islam more than made good what it lost in control over the acts of its followers by what it gained in spiritual power over their minds."[49] It neither broke custom nor destroyed itself by trying to give effect to its broad claims. By reducing its secular demands, it managed to maintain its hold in the spiritual domain.[50]

Respect for ideal form, despite the enervating effect it may have, extends to the "modernist" movements to adjust Islamic law and other doctrine to the social changes the Near East has experienced in the last century. Modernism is an essentially weak trend in Islam; no one takes easily to revising a system of divine origin. Instead of adapting the divine system to earthly reality, the Moslems have tacitly agreed to bypass perfection, leaving it intact as they adopt an entirely secular system borrowed from European codes. This is not to say that no attempts have been made to legislate in the traditional areas of the sacred law, but they have all been halting, irresolute, and without a firm rationale. Few reformers are willing to say flatly that much of the religious law of Islam derives from the secular practice of the Arabs at its inception and hence was a response to the social demands of that era which needs revision in this one, more than a millennium later. Unwilling to recognize the fact that the divine law is grounded in human experience, the modernists are driven to a device used by modernists in other religions: they seek to reinterpret the sacred texts. The result is, in Schacht's words, that they are "bold innovators" who "try to avoid the semblance of interfering with the essential

[49] Schacht, p. 82.

[50] One of the means by which the rigidity of Islamic law was overcome has been the legal "device" or fiction (*hiyal*), on which see Schacht, *ibid.*, pp. 78–80, and Vesey-Fitzgerald, p. 108.

contents of the sacred law."[51] Revisions of other religious doctrines take a similar form of reinterpretation, but in both cases, i.e., law and doctrine that is not strictly law, change proceeds largely by ignoring the traditional forms and adopting new ones from the West.

I have tried to show how social history and personal development have combined to produce a society in the Near East in which insecurity, hostility, suspicion and rivalry find their compensation in a strong adherence to religious ritual, patterns of ingratiation and hospitality, and a limited form of co-operation. To relate such "good" qualities as hospitality and generosity to such "bad" qualities as hostility and suspicion may seem unduly stern and pessimistic. I do not mean to be; it is surely unnecessary by now to remind ourselves that "good" and "bad" qualities are always mixed in any group and that they merge with one another. I do not believe that the traditional hospitality and friendliness of Arabs, which is still one of their most engaging personal qualities, is one whit reduced in its noble character or welcome effect by this linking.

Can personality and values change? They do, over long periods of time, for they are not eternally implanted in any group. Nor do all members of a group share all its widely distributed traits. The Arabs are seeking to change their institutions rapidly. This promotes the ascendance of leaders with a different conception of what the Arab is and may become, and the changes may in turn alter Arab predispositions and ways of doing things. Now that the Arab world is increasingly able to shape its own future, it is possible that the new spirit of enterprise, personal relations, and aspirations toward freedom held by a few will spread to others.

[51] Schacht, *ibid.*, p. 83.

Part Two

SOCIAL INSTITUTIONS

CHAPTER 6

Economic Life and the Population Problem

Arab history, values, and personality have shaped both the Arab response to the problems that human communities face and the way in which the Arabs have viewed the problems. Their special geographical position, dominant religious tradition, and conception of family life have, as I have tried to show in Part One, influenced their outlook and their creation of desert, village, and urban communities. In each type the economic base is important. Historically, the three types were economically interdependent but autonomous. Today, however, they are not only increasingly interdependent but are being brought into the world economy through national economic systems, into which they are more and more integrated. The bedouin in the desert camp is affected by changes in agriculture, the fiscal policy of Arab governments in the far-off capitals, and the oil policy of governments and foreign companies. The peasant's income depends to a large extent on world commodity markets. And the factory worker in the city is the least insulated of all from the political and economic decisions taken by his employers, the national government, and others of which he has only a vague notion.

The Population Problem

Intimately connected with the economy of the Near East is its "population problem." This consists of the relation between the number of people and the rate and pattern of their increase, on the one hand, and the agricultural and industrial resources and their use, on the other.

Though the precise demographic position of the area must be expressed in seemingly dry birth and death rates, age structure and other apparently uninteresting statistics, the conditions revealed in such data touch the most significant and explosive features in the Near East today. The most dynamic Arab country politically, Egypt, is the one facing the most serious population problem—and this is hardly a coincidence. The drive to industrialize, the interest in economic planning, the drift from countryside to town, the unrest in the large urban centers, the political extremism to which the young people are susceptible, and the swelling of the ranks of the civil service which makes it difficult to improve public administration all hinge on the consequences of certain patterns of population growth.

Before using statistics on the population of the Near East, it is important to bear in mind their limitations of reliability and comparability. Behind the neat and internally consistent demographic tables for most of the world lie the very untidy procedures involved in getting information from people who are often hard to locate and to persuade. Of the five countries we are interested in, only Egypt has taken regular censuses, and even these are in some respects not comparable because of changing definitions of categories and different degrees of reliability from one census year to another. In urban, economically advanced countries, where census-taking has become familiar, post-census tests reveal a serious margin of error. In the Near East this is all the more true, for a census there is frequently resented as an unfamiliar prying into private affairs that may be put to uses harmful to those whose heads are counted.

One hundred and twenty-five years ago Muhammad Ali, the despotic ruler of Egypt, took a census. An engineer in his employ later told the British economist, Nassau Senior, that it was an underestimate. "The Sheykhs," he said, "were anxious to diminish the numbers in their villages, in order to diminish the taxation and conscription."[1]

[1] Senior, Vol. 1, p. 32.

This anxiety remained an obstacle to an accurate census in the Near East for a long time. Though conditions have changed, the general suspicion of a central government seeking such information remains. An Egyptian scholar who studied life in one province about twenty years ago was told by a *shaikh* that when the bedouins were ordered to register every birth, the leaders of one tribe resigned in protest against the "grave violation of the rights" of nomads.[2] More recently, in five Egyptian villages it was found that both deaths and births were considerably under-reported. Trained health teams found only a third of the actual deaths reported in 1950; in the two previous years the reported birth rate was 44 to 50 per 1000 persons, but the true birth rate was established at 56 to 61.[3] In studying his own village, an Egyptian anthropologist found a wide gap between the census data on occupations and the testimony of a well-informed villager.[4]

Demographic data from other Near Eastern countries are even less reliable. Lebanon, indeed, resists taking a census because the people and the authorities prefer not to test or upset the complicated political balance which yields tolerable Moslem-Christian relations based on the assumption that the population is about evenly divided between the two religions. An American consultant to the Lebanese Ministry of National Economy, trying to carry out a census in one region a few years ago, reported that the "enumerators were heckled and the villagers gave them answers that were not reasonable."[5] It is thus with good reason the demographic experts of the United Nations give the lowest rating, "poor," to the population statistics of the Near East—that is, the "basis of estimates is very weak and even the general direction of the indicated changes is open to question."[6] In the following analysis

[2] A. M. Ammar, Vol. 1, p. 219.
[3] Weir, p. 104.
[4] H. Ammar, pp. 17–18.
[5] Prescott, p. 7.
[6] United Nations, Department of Social Affairs, *World Population Trends 1920–1947*, New York, 1949, p. 3.

Egypt is referred to most often, not because it is "typical" of the area (it is not) but because it is the largest, has more than 60 per cent of the population of the five countries we are interested in, faces the most serious demographic problem, and has the most ample statistics subject to fewest limitations.

Population, area, and density are shown in Table 1.

TABLE 1. *Estimated Population, Area, and Density, 1960*

	POPULATION	AREA (sq. miles)	DENSITY (persons per sq. mile)
Egypt	26,080,000	390,625	67
Iraq	6,942,000	173,610	40
Jordan	1,678,000	37,738	44
Lebanon	1,639,000	4,062	403
Syria	4,561,000	72,062	63
Total	40,900,000	678,097	60

SOURCES: Population: Egypt and Syria, from preliminary official report of 1960 census, New York *Times*, Oct 24, 1960, p. 9; other countries, calculated from estimates in U.N. Department of Economic and Social Affairs, Statistical Office, *Demographic Yearbook 1959*, New York, 1960, Table 4, pp. 138–39. Area: from U.N. Department of Economic and Social Affairs, Statistical Office, *Statistical Yearbook 1959*, New York, 1960, Table 1, pp. 21, 31. Density: population divided by area.

With about 41 million people, this Arab core contains less than half the number in the Near East, defined as the area from Egypt and the Sudan eastward and northward to Afghanistan. Its density of 60 persons per square mile is well above the world average but conceals large differences between the settled areas of town and countryside and the vast stretches of desert and steppe. Though this region's expected rate of population growth in the next quarter-century is not among the very highest in the world, it is enough to put an increasing burden on the economy. According to U.N. estimates, the population of the five countries in the Arab core in 1975 will be almost 60 million. This would be an increase of about two thirds over the estimated population in 1955, giving the region a moderate expected rate of growth compared to the rest of Asia and the less developed areas of Africa and Latin America, as Table 2 shows.

TABLE 2. *Estimated Growth of Population*

	1955	1975	PER CENT INCREASE
Egypt	23,000,000	38,300,000	67
Iraq	5,730,000	9,230,000	61
Jordan	1,430,000	2,300,000	61
Lebanon	1,420,000	2,320,000	63
Syria	4,140,000	7,210,000	74
Total	35,720,000	59,360,000	66

SOURCE: U.N. Department of Economic and Social Affairs, *The Future Growth of World Population*, Population Studies, No. 28, New York, 1958, App. C, Table II, p. 72ff. For comparison of these countries with other regions, see *ibid.*, Table 9, p. 26.

Predictions of population change are chiefly based on birth rates and death rates, both of which are so volatile and unreliable for the Near East as to make it pointless even to cite the figures. About all that can be confidently said is that birth rates are high and stable, death rates high and declining.[7] The data for Egypt are the most reliable. Its annual birth rate, estimated at about 43 per thousand of population during the first half of this century, is among the highest in the world.[8] Its annual death rate fluctuated

[7] See for partial data, United Nations Department of Economic and Social Affairs, Statistical Office, *Demographic Yearbook 1959*, New York, 1960, Tables 9 and 25.

[8] *Ibid.*, Table 9, and Republic of Egypt, The National Population Commission, *The Population Problem in Egypt*, Cairo, 1955, p. 7.

between 25 and 28 per thousand during roughly the same period, but began to decline after World War II until it stands now at about 17, still among the highest in the world.[9] The rest of the Near East probably has birth and death rates somewhat lower than Egypt's.

The combination of a high rate of population growth, limited agricultural potential, and the undeveloped state of industry gives the Near East a low level of living. Table 3 shows the amount of land under cultivation, the amount which can still be cultivated without prohibitive costs, and the amount of cultivated land per person.

Table 3 shows that only about a tenth of the area can be cultivated at all. Of this cultivable total, about two thirds are actually under cultivation. There are, however, wide differences within the region. Nearly two fifths of the total land of Iraq and Syria can be put under cultivation, compared with only 4 per cent for Egypt. Syria and Jordan are now cultivating well over half of the land that is cultivable; the proportions for Egypt, Jordan and Iraq are considerably higher. Most of the area, therefore, has made productive a high proportion of the land that is appropriate for agriculture—that proportion is itself unfortunately low. The result is that the amount of cultivated land per person is rather low, less than half a hectare or not quite an acre. Again there are wide differences, Iraq and Syria being far better off than the others. Lebanon and Egypt have .2 and .1 hectare per capita (a half and a quarter acre, respectively), but while this low figure spells poverty for Egypt, which is largely agricultural, it does not mean the same thing for Lebanon because that country relies far less upon agriculture for its national income.

The rate at which cropped land (which counts a piece of land as many times as the number of crops it

[9] *Idem.*, and *Demographic Yearbook* 1959 (note 7 above), Table 25.

TABLE 3. Cultivable and Cultivated Land, Early 1950s

	TOTAL AREA (000 ha.*)	CULTIVABLE LAND		CULTIVATED LAND			No. OF CULTIVATED HA.* PER PERSON
		AMOUNT (000 ha.*)	PER CENT OF TOTAL	AMOUNT (000 ha.*)	PER CENT OF CULTIVABLE	PER CENT OF TOTAL	
Egypt	96,467	3,495	4	2,445	70	3	.1
Iraq	44,500	6,600	15	5,664	86	13	1.0
Jordan	9,750	945	10	530	56	5	.4
Lebanon	1,038	388	37	273	70	26	.2
Syria	18,448	7,000	38	3,668	52	20	1.0
Total	170,203	18,428	11	12,580	68	7	.4

* One hectare equals 2.47 acres.

SOURCES: UN, Department of Economic and Social Affairs, Economic Developments in the Middle East 1945–1954, New York, 1955, pp. 93–4, 152, 181. Republic of Syria, Statistical Abstract of Syria, 1957, Damascus, 1958, p. v. UN, Department of Economic and Social Affairs, Review of Economic Conditions in the Middle East, New York, 1951, p. 69, and Review of Economic Conditions in the Middle East 1951–52, New York, 1953: p. 16. Official Jordanian estimates given in Norman Burns, "Middle East Economic Problems, 1951–1952," mimeographed lectures at Johns Hopkins University, 1951, ch. VI.

grows) is expected to increase by 1975 is shown in Table 4. Only in Iraq is it expected that the increase in cropped land will keep pace with the increase in population. This is not a sure indication that population will outrun agricultural resources, because production can be increased not only by increasing cropped or cultivated land but also by more scientific methods of cultivation on the same land; moreover, industry and trade can be expected to absorb some of the increase in population. Yet Table 4 does indicate the kind of problem the area faces as population grows rapidly and presses hard on all resources.

TABLE 4. *Estimated Percentage Increase of Population and of Cropped Land, 1955–75*

	POPULATION	CROPPED LAND
Egypt	67 per cent	39 per cent
Iraq	61	92
Jordan	61	53
Lebanon	63	20
Syria	74	39

SOURCES: Population: see Table 2 above. Cropped land: United Nations Relief and Works Agency for Palestine Refugees, *Quarterly Bulletin of Economic Development*, No. 11, Beirut, 1954, p. 1.

This problem is particularly serious for Egypt, with the largest area and population in the region. Like other countries in Asia and Latin America, Egypt has had a high birth rate but a declining death rate; the latter has been the result of the introduction of inexpensive methods of public sanitation and innoculation against disease. These have been especially effective in reducing the death rate among infants, which has nevertheless been among the world's highest.[10] Until 1950 the situation was stark, for national

[10] New methods of calculation have yielded misleading fluctuations but there is little doubt, whatever the changing statistics show, that a high proportion of infants are surviving beyond the

income was declining. Recovery came with the war in Korea in 1950, which sent up the price of cotton, and since then austerity measures have prevented further deterioration.

The full measure of the pressure of population upon agricultural resources in Egypt may be seen in the relation between the growth of each. During the first half of this century the population doubled, while the cultivated area increased by only a sixth and the cropped area by a third. As a result the number of persons supported on an acre of agricultural land rose from two to four.[11] A considerable rise in yields, especially in the chief export crop, cotton, coupled with some industrialization, kept the level of living from falling as much as would seem inevitable from such population pressure. Yet the imbalance showed up clearly in the decline, between World Wars I and II, of consumption of food per capita.[12] The cause of rural poverty seems to be overpopulation rather than an inefficient agriculture, as a study by the National Bank of Egypt shows for the decade 1937–47.[13] The greatest increases in rural population occurred where population was sparsest, in the Northern Delta. Conversely, places of high density showed smaller gains, so that there was a definite inverse relationship between growth and density. This relationship is illuminated by another: the higher the density, the lower the income per person. Thus high density, low income, and a capacity for only limited population growth go together in rural Egypt. Until now the increased rural

first year of life. See *The Population Problem in Egypt* (note 8 above), p. 8, and U.N. *Demographic Yearbook* 1959 (note 7 above), Table 28, p. 599.

[11] *The Population Problem in Egypt*, (note 8 above), pp. 11–12.

[12] *Ibid.*, pp. 14–15.

[13] "Observations on the Urbanization and Distribution of Agricultural Population in Egypt," National Bank of Egypt, *Economic Bulletin* (1955), 8:171–81.

population has remained on the land rather than being absorbed in urban industry. The government is therefore engaged in two major efforts: to raise the capacity of industry to absorb increases in the labor force, and to increase the area of cultivable land by building a new dam at Aswan to irrigate a great deal more land. Both will take several years to arrest the present trend.

There is some awareness of the population problem in the Near East but little has been done to determine the possible effect of a drive to convince the people of the value of birth control and to educate them in the most effective methods. This is less a matter of explicit religious prohibition of birth control than of a simple traditional sentiment against it. To understand the problem better, we must see the particular pattern of fertility among Arab women, on which reliable studies are only now becoming available. The fertility ratio, a more precise indication of the capacity for population growth than the birth rate, is the number of children under five years of age per one thousand women in the reproductive age group fifteen to forty-nine. Recent studies[14] of fertility among Egyptian and Lebanese women show that Moslems have a much higher ratio than Christians. The largest gap between the two groups occurs not in the rural but in the urban population. Among the Christians, therefore, the urban fertility ratio is much lower than the rural, while among the Moslems urban and rural ratios are about the same. Among urban Christians, on the other hand, differences in socio-economic status are not accompanied by appreciable differences in fertility, whereas among the urban Moslems those with higher socio-economic status have a definitely lower fertility ratio. All this means that the reduction in fertility among Christian women is a concomitant of urban life while the reduction in fertility among Moslem

[14] Hanna Rizk, "Fertility Patterns in Selected Areas of Egypt," pp. 47–50, and Yaukey, Ch. 3.

women occurs only when urban life brings with it higher income and education.

Since the Near East, and especially Egypt, is overwhelmingly Moslem, the lesson is clear: the voluntary control of births comes with a higher level of living and urbanization. The question is not one of knowledge and availability of contraceptive devices but of the willingness to use them. Such willingness comes only with a new way of life and broader horizons for each person. In the traditional agricultural society, men and women simply accept the idea that they will have the number of children their capacity and relationship bring them. Children are economically productive and not expensive to rear in the rural Near East; moreover, a large brood gives a man and his wife status in the community and is viewed as a good thing in the eyes of God. The voluntary desire to reduce the number of children comes when, as in the cities, children are not so productive in their early years but indeed are expensive to rear because they go to school longer each day and for many more years than they do on the farm. The opportunities for children to become economically useful in the cities are far more limited. Finally, parents in cities are themselves more educated and value education more; their aspirations for their children put a greater burden upon urban than upon rural parents. It is under these conditions, where status is determined by occupation, income, and education, and one's ability to ensure the proper type and amounts of each for one's children, rather than by the number and sex of one's children, that ideas of voluntary birth control take hold. According to innumerable accounts of travelers and residents in the Arab world, there is much dissatisfaction among women with the unending burden of childbearing. My impression, from various informal sources,[15] is that there is also a considerable amount of intentional abortion both in cities and villages. Nevertheless I believe that a campaign for

[15] E.g., Loutfy, pp. 6, 39–40.

birth control would have little effect in the rural areas, though it would probably be better received in the cities.

The Economy

For more than a century the Near East has been undergoing a transformation in its economic life. Upon an agricultural society with some international trade a growing amount of industry has been built; agriculture itself has moved from almost total dependence on home markets to involvement in the whole economy of the world. Though large numbers of people are still insulated from changes in world markets, the Near East, through its industry, crops grown for export, and oil, is now closely tied to them.

Still largely agricultural and traditional, the Near East is economically poor, as the national income figures in Table 5 show. Only a few things may be confidently stated on the basis of the table and other available information. First, we may conclude that the level of living has not changed much in the last decade or so in Egypt and Jordan, but has risen somewhat in Syria, Iraq and Lebanon. Second, Lebanon enjoys the highest level in the group, Egypt and Jordan the lowest.

TABLE 5. *National Income and Income Per Person*

	NATIONAL INCOME (in millions of national currency unit*)	INCOME PER PERSON (in U.S. dollars)
Egypt		
1950	789	111
1960	1,282	146
Iraq		
1950	158	83
1956	303	134
Jordan		
1952	44	93
1954	49	100

	NATIONAL INCOME (in millions of national currency unit*)	INCOME PER PERSON (in U.S. dollars)
Lebanon		
1950	1,042	262
1957	1,503	318
Syria		
1950	1,187	104
1959	2,400	147

* Rates of exchange: 1 Iraqi dinar equals $2.80, 1 Jordanian dinar equals $2.80, 1 Lebanese pound equals $.32, 1 Egyptian pound equals $2.87, and 1 Syrian pound equals $.27.

NOTE. This table must be used with caution. National income studies in the Near East are in their infancy and hence are unreliable, based on shifting criteria and methods, and are not available for each year. They are also subject to these limitations: (1) most are not internationally comparable, (2) some are calculated at official rates of exchange, which are usually 20 to 30 per cent higher than the rates prevailing in free markets. The table can only show long-range changes, taking into account the inflation that has occurred.

SOURCES: The basic source for this table is the national income series, based on U.N. data, published monthly by the International Monetary Fund in *International Financial Statistics* (see, for example, issue for January 1961). Supplementary data have been taken from (1) U.N. Relief and Works Agency for Palestine Refugees, *Quarterly Bulletin of Economic Development*, No. 14, Beirut, 1956, p. 120; (2) U.N. Department of Economic and Social Affairs, *Economic Developments in the Middle East, 1958–1959*, New York, 1960, p. 48; (3) National Bank of Egypt, *Economic Bulletin* (1960), 13:81, 189.

The contribution of the various economic sectors to the national income is shown in Table 6. In Egypt, Jordan, and Syria agriculture contributes about a third to two fifths and industry an eighth to a quarter. In Lebanon agriculture and industry contribute less, but trade contrib-

utes more than a quarter. In Iraq the situation appears to
be the reverse of that in Egypt and Jordan, with agriculture contributing only a quarter and industry about two
fifths. This relatively high contribution from industry is
the result of oil production; if that were omitted from the
accounting, the contribution of industry to Iraq's national
income would decline from 39 to only 16 per cent.

TABLE 6. *Proportion of National Income Contributed*
by Economic Sectors
(In percentages)

		AGRICULTURE	INDUSTRY	TRADE	OTHER	TOTAL
Egypt	1960	31[1]	21	10	38	100
Iraq	1956	24	39	11	26	100
Jordan	1954	39	6	16	39	100
Lebanon	1950	20	13	28	39	100
Syria	1959	40[1]	11	16	33	100

[1] These proportions are considerably lower than those given in
other estimates for previous years.

SOURCES: Iraq—U.N. Department of Economic and Social
Affairs, *Economic Developments in the Middle East, 1956–
1957*, New York, 1958, p. 32. Jordan—estimate of Economic
Research Institute, American University of Beirut. Lebanon—
Albert Y. Badre, "National Income of Lebanon," *Middle East
Economic Papers 1956*, Economic Research Institute, Ameri-
can University of Beirut, Beirut, pp. 1–37. Egypt—I. H. Ab-
del-Rahman, "The Institute of National Planning. A General
Review," The Institute of National Planning, Documents and
Occasional Notes, No. 2, Cairo, 1960, p. 5; and National
Bank of Egypt, *Economic Bulletin* (1961), 14:6. Syria—
National Bank of Egypt, *Economic Bulletin* (1961), 14:11.

To get a more meaningful picture of the area's dependence on agriculture we must also examine the data on the
distribution of the labor force in the various sectors of
the economy, as shown in Table 7. From a half to nearly
two thirds of the employed population is in agriculture,
though that sector of the economy, as Table 6 shows, contributes only a fifth to two fifths of the national income.

Industry employs only about a tenth of the total labor force, while commerce and retail trade engage a slightly higher proportion, except for Lebanon, whose higher level of living is the result of the special development of international and domestic trade and other services.

TABLE 7. *Distribution of Labor Force, by Economic Sector*
(In percentages)

		AGRI-CULTURE	INDUSTRY	COMMERCE	OTHER	TOTAL
Egypt	1958	56	11	10	23	100
Iraq	1951	60	7	9	24	100
Jordan	1957	63	4	14	19	100
Lebanon	1960	50	12	14	24	100
Syria	1955	62	4	32	2	100

SOURCES: Iraq—International Bank for Reconstruction and Development, *The Economic Development of Iraq*, The Johns Hopkins Press, Baltimore, 1952, pp. 128–30. Jordan—International Bank for Reconstruction and Development, *The Economic Development of Jordan*, The Johns Hopkins Press, Baltimore, 1957, p. 444; and U.N. Department of Economic and Social Affairs, *Economic Developments in the Middle East 1958–1959*, New York, 1960, p. 21. Lebanon—estimates supplied in 1961 by Middle East unit of U.N. Department of Economic and Social Affairs. Egypt—National Bank of Egypt, *Economic Bulletin* (1960), 13:88. Syria—very rough estimates (overstating the proportion in commerce), based on various kinds of data in Edmund Y. Asfour, *Syria: Development and Monetary Policy*, Harvard University Press, Cambridge, 1959, pp. 13–15, 133; International Bank for Reconstruction and Development, *The Economic Development of Syria*, The Johns Hopkins Press, Baltimore, 1955, pp. 10–11.

As Near Eastern governments have assumed increasing functions regarding social welfare and economic development (not to mention military preparedness), their income through taxation, loans, and grants has risen considerably. Table 8 shows that ordinary budget receipts in 1960 were two to three times greater than in 1950. "Development" budgets are absorbing an increasing proportion of governmental expenditure. This is especially the case in Egypt, where the development budget in 1959–60 was 98 million Egyptian pounds, or about a fifth of total expenditure. In 1960–61 it was almost 300 million pounds, or two fifths of the total.[16]

TABLE 8. *Index of Ordinary-Budget Receipts[1] of Governments, 1950–60*
(1950–51=100)

INDEX FOR 1960–61[2]

Egypt	183
Iraq[3]	248
Jordan	311[2]
Lebanon	276
Syria	283

[1] 1960: estimates for all countries except Iraq, for which the basic data were final.

[2] Adjusted for price changes in accordance with wholesale price index series in International Monetary Fund, *International Financial Statistics*, various issues in 1955, 1961. The index for Jordan is not adjusted because the index series is too short, but the resulting distortion is slight.

[3] 1958–59.

SOURCES: For base year data, U.N. Relief and Works Agency for Palestine Refugees, *Quarterly Bulletin of Economic Development*, No. 13, Beirut, 1956, p. XIX. Iraq—Republic of Iraq, Central Bureau of Statistics, *Statistical Abstract, 1959*, Baghdad, 1960, p. 299. Jordan and Lebanon—*Le Commerce du Levant*, Beirut, April 2, 1960, and Oct. 5, 1960. Egypt and Syria—National Bank of Egypt, *Economic Bulletin* (1960), 13:254.

[16] National Bank of Egypt, *Economic Bulletin* (1960), 13:252 (Table I), 259 (Table VI).

The sources of governmental revenue are chiefly taxation, of course, but the proportion that this source contributes in the Near East is lower than in the more developed countries. Table 9 shows that the highest proportion of receipts from taxes is Lebanon's. Without oil and with only limited royalties from the transit of oil by pipeline, Lebanon must rely chiefly on taxation. But, as a country depending a great deal on trade, a large portion of its tax revenue comes from indirect levies, mainly custom and excise taxes. Indeed, this is true of the other governments as well, though to a lesser degree. Iraq derives only 57 per cent of its governmental income from taxes because

TABLE 9. *Sources of Governmental Revenue for Ordinary Budgets*
(In percentages)

	IRAQ 1958–59	JORDAN 1959–60	LEBANON 1961	EGYPT 1959–60	SYRIA 1959–60
Taxes-direct[1]	6.8	3.1	24.4	28.3	19.3
Taxes-indirect[2]	40.2	14.5	56.4	34.9	42.6
Fees	10.0	3.0	5.0	[3]	8.7
Current non-tax[4]	39.5	8.6	14.2	9.6	3.9
Extraordinary[5]	3.5	70.8[6]	—	27.2[7]	25.5
Totals	100.0	100.0	100.0	100.0	100.0

[1] Income, agricultural, urban buildings and land, inheritance.
[2] Customs, excise, and other duties.
[3] Included with direct taxes.
[4] Mainly oil royalties and revenue from government enterprises.
[5] Withdrawals from reserves, grants, and loans.
[6] Loans from abroad.
[7] Classified as "sundry receipts" in the source.

SOURCES: National Bank of Egypt, *Economic Bulletin* (1959), 12:242–51. Republic of Iraq, Central Bureau of Statistics, *Statistical Abstract*, 1959, Baghdad, 1960, p. 301. *Le Commerce du Levant*, April 2, 1960, and Oct. 5, 1960.

it receives large royalties from its oil. Jordan, living mainly from grants and loans from the United States and Great Britain, receives only a fifth of its governmental revenue from taxes.

Like most governments in the less developed countries, Near Eastern regimes depend more on indirect taxes than on direct taxes on income and property. Table 10 shows in greater detail than Table 9, the degree to which governments rely on indirect taxes such as customs and excise duties, which account for a half (for Jordan) to two thirds (for Lebanon and Iraq) of total tax receipts. Income and inheritance taxes, on the other hand, are relatively light, and bring in only a twelfth (for Iraq) to an eighth (for Egypt) of the total tax revenue. The annual tax load per person is relatively low, varying from $8.28 for Jordan to $25.72 for Lebanon. The situation in the economically advanced countries is just reversed. In the United States, for example, the annual tax load per person has been about $500, with direct taxes on income and inheritance accounting for about five sixths of all federal tax receipts.

Poverty and the greater facility of collection help explain the Near Eastern governments' heavy reliance on indirect taxation. An income tax is a rather new thing in the Arab world. Most occupational groups are difficult to reach for tax purposes. The civil servants, of course, are an easy target. In Iraq, for example, it has been reported that of 27,111 persons who paid the income tax in 1952–53, nearly a third were government workers.[17] Personal income taxes thus take much less of a man's income in the Near East than in the wealthier, industrialized countries. Calculations for 1950, which are still relevant today, indicate, for example, that an Egyptian with a wife and three children could earn almost four times the per capita income before he would have to pay a tax on it. If he earned ten

[17] Iversen, Table 13, p. 65.

TABLE 10. Per Capita Tax Revenue for Ordinary Budgets,
Annual Average 1945-55

	TOTAL TAX REVENUE	INCOME AND INHERITANCE	AGRICULTURAL, URBAN BUILDING AND LAND	CUSTOMS AND EXCISE	ALL OTHERS
	(In U.S. dollars)				
Egypt	$20.14	$2.73	$2.35	$12.65	$2.41
Iraq	15.14	1.07	2.05	10.21	1.81
Jordan	8.28	.60	.90	4.22	2.56
Lebanon	25.72	2.84	1.20	17.34	4.34
Syria	15.30	1.55	2.77	8.08	2.90
	(In percentages)				
Egypt	100	13.6	11.7	62.8	11.9
Iraq	100	7.1	13.5	67.4	12.0
Jordan	100	7.2	10.9	51.0	30.9
Lebanon	100	11.0	4.7	67.4	16.9
Syria	100	10.1	18.1	52.8	19.0

SOURCE: United Nations Relief and Works Agency for Palestine Refugees, *Quarterly Bulletin of Economic Development*, No. 13, Beirut, 1956, selected from Table 2, p. VI.

times the per capita income of Egypt he would have to
pay only about three per cent in taxes, whereas an English-
man or an American in the same relative position would
have to pay taxes amounting respectively to a quarter and a
fifth of income.[18]

FOREIGN TRADE

Economic relations between the Near East and the rest
of the world have been increasing with the growth of industry, the long-term rise in the level of living and, especially, with the changes in popular demand that have come
with increased communication. Though Arab foreign
trade accounts for only a minute part—less than 3 per
cent—of total world trade, it is of great importance to the
area itself, for exports provide the means by which the
Arab states acquire machinery for industrialization and the
myriad consumer goods that a modernizing population requires. In exchange for such goods the Arab countries export
chiefly raw materials such as cotton, grains, fruits and vegetables, and, of course, oil. They each depend heavily on one
or two products in exports. Cotton and its products have
for years accounted for more than three quarters of the
value of all of Egypt's exports. About 70 per cent of
Syria's exports have been made up of raw cotton, cotton
products, and other textiles.[19] Iraq exports chiefly oil, but
among its other exports cereals and dates make up more
than half. Fruits and vegetables account for a third of
Lebanon's exports as well as Jordan's.[20]

Owing largely to Western European political control,
the Arab world's trade has been mainly with that area and,
beginning in World War II, with the United States. There

[18] Harvard University Law School, Tables 1 and 2, pp. 98
and 100.

[19] National Bank of Egypt, *Economic Bulletin* (1960),
13:304-5, 318.

[20] United Nations Department of Economic and Social Affairs, *Economic Developments in the Middle East, 1958–1959,*
New York, 1960, pp. 102-3.

has been a major shift, however, in the Egyptian pattern since 1955, as Table 11 shows. Except for Iraq, which has large oil exports, all the countries import more than they export. Since Iraqi oil goes to Western Europe, most of its exports, in value, go there, while over half of its imports come from that region. Jordan exports very little, and most of that goes to other Near Eastern countries; its imports come largely from those countries and Western Europe. Half of Lebanon's exports go to the Arab countries, and about half of its imports come from Western Europe and the United Kingdom.

Until the middle 1950s, the pattern of Egyptian trade was similar; nearly half of its exports went to the United Kingdom and Western Europe, which in turn provided well over half of Egypt's imports. In 1955, however, when Egypt concluded an arms agreement with the U.S.S.R., the pattern changed. Eastern Europe and the U.S.S.R. bought from Egypt and sold to it in increasing amounts until in the first half of 1960 Egypt was sending that area almost half of its exports and obtaining from it almost a quarter of its imports. Previously, Egypt had been sending the Soviet bloc only a tenth of its exports and had been buying from it only about 5 per cent of all its imports. Syria maintained the older Near Eastern pattern of trade until 1958, when it joined Egypt in the U.A.R. Up to that time Syria had bought from and sold to the U.S.S.R. little or nothing, while its trade with the rest of Eastern Europe was relatively small. It began to increase in 1958, and in the first half of 1960, Syria sent to the Eastern bloc nearly a quarter of its total exports and was obtaining from that area a tenth of its total imports. Jordan and Lebanon have had little trade with the Eastern bloc and there has been no tendency for it to increase. Iraq, since 1958, when it became a republic, has slightly increased its trade with Eastern Europe, which had been virtually nil. Because Iraqi oil still goes to the West, its whole pattern of trade remains virtually the same.

TABLE 11. *Geographic Pattern of Foreign Trade*

	TOTAL (millions of $)	NEAR EAST	U.S.	U.K.	W. EUROPE	U.S.S.R.	E. EUROPE	OTHER
					PERCENTAGE DISTRIBUTION BY AREA			
Egypt 1960[1]								
Exports	321.2	6.6	6.9	2.9	16.0	19.9	25.7	22.5
Imports	327.8	5.2	20.0	6.1	33.5	8.0	15.6	11.7
Iraq 1958								
Exports	567.0	9.4	4.0	10.6	53.4	—	—	22.6
Imports	307.4	4.6	13.9	27.5	31.7	—	1.9	20.4
Jordan 1958								
Exports	8.8	22.6	—	—	1.1	—	10.2	2.7
Imports	95.3	67.0	8.6	12.4	27.5	—	5.6	23.3
Lebanon 1958								
Exports	34.7	49.3	5.5	4.0	17.0	4.0	3.5	16.7
Imports	236.4	23.3	12.9	16.8	33.5	0.5	2.2	10.8
Syria 1960[2]								
Exports	39.1	32.7	3.4	4.6	21.5		23.2[3]	14.5
Imports	93.0	8.9	15.4	7.9	40.6		10.0[3]	17.2

SOURCES: For Egypt, Syria, National Bank of Egypt, *Economic Bulletin* (1960), 13:307, 319. For other countries, U.N. Department of Economic and Social Affairs, *Economic Developments in the Middle East 1958–1959*, New York, 1960, Table XXX, pp. 93ff.

[1] January–June. [2] January–May. [3] U.S.S.R. and Eastern Europe.

Trade among the Arab countries constitutes only about 10 per cent of their total foreign trade, including imports and exports. This is probably the result of the general low level of economic development, which means that each country has very little surplus of any manufactured product the others want, and of the fact that all have roughly similar agricultural economies. It is probably also the result of the area's traditional economic connections with Europe, and of the general belief in the superiority of foreign-made goods. That this reliance on Europe (West or East) need not persist forever is indicated by the growth of trade between Egypt and Syria following their union early in 1958. Several months later customs duties were abolished on most locally produced commodities, and export licenses were no longer required. Trade between the two regions more than tripled very rapidly, rising from a total of $12.6 million in 1958 to $39.9 million the following year. Egypt imported mainly fruits and textiles and exported mainly rice, mineral products, and textiles.[21]

This review of the broad economic features of the Near East reveals an area largely poor and agricultural but straining to increase wealth by industrializing. All of the countries have been plagued by political instability, domestic and international, by a lack of experience in creating and investing capital, and by a labor force inadequately trained for modern industry though adaptable enough to it.

Iraq, with considerable oil income, is in a good position to raise its economic level if it can achieve political stability and train a working and supervisory force. Lebanon is now in the best position of all. It has the highest and most evenly distributed income per person, the best educated population, and an established place in world and regional trade. A very high proportion of its income comes from this trade, finance, communications and tourism. Moreover, most of its trade is in goods of foreign origin and

[21] *Ibid.*, p. 37; and National Bank of Egypt, *Economic Bulletin* (1960), 13:136.

involves the other Arab countries. Lebanese welfare thus
depends on its capacity to maintain confidence in its
domestic stability and good relations with both the Arab
countries and Europe.[22] In Syria a certain balance between
an energetic population and natural resources has enabled
a fair proportion of the population to enjoy a level of living above that of mere subsistence. But union with Egypt
in 1958 produced economic, political and administrative
problems that severed the union a few years later and set
Syria on a new course once again.

Egypt, the largest country in the Arab Near East, remains the biggest problem, for it is by no means clear that
the plans for industrialization and increase in crop area
will provide enough jobs and food for the rapidly growing
population. The structure of Egypt's entire economy must
still be geared to meet the most basic needs of the people
before it will be possible to produce enough surpluses of
any kind to raise material welfare appreciably. As for Jordan, it lives off loans from England and the United States
which it has not repaid and probably never will. It has
few resources and little prospect of using even those fully.
Without a sense of nationality beyond that of being Arab
(a sense which the other countries do have), and without
a chance of becoming self-supporting in the calculable future, Jordan's justification for separate existence is only the
political convenience of others (which may indeed be justification enough, judging from the nature of the scores of
independent states that have appeared since World War
II).

Agriculture and Land Reform

It is surely unnecessary to belabor the point that agriculture is important in a region where it contributes a
fifth to two fifths of the national income, absorbs well over
half of the labor force, brings in most of the foreign exchange, provides support for perhaps three quarters of the

[22] On the second point, see especially Sayigh, "Lebanon
. . . ," pp. 84–85.

population, and indeed constitutes the entire mode of life for most of the people. Having reviewed the types of land-holdings in Chapter 3 and the relation between land and population earlier in this chapter, we need to consider here three other major issues: the general level of living of the farm population, the distribution of land, and recent programs of land reform.

LEVEL OF LIVING

We commonly associate disease with urban slums, but in the Near East the rural villages, which tend to be crowded too, are great breeders of illness and lack even the scarce medical facilities to be found in the cities. As we have already seen earlier in this chapter, in Egypt the most densely populated rural districts have the lowest incomes. In rural Egypt, too, the diseases (and statistics on them) are more abundant than in the rest of the area we are considering. A decade ago a group of Egyptian and American doctors and public health experts completed detailed studies in several villages over a four-year period. They found that in 1948 one "test" village of about 4200 people harbored an extraordinary amount of disease.[23] Half of the people were infested with lice, three quarters with fleas. Nine out of ten suffered from some degree of trachoma, and one in twelve was blind in one or both eyes. Bilharziasis, the debilitating disease that is the scourge of the Egyptian irrigated areas, afflicted no less than 95 per cent of the boys and men in the village. These statistics represent the worst conditions of a decade ago; since then there has been some improvement. In the rest of the Near East, health in the rural areas is poor by advanced standards but not so bad as it is in much of Egypt. In Lebanon and Syria, conditions are far better and approach the level of, say, eastern and southern Europe.

In several countries of the Near East awareness of such miserable conditions of rural life has stimulated the building of rural welfare centers. Egypt pioneered this move-

[23] Weir, Tables 10 and 11, p. 77, and Table 23, pp. 90–91.

ment to bring medical care and elementary sanitation to people who knew neither. Far from enough of these centers have been built and even those that have, have not been adequately staffed.[24] Very often the centers have modern equipment beyond their needs but are themselves guilty of violating elementary rules of sanitation. The United Nations, in collaboration with the Arab governments, has since 1955 conducted the Arab States Fundamental Educational Center at Sirs al Layyan, near Cairo, where experts train students to go into the villages to teach people hygiene, reading and writing, how to improve their farming, and some elements of co-operation.

Such efforts by governments and international and voluntary foreign agencies have not yet made a great dent in the problem. As recently as 1953, a United Nations study group reported, after a field survey, that the rural health centers in Egypt, where they are most highly developed, were inadequately used. The mission reported: "It is estimated that at most not more than 10 per cent of the families take advantage of the facilities provided. It would thus seem that the principle of self-help which is the very basis of the philosophy of the movement has so far failed to establish itself very deeply."[25] The group also found that the mere fact of great need was not enough to convince Near Eastern governments to seek aid in the establishment of health centers in adequate numbers and with appreciation of their significance. "There has been no firm demand," according to the mission, "from the Governments concerned for assistance of this character, and, in our view, it ought not to be stimulated on a piecemeal basis or accepted without full understanding of its implications."[26]

Improvement of the level of rural living depends not only upon a rise in income but upon general education

[24] Weir, pp. 96–99.
[25] U.N. Technical Assistance Administration, *Report of the Mission on Community Organization and Development in Selected Arab Countries of the Middle East*, New York, 1953, p. 10.
[26] *Ibid.*, p. 25.

and special efforts to instruct people in sanitation. A gigantic, co-ordinated effort seems to be required, according to the Egyptian-American public health group, to improve at least the worst conditions.[27] To control disease, they point out, a water supply and latrines must be installed; but without improvement in housing the effect of these changes would be somewhat dissipated. Along with insecticides more sanitary methods of handling manure and animals are needed. The task is so huge that it cannot be done without governmental assistance in the provision of medical care and the reconstruction of villages with more concern for sanitation. Villagers are simply too poor and ignorant to obtain proper care and advice. In one village, the group found that of those who obtained medical care at all, nearly three quarters relied wholly on the government and only a fifth could go to private doctors for the most serious diseases.

PATTERN OF LAND OWNERSHIP

The Near East suffers from an imbalance between population and land and from a serious inequality in the distribution of land. As in other less developed areas, relatively few cultivators of the land own their plots, a large proportion of those who do own land own a very small amount, and all must pay high rates of interest for capital.

What is "a very small amount" of land? A "small" holding in one country may be a "large" holding in another. In the United States fifty or seventy-five acres is small but in the Near East and parts of Europe such a plot is considered very large. How much land is needed to provide a minimum of subsistence for a family? This depends on productivity. Though the question of "optimum" or "adequate" size is a difficult one in general, there is no doubt that in the Near East a great proportion of the farm holdings are too small to support even a family. The data on land holdings, as the following tables show, refer to the 1950s, but the situation has not materially changed since

27 Weir, pp. 109–11.

TABLE 12. *Iraq: Agricultural Land Holdings, 1953*

SIZE OF HOLDING (in acres)	NUMBER OF HOLDERS	PER CENT OF TOTAL HOLDERS
under 2½	24,270	19
2½ – 11	25,849	21
12 – 37	27,214	22
38 – 62	14,691	12
63 –124	17,374	14
125 –624	12,028	9
625 and over	3,619	3
Total	125,045	100%

SOURCE: J. A. Salter, *The Development of Iraq*, Iraq Development Board, London, 1955, p. 190, based on official agricultural census of 1953.

then. Table 12 shows that in Iraq, before the recent land reform, about a fifth of the holdings were less than two and a half acres and another fifth were less than 12 acres. A consequence of this pattern of distribution is the high proportion of total land held in large holdings, as Table 13 shows. Only about a sixth of the total land is held in

TABLE 13. *Iraq: Proportion of Agricultural Land Held in Certain Sizes of Holdings, 1951*

SIZE OF HOLDING (in acres)	PER CENT OF TOTAL LAND
under 62	16
62–309	11
310–619	6
620 and over	67
	100

SOURCE: International Bank for Reconstruction and Development, *The Economic Development of Iraq*, The Johns Hopkins Press, Baltimore, 1952, Table 4, p. 142, based on an official survey of half the agricultural land.

plots of 62 acres or less while two thirds is held in vast holdings of 620 acres or more. A similar pattern prevails in the other countries. In Jordan, as Table 14 shows, 85 per cent of the holdings are under 25 acres but comprise only

TABLE 14. *Jordan[1]: Distribution of Agricultural Land,* 1950

Size of Holding (in acres)	Per cent of Total Holdings	Per cent of Total Land
under 25	85.0	36.3
25– 49	8.7	17.0
50– 74	2.8	9.4
75–124	2.0	12.1
125 and over	1.5	25.2
	100.0	100.0

[1] East Jordan only, a region larger and poorer than West Jordan.

SOURCE: International Bank for Reconstruction and Development, *The Economic Development of Jordan,* The Johns Hopkins Press, Baltimore, 1957, Table 5, p. 130.

a little more than a third of the total land. At the other end of the scale, only 3.5 per cent of all holdings are 75 acres or more in size, but they also constitute more than a third of the total land. In Lebanon, Table 15 shows, virtually all holdings are less than 13 acres but comprise

TABLE 15. *Lebanon: Distribution of Agricultural Land,* 1948

Size of Holding (in acres)	Per cent of Total Holdings	Per cent of Total Land
under 13	98.6	35
13–24	1.2	15
25 and over	.2	50
	100.0	100

SOURCE: Norman Burns, "Middle East Economic Problems, 1951–1952," mimeographed lectures at Johns Hopkins University, 1951, Ch. VII, p. 2, based on 1948 estimates by Ministry of Lebanon.

only about a third of the total land, while a very minute fraction—less than 1 per cent—includes half the land in that small country. In Syria, on the other hand, the concentration in large holdings is not nearly so great, as Table 16 shows. There the smallest plots do not take up a very

TABLE 16. *Syria: Proportion of Agricultural Land Held in Certain Sizes of Holdings, 1952*

SIZE OF HOLDING (in acres)	PER CENT OF TOTAL LAND
under 2½	1
2½ – 12	5
13 – 24	7
25 – 62	17
63 – 124	11
125 – 249	10
250 –1,249	24
1,250 –2,499	9
2,500 and over	16
	100

SOURCE: International Bank for Reconstruction and Development, *The Economic Development of Syria*, The Johns Hopkins Press, Baltimore, 1955, pp. 354–55, based on official survey at end of 1952.

large proportion of the total land. Holdings of less than 25 acres constitute only 13 per cent of the total land, while holdings of 25 to 250 acres make up nearly two fifths of the total. As for the vast estates of 1250 acres and more, they constitute a quarter of the total land.

It is Egypt, with its large population and limited amount of cultivable land, that faces the most serious problem of small holdings by owners, as shown in Table 17. Even in 1956, after at least half of the land to be distributed under the agrarian reform law of 1952 had already been parceled out, almost three quarters of all holdings by owners were still only an acre or less in size. This vast majority of the owners held only about a seventh of the total land.

TABLE 17. *Egypt: Distribution of Agricultural Land, 1952 and 1956*

SIZE OF HOLDING (in acres)	PER CENT OF TOTAL OWNERS[1]		PER CENT OF TOTAL LAND	
	1952	1956	1952	1956
1 and under	72.0	72.0	13.0	13.7
2 – 4	22.2	22.4	22.5	24.0
5 – 9	2.8	2.7	8.8	8.9
10 – 49	2.6	2.5	21.4	22.2
50 –199	0.3	0.3	14.5	15.5
200 and over[2]	0.1	0.1	19.8	15.7
	100.0	100.0	100.0	100.0

[1] The data on *holdings*, by owners and tenants, reveal much the same picture for 5 acres and less; see National Bank of Egypt, "Land Tenure in Egypt," *Economic Bulletin* (1957), 10:46, Table I.

[2] Since land reform of 1952 all holdings over 200 acres have been regarded as owned by the government and subject to compensated expropriation.

SOURCE: Egypt, Statistical Dept., *Statistical Pocket Year-book, 1953,* Cairo, 1954, Table 24, p. 33; and *Statistical Pocket Year-book, 1957,* Cairo, 1958, Table 25, p. 39.

At the other end, less than half of one per cent of all owners held large plots of 50 acres or more but they owned almost a third of the total land. This situation has been plaguing Egypt for a long time. From 1896 to 1948 the number of holdings (by owners or tenants) of 5 acres or more remained about the same, as did the total amount of land occupied by holdings of that size. But for plots of less than 5 acres the number of holdings more than quadrupled while the total area they occupied only doubled.[28] The smaller holdings have thus been even further fragmented.

Not only are holdings small; ownership of land of any size is not widely diffused in the Near East. There are no

[28] See data in Issawi, *Egypt at Midcentury,* Table XVIII, p. 126.

reliable data on the proportion of landless agricultural workers for the whole area. The proportion varies for each country, being higher in Egypt (and Lebanon) than elsewhere. There is reliable information for Egypt, which indicates that even there in 1950 the proportion of *holders* who *owned* the land they cultivated was only 29 per cent; in 1956, after the distribution of some land expropriated under the reform of 1952, the proportion rose slightly to 30 per cent.[29]

Fragmentation of holdings (whether worked by owners or tenants) continues to trouble the Arab world. Though it is sometimes (but not necessarily) accompanied by a rather wide diffusion of ownership, it makes efficiency impossible in national or regional terms. Combined with primitive methods of agriculture, it results in low yields, which in turn mean low income. In the Near East output *per acre* is generally low except for cotton in Syria, several products, in Lebanon and several important crops in Egypt. The output *per person* is also low throughout the area, even in Egypt, because of the density of the farm population. Though productivity is low in Egyptian industry and other urban enterprises, it is even lower in agriculture.[30] A final weakness in Near Eastern agriculture has been the probably excessive taxation of small holdings of owners and tenants.[31]

These weaknesses make capital scarce among smaller owners and tenants. How do they obtain the capital they need? By borrowing, of course, and in this process they undergo another type of impoverishment. Special agricultural credit facilities, either private or governmental, have

[29] National Bank of Egypt, "Land Tenure in Egypt," *Economic Bulletin* (1957), 10:48, for 1950; similar calculation for 1956 based on *ibid.*, Table II, p. 47, and U.A.R. (Egypt), Statistical Dept., *Statistical Pocket Year-book, 1957*, Cairo, 1958, Table 25, p. 39.

[30] Hosny, pp. 14–16.

[31] See, for example, U.N. Department of Economic Affairs, *Land Reform*, New York, 1951, pp. 43–45, and Harvard University Law School, Part Three, Ch. 1, and Part Four, Ch. 1.

been available chiefly to large holders and owners. The small owner or tenant has been forced to obtain credit from three other sources: local merchants, landlords, and professional money lenders. Governmental and quasi-governmental lenders charge interest rates of only 5 to 10 per cent but the small farmer either does not know of such sources, or finds them too formal and distant, or does not have the security to warrant a loan. The merchants, landlords, and money lenders are more easily approached but charge rates of from 25 per cent to 200 per cent, with 100 per cent rather common.[32] They are not entirely culpable, because they are not merely impersonal "sources of credit" to the peasants but, rather, advisers and partners in some respects; the local lenders often pay the peasants' taxes in advance, help them harvest the crop efficiently and then transport it, and lend money for personal or family needs and often even to delinquent borrowers.[33]

Very often the peasants find such a personal relationship with the lender more satisfactory despite the high rates of interest. Hamed Ammar has reported the failure of the quasi-governmental Agricultural Credit Bank.[34] In 1938 it established a branch in the village of Silwa, in Upper Egypt, hoping to "rescue" the peasants from local usurers. The villagers, according to Ammar, were not attracted by the bank's benefits, "partly because it involved becoming implicated with Government procedures, and partly because it implied loss of prestige, due to dealing with interest, which is religiously forbidden." The branch was closed in 1950. It is interesting that the villagers were unwilling, on religious grounds, to pay the formal, recognized, but low interest rates to an established organization like the bank, while they were perfectly willing to pay high rates of interest to informal lenders whom they could consider partners or benefactors in some sense not forbidden by Islam. Co-operative credit societies, however, have been

---

[32] See U.N., *ibid.*, pp. 37–38, and Iverson, pp. 82–83.
[33] Wilmington, especially pp. 142–45.
[34] II. Ammar, p. 81.

resorted to by increasing numbers of small holders and owners in Egypt.[35]

Endemic and persistent indebtedness has resulted from rural poverty, traditional methods of farming, and other social habits. Though there are no current data for the entire Near East, there is a reliable study of indebtedness in a sample of 238 households in 1939, in the province of Sharqiya, one of the more prosperous ones in Egypt.[36] It is impossible to say how representative this study is of the whole Near East or how much the situation even in that province has changed and in what direction, but at that time, about two fifths of the landowners and tenants were in debt; of the farm laborers, only a fifth were in debt, probably because they did not need loans for agriculture and lacked the security upon which to obtain them. Among the owners in debt, about a quarter were moderately or considerably so in relation to their resources; among the tenants in debt about two thirds were considerably so; and among the landless workers all who were in debt were moderately or considerably so. Indebtedness among the people sampled was chiefly the result of daily expenditures, taxes and rent, and weddings rather than the need to purchase land or animals.[37]

RECENT AGRARIAN REFORM PROGRAMS

The picture of Near Eastern agriculture just given has not been much altered as yet by programs of land reform since World War II. The potentialities of the reforms since 1952 in Egypt, Syria, and Iraq are great, but they will have to be extended to change the distribution of agricultural wealth materially. The land reforms in Syria and Iraq, since 1958, have not yet been carried very far. The program in Egypt, instituted in 1952, will therefore be discussed in greater detail.

Land reform programs in the Near East have had three broad elements. The government (1) expropriates with

---

[35] Issawi, *Egypt at Midcentury*, pp. 221–23.
[36] A. M. Ammar, Table 131, Vol. I, p. 310, and p. IX.
[37] *Ibid.*, Table 132, p. 312.

compensation all land above a stated maximum holding and sells it in small plots, on easy terms, to farmers with little or no land, (2) organizes the new owners into co-operatives for loans, purchase of materials and tools, and marketing of products, and (3) establishes some safeguards for farm workers and tenants who are landless.

Soon after the revolution of July 1958 the new Republic of Iraq revised earlier programs of land reform established in 1945 and 1951. These earlier efforts, except for one successful venture on a limited scale, were either not carried out systematically or were diverted to the benefit of large landholders and tribal rulers.[38] The 1958 reform came at a particularly trying time, for adverse weather had already caused substantial declines the year before in the wheat and barley crops. The law[39] limited ownership to 618 acres of land irrigated artificially and 1236 acres of land irrigated by rainfall. Land beyond these limits was subject to expropriation by the government, which agreed to compensate the former owners with government bonds paying 3 per cent interest and redeemable within 20 years. This land, in plots of 19 to 37 acres if irrigated artificially and double that range if irrigated by rainfall, is sold to landless peasants and small owners, who pay the government the price paid as compensation to the original owner (plus 20 per cent for administrative costs), at 3 per cent interest in equal annual installments within 20 years. The law sets up co-operatives which the new owners must join. Supervised by appointees of the Ministry of Agriculture, these co-operatives are charged with obtaining loans, supplying materials and implements, regulating cultivation, marketing crops, and performing certain welfare functions. Finally, the law regulates relations between owners and sharecroppers, and sets minimum wages for farm workers and assures them the right to organize trade unions.

[38] I.B.R.D., *Iraq*, pp. 13–16, 268–71, and Warriner, pp. 158–64.

[39] See U.N., *op. cit.* (note 20 above), pp. 3–4, and text in Republic of Ministry of Guidance, *The Weekly Gazette of the Republic of Iraq*, No. 20, Dec. 3, 1958, pp. 206ff.

According to an official report,[40] about 4.7 million acres belonging to 3253 landowners were subject to requisition; more than a quarter of this land had been taken over by the end of 1959. It appears that by the end of 1960 the government had distributed 7783 deeds covering 580,000 acres, or 74 acres per deed. This seems to be land irrigated by rainfall, for the law sets 74 acres as the maximum plot of such land to be distributed. How much of this land was actually occupied and farmed by the new holders of these deeds was not explicitly stated. Meanwhile, a much larger amount of land was being rented, rather than sold under the terms of the agrarian reform, to peasants by the government. At the end of 1959, according to the same official report, the government was renting 2.9 million acres to 137,292 farmers, or an average plot of 21 acres. This is probably the more desirable artificially irrigated land, which, the law stipulates, is distributed in plots of 19 to 37 acres.

In Syria an effort at land reform was made in 1952 but, as in Iraq, it involved only state-owned land.[41] Shortly after Syria joined Egypt in the U.A.R. in 1958, it adopted a law patterned after the latter's.[42] It limited each person to 200 acres of orchards and artificially irrigated land or 750 acres of other land; each owner could also retain for his wife and children up to 100 additional acres of the first type and 400 of the second. Compensation for expropriation was set at ten times the average rent of the land, with payment to owners in government bonds paying 1.5 per cent interest and redeemable within 40 years. Land taken over by the government in this way is sold to farmers in plots of no more than 20 acres and 75 acres respectively

[40] Embassy of the Republic of Iraq, Washington, D.C., *Bulletin*, No. 2, Feb. 1961, p. 12.

[41] Warriner, pp. 101–4, and I.B.R.D., *Syria*, pp. 67–68.

[42] See U.N., *op. cit.* (note 20 above), p. 13. For text of law on redistribution of land, see *L'Economie et Les Finances de la Syrie et des Pays Arabes* (Damascus), Oct. 1958, No. 9, pp. 84–93. For summary of law concerning workers and tenants, see Asfour, p. 157, n2.

for land irrigated artificially and by rainfall. The peasants
pay the same price for the land that the government paid
(plus 10 per cent to cover administrative costs) at 1.5 per
cent interest over 40 years. An earlier law of 1958 fixed
minimum wages, maximum hours, and other standards for
agricultural workers, and established certain standards for
tenants too.

Several million acres were earmarked for expropriation
and sale to about 150,000 families comprising a quarter
of the rural population. At the end of the first year, it
was variously estimated that about 85,000 acres had been
sold to 7300 families. There was some criticism that the
Syrian law followed the Egyptian pattern too mechanically
in fixing the maximum at 200 acres, for that amount of
land in Syria is much less profitable than in Egypt, with
its higher yields per acre. The law also regulates landlord-
tenant relations, fixes the shares of owners and sharecroppers, provides for minimum wages for farm laborers,
and assures their right to associate in trade unions.

The model for the Iraqi and Syrian land reform of 1958
was Egypt's law of 1952.[43] It limited ownership to about
200 acres while permitting the transfer to children of no
more than an additional 100 acres. The government was
entitled to buy land in excess of these limits at ten times
the rent (which in turn was fixed at seven times the land
tax). At first, compensation to the former owners was
to be in government bonds at 3 per cent interest and redeemable within 30 years, while new owners were to repay
the government the price of the land (plus 15 per cent for
administrative costs) at the same rate of interest and in
installments over the same period of time. In 1958 the
terms for compensation to former owners and repayment
by new owners were reduced to 1.5 per cent interest over
40 years (and administrative costs to 10 per cent). The
plots to be sold were fixed at 2 to 5 acres each, and the

[43] See Warriner, pp. 31–40; for the text of the law and
amendments see Marei, pp. 361ff. and National Bank of Egypt,
"Land Reform in Seven Years," *Economic Bulletin* (1960),
13:37.

new owners had to be persons previously engaged in agriculture and owning less than 5 acres. The new owners, or their heirs, may not sell their land before paying its full price to the government. The law establishes co-operatives for the new owners of 5 acres or less. Supervised by central government officials, these local co-operatives lend money to the members, provide them with materials and tools, organize the cultivation of the land, sell the product (after deducting the amount due the government in payment for the land, taxes and loans), and offer other services. The law altered the relations between owners and their tenants and sharecroppers. Maximum rents were fixed at seven times the land tax, while in the case of sharecropping the portion going to the landlord was set at a maximum of one half the crop after deduction of all expenses, including the cropper's. Further protection to tenants was given by the provision that land leases must be for a minimum of three years and contracts must be in writing. Finally, the law authorized the establishment of minimum wages for agricultural workers and asserted their right to form trade unions.

What have been the effects of almost a decade of agrarian reform in Egypt? If its goals are viewed as modest (often they were inflated), then it may be said to have realized much of what it set out to do. Many landless peasants have acquired small plots, tenants and sharecroppers are economically better off than before, farming is probably more efficient and production higher. Politically, the control that large landowners exercised nationally and over their own tenants and workers has been considerably reduced.

The amount of land expropriated and sold under the law has regularly been the subject of contradictory reports. The National Bank of Egypt has published[44] what seems to be the most reliable one. It states that the law in 1952 applied to 600,000 acres, or 10 per cent of the country's total cultivated area, which were held in excess of the

[44] *Economic Bulletin* (1960), 13:37.

maximum. Of this amount, 109,000 acres were excluded as barren or for other reasons, while another 145,000 were sold before expropriation until an amendment soon prohibited sales of land subject to expropriation. Thus, 346,000 acres were ultimately available for resale in plots of 2 to 5 acres. By the end of 1959, 295,000 acres had been sold to 111,000 new owners; the average size of plot was about 2½ acres. There remained 51,000 acres to be disposed of after 1959. (The government meanwhile sold to peasants thousands of acres of land acquired in other ways.)

Though these 111,000 farmers and their families have benefited from acquiring land, their new status has not seriously affected the traditional pattern of ownership. Most of the land appears to have been distributed by the end of 1955, according to most accounts,[45] so that a comparison of ownership in 1952 and 1956 reveals the extent of change.[46] The number of owners of plots larger than 1 acre but less than 5 (approximately the size sold to new owners) increased by 36,300, from 623,800 to 660,000. These owners were 22.2 per cent of all owners in 1952 and only 22.4 per cent in 1956. In 1952 they owned a total of 1,344,000 acres, or 22.5 per cent of all agricultural land, while in 1956 they owned 88,000 acres more, or 24 per cent of the total. At the other end of the scale of ownership the change was greater. In 1952 there were 2100 owners of 200 acres or more, who constituted less than one tenth of 1 per cent (.08 per cent) of all owners but owned about 20 per cent of all land. In 1956 this group fell to 1700. This was a large drop, about 20 per cent, in comparison to the number in 1952, but these 1700 owners in 1956

[45] For example, Warriner, p. 35.

[46] The comparison of ownership in 1952 and 1956 is based on data given in Republic of Egypt, Statistical Dep't., *Statistical Pocket Year-Book*, 1953, Cairo, 1954, Table 24, p. 33, and the edition for 1957 (Cairo, 1958), Table 25, p. 39. The figures above do not take account of other transfers of land affecting the number and proportion of owners of this size of plot; such transfers, however, were probably very few compared to those made under the land reform act.

remained roughly the same minute proportion (.06 per cent) of the total number of owners. But if we assume that because of the reform law, they held no more than 200 acres each in 1956, then the amount of land they owned fell about 837,000 acres and constituted only about 6 per cent of all agricultural land, as against 20 per cent in 1952.

Yet the effects were substantial on the few hundred owners who had to reduce the size of their estates and the many thousands who acquired land. Because of reasonably good planning and administration, production did not decline on the transferred land. The new owners were organized into co-operatives which put their plots of land on the same basis as large estates, which can be run more productively than small holdings. The income of the new owners increased, chiefly because the annual rent they had paid as tenants and sharecroppers had been much higher than the annual payments to the government to buy the land.[47] Peasants who have remained tenants and share-croppers have also enjoyed a rise in income because rents have been reduced by the law[48] (although there have been violations because the continuing scarcity of land makes peasants willing to pay higher rents).

A substantial change in the agrarian law was made in July 1961, as part of the regime's new economic program. The maximum holding of land was reduced from 200 acres to 100, making available perhaps 400,000 more acres for sale to the landless in small plots. The government also reduced by half (1) the amount of money still owed it by peasants who had received land earlier, and (2) the interest rate on these debts to the government. (U.A.R., *Official Gazette* (in Arabic), July 25, 1961, No. 166, pp. 1076–77.)

In two important respects the land reform has not yet succeeded. First, the landless agricultural laborers, the poorest and most numerous of all peasants, have not

[47] Marei, p. 245, and Warriner, p. 37.
[48] Marei, p. 251, and Warriner, p. 39.

gained much. Minimum wages have been established but, in the face of the large oversupply of workers on the land, have not been enforced. Second, the progressive fragmentation of the land has not been arrested, despite the authorities' efforts.[49]

According to Dr. Sayed Marei, who has ably guided the land reform from its inception, its goal has been to give the peasant both a higher income and the dignity, independence, and initiative that are said to accompany individual ownership.[50] Nevertheless the authorities, fearing a decline in efficiency if the distributed plots were farmed entirely in accordance with individual initiative, required the new owners to join government-directed co-operatives that leave them little freedom of choice in the business of farming. "This could be interpreted," Dr. Marei admits, "as interfering with the rights of the individual. But we have to face things in a practical manner. It is well known that farmers are individualistic by nature, they are reticent and reluctant to help one another. We have to create the spirit of cooperation and with the passage of time it becomes no more a question of compulsion."[51]

Doreen Warriner, who has studied Near Eastern agriculture intensively, observes of the Egyptian land reform: "In practice, though not in theory, the redistribution of property means that the land is nationalized." Though less independent, the new owners are more secure economically. The government, through the co-operatives, really controls cultivation of the distributed land and the sale of its crops. Though he is called the owner, the peasant who receives such land does not get title to it for thirty years, during which he may not sell or rent it. As Warriner concludes: "The reform in practice is very managerial. The idea of creating a small-peasant class, which influenced liberal opinion when the law was passed, has disappeared completely."[52]

[49] Marei, pp. 197ff.
[50] *Ibid.*, p. 99.
[51] *Ibid.*, p. 107.
[52] Warriner, pp. 42, 47, 48.

The effects of nearly a decade of land reform in Egypt are likely to be the same in Syria and Iraq. Owners of large estates are weakened in two respects by the distribution of their lands beyond the maximum: they lose income and power. The income they lose goes chiefly to the new owners of small plots and to tenants and sharecroppers. But the power they lose, the power to decide what is produced on the land and how, goes to the government. Land reform is thus as much a political as an economic measure. By it, certain Near Eastern regimes reduce the economic power of a small group of wealthy owners and with it their traditional control over the beliefs and attitudes of the peasants who once depended on them utterly. The national political power of this small landed group is reduced not by agrarian reform itself, but by the new orientation and loyalties of the regimes (such as now rule Egypt and Iraq) that introduce it.

Industrialization and National Planning

The Arab countries, along with others where the level of living is low, associate their poverty with their dependence upon agriculture and the undeveloped state of their modern industry. All of them equate industrialization with national power and individual welfare; and Egypt and Iraq, especially, have adopted national plans toward these ends.

The place of manufacturing industry in the Near East is broadly shown in Tables 6 and 7 above. Excluding Iraq's oil production, industry contributes only 6 to 25 per cent of national income, while employing only 4 to 12 per cent of the labor force. Even these low figures exaggerate the place of really modern industry, for much manufacturing still takes place in small workshops in which few people outside of the owner's family are employed. In Syria it was estimated only a few years ago that of 100,000 workers in "manufacturing" only 40,000 were working in establishments using machinery; the textile industry alone employed 20,000 workers.[53] In Iraq there is little "modern industry" except oil, which is owned and operated by foreign companies.

Near Eastern industry consists mainly of processing food and local raw materials for the domestic market. Even in Egypt, with the largest manufacturing industry in the area, textiles and foods, both largely for domestic uses, have in recent years accounted for about 60 per cent of the industrial labor force and of income from industrial sources.[54] Industrial production has been increasing but the base has been so low that both absolute and percentage differences can be misleading. In 1954, for example, Jordan had 421 establishments with 5 or more workers, employing a total of 8198 workers. Only three years later it had over a thousand such establishments, employing a total of 13,453 workers, while the payroll doubled.[55]

Jordan is, of course, the least developed country industrially of those we are considering. Since Egypt is the most developed in this respect, has the greatest need for further industrialization, and is the most important populous country in the region, we shall consider its industrial position and prospects in greater detail.

Industrial production has contributed an increasing proportion to the national income of Egypt. In 1960, as Table 6 shows, its contribution was 25 per cent. The volume of manufacturing production has, of course, grown too. From 1954 to 1959 it rose 40 per cent, or about 8 per cent annually, according to an index prepared by the able research section of the National Bank.[56] Employment in factories with 10 or more workers has likewise risen considerably in recent decades, doubling between 1927 and 1947 and in-

[53] I.B.R.D. *Syria*, pp. 10–11, and National Bank of Egypt, "Economic Survey of Syria," *Economic Bulletin* (1958), 11:15–16.

[54] Hosny, pp. 35–38.

[55] U.N., *op. cit.* (note 20 above), p. 21.

[56] National Bank of Egypt, "A Preliminary Index of Industrial Production," *Economic Bulletin* (1957), 10:6–14, esp. p. 7, and 1960, 13:360.

creasing since then too.[57] Despite these important gains, manufacturing industry has not been able to absorb workers at the rate at which the labor force has grown. Thus

TABLE 18. *Egypt: Percentage of Workers in Manufacturing to Total Employed Population, 1927–57*

YEAR	PERCENTAGE IN MANUFACTURING*
1927	8.2
1937	6.4
1947	8.4
1957	8.6

* Excludes mining, quarrying, construction, and includes manufacturing and power.

SOURCES: 1927, 1937, 1947—U.N., Department of Economic and Social Affairs, *The Development of Manufacturing Industry in Egypt, Israel and Turkey,* New York, 1958, Table I, p. 90. 1957—computed from National Bank of Egypt, "Statistics of Labor Force in the Southern Region," *Economic Bulletin* (1960), 13:88, Table II.

the proportion of workers in manufacturing to the total employed population remained about the same during the period 1927–57, as Table 18 shows, that is, about 8 per cent. Moreover, according to a U.N. calculation, the volume of production increased by three quarters from 1947 to 1955, while the number of workers employed in the larger factories actually declined slightly.[58]

Official agencies are aware of this situation. The National Population Commission pointed out in 1955 that "in spite of sustained government support, the growing industry has absorbed only a very small percentage of the increase in population . . ."[59] And the National Bank

[57] U.N., Department of Economic and Social Affairs, *The Development of Manufacturing Industry in Egypt, Israel and Turkey,* New York, 1958, p. 28 and Table XIII, p. 103.

[58] *Ibid.*, from Table 9, p. 14.

[59] *Op. cit.* (note 8 above), p. 17.

research department in 1957 noted the same problem.[60]
It is for this reason that Egypt is so eager to expand industry and, as we shall see in the section on planning below, is emphasizing this in its programs for economic development.

THE PLACE OF OIL

The oil industry has a special role in the Near East. Of
the countries we are considering, only Iraq produces oil in
great quantities but Egypt, Syria, Lebanon, and Jordan all
receive income from the movement of oil through the
Suez Canal or overland by pipeline. In dealing with oil,
therefore, we must take in a larger geographical area, for
oil affects the whole Arab world intimately. It is important
in the economy of the region and has great potential effects
on its social life as well. Unfortunately, neither of these
features of the oil industry in the Near East has been
systematically studied. Because Europe has been obtaining
about two thirds of its oil from the Near East, the industry
is charged with political dynamite too, involving disputes
among Arab states, between Arab and European states,
and between the Soviet Union and the Western powers.
The fact that oil in the Arab world is extracted and
marketed by private and state companies in the West only
complicates the economic and political issues that are explosive in themselves. Arab oil is still important to both
the Arabs and the West. But other sources of oil and new
sources of energy portend great changes in coming decades. North African oil under Western or local control
and Russian oil are flowing in increasing amounts to
Europe. The question is already raised of the effects of reduced European dependence on Arab oil east of Suez. The
trend will reduce Arab revenue and perhaps Arab political
leverage against the West as well. It will also reduce the
income of the Western companies that now operate the
oil industry in the Arab world.

Russian competition in particular is growing. Most of

[60] *Economic Bulletin* (1957), 10:346.

the increase in Russia's exports of oil and oil products has gone to Western Europe and other countries not in the Soviet bloc. In 1960 Russia was already supplying Western Europe with a tenth of its oil requirements, and was planning to increase exports until it recovered the position it had in the international oil market before World War II. It can make a strong bid to do so because, with state control, it can provide stiff price competition. Moreover, Russia has been accepting European products for its oil, thus enabling certain countries to conserve foreign exchange.[61]

The Arab world, including Iraq, Saudi Arabia, and the Arabian peninsula, has over half of the proved oil reserves of the entire world; with Iran, a non-Arab country, the Near East's reserves reach about two thirds.[62] Near Eastern oil, besides being plentiful, is cheap to produce. During the 1950s the cost of producing a barrel of oil there was 16 cents, compared to $1.66 in the United States, 57 cents in Venezuela and 87 cents in the Far East.[63] The Arab countries' share in the world's total production has been steadily rising. In 1950 it was 11 per cent; in 1956, 17 per cent; and in 1959 it reached 19 per cent.[64] Accordingly, revenues to Arab governments have been rising too. As Table 19 shows, the governments in the countries that produce oil in substantial quantities received almost a billion dollars in royalties and taxes in 1959. Of the countries we are specifically concerned with here, only Iraq enjoys such a position. It has since 1951 set aside 70 per cent of its oil revenue for economic development projects. The full importance of oil to Iraq lies in the fact that income from it has constituted about two thirds of all gov-

[61] *Petroleum Press Service* (1960), 27:124, 329; (1955) 22:38; The New York *Times*, Oct. 30, 1960, Sec. 3, p. 1, and May 14, 1961, Sec. 3, p. 1.

[62] The Economist Intelligence Unit, *Three-Monthly Economic Review*, Annual Supplement, "Middle East Oil and the Arabian Peninsula," Sept. 1960, p. 2; and Lebkicher, p. 111.

[63] U.N., *op. cit.* (note 20 above), pp. 28–29.

[64] Calculated from *ibid.*, p. 72.

TABLE 19. *Revenues to Governments of
Oil-Producing Arab Countries, 1955–59*
(millions of U.S. dollars)

	1955	1956	1957	1958	1959
Kuwait	282	293	308	354	345
Saudi Arabia	275	283	303	302	315
Iraq	223	194	144	236	252
Qatar	35	36	45	61	53
Bahrain	9	10	10	12	13
Totals	824	816	810	965	978

SOURCES: U.N., Department of Economic and Social Affairs,
Economic Developments in the Middle East, 1958–1959,
New York, 1960, p. 77. Iraq, 1955: the Economist Intelli-
gence Unit, *Three-Monthly Economic Review,* Annual
Supplement, "Middle East Oil and the Arabian Peninsula,"
Sept. 1960, p. 13.

ernment revenue in recent years.[65] The other four countries, Egypt, Syria, Lebanon, and Jordan, derive income
from the movement of oil. Table 20 shows that the total
they have received has increased from 10 million dollars
in 1950 to over 100 million dollars in 1959. These large

TABLE 20. *Revenue to Arab Governments from
Movement of Oil, 1950–59*
(millions of U.S. dollars)

	1950	1955	1959
Egypt	9.5	17.6	87.0
Jordan	0.3	1.0	1.0
Lebanon	0.1	2.4	3.8
Syria	0.4	2.9	17.8
Totals	10.3	23.9	109.6

SOURCE: U.N., Department of Economic and Social Affairs,
Economic Developments in the Middle East, 1958–1959,
New York, 1960, p. 78.

[65] U.N. Relief and Works Agency for Palestine Refugees, *Quarterly Bulletin of Economic Development,* No. 13, Beirut, 1956,
p. 45.

incomes from production and movement of oil are made possible by a huge capital investment by Western private and governmental interests, including the United States. This gross investment in property, plant, and equipment amounted (before depreciation) to a billion dollars in 1946 and rose to almost 3 billion in 1955 and to nearly 4 billion in 1958.[66] Another way to measure the economic impact of oil in the Arab world is to consider the number of Arabs employed by the oil companies in the producing countries and the number in other countries who depend on the movement of oil. The latter is not possible with the information at our disposal but we can estimate that there are 55,000 to 60,000 people of all nationalities employed in the production of oil in the Arab countries, of whom two thirds to three quarters are Arabs.[67] In the higher supervisory positions, of course, there are only a few Arabs but their number has been increasing steadily as they are trained on the job and in special courses at home and abroad. In terms of employment, therefore, the oil industry makes only a slight dent in the economy of the Arab world.

The oil industry, nevertheless, has had a significant impact on labor as a demonstration of relatively advanced policy on recruitment, training, wages, and welfare. Wages paid by the foreign oil companies are higher than those for comparable skills in other industries.[68] The companies have also introduced personnel practices such as aptitude testing, training, safety, and discipline, which are more systematic and humane than those prevailing in the area. Finally, they have provided services that few, if any, local employers provide, such as medical care, housing, restaurants, shopping facilities, recreation, transportation, and even prayer. The Arabian American Oil Company, operating in eastern Saudi Arabia, has gone farthest in this respect. It has paid for the building and operation of government-run schools for almost 3000 children, helped

[66] U.N., *op. cit.* (note 20 above), Table XIV, p. 76.

[67] Based on estimates in Finnie, p. 127.

[68] Badre and Siksek, pp. 56–63, 241.

the central government to build port facilities and a railroad, and helped municipalities and private businesses with community and industrial development.[69]

As often happens, the higher level of living and the widened horizons that workers in the oil industry enjoy have heightened their dissatisfaction, for they have now become aware of material wealth of which they had hardly known. Their sense of injury has been expressed chiefly against the oil companies but extends to the governments despite the authoritarian character of the regimes. In the major producing countries trade unions are not tolerated in the oil industry.[70] So far as material benefits are concerned, the governments seem to be the bargaining agents for the workers; the governments, indeed, are probably able to obtain from the foreign companies better conditions than even independent local trade unions could without official backing.

As extraordinary examples of modern private and public enterprise in the Near East, the oil companies might be expected to have a great impact on entrepreneurship there. This subject has not been given much study. On the face of it, however, it would appear that as a model of entrepreneurship the oil companies are so overwhelming as to inhibit rather than stimulate Arab entrepreneurship. In any case, the countries with formidable oil operations are in general the least advanced industrially and hence in the worst position to benefit from the example. It is more likely that the more highly industrialized countries, especially Egypt, are impressed with the Western model of productive gigantism and efficiency to the point of learning from it in some ways—but with the clear realization that in the Near East such enterprises can be undertaken only by governments or with government capital and other resources. On a small scale, however, the Arabian American Oil Company has helped Saudi Arabs to create and expand businesses that provide products or services the company

[69] Kinch, pp. 198–201, and Lebkicher, pp. 216, 219, 221.
[70] Badre and Siksek, p. 191.

needs but prefers not to produce itself. Company experts have designed small plants and equipment for irrigation works, machine shops, garages, ice factories, water and sewage systems, and even barber shops. The company has also guaranteed loans from banks to local entrepreneurs but has not itself lent money to them.[71]

ENTREPRENEURSHIP: ROLE OF THE STATE

The two issues involving resources in industrial growth, entrepreneurship and labor relations, are, of course, important for the entire economy as well as for the oil industry.

Political developments in the leading countries of the Arab world have made it clear that the state itself will be the chief direct stimulant to industrialization and probably the largest operator and owner of industrial enterprises. This is the current stage in the evolution of entrepreneurial functions in the last century. On the basis of developments in Egypt, on which the information is best, we may mark three such stages: a period in which big entrepreneurs were mainly private persons of non-Egyptian origin, followed by one in which Egyptians became increasingly active in industry through family firms and corporations, followed by the present period of government domination. It must be remembered, however, that the government played an important role in the early stages too by providing entrepreneurs with monopoly conditions and then protective tariffs.

According to Dr. El-Gritly, the prominent Egyptian economist who intensively studied the growth of industry in Egypt down to the period just following World War II, in the third quarter of the nineteenth century the industrialists "were almost all foreigners or local residents of foreign extraction." At first, he adds, "French capital and entrepreneurship predominated and . . . were later reinforced by British and Belgian capital." The Europeans often obtained monopoly privileges from the rulers

[71] See Lebkicher, p. 216, and Coon, pp. 322–26.

of Egypt to build transport and utilities, to extract minerals, and to put up factories for the processing of local agricultural products.[72] In latter part of the nineteenth century the next stage began, as local businessmen and bankers who were associated with foreign interests lent money and developed industry and trade on their own accounts. World War I proved especially profitable to them. In the first quarter of the present century, as religious restraints upon banking weakened, Egyptians became increasingly active in finance and industry too. Between 1902 and 1934, Dr. El-Gritly reported, the proportion of the Egyptian public debt held in Egypt itself, rather than abroad, increased from 10 per cent to 59 per cent. At the same time the proportion of company shares held in Egypt rose from 22 per cent to 46 per cent. After World War II Egyptian capital even went into industries where it met "severe foreign competition" for the domestic market but "on the tacit assumption that adequate protection would be forthcoming."[73]

Since 1952 Egypt has entered the third period, that of government domination of entrepreneurship. In the wake of international disputes, the state has taken over the Suez Canal and leading banks in which British, French, and Belgian capital was dominant. It has also taken over the leading Egyptian-owned banks and the newspaper and periodical press. In the manufacturing industry itself the government has pursued a different course. In 1957 it created the Economic Organization to unify and extend the government's role in the creation and expansion of industrial firms through the investment of public funds. Where the Organization owns 25 per cent or more of the capital of a company, it has effective control because the government then appoints the chairman of the board and the managing director. In 1960 a similar agency was established for the Syrian region of the U.A.R.[74] At the end

[72] El-Gritly, pp. 372–74.
[73] *Ibid.*, pp. 374, 376, 383–84.
[74] National Bank of Egypt, *Economic Bulletin* (1957), 10:37, and (1960), 13:42.

of 1957, the Egyptian Organization's total capital was 58 million Egyptian pounds. The sources of these investments were: 40 per cent from shares already held by the government, 42 per cent from the British and French companies nationalized after the Suez crisis of 1956, 12 per cent from companies created by the Organization, and the remaining 6 per cent from purchases in existing companies. Of the total capital, two thirds was in industrial companies, an eighth in banks and another eighth in mining and petroleum.[75] By the end of 1959, two years after its inception, the Organization held about the same amount of capital but had established several new companies. It held, at that time, about half of the total capital of the 58 companies in which it had an interest.[76] The intention of the government was ultimately to sell its shares to private corporations rather than to remain the owner and operator of so many firms.[77]

In the summer of 1961, however, the U.A.R. took several steps that brought virtually all economic activity under full or partial government ownership and control. These drastic decrees were to apply to the Syrian region only in modified form, but just a few months later political power there was assumed by local leaders who re-established the country's complete independence. The decrees thus apply only to Egypt. They nationalize many firms, severely limit income, and alter working conditions. (The decrees appear in the U.A.R. *Official Gazette* (in Arabic), July 19, 1961, No. 161, pp. 1042–43, and July 20, 1961, No. 162, pp. 1046–53; *Egyptian Gazette* (official, in Arabic), July 25, 1961, No. 59 (supplement), and July 30, 1961, No. 59 (b). See also National Bank of Egypt, *Economic Bulletin* (1961), Vol. XIV, Nos. 2 and 3.)

All banks and insurance companies and forty-eight additional large firms were nationalized. In each of eighty-three more firms the government was to buy not less than 50 per cent of the capital and to have the authority to

[75] Egypt, Economic Organization, pp. 21–22.
[76] U.K. Board of Trade, pp. 54–55.
[77] Egypt, Economic Organization, p. 16.

remove and appoint directors. Compensation for the expropriated property was to be in fifteen-year government
bonds at 4 per cent interest. As for companies of all kinds,
no matter by whom owned, they may now have no more
than seven directors, two of them elected by and representing the workers. Foreign trade, too, was put under
government control. Government corporations were authorized to acquire 50 per cent of the capital of companies
exporting cotton (which supplies most of Egypt's foreign
exchange), while the import trade was almost entirely
lodged in the hands of these public bodies.

Several measures put a ceiling on income. In the remaining large private companies, no one may own shares worth
more than 10,000 Egyptian pounds (about $28,000). The
government takes the excess and compensates the owners
with fifteen-year bonds at 4 per cent interest. A maximum
salary of 5,000 Egyptian pounds (about $14,000) was set
for all directors in public and private establishments. An
amendment to the income tax law stiffened the tax on
higher incomes. Finally, the distribution of company
profits is strictly prescribed: 75 per cent goes to share-
holders and 25 per cent to the workers in the form of
cash and welfare.

Labor is benefited in other ways. The maximum work-
day was set at seven hours and the maximum work week
at forty-two hours. To keep unemployment down, the regime decreed that more than 300 companies, public and
private and designated specifically by name, must take on
about 25,000 more workers within a year.

The Egyptian government has clearly decided that industrialization and the improvement of living standards
can come only through direct government ownership and
control of practically the entire system of production and
foreign trade. The regime may have felt that such measures were required to fulfill its claim that it is building a
socialist society. It is likely, too, that the regime felt increasingly frustrated at its own economic difficulties while
some sectors of private enterprise continued to thrive despite regulation; so it decided simply to put all profit in

the country at the disposal of the government. Whether the same level of profit will be earned by government corporations remains to be seen.

The government's many-sided role in entrepreneurship today is facilitated by two conditions: the prominence of the corporate form of enterprise, and a lingering skepticism of risk and uncertainty.

The corporation was introduced into Egypt in the last quarter of the nineteenth century by Europeans. Registered and financed in Europe, these firms conducted such large-scale enterprises in Egypt as were not a function of the government itself.[78] As industry grew, the corporation was increasingly resorted to, until it became common even for smaller enterprises. In 1954 the corporation was the chief form of ownership of manufacturing firms with ten or more workers each. Of all such firms, 52 per cent were corporations, 30 per cent partnerships, 15 per cent individually owned, and 3 per cent other forms. In this category, the 300 corporations employed more than half of all the workers.[79]

We saw in Chapter 2 the traditional suspicion of risk in Islam. Though it is difficult to apply a general predisposition of this kind to a specific case like entrepreneurship, there does seem to be some relationship between the two. Arab business is widely reported to prefer large profit margins and small turnover to lower margins and greater turnover, and investment in agricultural land and urban real estate to investment in industry. El-Gritly has made the significant point that even textbooks in Egypt have "unduly exaggerated" the advantages of bonds over stocks from the standpoint of security.[80] Very likely the general political and economic insecurity in the Near East has also been at work in the creation of these attitudes toward

[78] El-Gritly, pp. 380–81.
[79] U.N., *op. cit.* (note 57 above), Table 48, p. 58. On the similarly important place of the corporation in Syria, see Asfour, pp. 31–32.
[80] El-Gritly, pp. 391–92.

risk. It is interesting to note that emigrants from the Near East (chiefly Lebanon and Syria) to the Americas find the new environment congenial to a keen spirit of entrepreneurship.[81]

LABOR RELATIONS

Labor, the other major human resource in industrialization, has likewise raised problems in the Arab world. The chief one is the creation of a labor force trained for modern industry but not so politically radical as to threaten economic development or political stability. Until now Near Eastern governments have been mainly concerned with preventing the working class from achieving autonomous power and with using its power in the cause of Arab nationalism. More recently, however, they have sought to improve the conditions of labor and have begun to attack the entire problem of the recruitment, training, and adjustment of manpower to industry.

The Near East has suffered from a vicious circle: low wages and poor health lowers the productivity of the workers, which helps keep industry inefficient, which perpetuates low wages, and so on. Conditions of factory labor are poor by Western standards, with unsanitary conditions, harsh discipline, and general insecurity of employment. With only few and weak trade unions, the workers are not able to improve their own situation,[82] especially in regard to wages during inflationary periods. There is reasonably reliable information on this only for Egypt, where wages are somewhat lower than in the rest of the area[83] and where industry is more developed. Egyptain wages for factory workers vary from the equivalent of 7 to 12 dollars a week (which of course buys much more in Egypt than in the United States). Although, real wages have been rising in the last decade, after having declined considerably

[81] On emigrants to the United States, see, for example, Berger, "Americans from . . . ," pp. 353–55.

[82] Sayigh, "Management-Labor Relations . . . ," *passim.*

[83] See, for example, I.B.R.D., *Jordan,* pp. 60, 453, and Asfour, p. 133, note 10.

during World War II and for several years after it, according to the estimate of the research department of the National Bank, by 1955 they had not yet climbed back to the prewar level.[84] Since then, however, rising money-wages and government control over prices of staples have combined to bring real wages to a postwar peak.

Because of the weakness of the working class, the governments have had to intervene with legislation concerning wages, hours, trade unions, safety, and other conditions of labor. Yet much of this protection has availed little because the workers have not been alert enough or strong enough to maintain adequate vigil and the enforcement machinery has been weak or inefficient. More recently trade unions have spread under the watchful eye of the governments; the new regimes in the U.A.R. and Iraq ideologically committed themselves to improve working conditions. The result has been an increase in governmental regulation of both labor and management. The governments reserve the right to inspect the most private details of trade unions, and discourage the development of professional leadership and staff as well as contact with labor in other countries.[85] Management is likewise restricted in its freedom to hire and fire, and is required to provide workers certain educational and health services which in other countries are assumed either by the government or trade unions, or are the responsibilities of the individual citizen.[86] The reason is that both the workers and the governments in the Near East are ill-prepared or simply unwilling to carry the burden of welfare. This extends to the provision of housing, transportation, and community facilities, for most municipalities outside the main cities are not equipped to receive large numbers of workers whose needs outside the factory must be met if the work is to go forward. The larger enterprises thus

[84] "Statistics of Wages and Working Hours in Egypt," *Economic Bulletin* (1957), 10:105.

[85] See, for example, Hallsworth, p. 383, and on Egypt, Harbison and Ibrahim, pp. 181–82.

[86] See Harbison and Ibrahim, pp. 83, 113.

find it useful to provide for such needs in order to recruit
and hold workers, and the government finds it easy to adopt
regulations requiring large employers to do so instead of
meeting such needs itself.

With a small working class only recently introduced to
modern industry, it is no wonder the Arab countries do not
have a strong trade union movement. Table 21 shows that
in 1957 there were about 340,000 trade union members in

TABLE 21. *Trade Unions: Membership and International
Affiliation, 1957*

	NUMBER OF MEMBERS	INTERNATIONAL AFFILIATION			
		ICATU[1]	WFTU[2]	ICFTU[3]	NONE
Egypt	275,000[4]	275,000			—
Iraq	821	—	—	—	821
Jordan	11,248	5,953	—	—	5,295
Lebanon	21,478	5,715	2,400	4,000	9,363
Syria	32,213	32,213	—	—	—
Totals	340,760	318,881	2,400	4,000	15,479

[1] International Confederation of Arab Trade Unions

[2] World Federation of Trade Unions

[3] International Confederation of Free Trade Unions

[4] A much higher figure for Egypt, 373,000 in 1955, is given
by the research department of the National Bank of Egypt,
Economic Bulletin (1957), 10:108, Table V, and higher
figures for all countries in 1953–54 are given by J. A.
Hallsworth, "Freedom of Association and Industrial Relations in the Countries of the Near East," *International Labor
Review* (1954), 70:366.

SOURCE: Willard A. Beling, *Pan-Arabism and Labor*, Harvard
University Press, Cambridge, 1960, Table 9, p. 73.

the five countries, with Egypt having the vast majority.
Controlled by the government in the most cases, with uneducated and inexperienced workers and leaders, and having few contacts with stronger trade unions in other
regions, these unions are only beginning to perform some
union functions effectively. As yet, they have been able to

obtain few collective agreements.[87] The more the governments have encouraged the growth of unions, the more they have also controlled them and used them for political purposes. Recently this use has extended from domestic to international politics when, in 1956, several Arab countries formed the International Confederation of Arab Trade Unions. Suspecting the Western group, the International Confederation of Free Trade Unions, of imperialist and Zionist affinities, and wishing to avoid too close identification with the Communist-sponsored World Federation of Trade Unions, the Arab leaders decided to form a separate federation. According to a student of the Arab labor movement, the International Confederation of Arab Trade Unions is interested chiefly in politics, is the "unofficial regional labor arm" of the Arab League, and has been "involved in every Egyptian-sponsored international action."[88] Thus the governments in the leading Arab countries have in a sense established the trade union movement and have used it, first in the nationalist struggle against foreign enterprise and foreign occupying powers, then in internal politics in the struggle for power, and now in the international political arena.

SOCIAL AND ECONOMIC PLANNING

Like other poor and industrially undeveloped regions, the Arab world has, especially since World War II, caught the fever of planning for economic growth. All the five countries we are considering have plans of varying duration and detail and have varying capacity to plan realistically. The Egyptian Ministry of Industry, for example, has pointed to the magnitude of the task. "We are attempting," it has observed, "to narrow the gap between our standard of living and that of economically advanced countries" as the latter are advancing too. "It is our duty therefore," it continues, "not only to keep pace with the present ad-

[87] Hallsworth, p. 528.
[88] Beling, pp. 22–23, 97.

vancement in other countries but also to exert extra efforts if our objective is to be reached."[89]

Has the Arab world the capacity to raise its material level substantially? Apart from the questions of the human resources of labor and management and a knowledge of economic forces, which we have already discussed, there is also the simple matter of the availability of capital in adequate amounts to finance development. If the Arab Near East were unified to such an extent that the oil royalties of the less developed countries were available to the more advanced ones without oil, there would undoubtedly be enough domestic capital to insure a modicum of economic growth and the absorption of the normal annual increase in the labor force. But this degree of unity does not now seem likely to be achieved, peacefully or by force, for many years, if ever. The Arab countries that want to raise national income through industrialization must therefore obtain capital from outside, through governmental or international loans and grants and private investment. Until now there has been a large gap between their need for foreign capital and their ability to attract it.

Some of the Arab countries are nevertheless going ahead resolutely with plans for economic development within their present capacity to raise domestic capital and to attract foreign capital. The ones that have been at it the longest, Egypt and Iraq, have learned two important lessons. First, after several disappointing trials, they have improved the administrative machinery for national planning. Egypt now has a special Ministry of Planning (which is responsible to a planning committee in the cabinet), as well as planning sections in each ministry. In 1960, an independent Institute of National Planning was established with a competent staff and good leadership, to train the officials engaged in planning at all levels and to undertake theoretical as well as practical studies.[90] Second, they have learned that planning does not mean simply the

[89] Republic of Egypt, Ministry of Industry, *Industry After the Revolution and the Five Year Plan*, Cairo, 1957, p. 89.

[90] Abdel-Rahman, pp. 1, 11, 25.

hurried and random building of factories but more importantly the establishment of the basis for economic growth: an educated, literate, healthy population trained at all levels of skill and in various functions; transportation and communication facilities; agricultural reform; and sources of energy.

In most of these plans the state is playing an increasingly prominent role. This is less the case in Lebanon[91] and more the case in Egypt than elsewhere. We have already seen the influential role of the Egyptian Economic Organization in creating and expanding industries and banks. Government expenditure for economic development, it is estimated, increased from 2 per cent of gross domestic product in 1945–47 to 4 per cent in 1954–56. Accordingly, the share of the public sector in gross capital formation rose from 19 per cent of total in 1950 to 60 per cent in 1956.[92]

The planning apparatus and goals of the U.A.R. were the most elaborate in the region. In 1960 it adopted the goal of doubling national income in a decade.[93] Detailed goals for both Syria and Egypt were announced for the five-year period 1960–65, in which it was planned to increase national income by 40 per cent through the expenditure of two billion Egyptian pounds (or about 5.6 billion dollars at the official rate of exchange). In the Egyptian region the rise in national income is expected to come chiefly from the expansion of power resources and industry, while agriculture is not expected to contribute much to growth until after 1965, when the benefits of the high dam at Aswan, now in construction, will be enjoyed. Domestic savings, according to the plan, will rise from 11 per cent of national income in 1960 to 21 per cent in 1965. Domestic financing is thus to cover about two thirds of capital needs, the remainder to come from foreign gov-

[91] Sayigh, "Lebanon . . . ," pp. 72–73.
[92] U.N., op. cit. (note 57 above), p. 5 and Table 18, p. 21.
[93] On the plan, see National Bank of Egypt, "The Budget and the Plan," Economic Bulletin (1960), 13:80–5, and (1961), 14:5–9, 11–18. Also Abdel-Rahman, pp. 4–6.

ernments in loans and grants. The labor force is expected to grow by about one million persons, who are to be absorbed mainly by the industrial projects envisioned. In order to raise the worker's level of living it is planned that wages will rise by about a third, while the labor force will increase by less than that proportion. Consumption is planned for an increase of 24 per cent, less than the 40 per cent planned for national income; the gap, it is hoped, will provide additional sources of capital to finance future plans.

CHAPTER 7

Social Groups:
Economic, Religious, and National

To the world outside, the Near East appears to be a homogeneous culture, Islamic in religion, Arab in nationality, agricultural and poor economically. This popular impression is far from the truth about an area that includes Israel, Iran, and Turkey. It is closer to the truth if we speak only of the Arab core we are treating in this book: Egypt, Syria, Lebanon, Jordan, and Iraq. Yet even in this limited area there are many group loyalties and class differences. There are, first, as in other societies, the poor and the rich and the groups between them, as well as the peasants and large landowners, workers and employers, laborers and professionals, and so on. And beyond these economic and occupational divisions are others which sometimes coincide with them but more often produce additional differences among groups, in religion, nationality, and language. These differences have emerged during the long and varied history of the area, with the rise of several religions and sects within each, the growth of nations and their mixture. Each sweep of religion or nationality has left corners in which groups formed earlier have survived to this day.

These two types of division, one according to wealth and economic function, the other according to religion or nationality, have co-existed in the Arab world for centuries. Traditionally, the second has been the main mark of distinction—a man was known as a Moslem or Christian or Jew, and later as an Arab, Turk, Armenian, or European. Distinctions of wealth and occupation were likewise important, of course, but primarily within each religious, national, or racial community. Such socio-economic differences were traditionally not made between, say, a Moslem and a Christian. Occupation and religion, however, often went together. In Egypt the Christian Copts were numerous in the civil service, and almost everywhere Jews were prominent in trade and finance. But although an economic calling might be dominated by a certain ethnic or religious group, that group was by no means engaged only in that calling. In other words, the ethnic or religious group has been more inclusive than the occupational or economic. In recent decades, the growth of modern industry, nationalism, and secularism have given greater importance to distinctions based on wealth and occupation and the Arab world has taken on a type of social stratification more nearly like the general type prevailing in Europe and America. But the persistence of the older type of ethnic-religious distinction has produced a crisscrossing of social differences and prestige rankings that within even a single Arab nation-state cannot be fully encompassed within the terms of the conception of social class as it has applied to the industrial, secular society of the West. To understand the Arab world today we must take account of these socio-economic, ethnic-religious differences, for these groups into which an Arab is born influence his behavior and ideas no less than does the family. They exert varying degrees of power in the Arab world, and the relations between them are changing rapidly.

Ethnic and Religious Differences

The main distinction among the people of the Near East is that of religion. Islam, Christianity and Judaism define the major communities and their cultures.[1] Islam, as

[1] There are, of course, differences in physical appearance. We shall not consider these in detail because they do not seriously affect social relations among the Arabs today. Moreover, the physical types are so mixed that no precise, consistent, and socially relevant ones can be established. Roughly, the single most numerous group would be what is called the Mediterranean "race"

TABLE 1. Main Minority Groups,[1] 1960

Country	Total Population	Per cent Minorities	Religious Minorities[2]	National Linguistic Minorities
Egypt	26,080,000	8.3	Christians Copts 2,000,000	
			Europeans[4] 100,000	
			Arabs[5] 40,000	
			Jews 14,000	
			Total 2,154,000	
Iraq	6,942,000	19.5	Christians 150,000	Kurds 1,200,000
			Jews 5,000	
			Total 1,355,000	
Jordan	1,678,000	6.5	Christians 110,000	
			Total 110,000	
Lebanon[3]	1,639,000		Christians 904,550	
			Moslems 728,450	
			Jews 6,000	
Syria	4,561,000	18.5	Christians 550,000	Kurds 300,000
			Jews 5,500	
			Total 855,500	
Totals[3]	40,900,000	13.2	Christians 3,854,550	Kurds 1,500,000
			Jews 30,500	
				Grand Total 5,385,050

1 Based on ancestry as well as citizenship.

2 Excludes Moslem minorities. Some of the Christian groups can be classified as "national-linguistic" minorities but in the Near East they are still identified mainly by religion.

3 For Lebanon, estimates are given for both Christians and Moslems because neither is regarded as a "majority" or "minority" group in the usual sense. For this reason, also, the total number and percentage of the "minorities" is not given. But as the Lebanese Christians are regarded as a religious minority in the Near East as a whole, they are included in the *total* number and proportion of the minority population.

4 Chiefly of Greek, Italian, and Armenian ancestry.

5 Chiefly of Lebanese ancestry.

SOURCES: Population—see Ch. 6, Table 1. Figures for minorities are rough approximations based on other estimates, inferences from scanty census data and on the author's talks with representatives of the minority communities. For Lebanon the estimate is based on the distribution of parliamentary seats to Christians and Moslems. The chief published sources used are (1) Royal Institute of International Affairs, *The Middle East*, 3d ed., Oxford University Press, London, 1958; (2) Albert H. Hourani, *Minorities in the Arab World*, Oxford University Press, London, 1947, and "Race and Related Ideas in the Near East," in *Race Relations in World Perspective*, ed. Andrew W. Lind, University of Hawaii Press, Honolulu, 1955, Ch. 6; (3) *The Jewish Year Book 1958*, Jewish Chronicle Publications, London, 1958, Table I, pp. 213–14; (4) *The American Jewish Year Book*, 1960, The American Jewish Committee, New York, 1960, Table 3, p. 353 and Table 5, p. 354.

we saw in Chapter I, was intended for Arabs; the Arab Moslems did not distinguish between their religion and their nationality. This unity of what we now call religion and nationality has persisted among Arab Moslems to this day. A former president of the American University of

which (contrasted with the most numerous of Northern Europeans and North Americans) is dark in complexion, with dark and wavy hair, of short and slight build. Egypt has a large proportion who are African Negroid.

Beirut has reported that students asked to give their nationality on the registration card would usually write
Moslem rather than Syrian, Palestinian, and so on.[2] Islam
not only came first to Arabs, it was the structure within
which the Arabs were unified. In several places in the
Koran[3] Moslems are enjoined to ignore sexual, national,
tribal, and other differences among themselves, for all are
united in a single community embracing all such loyalties
which we now distinguish.

But Islam did not absorb all the religious and tribal-
national groups it met as it expanded, nor did it succeed
in remaining united within itself. The result is that there
are Moslem and non-Moslem communities, and differences
within the Moslem community, the most important of
which is between the Sunnites and Shi'ites. The Sunnites
are the Moslems who stress their adherence to the path
(*sunna*) of the Prophet; they constitute the majority and
are known as the orthodox group. The Shi'ites, whose
greatest strength in the Arab world today is in Iraq, are the
adherents of the party (*shi'a*) of Ali, the son-in-law of the
Prophet; they believe that Ali should have become caliph
after the Prophet's death. Though it arose in dissent on
the question of succession, Shi'ism later became a religious
opposition to orthodoxy and then attracted the non-Arab
minorities among the Moslems who had social grievances
against the ruling Sunnites.

The preceding table gives the approximate number and
proportions of the most important ethnic minority groups,
taking the Arabic-speaking Moslem group as the majority.

As the table shows, the chief religious and national minorities constitute about an eighth of the population of
the Arab world. Christians alone are almost a tenth. Kurds,
a group of Moslems with their own language and separate
national traditions, are found in the Arab countries of Iraq
and Syria (as well as in Iran and Turkey). The Jews formerly numbered about a quarter of a million but emigration since the establishment of the state of Israel in 1948

[2] Penrose, p. 131.
[3] See especially Ch. 49, verses 10ff.

and the Sinai war of 1956 has reduced them to about 30,500.

Religious differences produce other differences that take on a national aspect. Just as Moslems in the Near East see themselves as a nation of Arabs, so the Christians feel less a part of that nation and are less enthusiastic about plans to create a single nation-state in the Arab world. The Egyptian Copts consider themselves more Egyptian than Arab and are thus in two senses, religious and national, removed from the Arab Moslem community. The Christians in Syria, especially the largest group of them, the Greek Orthodox, are closer to the Arab majority in national feeling. The largest Christian community in Lebanon, however, the Maronites (an autonomous group affiliated with Roman Catholicism), have a very strong sense of Lebanese nationality which they like to trace back to the pre-Arab Phoenician culture of that area. The curiously conducted civil war in 1958 revealed the depth of Christian Lebanese suspicion of even unspoken or implied schemes for Arab unity that might threaten the continued separate identity of Lebanon as a state. In Lebanon, as in Egypt, the Christian community lives in all parts of the country (but least in the South). Also, in both countries and in Syria as well, the Christians enjoy a higher educational and economic level, although this gap is not so great in Lebanon. In Jordan the only considerable minority is the Christian one, living mainly in and near Jerusalem and the Holy Places; here, too, Christians enjoy a higher standard of living than the country as a whole.

In Iraq the situation is different, for there we find the only important minority question within the Moslem community as well as the largest national minority, the Kurds. There are only a few Christians, the largest concentration of them being in the northern district of Mosul; most of them are better educated and enjoy a higher standard of living than the average Iraqi, and they work in services and trades and industries connected with Western interests of all kinds. The Jews, of whom there were about 130,000 before their large-scale emigration (mainly to Israel) in

1950–52, were nearly as numerous as the Christians and enjoyed even higher living standards; they were prominent in commerce, banking, and the crafts. The small number of Christians and Jews today, 150,000 and 5000 respectively, accentuates Iraq's two main minority issues: the Moslem difference between Sunnites and Shi'ites and the Kurdish national question. It is generally conceded that the Shi'ites slightly outnumber the Sunnites in Iraq, a reversal of the situation elsewhere in the Arab world. But the Sunnites hold the major positions in the government and the economy. Largely agricultural, the Shi'ites live along the banks of the two rivers, the Tigris and Euphrates, in the central and southern districts. The Sunnites are less concentrated geographically and occupationally. Controlling the main sources of power, they also have had more sympathy than the Shi'ites with the rest of the Arab world.

The Kurds are a Moslem (largely Sunnite) group speaking an Indo-European language and divided among several countries bordering on one another. In Iraq there are more than a million of them, constituting almost a sixth of the total population. Concentrated in the northern and northeastern districts (bordering on Iranian districts also heavily Kurdish), they have been rapidly emerging from a tribal form of life in the mountains and have moved into the plains and cities. Their growing nationalistic feeling, encouraged by the Soviet Union and its followers in the area, has caused political disturbances in Iraq and has been a potential or active source of unrest there and in Syria, Iran, and Turkey, where they also form a sizable minority group. The Sunnite-Shi'ite division and the nationalist tendencies of the Kurds were both important influences, together with the purely political one of the Communists, working against unity with the United Arab Republic after the 1958 revolution which overthrew the Hashemite dynasty in Iraq.

For many years the Christian and Jewish communities in the Arab Moslem world were the chief agents through whom Western techniques and products, tastes and ideas, were introduced. Christians and Jews were the leading traders, bankers, and manufacturers; many of them were the first managers and clerks in the businesses set up by Western firms and individuals and in the regimes controlled by the Western powers. Politically, they usually remained outside the struggles against Western rule, except for a small number of Christians who became leaders of Arab nationalism and other local nationalist movements such as the Egyptian. In this role, too, however, they introduced a Western idea because as Christians, their nationalism was purely secular and lacked the religious character of Arab Moslem nationalism. During the 1920s and 1930s, the Arab Communist parties had a large proportion of Christians and Jews, before international communism began to ally itself with the dominant nationalist Arab sentiment rather than with the discontented, more Westernized minority groups.

It is clear from the nature of this activity by minority groups that they have enjoyed considerable economic and social freedom in the Moslem Near East. From the very beginning the Prophet displayed a special attitude toward Jews and Christians to whom had been revealed the Old and New Testaments which Moslems were bidden to accept in part. The early spread of Islam was not always viewed as a calamity by these "people of the Book," for in many respects the new rulers were more lenient than the Christian Byzantines they displaced. A Christian or Jew was early considered a *dhimmi*, a protected person who had to pay higher taxes and endure certain inequalities but who was permitted to practice his religion freely; indeed, the Christians and Jews were allowed to regulate their own religious and personal affairs. Traditionally this policy is reported to be based upon the Koran[4] which calls upon Moslems to "make war" upon those who have received the Scriptures but do not accept Islam, "until they pay tribute out of hand, and they be humbled." Lewis sums up their status in this way: "The Dhimmis were second-class citizens, paying a higher rate of taxation, suf-

[4] Ch. 9, verse 30.

fering from certain social disabilities, and on a few rare occasions subjected to open persecution. But by and large their position was infinitely superior to that of those communities who differed from the established church in Western Europe in the same period. They enjoyed the free exercise of their religion, normal property rights, and were very frequently employed in the service of the State, often in the highest offices. They were admitted to the craft guilds, in some of which they actually predominated. They were never called upon to suffer martyrdom or exile for their beliefs."[5]

As Lewis also remarks, tolerance was not equality. The status of the Christians and Jews differed from time to time and place to place as laws were enforced or ignored in turn. They were required to assume certain dress, ride certain animals only in certain ways and sometimes not at all, and to mark their houses in a special way.[6] Though allowed to retain their own beliefs and practices, this very freedom served to make them conspicuous as non-Moslems in a Moslem world which had absorbed and converted the pagans—they became the recalcitrant unbelievers in a world of believers. Under the Ottoman Empire the autonomy of the religious minorities took the form of *millets*, each conducting its own communal affairs and regulating the personal status of its members. As Gibb and Bowen observe,[7] because religion was the unifying feature of the empire, the various *millets* were "condemned . . . to exclusion from effective incorporation in the Ottoman structure of society . . ." So pervasive was the Moslem feeling of tolerant separation from non-Moslems that the Ottomans granted even to European Christians certain personal, commercial, and religious rights, and a degree of autonomy on Ottoman territory. These rights, beginning in the sixteenth century, were known as the Capitulations and, far from being wrung from the Ottomans by superior Western pow-

---

[5] Lewis, *The Arabs in History*, p. 94.
[6] See, for example, Strauss, *passim*.
[7] Gibb and Bowen, Part II, pp. 78–79.

ers, were offered to the foreign non-Moslems as virtually an extension of the Moslem policy toward the *dhimmis* who were Ottoman subjects.

The persistence of these religious-national minorities in the Arab Moslem world is the result not only of the early attitude toward the "people of the Book" and of the Ottoman *millet* system but also of other influences which Albert Hourani, a leading British historian of the Arab world, has mentioned.[8] First, tribal and national differences were reinforced by religious differences, as has happened among the Druzes, a small Moslem sect in Lebanon, Syria and Israel which has doctrinally wandered far from orthodoxy. Second, differences of religion, language, and custom were perpetuated through the social isolation of community from community in the centuries preceding the introduction of modern means of communication, and through the geographical isolation resulting from a vast and difficult terrain of mountains and deserts. Finally, partly because of these difficulties of communication, governments had little control outside the towns and the plains and even there ignored many spheres of life. As a result, local cultures could grow, flourish and, when threatened, withdraw into the less accessible areas where they easily preserved their own character. Within the Ottoman Empire local dynasties and feudatories were thus able to maintain themselves.

In recent years the tides of nationalism throughout the world have affected the way in which minority groups in the Near East look at each other and themselves. Not only has national feeling become a greater divider of peoples than religion, but even the religious differences that remain are being expressed increasingly in secular, national terms. Arab nationalism itself is a prime example of this tendency; behind its secular appearance there is still much religious fervor among the millions of Moslems who feel their Arabism without making speeches about it which get into the Western press.

[8] Hourani, *Minorities in the Arab World*, pp. 15–21.

Evidence of the change of emphasis, among the articulate Arabs at least, appears in a study of "social distance" made by the psychologists Prothro and Melikian[9] in 1951. They repeated an earlier questionnaire given to students at the American University of Beirut in 1935 and compared the two sets of results. The questions were designed to elicit the respondents' degree of "social distance" from other Arabs and several Western nations, as well as from other main religious groups and minor sects in the area. The 130 students—the large majority males between 17 and 22 years of age, about half of them Christians and half Moslems—were given a list of nations and religions and were asked to state which of the following intentions represented their attitudes toward each group: (1) willing to marry one of that group; (2) willing to have one as a guest for a meal; (3) prefer only as an acquaintance; (4) do not enjoy companionship; (5) wish someone would kill the members of the group.

Responses to such questionnaires tend to follow political events, so it must be recalled that this one was given a few years after the creation of the state of Israel (which Arabs attributed to Western policy) but before the Egyptian revolution which brought Nasser to prominence and before the Anglo-French-Israeli attack upon Egypt in 1956 and the Iraqi revolution of 1958. The most general finding relevant here is that in 1951 the distances based on national differences were greater than those based on religious differences. In 1935, exactly the opposite had been found. Though the Moslem students expressed greater national feeling than the Christians (whose Arab sentiment is complicated by their Western loyalties), their attitude toward Christians improved from the first to the second study. Toward Jews it worsened; but this was not a purely religious affair since it followed the establishment of a Jewish *national* state in Israel. Zionism has stimulated in the Arab world a certain amount of anti-Semitism of the classical type to be found in Europe. Islam hardly knew

[9] Prothro and Melikian, "Social Distance . . . ," p. 7.

this social doctrine despite its opposition to Judaism on religious grounds from the very moment the Jews resisted conversion by Muhammad and his successors. As Dr. Sylvia Haim, a keen student of Arab Moslem contemporary thought, points out,[10] anti-Semitism was a Western importation through the Westernized Arab communities: "The flow of antisemitic doctrine from Europe did not originate in one country nor was it confined to a single decade. In the nineteenth century it emanated from France at the time of the Dreyfus Affair and, for obvious reasons, the Eastern [Orthodox] Christians became the agents through whom the doctrine was propagated." With the exacerbation of Arab-Jewish relations on the Palestine question, Nazi propaganda flooded the Near East and found a large audience willing to listen to it, and a few influential Moslems willing to learn the technique. Since the creation of the state of Israel in 1948, anti-Semitic propaganda has not needed to be imported from Europe; "Westernization" has made the Near East self-sufficient in this as in some other kinds of production, though criticism of Israel and Zionism is of course not in itself necessarily anti-Semitic.

Yet it is significant that the wave of swastika-painting on synagogue walls in Europe and America in 1959–60 did not spread to the Arab world, except to Beirut, the Arab city with the highest proportion of Christians.

While hostility between different religions as religions probably has declined, hostility between different branches of the same broad religious group seems to have continued unabated. Among the Moslems, Sunnite-Shi'ite hostility increased from the earlier to the later study; indeed, in the later one the Sunnites expressed greater hostility toward Shi'ites than toward several Christian denominations. This, too, may have reflected only growing national feeling within the Arab world, for Shi'ites are usually assumed by Sunnites to be either Iraqis, or not Arabs but Iranians. The later study also gives additional evidence of an in-

[10] Haim, "Arabic Antisemitic Literature."

teresting phenomenon: the frequently greater enmity between two related groups having the same goal but advo-
cating different means than between two groups seeking
different goals entirely. Thus only one of forty-nine Moslems stated that he wished someone would kill all Maronite (Catholic) Christians but five of fifty-four Christians expressed this intense hostility toward Maronites.

Nationalism is a sentiment that reduces differences
among those who share it but magnifies the contrasts between those who adhere to varying national groups. Because of the numerous ethnic groups in the Arab world,
nationalism there has had an unsettling effect. Although
it has been a unifying sentiment, it has also presented the
groups who find Arab nationalism uncongenial with a different choice: to "become" as Arab as possible or to refuse
and thus incur hostility from the majority. In the loose
social structure of the past, the minorities were able to
retain their identity with greater ease and at less social
cost than they can now with the advent of a nationalist
spirit which demands positive loyalty and homogeneity
rather than mere separation and tribute. Though it is now
easier for anyone in a minority group to "become" an
Arab, it is worse for those who do not. As European power
has waned in the Near East, minorities have found it increasingly difficult to retain their communal identity. The
Jews, as we have seen, have emigrated almost entirely
from Iraq and Egypt (as well as Yemen), where they
were most numerous. Many Christians of European descent have also emigrated, some have become citizens of
the Arab states in which they live but continue to live as
Europeans, and the remaining ones find themselves more
and more alienated from the life around them. The Christian Arabs (including the Egyptian Copts) have, on the
whole, adopted or adjusted to Arab nationalism but with
less enthusiasm for a single Arab nation-state in which
Moslems would be even more predominant than in the
individual ones. Two developments since World War II
have impelled the Christians in this direction. First, the
decline of Western influence left them without a "pro-

tector" and hence forced them to seek accommodation to the Arab Moslem majority. Second, the rise of the Palestine question stimulated Arab nationalism and became a test of loyalty for the Christians. On both counts, they found it easier and safer to identify themselves with the growing nationalist trend, for, after all, culturally and linguistically they have a great deal in common with other Arabs despite the great difference in religion. As for the Kurds, the largest national-linguistic minority, their traditional weakness—the fact that they are divided among four countries—has recently been intensified by the modernization of national states in the area, which has made the governmental apparatus more efficient in controlling minority activity. The Kurds have stoutly preserved their differences, cultural and ideological, and show few signs of willingness to be absorbed in the nationalism within or among the Arab states.

So far as the ethnic minorities are concerned, Arab nationalism has thus far unsettled their status without producing, except to some extent for Christians with a long Arab heritage, a compensating degree of unity or an accommodation based upon closer association rather than, as in the past, upon separation. The result is that group relations are not friendly relations. The study by Prothro and Melikian, referred to above, reveals that "social distance" among national and religious groups in the Near East is greater than in the United States, according to similar studies made here. Yet there is a curious absence of public discussion of the minorities. Arabs themselves do not write books, scholars do not conduct research, and the newspapers and radio do not dwell on the problems of the ethnic and religious groups themselves, or their relations with the majority community. There is plenty of private conversation on these questions, but they are not great issues debated in legislatures or presented to the public by other means. One explanation may be that the various communities are so distinct and segregated that there is no basis for a national airing of issues between them. One has the feeling that public discussion, with its inevitable disagreements brought into the open, would only exacerbate differences and stimulate violence. There is as yet not enough common ground or communal discipline or social machinery to permit a public dialogue that might smooth out rather than sharpen the edges of contact between minorities and majority.

Social Classes

Ethnic-religious differences, we have seen, are declining as some minorities virtually disappear through emigration or absorption into the majority community. But as modern industry grows, urbanization increases, and communication becomes easier, other types of social distinctions which formerly overlapped with or were obscured by the ethnic differences have begun to emerge more clearly and to assume independent significance. These are the social classes or strata based on occupation, income and power. We call these distinct groups *strata* because they occupy, so to speak, different social layers in a vertical column, constituting a hierarchy from lowest to highest. Ethnic-religious distinctions also yield a hierarchy to a certain extent but not so satisfactorily, for they are highly subjective and less measurable. First, an ethnic or religious minority usually feels itself no lower than the majority and may even consider itself superior. The majority group takes the same view regarding itself. Moreover, where ethnic-religious differences do produce genuine strata, they do so in conjunction with differences of economic function and wealth. Social class differences, however, are less subjective and more easily measured for they are based on income and degree of social power; they are also based on occupational prestige, which in turn is partly derived from measurable differences of income and power. Finally, although in the Arab world most ethnic-religious groups do not admit the superiority or greater prestige of others, the social classes do admit the differences in prestige among themselves even to their own social detriment. Traditionally a European Christian would consider himself superior to a

Moslem while a Moslem would have contempt for this *franji* (foreigner, from "Frank" or European) who was outside the circle of believers who alone have status in the world of Islam. But a peasant accepts the fact that he is socially inferior to a landlord, merchant, or government clerk. An Arab laborer, for example, may resent the social class he is in and may seek to increase the power of the class itself or simply to rise into a higher one, but he is not likely to deny the fact of its low status.

It is easy to see that in the Arab world there are the rich and the poor. As elsewhere, the rich own the means of production and land, enjoy the occupations that are usually regarded as most desirable, have greater political power, are better educated and more articulate on public affairs. The poor, of course, do not own productive wealth or much land, are usually in occupations with little prestige, have less political power (as individuals, though not always as a class), are less educated and less articulate on public affairs. Apart from the paucity of studies, we face a serious difficulty when we try to go beyond these broad differences which apply everywhere and to specify in detail the various social strata in the Arab world. There is a confusion of criteria resulting from the interplay of the two sets of distinctions we have been discussing, ethnic-religious group and social class. The vast gulf separating the European from the Arab, the Christian or Jew from the Moslem, has created virtually independent communities with little social intercourse between them. It is therefore hazardous to compare economic positions across ethnic-religious boundaries, since this would mean trying to put on a single scale two elements that in social life are judged in different terms and without reference to one another. As we have already seen, these separate social orders traditionally overlapped very little in economic life. At least in the urban areas it was the minorities, for example, who were in trade, banking and in the skilled crafts involving modern machinery. How, therefore, could one determine the relative social positions of a Christian insurance company owner and a judge in a Moslem court? Both enjoyed high status but in completely different worlds. It is true that vestiges of earlier forms of social distinction still persist in most industrial countries too, but not to the extent that we find in the Arab world, which is only beginning to industrialize and in which only very recently there were still separate religious-national communities with autonomy grounded in law as well as in custom.

Though the Arab world is moving toward a system of social classes resembling that of the West, the process has only begun. Another difficulty confronting us is that industrialization in the Arab world is proceeding with greater participation by the state, so that we do not find there, to the same degree as in the West in a comparable era, the emergence of an independent middle class based upon manufacturing and commercial interests. Rather, the functions performed by such a middle class in the West are more likely to be carried out in the Arab world by technicians employed in government and business offices. Finally, the political changes in recent years affect the status of certain callings but it is difficult to know how enduring these changes will be. The advent of military regimes raises the prestige and power of the army leaders. Their attacks on the corruption of the regimes they displaced tends to lower the prestige of the civilian bureaucracy, but the accompanying enhancement of the state's role in industrialization, land reform, and so on certainly increases its power and perhaps its prestige as well.

With these limitations in mind, we may propose the following hierarchy of social classes in the Arab world today, going from highest to lowest in status, wealth, power, and occupational prestige:

1. Big landowners, bankers, industrialists, and highest governmental and military leaders.

2. Higher civil servants and army officers, independent professionals (doctors, lawyers, engineers, etc.), higher intellectuals, religious leaders.

3. Lower professions (teachers, journalists, pharmacists, etc.), white-collar workers in government and private enterprise.

4. Shopkeepers, skilled workers, artisans.

5. Peasants, laborers, service workers.

Two things are worth noting about this hierarchy. First, it has an urban bias in the sense that it distinguishes more among urban occupations than among rural. This is inevitable because rural society is less differentiated in occupation and social class; the vast majority live off the land and socio-economic status depends on the size of one's holdings and one's family, clan or tribal background. Second, it leans toward the kind of class system that is emerging, that is, one based more on occupation and income than on those ethnic-religious factors that, influential as they undoubtedly remain, are both declining in relevance and difficult to encompass without introducing so many gradations and qualifications as to make the list of classes unwieldy if not incomprehensible.

Though we have adapted to the Arab world concepts of social class based upon Western industrial society, we must be careful not to apply them indiscriminately. The relative positions of the classes in the Arab world differ; moreover, we may call the classes there by the same names we use to designate classes in the West, but it does not therefore follow that the values and attitudes and capacities of the classes similarly called are identical. The most important differences are, of course, in the relative size of each class and the degree of influence each exerts on the society.

The agricultural class in the Arab world is far more numerous, proportionally, than in the West, and is weaker politically; in addition, with only a few exceptions, it is a landless class or one with very small holdings permitting only a meager existence at or below the level needed to sustain life.

The working class is likewise weak but not numerous, for modern industry, as we saw in the previous chapter, employs only a very small proportion of the labor force. A great many artisans in the Near East cannot be included

in the working class because they really work outside the
structure and style of modern industry, while in income,
outlook, and loyalties—all of which still owe something to
the remains of the once-powerful guilds—they belong more
with the urban lower middle class. The workers are organized into a few trade unions but these are largely under state control. Indeed, the Arab countries in this respect have followed the pattern of Latin America, which
they resemble more in social structure than the West.
With a large peasant class, a small middle and working
class, and, until recently, a foreign community controlling
most of the capital invested in industry and commerce,
the Arab countries have encouraged trade unions and
adopted protective labor legislation as a nationalist
weapon to reduce the power of foreign investors and governments in the area. To cultivate new elements of political support, Arab governments have encouraged trade unions while retaining close control over them and using
them in the struggle against older combinations of power.
Thus it was the strike action of several important unions
in 1954 that enabled Nasser, with the support of most of
the army leadership, to remove Naguib from power and
thereby to prevent the revival of the old political parties
in Egypt. The workers have not been able to achieve such
goals on their own strength but only through the support
of the state apparatus.

The social classes formerly in control of affairs have lost
much of their power with the advent of military regimes
owing no allegiance to older classes. These are the large
landowners and their allies among the professional politicians, lawyers, newspaper owners and some writers, and a
few industrial leaders. Another group traditionally very
powerful, the religious leaders or *'ulama* (literally, the
learned ones), have likewise lost influence with the growth
of secularism and the nationalist goal of economic and
military power. They began to lose power decades ago
throughout the Moslem Near East. In Turkey and Iran
in the 1920s, Kemal Ataturk and Reza Shah were able to
defeat them early. In the Arab countries the *'ulama* have

either withdrawn quietly from the direct or implied challenge of secularism or have been simply ignored or converted into apologists for the new order. Without a central, unified organization and no longer in control of important state functions, they have been unable to overcome the weakness resulting from the absence of a genuine hierarchy in Islam or even within a single country.

The Middle Class

The middle class in Western society has been especially important because of its role in industrialization and the development of democratic institutions. In the Arab world the middle class is small and even less independent today than it was a few years ago before the shift toward military republicanism. The professional classes, especially lawyers and journalists, traditionally provided nationalist leadership just below the top level. As Arab parliamentary institutions grew under Western influence between the late nineteenth century and World War II, the professional class supplied the people to occupy the political posts along with the landowners and the big merchants in the major cities. With the growth of industry, political power was also shared with the few large capitalists. The civil service, meanwhile, constituted all along a substantial middle group. As military regimes have spread through the Arab world, with their emphasis on state regulation of and participation in economic affairs, the position of the independent middle class has not improved. Instead, it is the employed middle class that has grown—a class of technicians, administrators, and clerks employed by government and private industry and commerce.

However, the prestige of professionals seems to be rising in the Arab world as elsewhere. Traditionally, Islamic society has revered the man learned in religion, but this reverence appears to be shifting to secular learning. It is the middle class that has thus far profited most from the rapid growth of state-supported education. Ammar has shown[11] that in Egypt in the early 1940s the children of middle-class fathers constituted a much higher proportion of pupils in the public schools than that class did in the total working population. A decade later another study, this one of girls in the Alexandria secondary schools, showed a similar middle class predominance. As for prestige, in the same study 90 girls were asked the occupation they preferred for the men they hoped to marry. A majority selected engineer, and doctor, teacher, lawyer, and merchant followed in that order.[12] A similarly high rating for the independent professions was expressed by higher civil servants in a study made by this writer in 1954.[13] Asked to rank ten given occupations, the 249 replies yielded the following order: doctor, bank director, lawyer, factory owner, landowner, government bureau chief, government clerk, small merchant, factory worker, peasant.

Since industrialization in the West has been associated with the rise of an independent middle class, the question arises whether such a class can play the same role in the industrialization of the Near East. This issue is discussed at length in Chapter 11; here it can be said in summary that this is unlikely to be the case in the Arab world. These middle groups are, nevertheless, important enough to warrant further analysis as to their composition and role in Arab society.

The idea of socio-economic class can be a very simple one. Aristotle remarked that, "In every city the people are divided into three sorts: the very rich, the very poor, and those who are between them." This classification illustrates the elusive quality of the middle class: a residue after we easily identify the rich and poor. With the development of trade and manufacture, the criterion of function was systematically added to that of wealth, so that

[11] Hamed Ammar, "An Enquiry into Educational Opportunities in Egypt," unpublished M.A. thesis, University of London, 1949, Table 21, p. 174.

[12] Mito, p. 37.

[13] Berger, *Bureaucracy and Society in Modern Egypt*, Table 29, p. 99.

middle class came to mean not only middling income, but also the group managing an economy's exchange and manufacture. Later the criteria of status (or prestige) and socio-economic power were also added, giving us four bases for the ascription of class position of any kind.

The triumph of the industrial system in Western society brought with it vast social changes and the loosening of class positions. During the rise of capitalist enterprise urban merchants and manufacturers, formerly occupying a middle-class position in terms of income, status, function, and power, moved into the upper class when their incomes became large enough to enable them to adopt at least the outward aspects of upper-class life. Such movement was made possible by (and further stimulated) the eradication of feudal and other privilege embodied in law, by changes in standards of behavior, and by the advent of new social values. The upshot was to raise the middle-class capitalist to the level of the upper classes. Yet we still speak, often, of the large-scale entrepreneurs as middle class or "bourgeois." This is, in most parts of Western society, merely an anachronism of linguistic usage, for since the latter part of the nineteenth century the entrepreneurs, managers and merchants in large-scale enterprises can hardly be called middle class from any modern point of view.

The situation in the Arab world is somewhat different. There the changes we have just summarized are only beginning to appear, so that, in most cases, the merchant and the manufacturer (perhaps we ought to say, the artisan) still occupy a middling position in terms of status, function, power, and income. I put income last because it is in this respect that changes are occurring. As happened in Western society in the eighteenth and nineteenth centuries, the first break in middle-class position in the Near East has been in income. Many merchants and industrialists have the income commensurate with upper-class position but not the power or prestige.

We take the middle class, then, to encompass: (1) those self-employed merchants and small manufacturers whose income and influence are not great enough to place them among the really powerful men in political or economic life; and (2) a more mixed group including such independent professionals as doctors and lawyers; employed managers, technicians, and administrative workers such as clerks and bureau chiefs; and the civil service.

If we seek so simple a figure as the size of the middle class in the Arab world, we run into the problems posed by the lack of data. Only Egypt among the Arab states conducts a regular census and even it has serious limitations, as we shall see. The following table shows the composition and size of the urban middle class in Egypt in 1947, the latest census-year for which the results are available:

TABLE 2. *Urban Middle Class[1] in Egypt, 1947*

OCCUPATION	NUMBER	PER CENT OF ALL MIDDLE CLASS	PER CENT OF TOTAL POPULATION GAINFULLY OCCUPIED[2]
Merchants	254,388	51	3.00
Chief clerks and agents	127,876	26	1.51
Professionals[3]	94,339	19	1.11
Businessmen and clerks	22,561	4	.27
Totals	499,164	100	5.89

[1] We omit the agricultural middle class, however defined, as not sufficiently relevant as yet to our present interest in the middle class. If we define this rural middle class as the owners of holdings between 5 and 30 feddans (a feddan is slightly larger than an acre), then there were only 134,562 in this class in 1947, constituting 5 per cent of the 2,662,800 owners of holdings of all sizes (see République d'Égypte, Département de la Statistique et du Recensement, *Annuaire Statistique 1949–1950 et 1950–1951*, Imprimerie Nationale, Cairo, 1953, Chapter X, Table II, pp. 352–353). In 1952, on the eve of the land reform, there were 139,200 such holders,

again constituting 5 per cent of all 2,802,000 landowners (see Republic of Egypt, Ministry of Finance and Economy, Statistical Department, *Statistical Pocket Year-book, 1953,* Government Press, Cairo, 1954, Table 24, p. 33). In neither case would the addition of this agricultural group to the urban middle class in the table significantly alter the low proportion of the middle class to the total population gainfully employed. Nor does the agrarian reform since 1952 affect our point much either, since the holders who benefit from it are precluded, after the redistribution, from owning more than 5 feddans.

2 The figure used to calculate this percentage is 8,479,503 as the total number of persons gainfully occupied. The census data, however, give as this total 14,155,168 (see source indicated below, Table 11, p. 23). We prefer not to use this larger figure because it is based in part on what is apparently a mere redefinition of two occupational categories for women, rather than upon actual changes in the Egyptian economy between the two census years 1937 and 1947. Our use of the lower figure yields a higher proportion in the middle class but it is nevertheless a more accurate indication of its relative size.

3 Includes actors, doctors, chemists and pharmacists, school administrators, professors, teachers, authors and editors, lawyers, engineers.

SOURCE: Egyptian Government, Ministry of Finance and Economy, Statistical Department, *Statistical Pocket Year-book, 1952,* Government Press, Cairo, Table 12, pp. 24–29.

As we define it, the Egyptian middle class in 1947 numbered only about half a million persons, or about 6 per cent of the total gainfully employed population. Even if all possible miscalculations owing to errors in the original census data or to faulty interpretation are in the direction of an underestimation (which is not likely), the middle class in Egypt in 1947 could not have constituted more than 10 per cent of the gainfully occupied population. Information for 1957–58 confirms this analysis. A sample survey by the government, summarized in the following table, showed that middle-class occupations, not including small owners, constituted 6.1 per cent of the total labor force. This proportion, moreover, is undoubt-

edly larger than is the case in the other Arab countries
(with the exception of Lebanon) where industry and
commerce are less developed than in Egypt. Let us compare this proportion to the comparable one for the West,
where about one third to two fifths of the labor force is
in urban middle class occupations. I am not implying, of
course, that Egypt and the West are justly comparable in
this respect; my purpose is only to show the far greater
numerical strength in an industrial, urban society. Even
in the West, there are observers who say the middle class

TABLE 3. *Urban Middle Class Occupations in Egypt, 1957*

OCCUPATION	NUMBER OF PERSONS	PER CENT OF LABOR FORCE
Professional and technical	171,000	2.4
Managerial	65,000	0.9
Clerical	193,000	2.8
Total	429,000	6.1

SOURCE: National Bank of Egypt, "Statistics of Labor Force
in the Southern Region," *Economic Bulletin* (1960), 13:89,
Table III.

is weak, unorganized and with little economic power.
Whether or not we agree with this view of the middle
class in the United States or other Western societies, certainly the middle class in the Arab world shows little
economic influence in view of its numerical weakness and
the large proportion in it of "merchants," mainly owners
of small shops, and technicians, administrators, and clerks
in private and government offices.

It is, however, stronger politically. In the West the political strength of the middle class, at least on election
day, is proportionate to its numbers. In the Arab world
the political influence of the middle groups takes another
form. They are literate and articulate. The leaders who
emerge from this class, however, do not act especially in
its interests but usually in those of a combination of the
wealthiest urban and rural groups, or an aristocracy (where

one exists) in league with other upper-class groups, or a military class that exercises control. It is true that leftist politicians, whose influence has grown considerably in recent years, tend to come from the educated middle classes, but their power derives not from this fact but from their appeal to the depressed masses and their association with the wealth, prestige, and power of the Soviet Union.

Level of education, by itself, has been a useful guide to class position in the Near East. A secondary school graduate, for example, who was likely to become a clerk in the civil service or a private firm, could be considered middle class despite his low income. But with the rapid expansion of compulsory primary education in the last decade, it is possible that middle class status is no longer automatically assumed by secondary school graduates but that it now takes a university degree to confer that position. Emphasis on formal education as a means of social mobility has set up strong expectations in Near Eastern society that a certificate or diploma entitles one to prestige and a certain kind of employment. In a largely rural-agricultural economy, however, outlets for such a class have been too few. In response to this and other pressures, governments have been willing to swell the ranks of the civil service, fearing to increase the already large number of unemployed, educated, and articulate young men.

Table 2 above shows that about half of the urban middle class in Egypt are merchants, that is, small retailers who employ few people outside the members of their own families. Another quarter are clerical workers. The middle class in the Arab world is thus largely a self-employed or an employed class and is less an *employing* class than its Western counterpart is today or was in an earlier era. As a non-employing group, it has little economic power and has been, as a class, rather distant from the fount of all power in the Near East, the government. The other major component of the middle class, the civil servants, are, of course, closer to the seat of power but are a rather pliant instrument in the hands of the real holders of political and economic power.[14] And the recruits to the middle class even in an industrialized Arab world are not likely to be in a more independent position than their predecessors.

Despite its small number, lack of power, and the limited role it will probably play in industrialization, the middle class has had enormous influence as a vehicle of modernization and the introduction of Western elements into the Arab world. Since this is too vast a subject to discuss in detail, I want to mention only one very important aspect of this middle-class role: the education and emancipation of women. We might first, however, bear in mind that as a vehicle of modernization in social relationships, family roles, relations between the sexes, and patterns of consumption, the middle class has exerted an extraordinary influence simply in showing the Arab world that change itself is possible, that there are other traditions and ways of doing things, and that even the Near East itself has varied styles of life and attitudes.

In regard to the education and emancipation of women (a process, incidentally, not irrelevant to industrialization and urbanization), the middle class has been quicker than others to send its daughters into the public schools, the shops, and even the secondary schools and universities, especially in Egypt. The upper classes have sheltered their daughters or Westernized them abroad. The lower classes have as yet hardly been drawn into this process. So it is the middle class that has felt the impact of changing family roles and of new employment opportunities which have changed the status and behavior of women. We saw in Chapter 4 that a study by an Egyptian social scientist[15] shows the degree to which a sample of secondary school girls in Alexandria enjoy greater social freedom than their mothers did at the same age. One of its most interesting findings is that the daughters' degree of emancipation *increases* as the income and education of their fathers in-

[14] See *ibid.*, Ch. 7.
[15] Mito.

crease, whereas their mothers' degree of emancipation *declined* as *their* fathers' income and education increased. This means, if these findings are representative, that today the higher a family's socio-economic status, the *more* emancipated the daughters are likely to be, whereas a generation ago the higher the status of the family, the *less* emancipated the daughters were. In other words, a generation ago the daughters of middle-class families were more emancipated than those of upper-class families, which were apparently rather conservative. Thus emancipation and education of women seem to have spread upward and downward from the middle class. In this critically important realm of social relations it was the middle class that made the first tentative but unmistakable moves toward change.

Technological change is also stirring Arab society and shifting socio-economic classes. Once accepted, as it is coming to be in the Near East, it places different values on certain skills and brings with it new social relationships and ideological commitments. The most powerful and articulate elements in the Arab world want technological change, especially industrialization. In such change the middle class has played an important part by introducing the idea of change itself, by supplying leaders and an articulate if small following in nationalist causes, and by at least beginning to transform itself from a largely clerical administrative bureaucracy into a managerial-technological one.

Economic growth, if it takes place steadily and to a substantial degree, or even if it is sought seriously, may lead to an important change in orientation in the Arab world—from the high political concerns of the era in which it sought complete independence, to economic and technological goals as a means of raising living standards and of enhancing national power once independence is achieved. Military regimes and the decline of parliaments and political parties may reduce the immediate attractiveness of politics and administration as careers. If economic growth can open up new ones, and if new social groups can acquire a stake in continued economic advance and in the sharing of political power, the Near East may well enter a period of greater social and political stability. The middle class can play a limited but important part in such changes, especially by its example and through its flexibility and familiarity with the new patterns and its close relationship with those elements of the population that want to cling to the old. If the various types of elite groups in the middle class can develop a spirit of independence and of responsibility to the entire society rather than only to their own narrow and immediate interests, they may be able to provide a good measure of the leadership that could take some parts of the Arab world into a new era of orderly progress.

Significance of Class Differences in Traditional and Contemporary Society

The class structure of the contemporary Arab world reflects that of its past eras despite the elimination of slavery and the other major difference we have already discussed, that is, the gradual advance of occupation and wealth as the main criterion of class position at the expense of ethno-religious affiliation. The similarities between present and traditional patterns extend throughout the class structure. First, there is still a far greater gulf between the highest and lowest classes with respect to wealth, power, attitudes, dress, and style of life in general than in industrial societies. Second, the middle groups, as we have just seen, are relatively small and weak, and the military and civilian bureaucracy still comprises a large proportion of it. Third, the learned professions (traditionally connected with religion, now more secular) have high status. Finally, the peasants and urban workers are still so poor and depressed that, except for a very small section of the latter which has recently begun to find articulate leaders, they remain virtually outside the political community.

Arab class structure is not feudal, although this loose epithet has become fashionable among some Western observers who want to draw attention to rural poverty, and among Arab spokesmen who want to condemn the old regimes. Arab society, traditional and modern, has little similarity to feudal Europe with its autonomous manorial order and elaborate system of personal dependence of one social group upon another. In some parts of the Arab world, however, notably Egypt before land reform, landless farm workers and tenants were so tied to certain large estates that the complete control of their lives by the owners suggested a feudalistic relationship in practice though not in law.

Although there is a strong impulse toward equality in Islam (as we saw in Chapter 2), traditional Arab Moslem society was far from egalitarian in doctrine or practice. The Koran itself refers to the divine creation of class differences. One verse (ch. 6, verse 165) says that God "hath raised some of you above others by various grades, that he may prove [test] you by his gifts." Another (ch. 4, verse 36) admonishes the believer: "Covet not the gifts by which God hath raised some of you above others. The men shall have a portion according to their deserts, and the women a portion according to their deserts." Still other verses (e.g., ch. 17, verse 22 and ch. 16, verse 73) refer to such distinctions of wealth and station.

In early Islamic society Muhammad tried to create a sense of brotherhood that would exclude all social differences among believers except the one of degree of piety. But his very success as Prophet and the expansion and enrichment of Islam after him perpetuated familiar class distinctions and introduced still another one: prestige in virtue of one's relationship to the Prophet. Special honor was attached to those (the *muhajirun*) who accompanied Muhammad on the migration ("hegira") from Mecca to Medina, and to his helpers (the *ansar*) in Medina. Later on, when Islam had established its vast empire in Asia and Africa, Arab Moslems were superior to the non-Arabs in social status, although the latter's disabilities in economic and political life were mitigated with time. And even to this day, prestige is accorded to those who trace their ancestry to Muhammad's immediate family or to his tribe, the Quraysh.

At the bottom of traditional Arab Moslem society were the slaves. Muhammad accepted the slave system of his time, though the Koran called for improvement in their treatment. Considered inferior, many slaves were nevertheless able to rise to positions of great wealth and power; those who did not, nevertheless retained certain rights, including relatively easy access to freedom. The very first "muezzin" (or mosque official who chants the call to prayer) appointed by Muhammad himself, was a slave from Ethiopia.[16] Slavery in Islamic society was thus not the same kind of exploitative arrangement it was in the antebellum Southern United States, for example, where it was an integral part of a plantation economy. In traditional Islam slavery was chiefly confined to the household, and thus was associated more with the prestige of the owners than with their directly economic interests in a broad sense.

Traditional Islam recognized certain class distinctions which have now disappeared. We have already mentioned (in Chapter 4) the doctrine of *kafa'ah* (equality) according to which families sought to insure that their daughters did not marry into an inferior social class; and if such a *mésalliance* was contracted it could be legally annulled. In the theory of evidence in Islamic law, cross-examination was not known. The courts became bound to accept as fact something attested to by two witnesses whose status in the community was such that they were believed to tell the truth.[17] And in punishment as well as in receiving testimony as evidence, the traditional Islamic courts took social status into account.[18]

The importance of these traditional and modern class distinctions may be seen in the way they have influenced

[16] "Bilal b. Rabah," *E.I.* (*New*), Vol. I, p. 1215a.
[17] Vesey-Fitzgerald, p. 94.
[18] Tyan, *Histoire*, Vol. 1, p. 377.

the major struggles for power in the Arab world in the last half-century or so. During the last quarter of the nineteenth century the first nationalist stirrings had a strong religious tinge. The caliphate in Turkey still existed as a rallying point for Islam, and reformist efforts within Islam took on an anti-colonial aspect that gave certain religious leaders an important part in what was later to become an almost entirely secular movement. In these early disputes between the native elite groups and the Western governments or the European classes in the Arab world, the so-called "sheikhly" class of religious divines was thus prominent. After World War I the anti-colonial struggle was carried on largely by secular nationalist political parties led by large landowners, urban industrial and commercial interests, the professional upper middle classes, and in some countries by army officers. Meanwhile, native Arab elites were at odds with one another, for the religious leaders resented their declining influence and made several unsuccessful attempts to halt the trend. In addition, the growing class of army officers was beginning to feel its strength as the Western armies left the area or restricted their functions and became geographically less extended.[19] After World War II the growth of industry (which had begun earlier and which was stimulated by the war) and of international communism strengthened the urban working class, which the older upper class, the military, and the religious have all sought to influence or to control.

Differences in social class are reflected both in struggles among the elite groups and in the attitudes of the people who make up these classes and in their predispositions to act. In the nationalist movement, for example, the role of the various classes has differed. Today, the Arab leaders, especially in Egypt and Iraq, are striving to draw

[19] In neighboring Moslem Iran and Turkey in this period just after World War I army officers came to power and greatly weakened both the upper-class nationalists and the religious leaders, thus foreshadowing what was to come a generation later in much of the Arab world as well.

upon new groups, including the lower middle class, the urban workers and even the peasants, to give support to their regimes and to the larger goals of Arab nationalism. These are social classes that lay outside the nationalist tide under the Arab monarchies. Several descriptions (based upon the same data) of the class differences in Egyptian nationalism on the eve of the 1952 revolution indicate the importance of social class in this dominant ideology of contemporary Arab society.[20] Interviews with Egyptian professionals in 1951 revealed an ambivalent nationalism: they admired Western ways but felt hurt by the imputation of inferiority to Westerners; they wanted to drive out the British (then still occupying Egypt under a treaty the Egyptian government soon repudiated) but could not bring themselves to advocate resolute action to achieve this goal. The lower middle class respondents, the white collar workers, with fewer ties to the West through education and travel, displayed an "uncomplicated" form of nationalism in which emotional rejection of the British was matched by resolute dependence on direct action to drive them out of the country. Among the urban workers, uneducated, unorganized, concerned with maintaining their meager existence, nationalism was weakest; in this class national sentiment was reduced or diverted by resentment against the native Egyptian rulers as well. Among the peasants, finally, the interviews revealed a strong national feeling reinforced by religion and a sense of belonging to the land itself; this was not a kind of nationalism easily galvanized into political action. Like the nationalism of the urban dispossessed, that of the rural dispossessed was mitigated by extreme poverty and absorption in the struggle to keep alive. Such differences of social class have concomitants and consequences which place narrow limits upon what Arab society can do. It is these concomitants and consequences that Arab leaders are now trying to overcome.

[20] Lerner, pp. 221–31.

CHAPTER 8

Social Basis of Political Institutions

The Arab countries in recent years have displayed a para-doxical tendency as the waning power of the West has left them freer to shape their own institutions. They have (excepting Lebanon and, to some extent, Jordan) demol-ished the political structure of parliaments, parties, and elections erected during the era of Western occupation or influence, and have at the same time tried to push and drag themselves toward a Western industrial and secular system. They have found the Western democratic forms unsuited to their political heritage and a barrier to rapid modernization of economic and social life; they therefore reject Western political forms in favor of those features of Western technology and social relations that will, it is hoped, raise the standard of living and increase the na-tional strength of a unified Arab world. The result has been not only changes in broad ideology and economic organization but also considerable changes in internal po-litical structure.

The most obvious of these changes is the advent of military regimes in Egypt, Syria, and Iraq, the prominence of the army in Jordan and the resort even in Lebanon in 1958 to a military leader for the presidency. The military regimes have discarded the forms of parliamentary de-mocracy, while in Jordan the forms remain but with little effect; only in Lebanon has the parliamentary structure survived. In the military regimes, new social groups have been drawn further into political life—the urban workers through state-controlled trade unions, the peasants through land reform and state-directed co-operatives, and an en-larged technical and administrative class of younger men

and women who owe their higher income and status to
the increased activity of the government and its stimulation of private enterprise. At the same time the military
regimes have greatly expanded education and the use of
the media of mass communication, chiefly the press and
radio (but to some degree even the movies and television),
to create a greater sense of community and to heighten the
political participation of these new groups on the side of
government.

Traditional influences, however, still have force. Political indifference on the part of the impoverished urban
and rural masses remains a severe drawback to efforts to
incorporate them into the effective national life of the
Arab world. Despite the reduction of their political power,
large landowners, commercial interests, and the older generation of professionals who dominated the defunct parliamentary system and its parties still retain much of their
economic power. Family loyalties, too, which were influential even in the old parliamentary structures, still
have considerable force, especially in Lebanon and Jordan
(where tribal affiliation is also important). The use of
street demonstrations, violence, and the threat of violence
to bring down governments is still frequent even under
the military regimes, though these are now directed chiefly
at foreign governments (both European and Arab) because, except in Lebanon, they are outlawed as methods
of expressing opposition to a domestic regime.

Finally, the Islamic legacy of attitudes towards government in general and the relationship between political
and religious life and organization still exerts great force
throughout the Arab world. This is true even in Lebanon,
where a compromise has had to be worked out because
of the general assumption (which few care to test) that
the population is evenly divided between Moslems and
Christians. The effect of all these changes and the persistence of older patterns has been to provide the embryo
of a new context—secular, industrial and national—to traditional political institutions of autocracy, governmental
claims to control over vast areas of social life, and the

suffusion of civil government with elements derived from
a religious doctrine that to this day does not recognize
any distinction between "church" and "state." But it can
no longer be said, as it could until only a few years ago,
that in the Near East the wealthy control the government,
the middle classes work for it, and the poor seek only to
avoid it.

Politics and Government in Islam

Traditional Islam, as we mentioned in the introductory
chapter, has been both a religious and political society;
its code of behavior makes no distinction between the
rules to be obeyed out of religious loyalty and out of
political loyalty. The two are not even distinguishable
"aspects" of one code; they are identical and inseparable
in Islamic conception. What the West distinguishes as
civic, political, social, religious, and moral obligations are
in Islam all moral obligations deriving from a revealed
religion. In the very origin of Islam, religion and state
and nation were inextricably bound. Muhammad founded
a monotheistic religion which he brought to the Arabs
and in doing so he created a state and nation upon the
basis of religious faith.

Six hundred years ago the great Arab philosopher of
history, Ibn Khaldun, offered an explanation of this characteristic of Islam.[1] Muhammad and his successors (the
caliphs), he pointed out, protected the religion of Islam
and exercised political leadership as well. The caliphate
is thus both "religious and worldly" and "the religious
law governs all the actions of human beings." Human
beings in society, he continued, need such leadership in
both religious and worldly affairs. Especially in Islam, the
obligation to defend and spread the religion requires the
unity of religious and political authority—caliphate and
kingship—"so that the person in charge can devote the

---

[1] Ibn Khaldun, Rosenthal's translation, Vol. 1, pp. 388, 472–
73 (Ch. III, sections 23, 31), and Vol. 2, p. 4 (Ch. III, section 32).

available strength to both of them [religion and politics] at the same time." Since other religions, Ibn Khaldun concludes, do not impose such an obligation upon the believers, among them "the person in charge of religious affairs . . . is not concerned with power politics at all," while political leadership is acquired "in some way that has nothing to do with religion."

Though the identity of religious and political institutions in the conception and creation of the Islamic community did not persist long, it had enduring consequences. It confused political and moral obligations, leading to political quietism and hindering the evolution of clear civic obligations as well as a body of political thought independent of religious doctrine. These consequences we shall discuss more fully in this chapter. But two other confusions must be mentioned at least briefly. First, the various loyalties an Arab Moslem feels have not been sufficiently differentiated to permit the growth of a solid foundation for political life. The basis has been a shifting one, including the concept of nation (Arab, or more particularist, such as Egyptian or Lebanese or Iraqi) and of religion, and of a state apparatus pertaining to each. Language has been identified equally with nation and religion. Besides these loyalties, there are those to smaller social units, family, clan or tribe, and village, which still make considerable claims upon the individual and weaken his loyalty to nation though not to religion. Other societies have, of course, felt a similar plethora of loyalties but have managed to relegate the religious one to a special place, enabling them to relate the others in a stable and satisfactory hierarchy or at least to sort them out in such a way as to leave them autonomous but not in conflict. The Moslem communities are only at the beginning of this process.

The second confusion, between geographical boundaries, is a concomitant of the lack of order and stability in political-religious loyalties. (Other factors are involved here, which we shall not deal with: the wanderings of nomads, and the fact that boundaries in the Near East in recent decades have been drawn by the Western powers in response to their own needs rather than to those of the people in the area.) Except for Egypt, whose national existence is ancient, the other Arab countries have all had uncertain boundaries until recently. The separate Arab nations are only now beginning to identify themselves with the areas they occupy, but it is difficult to overcome the legacy of an expanse of Arab territory under the Ottoman Empire with no national or religious frontiers. Even today the sense of Arab unity cuts across boundaries. During 1958 and 1959, when every one of the five Arab states we are discussing was involved in political disputes with at least one other, none questioned the "right" of any Arab government to appeal across frontiers to the people presumably loyal to any other. Whatever harsh words were exchanged between Iraq and Egypt, for example, neither one questioned the "right" of the other to compete for the loyalty of Syria even after it had joined Egypt in the United Arab Republic. It was only the Western powers, the Soviet Union, and the United Nations which spoke in these terms. A U.N. observation group, reporting in July 1958 on a Lebanese complaint that there was infiltration of men and arms from the United Arab Republic, mentioned the uncertainty of the frontier, for example, between Lebanon and Syria. The report[2] stated that at many points the frontier was (1) difficult to reach, (2) not clearly marked, (3) still disputed, (4) generally ignored and not even treated as a national border. Four months later progress in this respect was reported.[3]

Islamic societies have had a somewhat ambivalent attitude toward the exercise of political power. Pious men have avoided such power as evil. But the nature of the Islamic community implies an opposite attitude: that Islam must have—rather, must itself *be*—a politically organ-

[2] U.N. Security Council, *First Report of the United Nations Observation Group in Lebanon*, 3 July 1958 (S/4040), par. 5–11.

[3] *Ibid., Fifth Report . . . ,* 17 November 1958 (S/4114), par. 24.

ized community to protect the religion. The most extreme form of this identity is the *jihad* (literally, an extraordinary effort, but loosely translated as "holy war"), the obligation of every believer to spread Islam by force when necessary. Hardly an issue today, this obligation nevertheless once implied the unity of religion with political and military power. The mosque in early Islam was the "centre of gravity for both politics and religion," the place of official proclamations and of what we would now call political investitures. The business of government was soon moved into a special place but the mosque even then continued to be used for some transactions requiring public meetings.[4] Non-Arab Islamic societies in Iran, Pakistan, and Afghanistan, have not retained Western or Arab Islam's degree of unity between the religious and the social elements. Non-Arab Islam in Asia, affected by Eastern traits which antedate it, has displayed a greater degree of mysticism, less emphasis upon social obligations, and more upon individual interpretations of religious duties, and a greater sense of unity with other religions.[5]

Although the traditionalists even today speak of the unity of Islam as a religion and a polity, it has been for many centuries now only doctrinal rather than institutional unity. As Gibb and Bowen show,[6] the early genuine unity was soon shattered. "No distinction was made at first," they point out, "between the secular and the religious offices of government . . . But in practice the religion had to create the larger community. The task, already difficult in the limited area of Arabia, became infinitely more so when, as a result of the conquests of the first century, the religion was spread from Central Asia to the Atlantic. . . . The imposing Empire of the early Caliphs, so far from forming a unity of any kind, consisted of an ill-assorted group of provinces held together by the military forces and moral prestige of the central government."

4 See article, "Masdjid," *E.I.*, Vol. III, p. 346b, 349a.
5 See Frye, pp. 180–81.
6 Gibb and Bowen, Part II, pp. 70–71.

Later divergences between what became distinguished as church and state in fact though not in doctrine have been puzzling for Western observers who seek a pattern in an unplanned patchwork. Gibb and Bowen[7] provide a helpful interpretation. They begin with the fact that though the religious insitutitons were said to be identical with the political they did not in fact control political life. The religious and political elites each performed its separate functions in tacit recognition of the other's sphere. Fearing anarchy more than bad government, the religious authorities taught political quietism while they were building up their own position outside the state and were conducting religious affairs without reference to any particular state system. Thus developed a paradox (to Western thought): a religion which claimed to be the state and a state whose theoretical function it was to protect and spread the religion, but each going its separate way. The religion, moreover, depended for its financial support upon private contributions rather than upon the state. "Each," say Gibb and Bowen, "had its own functions and rarely overstepped them. The state was concerned with military, administrative, and economic affairs; the religious institution with doctrine, law, education, intellectual life, and social relations." Set apart from the state that it claimed to be, the religion guided its followers without relation to the state. "On the contrary," Gibb and Bowen conclude, "the fundamental task of the 'Ulema [religious leaders] was to ensure that, no matter what political changes might come about, the religious institution, with all that it stood for, should remain unshaken."

This indeed remains the aim of religious leaders today, for in one respect the relation between "church" and "state" has not changed in the Moslem Near East: the government still "protects"—and therefore controls—the religious institutions and agencies, which are part of the administrative apparatus of the state.

Two special difficulties in the political life of Arab

[7] Ibid., pp. 79–80, 165.

societies have accompanied the several confusions we have
been discussing. First, they have been unable to develop
either a satisfactory and enduring relationship between
the people and the government which could be peacefully
adjusted to changing social life, or a coherent political
philosophy adapted to their new goals in modern times.
Second, they have not found a way to regularize succession
to rule in monarchies or republics.

Governments in the Near East have made broad claims
to control even minute aspects of the lives of the people
but have in fact fallen far short of these ambitions. Oppression has been limited by administrative inefficiency
and the tendency of the people simply to withdraw, to
live their lives outside the framework of governmental pretensions. A proverb[8] points to the popular belief in the
gulf between ruler and ruled: "The camel has his concerns,
and the camel-driver his." Even in societies where there is
public control of government, popular attitudes toward it
are ambivalent; government is not merely an agency of a
community; it is also a repressive force. The fact that a
government serves people does not make them forget that
it also frustrates them. The ordinary popular suspicion of
government becomes fear and avoidance when government
is clearly not attuned to the needs of the governed. This
has been the case for centuries in the Near East. Moreover, since the connection between economic and political
power there has been greater than in the West, and the
government has been the chief source of formal social
power, few persons have had the independent economic
position or the security of property needed to enable them
to risk incurring its hostility. This attitude has, of course,
extended to the civil service, which the public has held
in a combination of fear and contempt. Shaibani, a co-
founder of one of the leading schools of Islamic law,
pointed out that all the prophets followed a profession
or trade. Goitein remarks: "Shaibani strikes a note which
became commonplace in later Muslim literature: namely,

8 Burckhardt, no. 198, p. 62.

that the profession of the honest merchant, or indeed any trade, pleases God more than government service."[9] This did not prevent a civil service job from later becoming the goal of educated youth in the Near East for centuries down to this day, even while such employment has been denigrated.[10]

In the Ottoman Empire, the most recent system of government that shaped Arab political institutions and attitudes during a long period of time (for four centuries down to World War I), the gulf between rulers and ruled was wider than ever and seldom bridged. Especially after the rise of Arab nationalism, the Ottoman ruling class was felt to be a foreign one; it maintained a rather formal contact with the Arab community it dominated through a partly Arab provincial bureaucracy which both protected the masses from the far-off rulers and joined in exploiting them as well.[11]

This separation was converted by the powerless into an element of strength, for their very withdrawal from the political society enabled them to withstand the oppressive system. Apathy toward government became, from time to time, acute hostility in which various sections of the population armed themselves morally and militarily against incursions by the governing class. Down to the present, a well-organized paramilitary minority has been able to make itself stronger than the government in a limited sense. In 1932, for example, the government of Iraq could not carry out a program because it was weaker than those who opposed the plan; as Khadduri says, "no less than 100,000 rifles were owned by the people as against 15,000 which the Government had in its possession."[12] In 1953 I gave a lift to a Sudanese serving in the border patrol of the Egyptian army who told me that the dope-runners from Lebanon were usually better armed than the military

[9] Goitein, p. 588.

[10] On the present, see Berger, *Bureaucracy and Society in Modern Egypt*, Ch. 4.

[11] See Gibb and Bowen, Part I, pp. 209–11.

[12] Khadduri, *Independent Iraq*, p. 36.

forces assigned to keep them in check. In Lebanon in
1958 the government forces were unwilling, even if they
were able, to use their full strength to put down an armed
revolt in which a substantial proportion of the population
simply withdrew from the legally constituted system of
government. And in the same year and the following one,
after an army officers' revolt had established an Iraqi republic in place of the monarchy, paramilitary Communist
forces seemed to be at least as powerful as the government
in controlling daily life in the capital city. That such
violent contests for power between government and opposition have a long tradition is demonstrated by an old
proverb which draws attention to the suffering of the
masses in such situations: "Wind and sea are fighting each
other. 'Now,' the ships say, 'we're in for it.' "[13]

While the typical relationship of the individual to the
state in the Near East has for centuries been avoidance or
hostility on the part of those outside the ruling group, for
those who ruled or helped rule the aim was to use the
state apparatus only for their own interests so long as they
could control this elusive kind of power. Between these
two extremes there was no room for the growth of civic
responsibility in which the governed might see the state
as their own creation and servant and the governors might
see it as, in some degree, a trust to be discharged to the
entire community. There have been no agencies to inculcate a civic spirit in the Near East. If, as we have already
remarked, the wealthy controlled government, the middle
class was employed by it, and the poor tried to avoid it,
no group sought to improve it. The Near Eastern city,
unlike the Western one just after the Renaissance, was a
collection of autonomous communities which cultivated
no sense of loyalty to the city itself. There was loyalty
to family and religious community, perhaps even to profession or trade, but certainly not to the political unit of
city or state. Indeed, these units were not identified as
such in the Arab mind, for the individual enjoyed status

[13] Burckhardt, no. 167, p. 53.

and rights not (as in the West) by virtue of his membership in a city or national polity but in a particular family or tribe, trade and, above all, in his Islamic supranational community. That community inculcated a religious devotion which transcended political loyalty. So long as Near Eastern governments did not disturb the Moslem's relationship to his God and his religious community, he was content to let the government have its own way. The other important loyalty in the Near East was to the family (or clan or tribe), and this too was left undisturbed for all religions by Near Eastern governments. Between fidelity to family and Islam there appeared to be no room for loyalty to a body, the city or state, which was neither a kinship nor a religious group. Indeed, through most of Arab history the city or state has not been sufficiently differentiated from the religious community to permit the growth of civic or secular political loyalty. As the Italian scholar David de Santillana remarks, in Islam there is no concept of a system of law apart from the will of God. "Islam," he says, "is the direct government of Allah, the rule of God, whose eyes are upon his people. The principle of unity and order which in other societies is called *civitas, polis*, State, in Islam is personified by Allah: Allah is the name of the supreme power, acting in the common interest."[14] There are many virtues to such a belief but they cannot by their very nature create a sense of responsibility to a deliberate, secular creation of man.

Near Eastern governments have been oppressive. Those in power have had to use their advantages quickly and fully because tenure was always uncertain; the people's defense was deceit and evasion, resulting in a relationship hardly conducive to the growth of civic responsibility on the part of either group. Napoleon's private secretary described a classic condition, having already a long tradition and still to have a long future, which the great soldier found in 1798 when he established his headquarters at the house of a local dignitary in Damanhur near Alexandria.

[14] De Santillana, p. 286.

The house [Napoleon's secretary wrote] *'had been new whitened, and looked well enough outside, but the interior was inconceivably wretched. Every domestic utensil was broken, and the only seats were a few dirty tattered mats. Bonaparte knew that the sheikh was rich; and, having somewhat won his confidence, he asked him, through the medium of the interpreter, why, being in easy circumstances, he thus deprived himself of all comfort. "Some years ago," replied the sheikh, "I repaired and furnished my house. When this became known at Cairo, a demand was made upon me for money, because it was said my expenses proved me to be rich. I refused to pay the money, and in consequence I was ill-treated, and at length forced to pay it. From that time I have allowed myself only the bare necessaries of life, and I shall buy no furniture for my house." The old man was lame in consequence of the treatment he had suffered. Woe to him who in this country is suspected of having a competency,—a hundred spies are always ready to denounce him. The appearance of poverty is the only security against the rapine of power and the cupidity of barbarism.*[15]

Is there a real contradiction between two characteristics of Near Eastern political life we have pointed out—individualism, hostility to government, and a passion for equality on one side, and despotic governments making broad claims on the other? I think not. Individualism among Arab Moslems is not a political trait; it refers to equality of social status and individual freedom to follow the way of the Prophet, which have been jealously guarded. This is not equality and individualism in the Western sense, that is, political equality and the right of each citizen to share in the determination of public policy and to assume some responsibility for government by playing the

[15] De Bourrienne, Vol. I, pp. 164–65. Despite the errors of this witness in other respects and his and Napoleon's desire to emphasize the injustice they found (the better to display Napoleon's presumed civilizing influence), we may accept the general accuracy of this particular description.

role of an institutionally accepted opposition. I might go further and insist that the passion for individual equality outside the political realm is not merely compatible with despotic government but may even require it. Individualism that is not controlled and directed by politically oriented and responsible associations makes stable government difficult to achieve. Authority cannot, in such circumstances, be maintained by tacit consent but only by constant repression of recalcitrant wills which are themselves neither organized nor stable. Strong individualistic and egalitarian tendencies, when not stabilized in voluntary associations playing accepted political roles, can constitute only a perpetual challenge to governmental authority: the governors must maintain their command by force and broad claims or simply see their power and authority dissipated.

Thus fierce egalitarian individualism defeats itself, because by not permitting government to feel itself legitimate, it impels government to maintain itself by force alone. An egalitarianism which permits no differentiation into social classes or groups with different degrees of political authority makes everyone equal—but under a small, despotic ruling group. Under such an arrangement it is difficult to see how democracy can emerge and spread. All individuals and groups being equal below the rulers and unconcerned with the political community, power cannot be progressively shared in a responsible manner. This sort of egalitarianism is not civic but social and religious; it must be given organized political direction before it can become an institutionalized support for a legitimate system of shared governmental authority. There are some signs, which we shall consider later in this chapter, that such an arrangement is beginning to emerge in the Arab world. Until it does, individualism and despotism are not merely compatible but symbiotic.

Individualism and despotism have lived side by side in other cultures as well, notably the Latin, as in Italy under Mussolini and in much of South America for a

long time. An explanation[16] of the Spanish legacy in that
continent applies in part to the Arab world:

"The Spaniard loves liberty, that ideal liberty for which
there is no place in an imperfect world. . . . He is, indeed, a passionate individualist . . .

"But side by side with this passion for liberty is found
recognition of the fact that government is a necessity and a
consequent desire that government also should be ideal.
The function of the ruler is to rule. He must therefore
rule fully, absolutely, exerting his authority without restraint and upon all in every relationship of life. He must
be a despot or nothing . . . That very individualism which
impels the Spaniard to resist control leads him also to
welcome control when it is the result of a vigorous assertion of individuality by another . . . And hence, there
is a perpetual tendency to alternate between a degree of
liberty which amounts almost to the negation of all government and a degree of government which amounts almost
to a negation of all liberty."

Arabs themselves have been aware of their own oscil-
lation between rejection of government and acquiescence
in its worst repressions; they have a proverb that expresses
the apparent paradox: "Govern the rabble by opposing
them."[17] The very fact that, as we have seen, a state
system is believed to be a necessary part of Islam as the
protector of the religion has induced reluctance to jeopard-
ize the latter by permitting the former to be questioned.
Traditional Islamic thought, reinforced by recent interpretations, has warned against hasty overturning of governments even when they are tyrannical. A government in
Islam is not merely a secular regime but at least in doctrine is the protector of the religion; its overthrow and
even a readiness to question its acts are serious matters
which may weaken the religion and the law given by God.
The Koran bids rulers to be just but it does not confer
upon the ruled the right or duty to rebel. Nor do the
many Moslem philosophers who have written on govern-

16 Jane, pp. 26–27.
17 Burckhardt, no. 333, pp. 104–5.

ment go further to encourage a critical civic spirit. Such
long ideological traditions combined with oppressive governmental practice have instilled the political quietism we
have frequently mentioned. It was given its most characteristic expression in the eleventh century A.D. by al-
Ghazali, one of the greatest and most influential of Islam's
theologians and philosophers. He insists that religion needs
a leader whom the believers obey as well as a world in
which there is that security of life and property that can
be safeguarded only when such a leader is obeyed. Religion and worldly rule thus go together. The leader must
therefore be obeyed in order to protect the religion, avoid
violence and promote prayer and study. A leader who is
not qualified by his virtue and capacity to lead may be
deposed only on two conditions: that he can be replaced
by a leader who is qualified, and that his removal is accomplished without dissension or violence. "If this is impossible," says al-Ghazali, "then obedience is due to
him . . ."[18]

Just as political institutions in Islam have been theoretically undifferentiated from the religious order and canon
law, so political thought has been really little more than
an aspect of theology. Though actual political life early
strayed from this identity with religion, political thought
has only recently emerged from the smothering embrace
of theology. Because doctrine has been kept pure and un-
adulterated by practice, political thought has been weak.
An Arab writer recently commented that the literature on
Arab nationalism "is noted for its dearth of political theory"; and he finds this characteristic of the entire "cultural
legacy" of the Arabs. This weakness, he adds, is revealed
in the "negativism" of Arab nationalist writings, which he
dates only since 1918 and which he attributes to the
growth of "pessimism" following World War I and the
Arabs' disappointment when the Western allies did not
immediately grant them full independence.[19]

[18] Quoted in Haim, "Islam and the Theory of Arab Nationalism," pp. 305–6.
[19] Nuseibeh, pp. 56, 99–100.

Weakness in political theory is also displayed in the widespread inability to create a viable synthesis between Western and Arab political institutions, a goal which many Arab writers profess. And there is little systematic examination of the political and economic goals of the Arab states beyond the strong desire for "national freedom" and "economic development." The resulting ideological confusion of Western ideas and policies is covered by the Arabs' increasing resort to the claim that they are "pragmatic" and "flexible." We shall examine both nationalist and social thought and activity in the next chapter. Here we must add only that folk wisdom as expressed in proverbs and popular sayings seems to have taken the place of systematic political theory in the Arab world. We have already quoted some of these sayings. Many refer to political and personal power in a cynical way that betrays bitter experience of the effects of power upon those who wield it. One saying emphasizes the danger of being weak: "Anger without status leads to punishment."[20] Others stress the greed of the powerful. "Even when the kite is dying, his eye is still fixed upon his prey."[21] Another points to the ease with which those in power begin to oppress: "Once firmly mounted, the rider begins to spur the horse."[22] On the same tendency: "They displayed humility until they established themselves firmly."[23] On the tendency of success to encourage excess: "He has just become a Moslem and already he claims descent from the Prophet."[24] Perceptive as such popular wisdom is, it cannot provide a coherent, positive philosophy of political action.[25]

---

[20] Burckhardt, no. 207, p. 66.

[21] Ibid., no. 159, p. 50.

[22] Ibid., no. 135, p. 43.

[23] Ibid., no. 165, p. 52.

[24] Ibid., no. 136, p. 43.

[25] Some of these proverbs are found in other cultures, of course. Shakespeare gives a slightly different emphasis to one of them in Henry VI (Part 3, Act I, Scene 4): ". . . beggars mounted run their horse to death."

Succession to Rule in Fact and Theory

The early development of the caliphate and sultanate reveals the failure to maintain any reasonable degree of correspondence between political doctrine and political fact, and the failure of political theory itself to provide a consistent rationale for political practice. The history of this institution central to the government of Islamic society is one of endemic incapacity to develop a stable mode of succession to rule.

During Muhammad's own lifetime no provision was made for a successor (according to the dominant Sunnite view). A caliph (or "successor") was imposed upon the community by several of the Prophet's closest companions, and this immediately led to dissension. The first caliph and the three who succeeded him in turn were all chosen or "elected" by the notables without any regard to the issue of hereditary succession. It is significant, too, that the second, third, and fourth caliphs (and possibly the first too, though the evidence is not conclusive) were murdered in office. Clearly the question of succession was an unsettled one from the start. The Islamic community had no more definite mode of transferring leadership than the tribal society from which it emerged. In A.D. 661 just twenty-nine years after the death of Muhammad, a caliph was acclaimed who fifteen years later *nominated* his own son as his successor, thus preserving the myth of election while achieving the stability of hereditary succession. The confusion of practice and principle that followed is described by Arnold in his summary of the mode of succession in the Ummayad dynasty (to A.D. 750) and in the Abbasid dynasty (A.D. 750–1258): "The precedent thus established was generally followed in later times throughout the Abbasid period also. The reigning Caliph proclaimed as his successor the most competent of his sons, or his favorite son if affection or prejudice influenced his choice, or the best qualified of his kinsmen. The oath of allegiance was then paid to this prince as heir apparent, first in the capital, and then throughout the other cities of the empire. But the direct succession of father and son was so little exemplified in actual practice in the case of the first twenty-four Caliphs of the Abbasid dynasty, that for a period of more than two centuries (754–974) only six of them were succeeded by a son. When the power of the Abbasid Caliphate had sunk into insignificance, it became more common for son to succeed father, but throughout the whole period political theory maintained that the office was elective."[26] The leading systematic treatment of the caliphate, which became accepted orthodox doctrine, was written by al-Mawardi in the eleventh century A.D. Though he was writing at a time when the caliphate had for centuries remained within the same family (the Abbasids) and when the caliphs themselves were already designated by their Turkish mercenary troops, he nevertheless insisted that the caliphate was an elective office. He also held that the formal oath of allegiance to the caliph, which was already a fiction, was a genuine indication of election.[27] These two notions preserving the myth of genuine election of the caliphs were widely accepted and perpetuated in Islamic political thought. Thus an extraordinary gulf between fact and doctrine developed. As an Arab student of New Eastern legal institutions, Emile Tyan, says, "The hereditary and dynastic principle spread throughout the Moslem world. Every autonomous authority which established itself, in whichever part of the vast empire, tended immediately to become settled in a dynasty."[28] But he adds: "In speaking of the hereditary and dynastic principle in Islam, it is necessary to avoid ambiguity: never at any moment in the evolution of the institution of the caliphate was hereditary transmission recognized in doctrine as a legal method of transmitting power and it was never erected into principle in the strict sense of the

[26] Arnold, pp. 22–23.
[27] See "Khalifa," E.I. Vol. II, p. 884b.
[28] Tyan, Institutions, Vol. 2, p. 61.

term."[29] Tyan presents interesting linguistic evidence of
the early tendency to establish dynasties and of its influence in later Islam. The word now used for state, *dawla*,
once meant the dynasty itself. "This meaning," he continues, "was in perfect conformity with the grammatical
sense of the term, which implies the idea of rotation, of
succession, in time. The idea of sovereign authority was
thus closely associated with that of its transmission in time,
within the same family group. In fact, the expression could
be used to designate the state only when the state had
taken hereditary form; it was thus never applied to the
government of the earliest caliphs. By extension, it has
served to designate the sovereign authority monopolized
by a family group outside the ruling dynasty, when it was
desired to emphasize the idea of the continuity of the
power of this group."[30]

Why, we may ask, did the elective system of the four
earliest caliphs become a dynastic one so soon? The answer given by the great Moslem social thinker, Ibn Khaldun, illustrates again the fear in Islamic society that excessive disputation over leadership weakens the community
and jeopardizes the religion of God. He begins by pointing out that all human societies need a "royal authority,"
a leader who can rule by force if necessary in order to
keep the peace.[31] When the first four caliphs lived and
took office by election, such a "royal authority" was not
yet in existence to act as a "restraining influence" upon the
community; at that time, religion was still the "restraining
influence" which each believer exercised upon himself.
Consequently, the first four caliphs were able to elect in
turn the man they believed absolutely superior from the
point of view of Islam; and they could be confident their
decision would be accepted. But with the fifth caliph,
Mu'awiya, who came to power after a civil war in Islam,
the "restraining influence of religion had weakened," ac-

[29] *Ibid.*, Vol. 1, p. 256.

[30] *Ibid.*, Vol. 2, pp. 61–62.

[31] Ibn Khaldun, Rosenthal's translation, Vol. 1, p. 284 (Ch.
II, section 16).

cording to Ibn Khaldun. In its place "royal authority" had
developed, for Mu'awiya had taken command in Islam by
force, as the leader of the powerful Ummaya family. When
the time approached to think of a successor to Mu'awiya,
this family was too strong to be denied; they would agree,
says Ibn Khaldun, only to his son as successor even though
there were others superior to him from the point of view
of Islam. It was no longer possible to elect merely the best
man. If the notables had appointed someone not acceptable to the Ummayads, "the community would have been
split and torn by dissension." In order to "preserve agreement and harmony," Ibn Khaldun concludes, Mu'awiya
nominated his own son in preference to superior men; and
this was the proper choice, Ibn Khaldun insists (invoking
Muhammad in the effort to justify a later practice), because in the opinion of the Prophet it was more important
to preserve unity than to have the best man as caliph.[32]

By the tenth century A.D. the caliphs had already become so weak that they no longer really designated their
own successors; real power in this respect was exercised by
the Turkish military leaders who had for some time been
used by the caliphs as mercenaries. During several centuries these recent converts to Islam gained supremacy
over what is now the Arab Near East. Their own leaders,
the Ottoman sultans, became the effective heads of the
Islamic community and the protectors of the religion. In
the late eighteenth century the Ottoman sultans began to
call themselves caliphs in order to increase their prestige
with the European powers and to appeal for Moslem support beyond their own empire.

How were the sultans selected? In this process too, elaborate fictions were maintained. The Ottoman tendency
was toward hereditary transmission of power but it could
not establish a fixed mode of succession—for example, from
father to eldest son, with a regular system of determining
the heir in cases where there was no son. The sultans were
selected in the same manner as the caliphs: the ruling

[32] Ibn Khaldun, Vol. 1, pp. 432–33 (Ch. III, section 28).

group selected a successor from the family of the reigning
sultan. This was, like the mode of succession to the caliphate, a compromise between the principle of heredity and
that of election, the two poles between which Islamic communities have swung.[33]

The Ottoman sultans, despite the instability, the fictions and the lack of a fixed doctrine of succession, managed to keep rule within the family for six and a half
centuries down to 1924. They alternated between designa-
tion of the strongest son of the dead ruler and the eldest
male survivor in his family; half of the sultans were deposed before death could take the throne from them.[34]

The hereditary principle of government has had two
strong supports in Islamic societies: the fear of dissension
and consequent weakness in the political-military arm of
the religion of Allah; and the desire of a ruling family to
retain power. The elective principle has had the support
of tradition in the tribal society out of which Islam grew
and the practice of the early caliphs. It is also supported
by sheer rationality; for, as Guglielmo Ferrero has succinctly said, "Heredity is the principle of legitimacy that
gives the biggest role to chance and the smallest to intelligence, that is, it is the least rational and the most
absurd of all principles of legitimacy."[35]

It would be rash to attribute the recent instability of
governments in the Arab world exclusively to the heritage
we have been describing. There is nevertheless little doubt
that this tradition of ambivalence has played some part
in the failure of Arab governments to work out a peaceful
means of transfer of power. That the principle of election
still carries weight may be seen in the case of Egypt, where
the monarchy was taken lightly. The fundamentalist Moslem Brothers, who were among the most powerful groups
there until the regime destroyed the leadership in 1954–
55, had planned before the overthrow of the king in 1952

[33] Tyan, *Institutions*, Vol. 2, pp. 60–61, 64–65.
[34] Alderson, pp. 4, 5, 12, 37.
[35] Ferrero, p. 149.

to substitute an elective monarchy for the hereditary one.[36] And just before the plebiscite of 1956 which confirmed Nasser as president of the republic, an Egyptian magazine published in English remarked concerning the election: "In itself it will be only the normalization of a situation whose fundamental legality has never been seriously challenged. In the Moslem world the justification for leadership has been ability and capacity. The form of that leadership is secondary and relatively unimportant."[37]

This is true; leadership in Islamic societies has been "legitimate" if it could maintain itself in power. As expressed in a jurist's dictum which has become a popular saying, "To him who has power over you, obedience is due." Ferrero laid down a basic requirement for legitimacy in a hereditary monarchy: "that the rule of succession be clear, precise, and strictly observed."[38] This has not been the case in the Near East. Ferrero points out, also, that Christianity improved the chances of the hereditary monarchy when it stabilized the family by "making marriage a sacrament" and by "sanctifying the eminent and exclusive right of the legitimate wife."[39] Traditional Islam has not had the advantage of monogamy or primogeniture in following the hereditary principle. The existence of several sons by the same mother has been a disturbing influence at times in Christian monarchies. The existence of many sons by several mothers in Moslem ruling families has been even more unsettling, for it has encouraged rivalry and the choosing of sides not only within the family but among the powerful groups in the palace which sought by various means to enhance their own power. This has been especially so because inheritance by the eldest son has not been a fixed rule.

[36] See, for example, the account by El Sadat (who had been the liaison between the revolutionary officers and the Moslem Brothers), p. 61ff.

[37] *Egyptian Economic and Political Review*, Vol. 2, No. 9 (May 1956), p. 17.

[38] Ferrero, p. 147.

[39] *Ibid.*, pp. 147–48.

Some Characteristics of Domestic Politics

Since the elective principle was never genuinely followed in Islamic governments, the community could not acquire the experience we normally associate with that principle: toleration of the unsuccessful by the successful. Traditional governments did not practice such toleration, and even in the brief parliamentary era in the Arab world the rights and duties of majority and minority were not clearly defined. Neither the majority nor the minority has permitted the other to perform its functions in a stable manner; the majority has sought to suppress the minority, while the minority has sought by equally illegitimate means to depose the majority. Thus, the Near East has not been able to carry out the logic of hereditary or elective succession either in a monarchy or a democracy.

Under foreign rule and "tutelage" as well as under independence, governments and opposition groups in the Arab world have refused to tolerate one another. When, a century ago, the Western powers began to introduce "legislative councils," they meant only to demonstrate to the Arabs how a modern state is run; they did not intend these councils as oppositions. But that is precisely what the Arabs made of them: a focus of native opposition to foreign rule. In thus challenging the authority of government, the Arab leaders weakened the foreign regimes in the eyes of ordinary people who did not understand that criticism of government could still mean obedience to it. Now the leaders of the independent Arab states (except Lebanon) feel as the foreign rulers they ejected did: official recognition of the opposition would imply approval of what it might say and do, and where the public does not understand the role of an opposition, it invites disobedience of the government. The public sees the opposition as a *competing power*, not merely as a party competing *for* power. Hence governments suppress the opposition to demonstrate that their authority may not be challenged with impunity.

The parliamentary system has thus far failed in the Arab world. Except in Lebanon (where, one might say, it survives through inaction, leaving affairs to the government departments and private agencies), the legislatures established by Britain and France or by Arabs inspired by the West have now been discarded in Egypt, Syria, and Iraq, while in Jordan the legislature functions merely as an appendage to the authoritarian monarchy. Two phases of parliamentary institutions have passed. The first, in the latter part of the nineteenth century, saw the introduction in Egypt and Lebanon of appointive bodies to "advise" the foreign rulers, Britain, France, and Turkey. The second came in the 1920s with the varying degrees of independence granted the Arab states, which (except Jordan) proceeded to establish elective parliaments on the Western model. The earlier experiments were adopted at a time when the level of education, in Egypt, for example, was hardly adequate; the legislature in 1868 stipulated[40] that by 1884 every member should be literate and that twelve years later the electors should have reached the same level of education.[41] The elective legislatures were likewise transplanted to infertile ground. Small and uneducated electorates, mass indifference, domination by large landowners and a tiny urban professional class, timidity, and corruption—these were the characteristics of the parliaments. In the Syrian parliament of 1943, for example, 36 per cent of the members were landlords and another 18 per cent tribal leaders and "notables." The legislature elected ten years later was already somewhat different, with only 21 per cent of its members landlords and only 10 per cent tribal leaders and "notables." The later body's members had a younger average age, higher education, and a smaller proportion of veteran parliamentarians.[42] Though

[40] Radwan, p. 91.

[41] The Organic Law of 1883 did make such a stipulation. See Cromer, *Modern Egypt*, Vol. 2, p. 272.

[42] This information on Syrian legislators is from a paper by Professor R. Bayly Winder prepared in 1957 for a faculty seminar of the Program in Near Eastern Studies, Princeton University.

Arab parliaments seemed to be reflecting the changes in social and economic life that gripped the area after World War I, they failed to satisfy the demands of the extreme nationalists. They were never held in high repute and few mourned their passing. Lacking an educated electorate and a large class with economic strength independent of government, and having a very wide gap between the upper and lower social classes with only a small and weak middle class between them, the Arab countries do not have the socio-economic basis conducive to a thriving parliamentary system.

The economist Charles Issawi has shown that the Arab countries, again with the exception of Lebanon, also lack the socio-economic basis of democracy in general (as distinguished from one of its particular forms, the parliamentary). Taking as a standard those countries, chiefly in Western and Northern Europe and North America, where democratic institutions are found,[43] he points out that the Arab states are at a disadvantage in the size of their territory and population, type of economy, distribution of wealth, homogeneity of language and religion, level of education, and patterns of voluntary cooperation. "What is required," he concludes, "is a great economic and social transformation which will strengthen [Arab] society and make it capable of bearing the weight of the modern state. Such a development is a necessary, if not a sufficient, condition for the establishment of genuine democracy in the region." Some change in this direction, as we have seen in previous chapters, is already taking place. Issawi justifiably calls for "more understanding and consideration" of the Arab reliance on the state to achieve a large part of this transformation and even of the recent drift to military regimes; these may, without being themselves democratic, help build the socio-economic prerequisites of democracy.

It must also be remembered that progress toward democracy cannot be measured only in terms of the ups and downs of a parliamentary system, which is after all a form

[43] Issawi, "Economic and Social Foundations . . ."

of government found in only a small part of the world and only in recent times. Nor should we assume that the obvious connection between political democracy and freedom means that some forms of freedom cannot exist under other types of regime. Despite the failure of parliaments and the absence of political democracy in all the Arab states but Lebanon, some of them nevertheless enjoy a certain degree of cultural and artistic freedom. Moreover, all the Arab states are still under the broad cultural impact of the West, so that liberating ideas and practices are still spreading in educational policy, social welfare, sexual and family life, labor-management relations. Concomitant with the decline of Western formal democratic institutions of parliaments and political parties, there is a greater sense of personal freedom in all realms but the political. Such gains ought not to be dismissed by observers interested in the growth of individual freedom and political democracy. Just as the existence of the façade of democratic institutions did not mean that the entire reality of democracy lay behind it, so the disappearance of the façade does not mean that the long-range prospects of democracy are nil. Individual attitudes favorable to it are growing among the Arabs, and some of the socio-economic requisites to it are being constructed, though slowly and through means that are not themselves democratic in the purely political sense of the term.

The advent of the military regimes in most of the countries we are discussing has altered the character of Arab political life under the previous parliamentary regimes. Street demonstrations (by well-organized and disciplined "mobs") are no longer ordinary weapons of domestic political warfare. With the passing of political parties, the mobs are no longer mobilized to attack a regime, except in extraordinary situations such as in Iraq during the revolution of July 1958 and the ensuing months of political uncertainty. Rather, they are now normally the regime's weapon in international politics, and are mustered to support it against other Arab governments, the West, or other powers.

The same fate has been dealt the students' political movement, which was closely related to the street mobs in organization, function, and ultimate leadership. This was especially true of Egypt for several centuries. Historically, the religious leaders (the *'ulema*) at El Azhar, the center of Islamic learning in Cairo, were the link between the masses and the students who frequently demonstrated together against the ruling Mamluk dynasty. In the period of Western occupation of Egypt and then Western control of other Arab countries after World War I, the student movement was secularized and attached to the political parties. As one of the few articulate and literate groups destined to form the future backbone of the nationalist movements, students were virtually a distinct social class wooed by the government and opposition parties alike. Parties vied with one another in arousing the students in the secondary schools and universities to a high pitch of nationalist fervor and in catering to the preference of many of them for politics over study. The politicians, having encouraged the students to go on strike for one reason or another, were at least consistent; they were also willing to lower the standards so that the demonstrators would not be penalized for their patriotism.

When independence was achieved in the Arab world, the schools and universities remained a political battleground as revolutionaries sought converts and regimes tried to suppress all agitation except in their own behalf. The victorious revolts in Egypt, Syria, and Iraq were led by young men and have found their most enthusiastic supporters among the youth. Indeed, recent political and social conflict takes on the aspect of a struggle between generations rather than social classes. The new regimes have given younger men great opportunities to serve their countries and to advance themselves at the same time. The rhetoric of revolution and the ideologies of the governments that come to power through it are studded with tributes to youth and criticism of both "old politicians" and the "old ways."

As these "youth" regimes become accustomed to power, however, they are reluctant to keep aloft the same standard of rebellion through youth movements. Now stability is sought. An account of Nasser's career in a pamphlet published by the government describes him as a leader of student nationalists against the British in the 1930s. On his return to school following a demonstration in 1935, he learned of his dismissal; other students went on strike to force his reinstatement and were successful. The account, published in 1955, immediately adds: "It must be pointed out, however, that his patriotism never interfered with his assiduity in his studies."[44] The implication is clear: it is no longer necessary to desert the classroom for the street. With the banning of political parties there is less stimulation and fewer occasions to do so. Moreover, stricter discipline in the schools and especially the universities makes it more difficult and costly to engage in political demonstrations. For a time, perhaps, it can be expected that nationalist gains and socio-economic innovations will keep the students enthusiastic or at least loyal. The promise of a place in the technical bureaucracy may temporarily compensate youth for the elimination of political careers and the insistence on ideological uniformity. But, increasingly, force may have to be applied to contain the volatile student groups refusing to acknowledge the regimes' claims to permanence and rejecting the role of technical replacements in a controlled bureaucracy. Praised, pampered, and courted, the Arab students, like others in recent years, may become dissatisfied with the combination of adulation of rebellion in the past and passivity in the present. What they do will probably depend on how popular the new regimes remain, how much opportunity industrialization is able to offer, and how efficaciously force will be applied.

[44] *Gamal Abdel Nasser. Leader of the Revolution*, pub. by The Department of Public Relations of the Armed Forces, Republic of Egypt, Cairo, n.d. (probably summer or fall 1955), pp. 7–8.

One feature of politics under the previous parliamentary regimes remains unchanged: the emphasis upon personalities at the expense of issues. The political parties, now proscribed in Egypt, Syria, and Iraq, and hardly free in Jordan, have been largely small urban groups each animated by the homogeneous interests of the few leaders who dominated them. Following the paternalistic tradition of tribal and village life, many of the parties were identified by little more than these individual leaders and, in some cases, by a few prominent families associated with them.

In Lebanon, the major parties are organized largely, though not exclusively, along "confessional" lines, that is, according to religious community, for the composition of the legislature is itself fixed in such a way as to insure a certain degree of proportional representation by religion and denomination. This distribution is carried out among the highest political and administrative posts in the government. By custom the president of the republic is a Maronite Christian, the prime minister a Sunni Moslem, the president of the Chamber of Deputies a Shi'ite Moslem, and each community guards the informal allocation of ministerial and higher civil service appointments to see that its interests are protected.

Until recently, the struggle to eliminate Western political and economic interests produced a certain uniformity of aim and appeal in most of the parties in each country, thereby accentuating the tendency to distinguish them by the individuals and families prominent in them rather than by the programs they put forward. This emphasis goes very far back in Arab Moslem history and, indeed, in attitudes toward history. Von Grunebaum points to the Arab historians' justified recourse to genealogy as an explanation of politics. "Political relationships," he remarks concerning Islamic society in its classical era, "are seen in terms of kinship. Changes in political groupings are reflected in the pedigrees allotted to tribal ancestors. Allies are descended from common forebears."[45] In his study of Moslem historiography Rosenthal says that because the "dogmatic struggle in Islam was to a large part waged in the name of personalities and individual merits or demerits," biography became especially important for history. Moslems in general—leaders, masses, and the historians, too—firmly believed, he says, "that all politics was the work of individuals and understandable in the light of their personal qualities and experiences."[46]

The paternalistic character of leadership combined with the tradition of using government for personal advantage so long as one's rule endured to make political parties the agencies for the open distribution of the spoils of victory at the polls. Civil servants became known by their political protectors; changes in elections were soon reflected in wholesale changes in the administration down to very minor posts. Such practice was facilitated by the absence of an effective system of regulating government employment.[47] With the achievement of many nationalist goals in the years following World War II, it seemed that some of the Arab parties were beginning to base themselves more firmly on political issues and principles. But this incipient change was not fated to have the opportunity to develop; just when it came into view all the parties were banned.

Two exceptions to this general description of the political parties must be mentioned. The first is the Wafd in Egypt, which at times transcended some of the peculiarities we have been discussing. The other is the left-wing parties which, having stronger ideological origins, were less oriented toward personalities and less dominated by considerations of kinship (although in Lebanon, characteristically, one socialist party was created with a particular sect,

<hr/>

[45] von Grunebaum, *Medieval Islam*, p. 283.

[46] Rosenthal, p. 89.

[47] On the conduct of the Egyptian political parties before 1952, see Berger, *Bureaucracy and Society in Modern Egypt*, pp. 130–31. The same volume reviews Egyptian efforts to reform the civil service (Ch. 2).

the Druzes, as its popular base simply because the Druze leader became a socialist).

Partly because of the emphasis on personalities in general political life (not merely in parties), and partly because of the violence resulting from the inability to work out an orderly manner for the transference of power, political careers in the Near East are more volatile than in the West. Politicians in the Near East play for big stakes. Many have no established place in the community and, as leaders of underground groups or semi-outlawed parties, take great risks, go to jail frequently, and suffer various degrees of official hounding. This was especially true under the monarchy in Egypt before 1952 and in Iraq before 1958 and it continues to be the case in Jordan. In Egypt, however, the domestic political situation has been relatively clear and stable since 1954, so that it is chiefly the outlawed communist groups which from time to time suffer most from this form of political hazard. In Iraq, where the situation since 1958 has been less stable, the older pattern has persisted. Near Eastern politicians who vie for power have, as compared with Western ones, much more to gain by victory and to lose by defeat. In the West if a man bids for power he does not become a dictator if successful or an outcast if not. But in Arab politics this is often precisely the size of the stake. From obscurity and disfavor, respectively, Colonel Nasser and General Naguib rose quickly to share almost absolute power in Egypt in 1952, while the politicians they displaced (not to mention the royal family) fell into disrepute and were shorn of political power. When Naguib in 1954 lost his running battle with Nasser he fell in a matter of days from his exalted position to house arrest. Similarly in Iraq, Colonel Kassem shot up overnight from a "non-political" officer (under suspicion) to the leader of his country. One of his closest aides, Colonel Aref, rose to almost the same heights and then fell quickly and was sentenced to death when the program he advocated was rejected. These are, of course, revolutionary situations, but political careers even in times of less violence have been almost as changeable.

Again, the exception is Lebanon, where a weak government and the strong economic and communal position of political leaders have saved them from these extremes of honor and humiliation.

Western Influences on Domestic Politics

The effect of the Western domination of Arab political life from the last quarter of the nineteenth century to the middle of the present one has been contradictory, although the intention was consistent. By deliberate policy and sheer example, the West introduced ideas and technology that considerably changed social relations in the Arab world and have had profound political effects as well. At the same time, however, the Western powers studiously pursued a conservative policy regarding political life itself, seeking in effect to prevent the social and economic consequences of their presence from altering political institutions. They introduced revolutionary conceptions, but tried to keep them from making a revolution in Arab political life.

The West's impact on the Arab world in modern times came in the late nineteenth century, when the Ottoman Empire was still dominant in the region. The immediate effect was a conservative one. The introduction of political stability and economic order froze power in the hands of the individuals and the class then holding it. Previously, instability had made for a certain degree of rough social justice. Power being held uncertainly and not for long, the very harshness induced by the awareness of the transitory nature of power was mitigated by the rapid circulation of exploiting rulers. Under the old system, the exploited could always hope for the best under a new dispensation. Under the new system, stability made this hope forlorn. Nowhere was this so meticulously planned a policy as in Egypt under Lord Cromer's rule in the quarter century beginning 1882. As he himself expressed it in 1913, he set out to make Egyptians devoted to England rather than to nationalism: ". . . it was thought that by careful attention to the material interests of the people it might eventually be possible to bring into existence a conservative class who, albeit animated by no great love for their foreign rulers, would be sufficiently contented to prevent their becoming easily the prey either of the Nationalist demagogue . . . or that of some barbarious religious fanatic . . . or, finally, that of some wily politician . . ." So, he went on, Britain pursued a policy calculated toward this end: tax relief, abolition of fiscal inequality and the *corvée* (forced labor), improvement of irrigation, and several measures to strengthen and increase the class of propertied peasants. He thought his policy successful, as in fact it was for a time; but the whole region has succumbed since then to precisely those native leaders whom Cromer would consider the "demagogue," the "religious fanatic," and the "wily politician."[48]

Bent upon preserving order in these agricultural countries, the British and French soon leaned for local support upon the class—those large landowners who also had political influence—which likewise wanted most to preserve order. And Britain and France declined in the Arab world as that class itself declined. The introduction of industry, education of young men in the West, the inevitable nationalist resentment against foreign rule, and the spread of the press and radio gave rise to a new urban class of industrialists, lawyers, government workers, journalists, professionals, and army officers, all of whom owed little or no allegiance to the landed class upon which the British and French had based their rule. When these urban groups found the Western powers hostile to their nationalist goals and political programs, which were, of course, upsetting rather than conducive to "stability" in the short run, they became more and more intractable, more and more hostile to Western rule—in a word, more and more "extremist" in the Western view. As Berque says, "feudalism,"

48 Cromer, *Political and Literary Essays*, pp. 253–55.

the local bugbear, became identified with "imperialism"
even though ultimately Western influence created those
urban forces that have now largely displaced the old land-
owning class in the seats of political power.[49]

In later years, the British did not rely exclusively on
the landed class, but by this time its influence was already
on the wane. The United States, reflecting a different social order than the British and entering the Near Eastern
stage at a much later time, has tried to base its influence
upon a stable urban upper and middle class interested in
further industrialization. These efforts have been comple-
mented by American encouragement of land reform. Yet
this approach has been unsystematic rather than carefully
planned and consistently applied; it displays frequent
throwbacks to the old British-French pattern of reliance
upon the landed class in order to prevent further political
upsets. The Soviet Union alone, interested precisely in
political upsets, has sought to cultivate the friendship
and increase the power of those groups who likewise see
their own interests in rapid political changes. These groups
are the urban intellectuals, the middle and lower ranks of
the army officers and the upper civilian bureaucracy, and
through them the urban masses. Thus, to a considerable
degree, the three Western powers most influential in the
Arab world in recent years allied themselves, at the time
they entered the Near East, with those local groups em-
bodying their own political values: the British with a conservative landed class, the Americans with a techno-
logically-oriented class interested in expanded private
industrial enterprise, and the Soviets with a class interested in national power through the state and in a position
to organize and manipulate the revolutionary potential that
lies in mass poverty in the midst of great social change.

Their rule in the Arab countries posed an insoluble
problem for Britain and France. On the one hand they
introduced ideas and economic changes that tended to undermine the position of the classes upon which they de-

[49] Berque, *Leçon Inaugurale*, p. 18.

pended to retain their own power; on the other hand, they could not bring themselves to support those groups that wanted political change. The result was a compromise in which parliamentary institutions were to maintain stability while providing the means by which the Arabs could move toward self-government. In emphasizing parliamentary institutions, the West confused two issues: democracy and independence. It took the position that a country was not "ready" for independence until it had democratic institutions; this, of course, put off independence indefinitely. The Arabs, however, emphasized independence. To them, the main issue was self-government, after which Western conceptions of political maturity could be adopted or rejected as Arab leaders saw fit.

The West's failure to support Arab forces interested in political change caused considerable disillusion among many genuine Arab liberals. They studied in the West, absorbed Western notions of democracy abroad and at home, but found their teachers intractable when it came to applying the lessons in their own lands. The same process is now beginning in the less advanced Arab world, that of the Persian Gulf. A new elite is now rising there, just as in Egypt and the northern Arabian peninsula in the late nineteenth century, seeking at once to remove the native "feudal" landed aristocracy (now further enriched and entrenched by oil royalties) and to drive out the Western ruler. And again the West is confronted with the dilemma of supporting traditional autocrats or modern intellectuals who want to end Western influence. And again the "progressive" Arabs appeal to the West for help in their struggle against the West's own allies among the native rulers. This classic petition was expressed in 1957 when the British helped the Sultan of Muscat to put down a challenge to his authority. An Arab wrote to *The Economist:* "Britain could have served the interests of the British people and humanity best had it demonstrated its power in support of the national uprising of the peoples of Oman, and the other territories of the Persian Gulf protectorates who have been struggling alone against the despotic and feudalist regimes of their countries."[50]

The paramount passion for independence set the native Arab elites against the West that had done so much, deliberately and unintentionally, to create them. At home the British were famous for their absorption into the upper classes of talented youth coming up from the lower classes. They could not do the same in the Arab world, nor could the French, despite their emphasis upon education and culture. Instead, their practices guaranteed the growth of a native elite which, refused entrance into the foreign ruling group on equal terms, was obliged to exercise its talents in leading its people against the West. Unable to find for himself a suitable place under foreign rule, the outstanding Arab concluded that he must drive out the Westerner in order to create such a place in his own society. He was driven back to his own origins no matter what his aspirations may have been to move away from them. His nationalist feeling combined with his self-interest to produce an ideological fervor and a persistence that would brook no compromise on the issue of independence—not even those to which he actually agreed in treaties from time to time. The foreign rulers wanted to stay and govern but the native elite wanted them to leave so that *they* could govern—through their own political institutions, and not those the West had held up as the ones required for independence. Public opinion within Britain and France made more difficult the repressive and costly policies needed to maintain control over the Arab world. At the same time two great powers, the United States and the Soviet Union, without traditional colonial interests there, began to make their influence felt. In this combination of circumstances, the Arabs won independence without being "ready" for it in British and French terms, that is, without successfully building Western parliamentary institutions, yet establishing regimes concerned with the welfare of a broader range of the Arab population.

[50] Letter from H. Karami, *The Economist*, Aug. 17, 1957, Vol. 184, p. 535.

CHAPTER 9

Ideologies, National and International

For many centuries, ending only in our own time, the Arabs were objects in world politics, minor actors in a drama whose marginal position on the stage was determined by and in the interest of others. In recent decades they have not only briefly occupied the center of the stage from time to time but have done so on their own terms. As they became more conscious of their common history and destiny, they began to make demands as well as to comply with those others made upon them. The Arabs found new allies among the powerful enemies of those who had controlled them and among those peoples who likewise sought to assert their own sense of identity. In this process they acquired a set of beliefs, or ideologies, that fortified them by justifying their yearnings for national unity, self-government, an honored place in a world of nations, social reform through state intervention, and an independent approach to international politics which they conceived to be appropriate both to these goals and to their new status in the world.

An ideology serves many purposes. It provides an interpretation of reality that is consonant with the holder's self-image. It supports those who adhere to it by giving them a set of defenses for the things they value and what they would like to be. It is often impermeable because it lies beyond the realm of logic if not of dispute. An ideology can be useful or not, relevant to certain goals or not, popular or esoteric; it can turn people inward upon their own emotional resources or provide them the excuse for blaming other people or such vague abstractions as "history" or "fate." One can probe the ideologies that dominate the Arab world today—nationalism, neutralism, or reform-ism—but one cannot meaningfully ask whether they are "true" or "false." As a mixture of interpretation of one reality and a passion to create another one, an ideology transcends such sober categories. It changes through ex-perience rather than argument, loses or adds elements in accordance with their usefulness or relevance rather than their accuracy as description of the past or their reason-ableness in anticipating the future.

Main Features of Arab Ideology Today

From one point of view, modern Arab nationalism may be considered an effort to create a new self-conception for the Arab, a new identity. For centuries, the Near Easterner has seemed to the West to be religious, indolent, patient, grave—a narrow, unambitious person in a narrow, circum-scribed world which was static while Europe was going through brilliant periods of geographic exploration, scien-tific discovery, technological progress, and economic pros-perity. So pervasive did this image become that it was ac-cepted even by Arabs themselves. But nationalism now seeks to change both the Arab's self-image and the world's conception of him. Arabs look back upon a common past which includes descent, language, customs—and religion, the vessel that carried all the others. They look forward to a common future which they want to make better than their recent past. This common future is based upon the sense that all Arabs must expect to be affected similarly by what happens in the world; their physical well-being, moral condition, and standard of living are all viewed as a function of their being Arabs. They aim to conserve some-thing of their common past as they interpret it and to in-sure for themselves the best possible future in the light of modern, secular goals—and they mean to do this by cultivating their solidarity through the establishment of strong national states which are related to one another in varying degrees of intimacy.

Whether under republics, military republics, or monarchies, the Arabs display several attitudes the world has come to recognize easily. The most prominent is the desire for national independence, not merely formal self-government but the power to determine their own national future to the extent that this is possible in our era. If we judge by the withdrawal of foreign troops and of exceptional diplomatic influence, then this goal has now been achieved in Egypt, Syria, Iraq, and Lebanon, and only a trace of the old Western power remains even in Jordan. Nationalist goals, however, are by their nature easily extended. If independence of foreign control is realized, unity among the Arab states or Afro-Asian "solidarity" takes on greater importance. So does the effort to increase national power through military strength, industrialization, and a rise in the standard of living. In states that are only now emerging, all of these goals take on a nationalist aspect. Underlying them all and providing the fuel to keep them moving is the continuing ambivalence toward the former Western rulers and Western society: resentment leading to a desire to reject them, mixed with envy leading to a desire to approximate their power and wealth.

This ambivalence is aptly described by Hourani:

The Western Powers in act if not in word treated the Arab countries as if the desires and wishes of their inhabitants were matters of minor importance; individual Westerners showed only too often their contempt for a people who dressed, believed and thought so differently from them, and were so backward in the material arts. The contempt was no less wounding when it was concealed beneath a romantic admiration for the primitive or the exotic. It was the more unbearable to the Arabs because of their conviction that in essentials they were not inferior to the West, no less than because of their suspicion that in many other things they were indeed far behind the West and had much to learn from it. It gave rise to a desire to equal the West in those things on which the West set value, and to be recognized by the West as equals. Since the West set value upon the independence and

*power of the national State, upon economic prosperity and
a certain ordering of social life, the Arabs too must be
independent and powerful, and modern in their social organization.*[1]

The depth of anti-Western sentiment and of the desire
to assert independence of the West has become clear in
all five Arab countries we are discussing. As soon as each
was able to remove direct Western power, it adopted, along
with the familiar goals of economic development and social modernization, a policy of neutralism in international
affairs or, at times, a pro-Soviet policy. Iraq went through
this process most recently. Within days or weeks after the
revolution of July 1958, the new military regime proclaimed that Iraq (1) was an integral part of the Arab
nation; and would (2) refrain from taking sides in the
cold war; (3) be governed by efforts to build nationalism,
socialism, and democracy and to raise living standards
through industrialization and land distribution; (4) modernize certain institutions, for example, by eliminating
"tribal law," and by legislation for social welfare and land
reform; and (5) withhold political freedom until the danger to the revolution was overcome.[2]

The two sides of Arab nationalism, rejection of political
ties with the West and the building of national strength
through the state apparatus, are related to the emergence
of the Soviet Union as a leading world power. Russia's
diplomatic, military, and industrial prowess has been directed toward removing Western influence and, where possible, supplanting it with Soviet or local pro-Soviet forces.
The coincidence of this anti-Western goal with Arab nationalist passions has brought the independent Arab states
to neutralism and at times to the side of Russia in the
diplomatic struggles since about 1950, but especially since

[1] Hourani, *Syria and Lebanon*, p. 100.
[2] The New York *Times*, July 26, 1958, p. 4; July 27, 1958,
p. 17; July 28, 1958, p. 2; August 8, 1958, p. 3. *Oriente
Moderno* (1958), 38:623, 665–66, 744–45, 819. Republic of
Iraq, Ministry of Guidance, *The Weekly Gazette of the Republic
of Iraq*, issues of July–December, 1958.

1955. Russia has not merely given diplomatic support to Egypt, Syria, and Iraq (and to certain groups in Lebanon and Jordan) but has also granted them considerable military, financial, and technical assistance at critical times. Nor does this exhaust the reasons for which the new Arab regimes admire the U.S.S.R. despite recent animosities over Soviet attempts to influence domestic Arab politics. The U.S.S.R. also appears to provide Arab leaders with a model of a strong national state that claims to have overtaken the West in important ways in only two generations. No one is under the illusion that the Arabs can do the same with fewer resources, but Soviet methods are admired and at times emulated as the most appropriate ones for achieving quick nationalist results. This is why, despite their own nationalist fervor and Islamic background, Arab leaders are attracted to the Soviet model of statism and anti-Westernism.

As in pre-Soviet Russia itself, in the Arab world moderate liberalism or constitutionalism has never had a chance. Many of the elements of Arab nationalism today were introduced in the late nineteenth century by pro-Western liberals before disillusionment with the West blanketed the Arab world. As we saw in the previous chapter, however, the European powers did not find it in their interest to encourage Arab liberals in their espousal of moderate nationalism, industrialization, and the Arabization of control over economic and political life.

One reason for the moderate character of early Arab nationalism is that Christians were among its leading exponents. Educated in the West or by Westerners in the Near East, the early nationalists hoped for Western assistance in creating a liberal nationalist Arab world. As disillusionment grew with Europe's refusal to extend this aid, Arab nationalism itself became "nationalized"—that is, it spread to nativist Moslem groups with less affinity to the West and with fewer economic ties to property. Unmoored from these moderating influences, Arab nationalism drifted from the relatively calm waters of traditional liberalism into the violent currents of political extremism.

Neither as wards of Europe nor as independent nations could the Arabs construct a viable liberalism. The landlord class, not numerous but powerful, had little interest in combatting foreign control and none in arousing native political passions. The traditional middle class in the Western sense, the commercial, industrial, and banking groups, were foreigners, members of minorities, or foreign-oriented and not interested in nationalism or liberalism. The urban working class was small, uneducated, hardly organized, and too impoverished to care about ideologies. The peasants, numerous but weak and poor, lay outside the political community entirely. The professionals new to Islamic societies—the lawyers, doctors, literary men, journalists, and the students who aspired to join them—became the keepers of the nationalist conscience, both moderate and extreme. But these ideologues suffered from the lack of a solid social movement behind them. Without a strong liberal or socialist party, without trade unions or independent peasant organizations, liberalism was a hothouse plant that flourished among the intelligentsia and bore little or no relation to the social environment. Because political power lay with the landed class in alliance with the Western-dominated monarchies, Arab liberals were isolated from the centers of power and could make no contribution to political life except one tied to the all-pervading nationalism whose rhetoric no group could avoid or resist. When they were nationalist they were heeded, when they were liberal they were largely ignored, both by the Arab holders of power and the Europeans behind them. The liberals were free to fight against foreign but not against native despotism. Consequently they could make no palpable gains in their own political influence, or in promoting democracy or social welfare—they could not enjoy even the modicum of success that in the West moderated the extreme left and gave it a sense of responsibility as it realized some of its immediate goals and came closer to political power. Instead, Arab liberals were left with only their ideology to embrace. They became weaker and further removed from the growing nationalist spirit, or they too clutched at the extremist versions of their own doctrines in order to make themselves heard in the ideological din. Looking to European liberalism for inspiration and support, Arab liberalism found only the first, which cost the West little, but not the second, which would have cost it more at the outset but probably not in the long run.

Arab liberalism, never more than a tender shoot in an uncongenial environment, finally withered just after World War II in the white heat of the West's insistence upon maintaining its special position in the Near East and of the creation of the state of Israel in 1948 and the ensuing war. Moderation could not survive such blows to Arab hopes and expectations. The older propertied middle class lost influence as foreign power declined and a new, more nationalist middle class waxed—an employed middle class of civil servants dependent upon Arab states now governing themselves at least in domestic affairs, of technicians and professionals who were Westernized without having been in the West, the products of Arab higher education systems which were themselves secular, modern, nationalist. Especially in Egypt, Syria, and Iraq but also in Lebanon and Jordan to some extent, a new and fiercer determination, unmitigated by the Western loyalties of older generations and of the Christians now less prominent in nationalist leadership, was added to the earlier nationalist goals of full independence, Arab unity, industrialization and a rise in living standards. New goals were added too. First, a passion for military strength developed in the wake of the humiliation in the fighting against Israel, which has been partly responsible for the growing influence of the military elite. Second, the task of industrialization and raising the level of incomes, health, education and welfare in general was placed upon the state apparatus to a greater degree than ever. Third, the process of Arabization of wealth and culture was speeded up. Fourth, land reform was begun. Fifth, the state became involved, through the foregoing and other policies, in a prodigious effort to bring the dispossessed and despised urban and rural masses into the political community on the side of the new regimes that had set out to transform their lives. With the higher stakes now involved in political power, the new regimes considered political freedom for dissident classes and individuals a luxury they could not afford. So, while democracy was proclaimed the goal, authoritarian rule settled upon the Arabs in a more efficient manner than before. Social equality rather than political freedom was emphasized. National power rather than individual welfare was held out as the primary aim, to achieve which the masses had to be driven to a far more intense national pride than they had felt before.

"Extremism" in Arab politics is the concomitant of certain social conditions rather than of some racial quality which observers of the desert Arabs frequently find. T. E. Lawrence, for example, wrote: "Semites have no half-tones in their register of vision. . . . They exclude compromise, and pursue the logic of their ideas to its absurd ends, without seeing incongruity in their opposed conclusions. . . . Their convictions are by instinct, their activities intuitional."[3] It is too sweeping to say that they exclude compromise. In all kinds of communities, even in the desert, Arabs enjoy formal litigation and informal argument in which they compromise readily and indeed consider compromise a part of disputation.

Islam has been able to sustain a system of canon law that accommodates four different schools of jurisprudence. In doctrinal discussion, Arabs do not compromise so eagerly but then neither do other peoples. Especially in politics, they have rigidly adhered to their ultimate demands for complete independence.

Among the Arabs political extremism on the part of the articulate elite is the reciprocal of political apathy on the part of the inarticulate masses. The leaders of the independent Arab states, now engaged in a mighty effort to make the indifferent masses politically conscious, need to shout in order to be heard at all, to go to excesses to make

[3] T. E. Lawrence, Introduction to Doughty, pp. 21–22.

people care even in the slightest about matters still remote from their day-to-day concerns. It takes hyperbole to induce the masses to share the elite's enthusiasms and to enable the leaders to realize their ambitious national goals. Before they achieved independence, Arab leaders were impelled to take extreme ideological positions by their very weakness compared to the strong Western powers which controlled the Near East.

This legacy of extremism is today augmented by new developments. The need for national strength is apparent when the smaller states are drawn into one or another camp by invasion or the threat of it during hot wars and by external pressure and their own interests in cold wars. To preserve their hard-won independence, which the Arab leaders must do if they are to retain their positions in a highly nationalist atmosphere, they go to extremes to awaken the population to the need for determination, change, work. In their effort to enlist support, they go to all groups for testimonials of faith in the national goals, even if action does not follow or is irrelevant when it does. Sometimes this tendency becomes amusing, as when the Egyptian dental association announced during "Algeria Week" in 1959: "On this occasion, when free men all over the world declare their support for the Algerian people who are fighting imperialism to obtain their right to freedom, a decent life and self-determination, Egyptian Region dentists declare their support for the struggle of Algeria . . . Dentists also declare that they will spare no effort to support right over evil."[4] But such heroics must not lead us to underestimate the seriousness with which Arabs regard their own aspirations. This realization of the stark necessity for change sets the stage for "extremism," and the sound effects are produced by the vast communications apparatus of newspapers, magazines, radio, cinema, loud-speakers in the streets and squares, and even the mosques with their quasi-political tradition.

Political extremism comes easily to the Arabs for three

[4] *The Egyptian Gazette*, April 20, 1959, p. 1.

reasons stemming from their recent experience: their low level of living and education, the absence of democracy, and their strong resentment against the West.

1. The low level of living enables Arab leaders to pursue political goals with little regard for the immediate economic consequences; an agricultural society that is surviving at a subsistence level anyway is hardly aware that changes in the remote, slight superstructure of industry and commerce affect its own welfare too. Thus, when Britain, France, and Israel attacked Egypt in 1956, Syria damaged the pipelines to prevent oil reaching Western Europe, Saudi Arabia refused to load oil onto tankers destined for the same place, and Egypt sank enough ships to block the Suez Canal for many months. The Arab states, these and others, were hurt by these actions, but not profoundly, for most of the population lies outside the short-run range of the modern oil economy of the area. Countries with a higher standard of living, a more articulate and independent population, and a democratic system of government cannot afford to give such free play to political goals at the expense of economic interests. In the Arab world, however, a large proportion of the modern industrial-commercial sector of the economy, until very recently, has been owned by foreigners or a small foreign-oriented middle class. Nationalist regimes, therefore, have not been seriously restrained by a powerful, propertied middle and upper class. The native middle groups, employed rather than propertied, have identified themselves with the most uncompromising nationalist goals and have indeed profited from the steady weakening of the foreign-oriented middle class.

The low level of education, combined with the relative imperviousness of a poor agricultural society to crises in the narrow industrial-commercial sector, is conducive to political extremism in two ways. First, as we have already seen, it takes hyperbole and constant repetition to arouse the masses whose national consciousness is still inchoate. But the very monotony, brutality, and hopelessness of their existence makes them responsive, from time to time, to ideological appeals. On such occasions, which may be infrequent, their lack of knowledge of the outside world and their repressed hostility makes them a gullible prey to propaganda and extremism, easily swayed to violence. This is the social background, rural and urban, conducive to mob action; it provides the spontaneous mass base for the organized and paid mobs which so often set the larger movements in train.

The urban working class is highly susceptible to manipulative appeals because it is organizationally weak but potentially useful to governments and oppositions alike. Inexperienced in politics and industry, with leaders who are also neophytes, the urban workers are easily swayed by promises from various quarters. Many of the workers are of recent rural origin, aware of urban standards and new possibilities but with little experience in evaluating claims and offers.

In societies like the Arab, where the levels of formal education and political consciousness are low, students in the secondary schools and universities often constitute a special class and usually augment extremist tendencies. They are a large proportion of the educated population of all ages; and the university students especially know their importance to the regime as an articulate, compact group, as well as the society's future elite. Unlike the advanced economies and relatively stable democracies of Western Europe and North America, the Arab world does not afford educated young people a well-established transition from the university to a job commensurate with their expectations. They are thus an articulate, politically alert, and ambitious group, aware of the changes going on in the world, the product of new tendencies, and have little stake in existing social arrangements which they feel do not offer them adequate opportunities. They are, consequently, a politically unstable group seeking change, excitable and carefully treated by the regimes. American universities in the Near East have tried to reduce their political activity, which takes the form of demonstrations and strikes, by providing more opportunities for extracurricular activities such as athletics and clubs of many kinds. The logic behind this policy has been that such hitherto neglected aspects of Arab campus life might drain off the students' political energies into other channels. But this American technique has not worked. The new activities have only given the students additional stages upon which to play their political roles, more opportunities to disagree with one another, more arenas in which to extend their political attitudes on the campus. In Egypt and Syria, recently, the regime has been more successful in curbing political activities by increasing the number of examinations, stiffening the requirements to stay enrolled, trying to emphasize science and technology, prohibiting political parties and hence appeals to students, and by sheer policing of the campuses.

2. The absence or weakness of democratic processes in the Arab states encourages extremism in two ways. First, it has reduced or eliminated the means by which dissent can be registered in a legitimate, orderly way. Differences of a serious nature are not afforded a regular outlet. When disputes over doctrine and fundamental policy are not allowed expression, they become exaggerated and feed on the repression itself in a continuous process of self-magnification. This was the case when Arab nationalism was the victim under European domination, and it is the case today when a form of nationalism is in the saddle and has turned authoritarian except in Lebanon. Second, the lack of democratic checks upon the rulers enables them to ignore public opinion for substantial periods of time and to mold it to their own desires, at least in the short run. Public opinion often pushes a regime to extreme positions, but it is also true that its weakness or political irrelevance in the immediate sense allows a regime to go to such lengths as it pleases in maintaining its own power or in sacrificing the long-run economic interests of the nation to the short-run political goals of the few but articulate supporters of the ruling elite.

3. The universality of Arab resentment against Western control has made it difficult for Arab leaders, whatever

their personal opinions or their judgment as to the best policy to pursue, to adopt a position of compromise. Anything short of total nationalist rejection of the West has been taken as a sign of weakness or even of treason. Since everyone is free to be as critical of the West as he wants to be, all are driven to this extreme position for fear of attack by others. This situation produces endless stimulation to extremism. It began with anti-Western statements but soon extended to nationalist testimonials and self-glorification, until politics became in some degree a contest in verbal excess. The atmosphere of hyperbole still hovers over the Arab world despite the withdrawal of Western influence from most of it.

The combination of nationalist goals, resentment against the West and a low standard of living and education makes extremism an easy refuge for both leaders and followers. Competition for power is fierce and stark in the Arab world; the struggle is not, in most places, carried on openly and with certain rights guaranteed the losers. *Within* each country, therefore, the stakes are high. There is another struggle for power going on *between* the Arab countries in which competing conceptions of Arab nationalism are the main issue. Thus, after 1952 the official Egyptian view was at odds with the official Iraqi view under the monarchy. For a brief period after the Iraq revolution of 1958, the Cairo and Baghdad ideas converged but they soon separated and opposed one another again. Lebanese conceptions have differed seriously from the official ones in Egypt and Iraq, while the politically dominant Jordanian one has remained rather stable and therefore in conflict with the changing visions in surrounding countries. This international competition within the Arab world produces its own extremist tendencies as the regimes appeal to their own populations for support and to the masses in other countries. In this process public opinion becomes important—but it is uninformed, volatile, and subject to easy manipulation, with the result that the contest in verbal extremism within each country extends across the boundaries and becomes general. The importance of the

masses in politics is growing faster than their experience
in politics, perhaps even faster than their interest or capacity to participate in political life. Extremist politics
shakes them out of their torpor for brief periods in which
they tend to respond in excess to appeals made in excess.
Moreover, except in Lebanon, the Arab political pattern
is authoritarian, so that political participation cannot take
the form of public contests for power in which appeals to
the various groups in the electorate might be at least
tinged with the rationality and predictability of self-
interest. Instead, political life tends to become sharply
divided: extreme support of the regime, or extreme but
clandestine opposition to it breaking out in violence when
it becomes open.

Arab Nationalism and Islamic Loyalty

Nationalism in the Near East is intimately connected
with religion. As we have seen several times in earlier chapters, being Arab meant being Moslem after the rise of
Islam, and the connections between these two kinds of
self-identification have persisted to this day. Arab nationalism is sharpened against the whetstone of European
domination and the memory of the Crusaders, so that
religious difference is felt acutely. Late in 1959, for example, President Nasser harked back to great victories of
Saladin, the unifier of Egypt and Syria, builder of the
Citadel in Cairo, the Moslem who took back Jerusalem
from the Crusaders and pushed them out of all Palestine
except for a few coastal towns. "The victory of Arab nationalism," Nasser proclaimed (anachronistically), "means
the end of foreign influence and the beginning of independence and of a great state in this part of the world
which will bring back the first glorious days of Saladin,
days in which Arab nationalism united Arabs everywhere."[5]
When Arab nationalism was directed against the Otto-

[5] Speech at Port Said, Dec. 23, 1959, reprinted in *al-Jumhuriyah* (Cairo), Dec. 24, 1959, p. 4, and *The Egyptian Gazette*,
Dec. 24, 1959, p. 3.

mans more than a half century ago, the religious aspect
was less important because the Ottomans were also Moslems. Indeed, Syrian Arab nationalism at that time was
led by Christian Arabs. In Egypt, on the other hand, where
the target was British control beginning in 1882, the nationalist movement was largely Moslem. Even today the
Moslem element in the Arab nationalism of Egypt is more
marked than it is in Lebanon and Syria.

The state, indeed, is the pinnacle toward which Arab
nationalism strives, as did the East European national
movements before it and the African and Asian peoples
after it. Arab nationalism is like its European model in
that it presents a conservative and a liberal side. The emphasis upon sheer sentiment, military power, national
unity on the basis of any tradition that can be mustered,
is politically conservative. But the interest in social welfare,
economic development, and modernization in general is a
liberal influence. Perhaps the most liberalizing aspect of
Arab nationalism is its awakening of masses previously
untouched by new ideas of independence, self-respect,
freedom, and a standard of living somewhat higher than
endemic poverty, disease, and lack of education permitted.
For all its extremism, even its authoritarian character,
Arab nationalism has generated a new sense of the possibilities of life for the ordinary man. It has given him a
glimpse of the human capacity for self-development, opening up new conceptions of what a man may do and be.
It has stimulated in large numbers of people previously
bound by the immediate task of staying alive nothing less
than a new sense of self.

Thus far the expanding horizon of the Arab has produced psychological conflict as well as personal inspiration,
revolving around the problem of how he shall see himself—primarily as an Arab or as a Moslem. In the West the
competing loyalties of nationalism and religion have been
relegated to different realms in both doctrine and practice, but this process has not yet gone far in the Arab
world. So the conflict persists not only in the individual
Arab, whether Moslem or Christian, but also among the

political and ideological leaders who must find ways to arouse the people to new efforts. Arab nationalism without Islamic overtones appeals to an increasing number of people who are literate, urban, and enjoy a standard of living above sheer subsistence. It is not that such people reject overt Islamic appeals but that they easily respond to purely secular Arab nationalist rhetoric. The vast mass of the Moslems, however, are still more effectively stirred by the traditional religious symbols; and they supply the religious connotations themselves when their leaders do not, since they have always seen "Arab" and "Moslem" as the same. The question of religion intrudes into that of nationalism for a simple reason: not all Arabs are Moslems. Christian Arabs face the issue of their relation to their own Arab tradition, which is so heavily Islamic, and Moslems face the issue of the extent to which the traditional religion is compatible with building a powerful national, modern state.

Arab nationalism has changed with the changing position of the two major religions in the area, Christianity and Islam, in respect to the ruling powers, Turkey and then Britain and France.[6] In Syria and Lebanon nationalism and pan-Arab sentiments arose in the late nineteenth century among the Christians, who, looking to Europe as the model, found it easy to oppose Ottoman rule, which was non-Arab, Moslem, and oppressive. This movement was stimulated by an Arab cultural and literary revival just as Western education, introduced on an already increasing scale, was beginning to take effect among a small but articulate group of intellectuals and literary men. Later it was further stimulated by the rise of liberal ideas among the Young Ottomans and the Young Turks. At first, pan-Arabism's political goal was freedom within the Ottoman Empire, and this seemed possible of attainment with the growing revolutionary movement within Turkey itself, the center of the empire. Arab nationalists and Turkish reform-

[6] On the various strands of Arab nationalism, see Antonius, Ch. 6; Ireland, Ch. 12, 13; Kedourie, pp. 100–11; and Chejne.

ers co-operated in the Committee of Union and Progress, the secret association through which the Young Turks took power in 1908–9 on a liberal program that promised equality to the various racial, religious, and national groups. But the chauvinism of the Young Turks disillusioned the Arabs, who then adopted autonomy as their political goal. Christian leadership in the nationalist movement began to be shared with Moslems, who were also feeling the influence of new ideologies. Moreover, the illiberal turn of the Young Turks alienated the Moslem Arabs as much as it did the Christians. The Ottomanization policy meant the discouragement of Arabic language and literature and the imposition of Turkish in administration and education. To this repression of Arab culture the Young Turks added a secular, even irreligious, attitude and policy which alienated Moslems. These developments set the stage for the failure of the Ottoman effort to defend itself against the Allied powers by calling for a Holy War in 1914.

During these decades from the late nineteenth century to the outbreak of World War I, nationalism in Iraq and Egypt was pursuing a separate course. Iraq, somewhat isolated from the rest of the Arab world and from Western influences, developed its own strong nationalist ideology which early adopted the goal of autonomy and an Arab empire. In Egypt, meanwhile, nationalism took another tack, for the main problem there was not Moslem Turkey, which since the early nineteenth century at least had ruled only nominally, but Britain, a Western Christian power. The Arab revival flowered in Egypt too, which had long been the cultural center of the Arab world, and enjoyed greater intellectual freedom than other Arab lands. But strictly political nationalism was directed against the British ruler—it was Egyptian rather than Arab nationalism. Nevertheless, as the haven for many nationalist leaders driven from the Syrian provinces by the repressive policy of the Ottoman regime, Egyptian nationalism acquired a broader outlook than its immediate tasks imparted. Since the proportion of Christians was smaller in Egypt than in

Syria and Lebanon, nationalism there fed to a greater degree on religious resentment against the Western power.

When the Arab world came under British and French control following Turkey's defeat in World War I, the several particularist strands of Arab nationalism began to cross one another. Now there was only one imperialist foe, Europe. This fact might have been expected to produce uncertainty among the Christian Arabs, whose nationalism was itself derived from their Western connections and who had looked to the West for guidance and assistance. It did in fact lead to some ambivalence but two developments dissipated the tendency to express it strongly and convinced Arab Christians that they must accommodate themselves to the Moslem majority's sentiment. First, European power began to decline soon after World War I. Egypt achieved independence with respect to internal affairs, in 1922 and the British found it expedient to grant the same status to Iraq by 1932. It became clearer each year that Europe could not continue to play the role of protector of the Christian minorities for much longer. The Christians, in these circumstances, began to emphasize those elements of their culture that they held in common with the Moslem majority—that is, their Arab heritage. It became easier for them to stress their Arabism by virtue of the second development, the growth of Zionism in Palestine, which presented a serious challenge to the political aims of the Arabs. Here there was no occasion for ambivalence; the Christian Arabs could wholeheartedly oppose the European and American Jews who posed the threat. In this test of their fidelity, the Christians were able to satisfy the demands of nationalism for absolute Arab solidarity. Zionism and, later, the state of Israel, have continued to spur Arab unity and nationalism. As President Nasser himself put it in a speech commemorating the evacuation of Port Said in 1956 after the Suez invasion, "The Palestine tragedy was the torch which aroused Arab consciousness in every Arab country."[7]

7 See note 5, above.

The accommodation of the Christians to nationalism has been facilitated by the secular tendencies of the Near East in modern times, which has in fact meant the accommodation of nationalism to the Christians. As religion becomes less pervasive, it is easier for all Arabs to find common ground. For this reason, of course, the Christians among the nationalists have stressed secular nationalism. Many Moslem thinkers have done the same, but secularization presents a serious problem to Moslems who want to hold fast to the traditional claims of Islam in all domains of human relations, not merely as a religion with a circumscribed "place" in society.

Though Arab nationalism and Islamic loyalty nourish each other ideologically, their specifically political embodiments have flown two opposing banners, those of pan-Arabism and pan-Islamism. They are both reactions to Western domination and its display of scientific, economic and cultural progress in recent centuries but they draw upon their past in different ways and have different visions of the future. Pan-Arabism is chiefly a political movement among Arabic-speaking peoples to achieve independence of foreign influence and some degree of unity among Arab states on a secular basis. Pan-Islamism is a fundamentalist reassertion of the political unity of all Moslems irrespective of nationality, and of the applicability of Islamic doctrine to all of human affairs. Politically, it aims to stem the tide of secularization within each Moslem country and to promote unity among them all in order to re-establish a single community of Moslems.

Both ideologies, in their modern form, arose in the late nineteenth century, though pan-Arabism did not assume political significance until the twentieth. Pan-Islamism (as it has developed in the Arab world) was a plain rejection of the West, pan-Arabism an attempt to accommodate to it by accepting two of its leading tenets: national sovereignty and technological advance. Pan-Islamism was, of course, the creation of Moslems, pan-Arabism of Moslems and Christians. Pan-Islamism was at first the political instrument of the Ottoman ruler Abdul-Hamid II who during a long reign from 1876 to 1909 tried to use this sentiment as a means of keeping his empire together against the encroachments of powerful European states and the nationalism of those parts of both Christian Europe and the Moslem-Christian Arab world which he ruled. He aroused pan-Islamic feeling for two purposes: to keep out the West, and to discourage purely nationalist separatism. In a sense he pitted pan-Islamic loyalty against the new inchoate pan-Arab ideas. Only once since that time has the opposition between the two ideologies been so clearly expressed. Abdul-Hamid's pan-Islamic policy failed not only because of European force but because of the secular revolt that brought to power a nationalist movement stressing Turkish rather than Islamic sentiment and tradition. The Turks continued to suppress Arab nationalism in the name of Ottoman national unity in time of war rather than in the interests of pan-Islamism.

The next confrontation of pan-Islamism and pan-Arabism came when Abdul-Hamid's successor in 1914 issued the call for a *jihad* or "holy war" against the "infidel" British, French, and Russians. The proclamation was followed by propaganda and missions to the Moslem countries, including, of course, the Arab. But nationalism and disgust with Ottoman impiety and neglect of Islam had taken their toll of pan-Islamic sentiment among Arabs. British political promises to Arab leaders proved more attractive than Ottoman pan-Islamic entreaties. Even to Hussein, the protector of the holy Moslem cities of Mecca and Medina, Arab nationalist prospects looked far better than pan-Islamic appeals to "holy war" against one group of infidels rather than another.

When Turkey abolished the "caliphate" in 1924 it destroyed the institutional and geographic basis of pan-Islamic ideology. Paradoxically, this freed Arab pan-Islamic advocates from the incubus of a hated ruler who was both chauvinistically anti-Arab and impious as well. Pan-Islamism could now join forces with pan-Arabism in the political arena at least, even if doctrinally the two did not coincide at all points. In the decades after 1930 the two movements fused with one another in the struggle for independence from the Western powers. But once national victory was achieved, in Syria, Egypt, and then in Iraq, the old opposition asserted itself once more. The sharpest expression of this renewal of conflict came in Egypt, after 1954, when the military regime had succeeded, by diplomacy, in ensuring the withdrawal of all British military forces. Then the fundamentalist Moslem Brotherhood, seeing the secularizing trend gathering momentum, turned against their former comrades-in-arms, the officers who had seized power in 1952. The regime relentlessly suppressed the Brotherhood and its traditionalist pan-Islamic bid for power against secular nationalism.

Arab nationalist denial of pan-Islamic political pretensions does not mean denial of Islamic loyalty. The sort of violent break that Turkey made with Islam under Ataturk in the 1920s is not likely to be made by any Arab leader, however powerful or secure he may be. In the first place, the Islamic traditionalists are not so influential in the Arab world as they were in Turkey and Persia, for example, and hence there is less need to destroy every manifestation of their power; only when they overtly challenge the secular regimes are they systematically put down, and then it is only the purely political side that feels the brunt of state power. In the second place, there is little inclination even among secular Arabs to reduce loyalty to Islam, for it is still difficult for them to think of themselves as anything but Moslem Arabs, rather than merely Arabs. Turkey has a national tradition previous to and outside of Islam, which made it easier for it to relegate the religion officially to a special and limited place in the society. The same may be said of Iran, but the Arabs (including the Egyptians, for whom the culture of ancient Egypt is not a tradition they can use) have no viable and meaningful national experience outside of the absolute identity with Islam. Finally, because of this intense loyalty to religion among Arabs, nationalists have appealed to Islamic identification without feeling any sense of contradiction.

In Africa and Asia secular nationalism often impels the ideologues to reject religion along with other traditional barriers to modernization. This is less so in Arab Islam, where nationalism can in fact call upon the religious tradition as a unifying force. Because Islam was a community under one banner, nationalists need not disown the past but can easily adapt to contemporary goals that deep loyalty to Islamic unity which is even today daily reinforced in the mosque. Whatever doctrinal problems may be created for the theorists, for the masses of Moslem Arabs it is an easy transition in self-identification from thinking of one community of Islam to thinking of one nation of Arabs. This two-sided identity makes it possible, almost irresistible, for Arab nationalists to invoke Islamic loyalty when seeking mass support for anti-foreign policies. The ordinary Arab is still more intimately touched by direct or implied appeals to his sense of religious unity than to his feeling of Arab brotherhood of a secular kind. Secular nationalism is the ideology of the educated Arabs, those who have been influenced by the West through education and travel; it is spreading among the urban workers for whom religion is still strong but no longer governs their entire lives. Islamic loyalty remains the chief sense of identity and unity for the vast majority of the uneducated people in cities and villages. Though the nationalists use Islamic loyalty in mobilizing sentiment against the non-Moslem world outside, within each Arab country they promote reforms that pit them against the Islamic fundamentalists. It is convenient for this reason, as well as others, to stress the foreign peril even after it has receded and automatically to attribute national disappointments to foreign influence. By this means sharp ideological and political differences are muted and the inevitable confrontation postponed. Time is on the side of the secular Arab nationalists in this struggle, for they are everywhere in control of the state apparatus with its monopoly of force and propaganda, while religious loyalty is slowly declining as urbanization and industrialization create in the articulate classes new values that do not so much contradict traditional Islamic precepts as simply bypass them.

The demise of pan-Islamism as an overt, organized political movement in active competition for state power has left these religious impulses with a rather diffuse influence which flows into areas where it is not deliberately excluded. The secular political leaders therefore try to guide and contain these religious loyalties, to bend them to nationalist purposes. In this they have been successful despite the presumed opposition between the universalism of Islam as a religion and the relative narrowness of nationalism as a secular loyalty. As a Western scholar puts it, "The nationalist solution is . . . clearly opposed to the Islamic principle. No matter how sincerely nationalists may profess their devotion to the doctrines and the ethical teachings of Islam, they are committed to setting up a second principle alongside it; and there is no way to avoid the resulting division and conflict of duties except by separating the spheres of church and state."[8] Yet Moslem Arabs can in fact be loyal to both Islam and Arab nationalism. But the doctrinal problem has given rise to two current conceptions of Arab nationalism, one that sees Islam as a larger kind of unity between Arabs and non-Arabs, and one that sees Arab nationalism as the broader conception because it seeks to unite Moslems with non-Moslems.

The first conception is exemplified by the work of al-Bazzaz,[9] an Iraqi Moslem who studied in London and later became a teacher in Baghdad. Since Islam, he insists, is a religion that encompasses social and political principles, it does not conflict with Arab nationalism unless the political goals of the two doctrines are in conflict. Nationalism, he continues, aims to unite Arabs on the basis of their common language and cultural heritage, and their present interests. They are a special group in Islam because of their role in the origin and development of the religion. At this moment in their history, Moslems cannot unite politically because of geographical barriers and differ-

8 Gibb, *Modern Trends in Islam*, p. 115.
9 al-Bazzaz, *passim*.

ences in political systems and social life. But within the Moslem spiritual unity, the Arabs form a group for whom political unity is a practical goal. Thus "the call to unite the Arabs . . . is the practical step which must precede the call for pan-Islamism." This special position of the Arabs in Islam, al-Bazzaz maintains, does not threaten the Arabs who are not Moslems or the Moslems who are not Arabs.

The second conception is well expressed in a book[10] (written in English and published in America) by Hazem Zaki Nuseibeh, a Jordanian who studied in the United States and later became a high civil servant in his own country. Nuseibeh, cautiously approaching Islam as a "factor in Arab nationalism," finds religion now discarded as an element of Arab unity because of the importance of the Christian Arabs in the nationalist movement and the fear that religion is a barrier to modernization. He does not, however, minimize the importance of Islam to Arabs. "Not only is Islam the greatest fact in the Arabs' national history thus far," he asserts, "but their entire civilization has arisen and has developed within its all-embracing doctrines." It is, therefore, on the ground of expediency that Nuseibeh excludes Islam among the elements making for unity among Arabs. Indeed, it has, in his view as a Moslem, become a divisive influence among Arabs. He therefore insists that, in the Arab world as in Europe, "in order to forge a progressive and homogeneous nation, religion must be taken out of politics. . . . What is involved is whether or not the non-Moslems are to participate as full citizens and without any disabilities on account of their creeds, in the conduct of national life. This they cannot do if religion is the axis around which public life revolves." In this view he is joined, of course, by Christian Arabs but also by a growing number of Moslem thinkers.

Practically, the issue of separation of "church" and "state" is already settled in the Arab Moslem world: they are separated in fact, irrespective of doctrine or fundamentalist aspirations. The real issue is twofold: (1) to what extent

10 Nuseibeh, esp. pp. 88–97.

will the secular nationalists have to continue to appeal to religious loyalty to mobilize mass support for their foreign and domestic policies, and (2) to what extent will religious loyalty prove a barrier to the modernization goals of the nationalists? On the first point, the political leaders will undoubtedly continue to call upon Islamic sympathies in arousing feeling against Western—or other foreign—influence. On the domestic front, they will continue to suppress the political forms of Islamic fundamentalism while seeking at the same time to divert the religious attachments of the masses into non-political channels and to substitute secular loyalties more in harmony with nationalist goals. As to the second issue, Islam has not been, nor is it likely to become, a serious barrier to modernization in the sense that its values positively prevent modernization or that religious leaders seek to arouse the masses against it. Rather, Islam, like other religions, encourages its believers to occupy themselves with thoughts and actions of a spiritual kind, from which they must be wrenched if those values are to be developed which are required for economic development, national power, and social welfare through the apparatus of the state.

The Soviet Union: Catalyst and Model

Into the political and spiritual ferment of Arab life after World War II has come a new element, a Soviet Union which has demonstrated its power in international affairs and its internal strength owing to rapid industrialization under state socialism. In the new situation of the 1950s, the Soviet Union stood out as a catalyst and a model for the most cherished goals of Arab leadership: independence of the West, and domestic economic strength through industrialization. On the first goal, Russia was, of course, in sympathy with the Arabs and eager to play the role of catalyst in pushing the West out of the Near East. On the second, Russia was equally eager to have the less developed countries of Asia and Africa look to it as a model of economic and social modernization through its version of socialism. "Neutralism" in international relations and "socialism" at home have thus been erected by Arab leaders into guiding principles. I put both concepts between quotation marks because Arab neutralism has not always been neutral and Arab socialism has not been socialistic in a familiar way.

Before World War I, Russia's interest in the Near East was directed toward Turkey and Iran, two Moslem but non-Arab countries. It had had little contact with the Arab world until the Bolshevik Revolution stimulated the growth of Communist parties in many regions, including the Arab countries. The establishment of these parties under the guidance of the international Communist movement made the Soviet Union, as the ruling force in that movement, adopt some kind of policy toward the Arab world. This policy has usually been one aspect of a broader one toward the whole of Asia and Africa, the "pre-capitalist" world which we now call the "underdeveloped areas." As revolutionaries and internationalists, the Bolshevik rulers of Soviet Russia were at first unsympathetic toward Asian nationalism, which they considered "bourgeois" and tied to Western capitalist imperialism. In this period several other influences combined to turn Soviet leaders away from Asia and the Arab world. First, they were still trying to consolidate Bolshevik leadership in Russia and to establish it in Western Europe. Second, their ideology and political experiences made them emphasize the class struggle rather than nationalist revolt. Third, they hesitated to stress Asian nationalism for fear it might stimulate nationalist separatism among the Asian nations within the Soviet Union. Bolshevik uncertainty over Asian nationalism colored the statement of policy adopted in 1920 by the Second Congress of the Communist International, at which Lenin disagreed with those who wanted to write off nationalism. At his insistence it was proclaimed that: "The Communist International must be ready to establish temporary relationships and even alliances with the bourgeois democracy of the colonies and backward countries. It must not, however, amalgamate with it." This was to be a tactical move during a period when proletarian parties had not yet been created in these agrarian societies. To put the compromise in a better light for international revolutionaries, Lenin later explained that it had been unanimously agreed, too, that "we should speak of the national-revolutionary and not of the 'bourgeois-democratic' movements."[11]

As if to hedge against this compromise, the Communist International held, shortly after its Second Congress, a special meeting at Baku, which had just been the scene of the announcement of a federated Soviet Socialist Republic in Transcaucasia. In inviting representatives of the "enslaved peoples of Persia, Armenia, and Turkey," that is, a largely Moslem area, the Comintern said the meeting's purpose was to discuss how the European proletariat might join the Asian nationalist movement in "the struggle against the common enemy," identified plainly as the "British, French, and American capitalists." Fresh from the victory in Baku earlier that year, the meeting called for the establishment of soviet regimes in this Moslem area bordering Soviet Transcaucasia. Aware, however, that the Soviet form was associated with an industrial proletariat, the meeting hastened to add that it was "also the only suitable type of organization for the toiling masses in general."[12] With the general decline in the Soviet Union's active intervention in foreign countries during the 1920s and 1930s came a supreme effort to consolidate the internal power of the Communist regime and of its leader, Stalin. During this period, the Moslem areas in the Soviet Union were subjected to extraordinary pressure to destroy their religious life and separatist inclinations, to cut them off from the rest of the Moslem world.

Until World War II the Soviet Union had practically no direct contact with the Arab world (as distinct from the Moslem regions). Communist leaders gave little attention to Arab nationalism, a movement they believed to be

[11] See the relevant documents in Eudin and North, pp. 65, 68–69.

[12] See documents in *ibid.*, pp. 79–81.

controlled and used by the British. During the war the
Soviet Union, now an ally of the capitalist West, was permitted to establish diplomatic missions in Cairo, Beirut,
and Baghdad, which enabled Soviet representatives to
carry out a considerable number of political and commercial assignments as well. The creation of the United Nations and the onset of the cold war between the Western
democracies and the Soviet bloc greatly increased the importance of the "uncommitted" areas of the Near East,
Asia, and Africa, which were becoming independent of
various forms of Western control and seeking allies to
hasten the process. When Stalin died in 1953, the Russian leaders turned toward their highly successful policy of
supporting movements for independence directed against
Western powers. Without concerning themselves with arid
problems of Marxist or Leninist doctrine, they have helped
liberals, communists, reactionaries, kings, feudal lords—
anyone able to embarrass or weaken the West through
nationalist claims or revolutions.

Applied to the Arab world, this policy enjoyed great
success from 1955 to 1959. Under it the Soviet Union
was able to give considerable diplomatic, military, and economic aid to Arab countries and thus to help weaken the
position of the West in the Near East, to win great prestige
there, and to gain the diplomatic support of the Arab countries in that part of the cold war that is waged in the roll
calls at the U.N.

The Soviet Union has given substantial military aid to
Egypt and Syria since 1955 and began to send similar assistance to Iraq after its revolution in July 1958. Commercially, it increased both its exports to and imports from
Egypt and Syria and then Iraq. Economically, during the
four years following the arms agreement with Egypt in
1955, the Soviet bloc (including China and the European
members) agreed to deliver arms, machinery, materials,
and technical aid totaling over a billion dollars to Egypt,
Syria and Iraq. This was more than the United States
was willing to promise them and more, too, than it was
ready to supply to Israel and Turkey. In fact, the Soviet

Union concentrated more economic and military funds in Egypt and Syria than the United States was giving all of the Arab world.[13] Included was the agreement, made in the fall of 1958, to finance and provide technical aid for the first stage of the construction of a high dam at Aswan, a project that has been of great importance to the world as well as Egypt. It was when the United States announced, in the summer of 1956, that it could not agree to help finance the dam, that Nasser nationalized the Suez Canal, which was followed in the fall by the Israeli, British, and French attack upon Egypt. Psychologically, too, the dam has meant a great deal as a symbol to the entire Arab world of Egypt's capacity to carry through with the aid of powerful sponsors so bold a project and one so essential to the country's economy.

In diplomacy, the Soviet Union has given considerable support to Arab nationalist goals. When Egypt nationalized the Canal, the Soviet Union and its allies were the stanchest defenders of the move after the Arabs themselves. During the attack upon the Suez Canal, the Soviet bloc likewise gave Egypt strong diplomatic and propaganda support and even threatened military reprisals against Egypt's enemies. During 1957 and especially in the summer of 1958 in the Lebanese and Iraqi crises, the Soviet bloc supported nationalist goals.

Culturally and ideologically, too, relations between the Soviet bloc and the leading Arab countries, Egypt, Syria, and Iraq, flourished. Hundreds of young Arabs went to study science and technology in the Soviet Union and East Europe. An endless procession of cultural missions, dancers, singers, actors, flowed into Egypt and Syria. Russian literature, Marxist classics, and communist propaganda flooded the bookshops and kiosks in Egypt, Syria, and Iraq and took up the lion's share of the sidewalk space of the street vendors of books, magazines and

[13] *The Mutual Security Program, Fiscal Year 1961*. The President's Message to Congress on the Mutual Security Program, United States Government Printing Office, Washington, D.C., 1960, p. 6.

newspapers. Socialism, communism, the welfare state, "socialist realism"—all the cultural and ideological accompaniments to communism filled the press of these countries as hundreds of intellectuals made pilgrimages to the new Meccas in Russia, China, and Eastern Europe. The high point of the new co-operation between international communism and Arab nationalism came in the last week of 1957 with the convening of the Afro-Asian Peoples' Conference in Cairo. Hundreds of delegates came from the two continents, some representing governments, some only themselves, but the vast majority speaking for a variety of organizations friendly to Russia and international communism. The Conference adopted a large number of resolutions in harmony with Soviet policies and then established an Afro-Asian Peoples' Solidarity Council whose permanent secretariat, headed by Egyptians, was located in Cairo.

The greatest sensation was created by the leader of the Russian delegation, a Moslem with a Russianized Arabic name, who reminded the assemblage that his country, after taking over private enterprise and repudiating its foreign debts, began to industrialize so rapidly that in forty years it had multiplied its productive capacity thirty-three times. What the Soviet Union did, he went on, the underdeveloped world today could also do, presumably by similar methods, and more easily. "Today," he said, "the nations of Africa and Asia are in a more favorable position than the U.S.S.R. was forty years ago. The highly developed capitalist countries now no longer have a monopoly of equipment, nor of machines, credit or scientific and technical experience." The Soviet Union, with its rockets, sputniks, and achievements in the use of nuclear energy, has demonstrated the great value of socialism. All this apparatus, the Soviet delegate assured his listeners and the rest of the world, his country was ready to put at the disposal of the Afro-Asian peoples without seeking any gain for itself. "We can build you a factory or a transportation system, a research center or a university, a hospital or a cultural institute. We can send you our technicians to study your problems, and you can send yours to our enterprises and research centers. We can send our teachers to teach in your schools, or you can send your students to our institutions. Do what you think best for yourselves. Tell us your needs and we are ready to give you any kind of assistance, whether through credits, technical aid, or by any other means. We do not want profits, privileges, a share in the management, concessions, or raw materials. We do not ask you to join any bloc, to change your government or your internal or foreign policy. We come to help you as a brother helps brother, without any axe to grind. We know from our own experience how difficult it is to emerge from poverty. Our only condition is to help you without condition."[14]

It is doubtful that Arab leaders took such statements at face value; in fact, the student and cultural missions were greatly reduced in size. Nevertheless Soviet scientific achievements, diplomatic victories over the West, and promises of aid continued to be rather uncritically praised or accepted in most of the Arab press and by official spokesmen. For a long time it had been felt in the West that the Arab and Islamic world would resist even the slightest Soviet penetration. It soon became clear that this was not the case. The Soviet Union's espousal of atheism was soft-pedaled in order not to hurt the feelings of religious Moslems. At the same time a large proportion of articulate Arabs of the younger generation were not seriously religious anyway. Moreover, the Soviet Union made a great show of the freedom of Moslems inside its territory, ignoring the long years of suppression of Islam or concealing their effects. Indeed, the fact that Soviet Russia avows atheism is in some sense an advantage to it, for Moslems do not fear from it the kind of Christian propaganda and proselytism they have resented on the part of the Western powers. The Soviet emphasis upon state power does not violate the political conceptions in the Near East, which has been accustomed to authoritar-

[14] Jargy, p. 65.

ian governments. Finally, the new Soviet imperialism, deeply felt in Europe, has not seriously penetrated Arab consciousness because Russia had not been politically influential in the Arab world before 1955. It was the Western powers, notably Britain and France, that the Arabs had known as imperialists. For these reasons the Arabs and Moslems have feared and resented the declining imperialism of Western democracies more than they have the thriving imperialism of the Soviet totalitarian state.

Resistance to Russian influence, however, was not long in developing once the Soviets became deeply involved in the Arab world in 1955. It was in Syria that the Soviet Union came closest to success, and it was over Syria that the Arabs felt their first disillusionment with the U.S.S.R. For a long time the Communists in Syria had been in the best position of any Arab Communist party. They had good leadership, strength, and a fertile field in which to implant friendship for the U.S.S.R., distrust for the weak and changing regimes, and confidence in themselves. During 1957 it looked as if the Syrian Communists, with or without Russian approval, were moving rapidly to a point from which they might be able to take power. The leading political forces, feeling themselves in danger of destruction from pro-Soviet communism and perhaps pro-Western intervention by Turkey and Iraq, suddenly accelerated long-standing plans for Arab union by asking Egypt to unite with Syria in a single state. This was done early in 1958. If the Russians had hesitated to encourage the Communists to take power in Syria, they had no doubt that the new United Arab Republic would suppress the strongest Communist movement in the Arab world. They overcame their pique at the unexpected turn of events and the blow to their allies, and granted recognition several weeks later.

During the first half of 1958 Communist activity was forced underground in Syria where Nasser outlawed political parties as he had in Egypt several years before. When the revolution in Iraq was successful in July 1958, Arab Communists found a new base there, for they had long worked for the overthrow of the pro-British regime, which commanded no popular support in any case. Then a struggle began in the Iraqi revolutionary government between those who wanted greater Arab unity through some kind of federation or even a single state with the newly-formed United Arab Republic and those, led by the dominant officers group and the powerful Communists, who feared that such unity would mean the end of political parties in Iraq too.

At this point, in the early fall of 1958, the latter forces began a concerted propaganda attack upon Nasser and an effort to swing Syria from Egypt to the new Iraq. Nationalist pro-Nasser groups in Iraq were also active as each side tried to undermine the other. Syria became the battle-ground, and it was over Syria, primarily, that Nasser openly criticized the Soviet Union late in 1958 and then more severely the following spring. He did so only reluctantly, for Egypt was getting much aid from the U.S.S.R. and was on very bad terms with the West. As Nasser put it in a speech in the spring of 1959: "We tried by all means not to make the local activities by Arab Communists in Iraq or Syria a reason for any clash with the Soviet Union as long as the Soviet Union did not interfere in our affairs. We were trying to convince ourselves that the Communist parties in our countries were independent from international communism. We found out that they were not independent. . . . They carry out orders and instructions for the liquidation of patriotic and nationalist elements in order to place our country inside the zones of Communist influence."

Russians, Nasser asserted, called for freedom for Communist parties in the Arab world, but when the Communists took power in Russia in 1917 they outlawed all other political parties. Nasser went so far as to insist that the Soviet Union did not offer so much support to Egypt during the Suez affair in 1956 as had been assumed. It gave "moral and spiritual help" but so did Afro-Asian countries and "free men in Britain" as well as Europe and

elsewhere. As for military assistance, which the world believed was offered by Russia, Nasser denied Communist
boasts and insisted that Egyptians "were relying on God
and on ourselves only" during the Suez war: "But from
October 29 to November 6 [the last day of fighting] we
received no hint from any country, except Syria, that it
was prepared to stand by our side in the battle."[15]

These criticisms of the Soviet Union were accompanied
by strict suppression of all Communist and Communist-
front activity in Egypt and Syria and by a strong reaction
in Lebanon and Jordan as well. Even in Iraq in 1959 it
appeared that the Communists were losing influence, but
they were not suppressed and there was no criticism of
the Soviet Union. The Soviet Union itself, as in other
cases, soon dropped its open support of Arab Communists
and continued its proper diplomatic and economic relations with the United Arab Republic. At the very time
Nasser was having serious doubts about the trustworthi-
ness of the Russians—the fall of 1958—they finally promised, after several years of holding the Egyptians in sus-
pense, to help in the first stage of the construction of the
Aswan dam. In January of 1960 the work began, and the
Russians announced that they would provide help in the
second stage too. These moves were interpreted as evidence
that Russia does not withhold promised aid because it is
criticized; participation in the project also assured the Russians of continuing importance in the economy of Egypt
and of the presence of many Russians there for many
years.

The difficulties caused in the Arab world by the connection between the Soviet Union and international communism will arise again. Arab relations with the Western
powers will also continue to vary. But short of the advent
of outright Communist regimes, the earlier adulation of
the U.S.S.R. in the Arab world is not likely to return.
Russian influence will remain, for the country is too powerful to be excluded from areas it considers vital to its in-

[15] *The Egyptian Gazette*, March 31, 1959, pp. 2, 4.

terests, and the greater its power the more such areas there are. But the Arab countries seem to be settling down to a more stable and moderate relationship with the U.S.S.R. in which they will strive to keep on good terms and obtain aid but will not again willingly swing so close to the Soviet orbit as to be almost pulled in. The Soviet Union in its turn will continue to exert pressure upon Arabs toward "neutralism" in foreign affairs and "socialism" in the effort to promote economic development and social welfare—and to weaken Arab ties with the West.

Neutralism and Afro-Asian Solidarity

Until now the Soviet Union's greatest gain in the Arab world has been the withdrawal of Western influence and the "neutralist" policy of the Arab states in international relations. This policy has been exercised largely in the United Nations and received its most characteristic expression in the conference of Afro-Asian states at Bandung, in 1955. The meeting made a great impression on Nasser, who found himself highly regarded among the leaders of the many countries seeking independence and modernization. Egypt played a leading role at the conference, where Nasser met the heads of governments that, like his own, were looking for models of change, for allies, and for assistance. The Arabs as a group were buoyed by the prominence of their most famous spokesman and by the sense of solidarity they felt in the company of so many other peoples facing problems similar to their own.

In this atmosphere "neutralism" and Afro-Asian "solidarity" went together and attained the character of an ideology. They meant the strength of numbers—votes in the U.N. and millions of people. They meant righteous rejection of Western influence and control, and a sense of power and dignity, as the leaders of the Afro-Asian states dealt with one another as important equals. Whatever political advantages may be derived from neutralism, it has a psychological dimension as well, though it is of course related to the political motive. Neutralism has given Arab countries the opportunity to be courted and flattered, to be considered worth the concern of the big powers after centuries of being their pawns when they were noticed at all.

Egypt has displayed this feeling most intensely and consistently. Shortly after the evacuation of the Suez Canal zone by the British and French late in 1956, an English-language publication in Cairo reviewed Egypt's "strategy" in international affairs. As a country that would "face the threat of immediate occupation" in the event of war between the great powers, "one of Egypt's principal political objectives is *to do everything in her power to prevent a major war.*" The Egyptian and Arab policy of "non-integration" with the two major blocs "supplies the greatest deterrent to a war."[16] This confidence in the power of a neutralist Asia and Africa was characteristically expressed by Anwar El Sadat, one of the twelve officers who led the successful movement against the Egyptian monarchy in 1952. Speaking to the Afro-Asian Peoples' Conference in 1957 as head of the Egyptian delegation and presiding officer of the meeting, he proclaimed: "Gone forever is the era when the future of war and peace was decided in a few European capitals. Today we have the power to determine that future, for our weight in the international scale is great. . . . War is impossible if we insist upon peace. . . . Though the neutrality in which we believe means avoidance of international blocs, it also means exerting a positive effort to reconcile these blocs. In this way do we in Egypt understand our responsibilities to the family of nations."[17]

Arabs delight in their new prominence in world affairs.

[16] *The Egyptian Economic and Political Review*, Vol. 3, No. 6, Feb. 1957, special section, "The Strategy of Egyptian Defense," p. III. (Emphasis in original.)

[17] *Afro-Asian People's Conference, 26 December 1957–1st January 1958. Inaugural Addresses. Resolutions. Closing Addresses*, Permanent Secretariat, Cairo, n.d., pp. 9–10 in Arabic, p. 11 in English.

When the Commander-in-Chief of the U.A.R. army returned from Russia in 1958 with its promise of assistance on the Aswan dam, a leading Cairo newspaper welcomed him back in an editorial: "Field Marshal Abdel Hakim Amer returned to the fatherland yesterday from a trip of more than ten days during which he succeeded in discussions which dazzled the whole world and focussed its attention upon Cairo . . ."[18]

During a single week early in 1959 the following world figures were all present in Cairo: the president of the World Bank, the secretary general of the U.N., and the prime ministers of Lebanon, Italy, and East Germany. The visits of such personages lends weight to the belief, assiduously fostered in Cairo, that Egypt and the Arabs are important enough to influence and perhaps even to check the cold war. In the same vein, President Nasser told the 1960 meeting of the U. N. General Assembly, when many heads of state were present, that the leaders of the U.S.S.R. and the United States should immediately meet to reduce international tension. He was an active member of a small group of leaders, including those of such more prominent countries as India and Yugoslavia, who sought to play a very influential role between the two major powers.

Afro-Asian solidarity and neutralism are ideologies that have emerged from a belief among the less powerful nations that they must have their own bloc while denouncing the existence of blocs; the realization that their goals and needs have much in common; their sense of exploitation by the West and consequent distrust of it; and their understandable desire to use the cold war to the best advantage for themselves.

The Arab form of these twin ideologies went through many years of incubation in the heat of the discussion of Arab nationalism even before World War II. Under the control of Britain and France, the Arab states could hardly convert such ideas into policy, and they remained inchoate

[18] *al-Ahram* (Cairo), October 28, 1958, p. 5.

although efforts were made to capitalize first on the disputes and then on the war between the Allies and Germany. With the emergence of several more independent Arab states and the creation of the United Nations, neutralism and Afro-Asian solidarity were more sharply defined and then regularly applied as the cold war between the American-West European bloc and the Soviet-Chinese bloc intensified.

Early in this period Dr. Constantine K. Zurayk, a leading Syrian intellectual, expressed, in a searching self-examination following the defeat of the Arab armies in Palestine in 1948, the prevailing mood for a realistic neutralism and solidarity. The "great nations," he pointed out, "have in our country important interests over which we can bargain in order to obtain our goals . . ." The Arabs, however, must be careful to establish proper conditions in this relationship:

> One of these conditions is that the exchange should not be motivated by feeling, "traditional friendship," or "natural alliance," for in most cases these are only snares and traps which conceal greed and mask exploitation and colonization. The only basis for this exchange in the world of current international transactions is self-interest, nothing else. Thus another condition is that the price of any interest that is conceded must be the safeguarding of a corresponding interest. For instance we should not ally ourselves with the democratic states against the Communist states or persecute leftist parties in our country for no benefit or for the sake of friendship, or because of mere impotence.[19]

As to the idea of solidarity among Arab and Afro-Asian states, the author criticized Arab efforts in foreign affairs

[19] Zurayk, *The Meaning of Disaster*, pp. 27–28. There is here a hint of that disillusionment, referred to earlier, of Arab liberals with the West. They appeared to be shocked at discovering that the West had not only a liberal side but also followed its conceptions of national interest, a side that appeared rather less liberal to the Arabs.

as last-minute improvisations instead of careful, long-range programs. He stressed the necessity to improve relations not merely with the great powers:

> . . . there are other states with whom relations must be strengthened, such as the Latin American States. Despite the fact that most of these nations are subservient to American influence and Zionist pressure, it is not right to neglect them or give them up entirely. There are also the Asian nations further to the east who share with us the dangers of Western imperialism, who have looked with favor on our case and have assisted us, and with whom we must strengthen our relations in order to make this assistance secure and to fortify it. It is unfortunate that our ties with these nations are still weak, and do not on the whole go beyond contact between our delegations and theirs at international conferences at times when the danger becomes acute and when other powers ally themselves against us.[20]

Neutralism and Afro-Asian solidarity gained support in the Arab world after 1948 from several sources: the West's diplomatic and economic aid to Israel; the increase in Communist influence in Syria, Egypt and Iraq; and the Egyptian revolution of 1952, following which Nasser emerged as the most prominent spokesman for Arab nationalism. As a completely independent state, no longer occupied by Britain, Egypt was in a position to lead the Arabs toward the application of these ideas in world politics. Under the impact of Arab resentment against Western attempts to bring the Near East into military alliance, culminating in the Baghdad Pact in 1955, the Bandung Conference a few months later brought Egypt to the point where it converted the ideology of neutralism and Afro-Asian solidarity into a full-fledged policy. With such powerful pressure in that direction, the other Arab states had to move along to some extent until even Lebanon and Jordan took steps in 1957 and 1958, following the Anglo-

[20] *Ibid.*, pp. 19–20.

French-Israeli attack upon Egypt, to reduce Western influence further. The 1958 revolution in Iraq, which had previously talked the ideology without practicing it, brought that country's policy into line with that of Egypt and Syria (by then already unified in the United Arab Republic). Since then there have been some backing and filling and serious differences among the Arab states, but there is no question about the commitment to neutralism in the sense of refusal to align with the West, a large measure of agreement with the Soviet bloc in international questions, and Afro-Asian solidarity as a counter-weight to the two major blocs led by the U.S.S.R. and the United States.

Socialism and Social Reform

Socialist ideas have pervaded the Arab world since the advent after World War II of the new nationalists in Egypt, Syria, and Iraq. Even in Lebanon and Jordan the same mood has enveloped intellectuals and publicists although the government spokesmen do not yet share their rhetoric. For several years Nasser has spoken of the intention to build in Egypt (and then in the U.A.R.) a "socialist, co-operative, democratic society." In visits to several Arab countries in 1958 and 1959 I found many professors, writers, journalists, students, and government officials eager to discuss socialism. Indeed, an Egyptian who had just been appointed to one of the highest posts in the Ministry of Foreign Affairs was more interested, I found in talking with him, in socialism than in international relations. After we had thrashed out several issues, he said with determination: "Look, let me ask you three questions, and I want you to give me brief and direct answers. What is your attitude toward the class struggle, socialization of property, and dialectical materialism?" The situation today, throughout the Arab world, is far from what it was a generation ago when a prominent literary man complained that the Egyptian writer had no freedom of political belief because socialism could not count a single champion.[21]

There have been three sources of Arab socialist ideas. First, many Arabs studied in the West where, especially in England and France, they came under the influence of teachers and writers who expressed moderate to extreme socialist notions, chiefly with regard to domestic economic policy concerning the welfare of the working class, and a mild anti-colonialism. A later source was the U.S.S.R. itself, with its great emphasis on national power through state ownership and its full-scale attack on Western interests in Asia and Africa. Finally, current Arab socialism can draw somewhat on its native antecedents. Thus many of the socialist ideas of Nasser and the Arab Ba'th (Resurrection) Socialist party may be found in the Ahali ("All-Peoples") party in Iraq in the early 1930s. The main difference is the greater emphasis socialists give to Arab nationalism today.

Though there has been an Arab socialist movement not tied to the Soviet Union, Arab socialism cannot be considered apart from the position of that country as the model of rapid industrialization and rise to national power and as the catalyst for much of the underdeveloped world. As we have already seen, the Soviet Union as a state did not exert much influence in the Arab Near East until the middle of the 1950s. Prior to that, international communism, controlled by Soviet Russia under Stalin, had had contact with the weak and divided leftist movements but not with the mainstream of Arab nationalism, which the Communists considered merely "reformist," bourgeois and under the thumb of the British.[22] After Stalin's death in 1953, the leaders of the U.S.S.R. and world communism adopted a more favorable attitude toward the nationalist movements and the new states in Asia and Africa. The resulting favorable image of Russia in the Arab world gave socialism, as Arabs understood it, great prestige. With re-

[21] Farès, p. 230.
[22] On the Soviet Union and international Communism in the Arab world, see the full accounts in Laqueur.

spect to international politics, the new friendship between Russia and several Arab countries was made possible by the worsening of relations between the Arabs and the West as the United States, Britain, and France tried to push them into alliances against the Soviet Union, a danger of which the Arabs had no immediate and direct experience. The Soviet's prestige in the Arab world was also enhanced when it adopted a consistent anti-Israel policy after having first supported Israel and then rather ignored it. With respect to internal Arab developments, the Soviet-Arab friendship was facilitated by the emergence of new groups to power and influence in Egypt, Syria, and (later) Iraq, and the increase in the power of corresponding groups in Jordan and Lebanon. These groups were the army officers, professionals, civil servants, and a small number of business men and manufacturers—all of them without ties and obligations to either the Western powers and Western economic interests, or to the old native ruling groups based on landed wealth and connections with the West. Seeking to make the Arab world strong, modern, and united, they had little hesitation in looking upon the Soviet Union and socialist programs in a new light.

These new middle groups moving into positions of power found socialism and even communism attractive. The Marxist critique of capitalism, although no longer appropriate to the West after a century of democracy, economic growth, and social reform, seemed to them to be an accurate description of their own society. Intellectuals, especially, adopted a new attitude toward the West. Up to World War II the West had appeared in the Arab world as conqueror and as dangerous innovator in political and social relations. But with the prominence of Soviet Russia and Communist China, this image faded. The Arabs, reaching for a new conception of themselves, began to see the West as weak, retreating before the new and greater power of the Communist world led by Russia. The Arab intellectuals, seeking innovation, now had before them an even more revolutionary model which made the West, with its capitalism, moderate socialism and religion, seem conservative and old-fashioned. A generation ago Arabs had criticized the West for its secularism and irreligion. Now they began to criticize the West as traditional. The younger intellectuals, reaching positions of influence in the universities, schools, press, and even the government, switched their basis of opposition to the West from a religious to a positivist one, but their strong nationalism remained. The Soviet Union's rise was to them a daily demonstration of Western decline. Socialism and communism, then, even if not accompanied by pro-Russian sentiment, enabled the Arab intellectual to do two things he needed very much to do: to reject the West in the name of a progressive Arab nationalism, and at the same time to reject his own tradition, with its weakness and stagnation, in the name of social progress.

For many years it has been necessary to distinguish socialism from communism in the Arab world because, as in the West, there have been Arab socialists who opposed communism. In the late 1950s, however, it became even more important to do so, not because of the rival movements but because several *governments* proclaimed socialist goals while rejecting communism. We must ask, therefore, what it means to say, as many observers have, that "communism" is "gaining" in the Arab world. First, the Arab states have become increasingly neutralist, as we have seen, and this has meant that they have tended to vote with the Afro-Asian group in the United Nations. Egypt and Syria first individually and then together in the U.A.R., and Iraq since 1958 have gone farthest along this road, though Lebanon and Jordan have gone a considerable distance as well. This has usually put them at the side of the Soviet Union in international politics, deliberately or by coincidence. Second, since 1955 several Arab countries have sought and accepted military and economic aid from the Soviet bloc, and Egypt, for a time, tied its enonomy very closely to the Soviet's. Third, with the increase in its power and its technological advances, the Soviet Union's prestige in the Arab world has grown, in most cases with the enthusiastic backing of the governments themselves.

Fourth, the Arab countries have been increasingly impressed with Soviet economic growth and have been willing to consider adopting similar methods. Fifth, for a time Egypt and then Iraq allowed or encouraged the growth of domestic Communist influence in political and cultural life, through the local Communists and their front groups as well as through various types of Soviet-bloc missions, while deliberately excluding Western influences.

Undoubtedly the Soviet Union and international communism have gained ground in the Near East but, as this brief summary suggests, there are several aspects of this development that must be distinguished if we are to assess it properly. Arab voting in the U.N. and greater Soviet prestige in the Arab world are reflections of the bad relations between the West and the Arabs, the rise of Afro-Asian consciousness, and the impact of a powerful Soviet Union. All the world has been affected by these facts, and they do not mean that the Arabs are "going communist." Soviet aid to several Arab states and the growing interest in the U.S.S.R. as a model for industrialization have put Egypt and Iraq into a very close relationship with the U.S.S.R. and strengthened certain wings in both governments which have wanted to go much further. Egypt, as we have already seen, has succeeded in retreating somewhat from its extreme position and even Iraq has been able to avoid going the whole way to becoming a satellite economically or politically. A considerable increase in the Soviet Union's influence through economic and military aid was to be expected once its leaders chose to adopt that policy, but willingness to accept such aid must not be interpreted as readiness to "accept" communism in all respects. The desire of the new regimes in Africa and Asia for economic development and the modernization of their institutions are so great, and the example and power of the Soviet Union so persuasive, that it is difficult for the needy to reject offers from so prominent a source. The most serious evidence that the Arabs have been "going Communist" comes from the impact of these four aspects combined and from the fifth, the permission or encouragement of Communist and Soviet activity by several Arab regimes from time to time. It went furthest in the U.A.R. and Iraq but has receded considerably in both. Except in the case of a country actually succumbing to local Communist groups, which has not occurred even in Iraq, it is doubtful that the Arab states will voluntarily become more deeply involved with the U.S.S.R. than they have until now. After a period of heady attraction, they are now in a period of sober reconsideration out of which an equilibrium is likely to emerge in which they will try to maintain good relations with the Soviet Union and accept its aid but avoid becoming satellites. There are groups in the Arab regimes that believe that the combination of Russia and China will triumph in the cold—and any hot—war against the combination of Europe and America, but thus far they have not been able to achieve power or convince those who hold it.

The Arab regimes most friendly to the U.S.S.R. in the past now distinguish between socialism and communism and speak of their goals as socialist. The two leading spokesmen for this position have been President Nasser of Egypt, and the Ba'th (Resurrection) Socialist party. Socialism was not precisely defined in Nasser's statements but it means the use of the state apparatus to achieve public welfare through industrialization, agrarian reform and protective social legislation. The decision to rely on the state itself rather than upon incentives to private enterprise and voluntary co-operatives was revealed in the nationalization decrees summarized in Chapter 6.

Although never in power, the leading Arab socialist party, the Ba'th, has advanced a radical and consistent socialist program which nevertheless is still somewhat vague in its economic principles but yields to no group in the vigor of its Arab nationalism.[23] This party quickly achieved considerable influence in Syria, Lebanon, Jordan, and Iraq, but the more recent trend toward the elimina-

[23] On the Ba'th party, see its constitution in *The Middle East Journal* (1959), 13:195–200, 487–89.

tion of political contests has hurt it very much. The Ba'th party in Syria favored unity with Egypt in the U.A.R. early in 1958; as a result it lost its right to separate existence in the new state. In Iraq after the revolution of 1958 it was suppressed as pro-Egyptian, and in Lebanon and Jordan it leads a clandestine existence. The Ba'th position was influential in the U.A.R., for it combined socialist, neutralist, and nationalist ideas rather congenial to the regime though a bit too doctrinaire to suit it perfectly. The leading Ba'th intellectuals sought to supply a firmer ideological base for the U.A.R.; their success did not, however, extend to the organizational side.

Socialism has been made compatible with Arab nationalism and even with reformist Islam by the ideologues of both movements. In the period between the two world wars the small leftist groups in the Arab world were founded, led and populated by members of minorities such as Armenians, Jews, and Greeks. As international communism made its peace with Asian nationalism, and as Arab nationalism in particular grew rapidly as the leading ideology, the members of minorities dropped out and Arabs (Moslem and Christian) assumed direction—socialism, like so much else, had become nationalized.

The nationalization of Arab socialism has meant something else too: the emphasis upon national strength rather than individual welfare. Arab leftists are, of course, concerned with raising the standard of living of the population but socialism is to them primarily a means by which the Arabs can best achieve nationalist goals of unity and industrial and military strength. The rise in the standard of living is deemed important because national strength today requires a people who are educated and capable of adapting to a highly technological system. In emphasizing acquisition by the society as a whole while being suspicious of individual enrichment, the Arab socialists in and out of power face a fundamental contradiction which Bertrand de Jouvenel has aptly pointed out with respect to Western socialism. They seek to encourage people to value material goods highly but not for themselves, only for the nation or state. As de Jouvenel asks, "If 'more goods' are the goal to which society's efforts are to be addressed, why should 'more goods' be a disreputable objective for the individual?"[24] The Arabs have indeed always been doubtful about private gain, yet have been characteristically unable to develop a morality of individual sacrifice for any group larger than those one knows intimately, or for the extended family, on whom one could make demands for reciprocity. That is why nationalist leaders find it necessary to exhort endlessly for work and sacrifice to build national strength; this has not been considered, in the past, a good reason why a man should exert himself. He might do without the fruit of his labor for the sake of his God or religion or his family, but not for his village, city, or nation, or their governments.

The socialist critique of Western society and its affirmative goals have increasingly appealed to religious modernists who seek to give contemporary relevance to Islamic traditions. As one writer recently pointed out, Islamic economic principles encourage individual initiative but stress co-operation and sharing and condemn the evils of capitalist (Western) exploitation.[25] Religious Islamic theory has been as capable as secular Arabism in adapting to modern nationalism, as Haim has shown in an acute analysis of the way in which both doctrines have treated such terms as nation, nationality, community, state, people, and liberty.[26]

Socialism is thus supplying the social content to Arab nationalism (and to some extent to Islamic modernism) which many critics have insisted that the ideology has lacked. Nuseibeh, a Jordanian political scientist familiar with Western thought, has described nationalist writings after the disappointments of World War I as a "bitter monotone distinguished more by what it opposes than by what it proposes." He asserts that these "negative traits in Arab nationalism" are the legacy of its struggle against

[24] De Jouvenel, pp. 11–12.
[25] El-Araby, *passim*.
[26] Haim, "Islam and the Theory of Arab Nationalism."

Western imperialism; the activities and attitudes necessary
to win independence are not those needed for the appreciation of constructive goals such as "freedom, account-
ability, and constitutional limitations" which, he argues,
had "figured so prominently" in the nationalist literature
before World War I.[27]

This kind of criticism of nationalism has come more
from Western than from Arab observers but rather frequently from both. Since World War I democracy has
been one of the stated nationalist goals. Once the nationalists achieved independence, however, they did not
find democracy a feasible system for countries with the
Arab political heritage and at their level of socio-economic
development. So democracy had to be dropped altogether,
or qualified as "economic" or anything but familiar political
democracy, or put off to the future when the nation
would be "ready" for it. Furthermore, democracy offered
no economic program, or it was identified with "capitalism," for which the new Arab leaders had no special attachment, or with "imperialism," which all Arabs abomi-
nated. Socialism, however, offered both a political and
an economic program of sorts. For the new rulers and the
intellectuals it supplied the "social content" they felt to
be lacking.

The most powerful spokesman for nationalism in recent
years, President Nasser, has shown awareness of this criticism. In an important speech at the end of 1959, for example, he adverted several times to the theme that Arab
nationalism was not only a political but also a social doctrine, that just as it had led the Arabs in the political
revolution for independence it could also point the way
to the social revolution for a higher standard of living.
Apparently responding, implicitly at least, to the nettling
charge of "negativism," he insisted that Arab nationalism
is a constructive doctrine.

Arab nationalism [he maintained] *. . . is a deep-seated
constructive idea, a progressive and changing idea. It rep-*

[27] Nuseibeh, pp. 55–56, 113–14.

resents the social revolution as well as the political revolution. . . . We want to achieve a socialist, democratic, cooperative society . . . We shall transform this social revolution into material fact . . . we shall work in the future . . . to prove to the whole world that Arab nationalism is a constructive movement, a social as well as a political revolution. . . . The time has come for Arab nationalism to prove that it has a progressive creed . . .[28]

The emphasis upon the "positive" and "constructive" aspects of nationalism, now that the "negative" task of defeating imperialism has been achieved, has added still another dimension to this dominant ideology. In the same speech Nasser adopted a humanistic tone reminiscent of the optimism and idealism of early Arab nationalist writings. Indeed, harking back more to the confidence of the European Enlightenment than to the realism and pessimism of the Arab tradition of political philosophy, Nasser told his listeners: "Human progress opens vistas before us which are without limits, and our backwardness in the past will not impede our progress in the present."

The early leftist parties did not see clearly the dependence of socialism upon nationalism in the Arab world. They were dominated by the internationalist ideology of Leninism. Soviet Russia itself, having just come into existence, was suppressing Asian nationalist movements within its borders, and made only half-hearted efforts to use them against the West. For several decades this attitude persisted. It was accompanied by a super-revolutionary pose among the leftist parties which stressed that nationalist goals could not be achieved securely without a "peasant revolution and the establishment of a workers' and peasants' government"[29]—a rather utopian conception given

---

[28] Speech at Port Said, December 23, 1959, text in *al-Jumhuriyah* (Cairo), December 24, 1959, p. 5, and in *The Egyptian Gazette*, December 24, 1959, p. 4.

[29] Resolution of Communist parties of Syria and Palestine, 1931, in Spector, pp. 80–81.

the indifference of the peasants to politics and ideology, and the minute size of the urban working class.

An early theorist pointed the way to a more realistic Communist program in the underdeveloped countries of Asia still under Western control but his ideas were condemned as nationalist deviations from Leninism. He was Mir Sayid Sultan Oglu, known as Sultan Galiev in Russian, a Moslem Tartar of Kazan who reached high posts during the early years of the Soviet Union until his arrest in 1923.[30] Upon his release from prison he did not return to politics and then disappeared entirely during the purges of 1936–38. Sultan Galiev set forth a special theory of Asian socialism. The Asian countries dominated by the West, he asserted, suffered exploitation at the hands of both their own rulers and the foreign imperialists. They were the real proletarians, the most exploited human beings in the world. Hence they were far more revolutionary, potentially, than the Western working class among whom Marxism developed. He insisted also upon the need for a special Communist International of the colonial world against the West including the latter's own working class, which participated in the exploitation of Asia. His Asian nationalism led Sultan Galiev to oppose even the suppression of Moslem and Asian nations within the Soviet Union, which made him a political as well as a doctrinal threat and ultimately caused his banishment.

Arab socialism today, deeply colored by nationalism, closely resembles Sultan Galiev's theories and attitudes. It does not, however, appear to have borrowed directly from him; rather, he emerges as a prophetic thinker whose notions are far more appropriate now than when he advanced them. It is now quite clear that the socialist governments which have come to power in Western Europe since World War I have not been so favorable to Asian nationalism as either Western or Asian socialists had expected; these governments, in the eyes of Asian leftists, have been

[30] This account of Sultan Galiev borrows from Bennigsen and from Walter Z. Laqueur, "Sultan Galiev's Ghost," *The New Leader*, February 3, 1958, pp. 10–11.

no less assiduous than the "capitalist" regimes in defending "imperialist" interests.

Asian socialism's suspicion of Western socialism was confirmed in 1953, when the socialist parties of Burma, India, and Indonesia sponsored a meeting at Rangoon which established the Asian Socialist Conference. It was remarkedly unfriendly to the Socialist International, composed mainly of Western socialist parties.[31] The greatest hostility to Western socialism was displayed by the Egyptian and Lebanese delegates, who also quit the meeting early because of the presence of an Israeli group. (The Egyptian, it turned out, did not represent a socialist party because there were at that time no political parties at all in Egypt.) The socialist parties of Iraq and Syria did not even send representatives. As a moderate Lebanese socialist writer has remarked concerning the gulf between Arab and Western socialism, ". . . the struggle against imperialism has, for the Arab Socialists, as much importance as the raising of wage-rates has for the American or European worker. They regard it as the acid test for any Socialism or even reformism. Hence the lack of sympathetic contact between the Ba'th and the European Socialist Parties, especially those of France and Britain, who are accused of overindulgence towards capital interests in the colonies."[32] In many conversations with Arab socialists I have heard the same criticism of Western socialism over and over again: it is lukewarm toward the nationalism of the Arab world and Asia and Africa. Arab socialists freely admit their own preoccupation with nationalism, which Western socialists find chauvinistic, but they insist this is putting first things first.

Arab liberal and socialist movements have often been weakened by the necessity of pursuing a policy of extreme nationalism. In Iraq, for example, a 1936 *coup d'etat* brought to power a coalition of politicians and the army with "unprecedented popularity and prestige," according

[31] On this conference, see Rose.
[32] Majdalany, p. 339.

to an Iraqi scholar who is now in the United States.[33] Though the new regime was aware that it must introduce "immediate and spectacular reforms" not merely because of the country's condition but also to retain public support, it soon found itself attacked for not displaying the customary enthusiasm for pan-Arabism. Criticism came from the extreme nationalists not only in Iraq but also in the other Arab countries. Within Iraq, attacks came also from the moderate nationalists who were suspicious of the liberal reformers. To maintain itself in power, the regime had to drop its reform proposals and yield to the nationalist pressures.

Only in the 1950s did Arab socialism, mainly in Syria, reach the point where it could even perceive that its nationalism and socialism might be in conflict. A leading Syrian socialist of the Ba'th party, Akram El Hourani, who later became a vice-president of the U.A.R. (until his resignation late in 1959), was asked in 1957: "You are a socialist and you are an Arab. With whom would you feel a closer affinity, a sheikh from Saudi Arabia or a socialist from the United Kingdom?" His answer was: "The Saudi Arabian sheikh without any question." Then he indicated that at least to him socialism was at the point where it could distinguish among various political elements in the West. "But," he added, "if you had asked whether I felt closer to a British socialist or a British conservative, then you would have got a different answer."[34]

International communism has come, since Sultan Galiev's time, to ally itself with Asian nationalism more wholeheartedly. This has been facilitated by the secularizing of Arab nationalism, so that its socialist wing has not been embarrassed by the Soviet suppression of Islam within its borders. The Moslems in the U.S.S.R. are not Arabs, hence a secular Arab nationalism finds no difficulty in overlooking their fate. Though Islam is still basic to

[33] Khadduri, *Independent Iraq*, p. 95 and Ch. 6.
[34] "Face to Face with Akram Hourani," interview with Tom Streithorst, *Middle East Forum* (Beirut), Vol. 32, No. 3 (March 1957), p. 33.

the nationalist feeling of the ordinary Moslem Arab, the Soviet Union and the Arab socialists who seek its guidance are able to count on the ordinary man's ignorance of the fate of Islam in Soviet Russia. Moreover, the U.S.S.R. has permitted the Moslems a modicum of religious freedom which is well publicized in the Near East and which some Arab leaders have praised to show that the power they have become friendly with is not anti-Moslem. So long as the Soviets do not challenge the power of the Arab leaders over their own people, this arrangement is convenient for both sides. Arab socialists can claim the prestige of the U.S.S.R. without embarrassment on the Moslem question, and the U.S.S.R. can pose as the great protector of Arab nationalism without fear of arousing Moslem nationalism within its own borders.

Sultan Galiev's prophetic view had to wait for two developments until Arab socialism could conform to its vision. First, the Soviet Union had to ally itself with the nationalism of Asia rather than seek, through the international communist movement, to establish "proletarian" regimes there. Second, Arab nationalism had to achieve victory, to express itself through governmental regimes in the international arena, and not merely through political parties and movements. This occurred during and just after World War II with the emergence of Syria, Lebanon, and Jordan as independent states, and the removal of the vestiges of British power in Egypt in 1954 and Iraq in 1958. The conjuncture of these two developments came, of course, in the mid-1950s, and gave the Soviet Union considerable influence in the Arab world, and the domestic socialists (friendly or neutral to Russia) increasing prestige.

Socialism attracts Arab intellectuals for many reasons beyond the important fact that it provides a good means by which they may express criticism of the West. It has certain positive virtues of which perhaps the leading one is that it provides a persuasive rationale for many intellectuals who believe that they are the elite called upon to bring social progress even if the masses are reluctant to pay the price in the uprooting of their lives and the imposition of new controls and loyalties. Committed to Arab glory and to progress through modernization, this influential group is attracted by socialism's manipulative character. Its members derogate the "false democracy" of parliaments and elections dominated by the old "feudal" regimes and justify the use of authoritarian means to industrialize and modernize. The Soviet model is the one they understand best because the Bolshevik revolution was made by a small, highly disciplined party with a great sense of mission supplied by its intellectual wing. For intellectuals not reared in a democratic tradition this is an appealing prospect.

Many Arab intellectuals learned their Marxism and Leninism in the West in European and American universities; they absorbed the Western liberal self-critique of democracy and capitalism, which confirmed their own hostility to Western rule over their own lands but they failed to absorb the lesson in method, that is, the ability to look objectively at their own society and their own beliefs. Educated beyond the capacity of the economy to provide them the jobs and status they came to expect, these intellectuals were without a place when Westerners ruled the Arab world and reserved the best posts for themselves, and they were not much better off under independence in a poor agricultural economy that could offer them little more.

In the Arab world the intellectuals have been in favor of state intervention, not merely as an ideological position but also for their own economic interests. The independent, self-employed liberal professions of the West had little opportunity to grow in the Arab world, for mass poverty made professionals dependent upon state employment either directly or indirectly through the state's assumption of responsibilities, such as health and welfare, long retained by the individual in the West. This situation is reflected in the fact that a large proportion of physicians, for example, are employed by the government. According to data in one study of public health in the Arab countries,[35] in 1950 about two thirds of all the 811 doctors in Iraq were in government employment. In Jordan (1949) and Syria (1951) this proportion was about a fifth. In Lebanon (1948) it was less than a tenth. For Egypt comparable data were not presented but statistics in an official source[36] suggest that of the nearly 8000 physicians there in 1956, almost a third were employed in government hospitals.

The compatibility of authoritarian with "leftist" political attitudes is no longer surprising even in the West, where fascism and communism have accustomed us to this combination of political and cultural repression accompanied by the destruction of the entrenched economic interests that have only abused the democratic institutions in which they flourished. A study[37] among Arab students at the American University of Beirut, made in the early 1950s, clearly reveals the compatibility of illiberal attitudes regarding freedom and personal relations with what we usually consider liberal attitudes toward political and economic questions. Their answers to a set of questions, devised and used widely in the United States to measure these qualities, showed no connection between authoritarianism and a particular political outlook. Whereas in the West students who tend to be authoritarian in general outlook tend also to be conservative in political attitudes, many of the Arab students who were authoritarian in outlook were also liberal or leftist in political attitudes. Indeed, those Arab students who showed the highest tendencies toward authoritarianism also expressed the most "liberal" political views—that is, they were most in favor of governmental responsibility "to guarantee everyone adequate housing, income and leisure," higher taxes on the

[35] Simmons, Vol. III, pp. 35, 98, 122, 148, and Vol. II, p. 14.

[36] U.A.R. (Egypt), Statistical Dept., *Statistical Pocket Yearbook*, 1957, Cairo, 1958, Table 13, pp. 18–23, and Table 14, p. 24.

[37] Prothro and Melikian, "The California Public Opinion Scale . . . ," pp. 354, 360.

large corporations and the wealthy, and greater governmental control over economic affairs in general.

In Egypt and Syria after 1955 and in Iraq after 1958
there appeared a large number of articles and books favorable to socialism and the Soviet Union (though communism never became a popular term even among pro-Soviet
writers). They contrasted the advantages of the Soviet
economic system with the disadvantages of "capitalism" in
the West, of which America was usually taken as the
prototype. In literary circles, the doctrine of "socialist
realism" became fashionable until it disappeared from the
U.A.R. when Nasser began, late in 1958, to criticize Soviet
intervention in the internal politics of the Arab world.

One of the best examples of this kind of writing was
produced in 1957 by a leading Egyptian Marxist literary
critic upon his return from the Soviet Union and the
"people's democracies."[38] He described favorably the
state's control over jobs, housing, education, health care,
and so on.[39] He also testified that these regimes allow
freedom of opinion and that where they do not do so they
are justified in the restrictions they impose.[40] He was also
impressed—and this is one of the Soviet regime's attractive features to certain intellectuals—by the status of intellectuals in the countries he visited. The minister of education in the U.S.S.R. told him, for example, that but for the
help of the intellectuals it would have been impossible to
redirect students from the liberal professions into the
socially more useful technological fields. Thus, the writer
points out, the state in the U.S.S.R. and the "people's
democracies" not only welcome the work produced by the
intellectual classes but also seek their aid in guiding the
whole society.[41] He was, moreover, particularly pleased by
the status of the creative writer in these countries, where
the state provides a modern printing press, a publishing
house which considers all proposals for books, provides

[38] Mandour.
[39] *Ibid.*, pp. 23–24.
[40] *Ibid.*, pp. 29–34.
[41] *Ibid.*, pp. 57–58.

the writer a good place to work and advances money to support him while he writes, and provides the remaining royalties after publication. He contrasted such a system with Egypt's, for example, where some writers cannot do their best because of financial worries.[42]

Arab (or Asian and African) intellectuals are not the only ones attracted by socialism's manipulative aspects, for socialism in Europe had already taken on this anti-humanist, exploitative character among those who admired its Russian embodiment after World War I. A European economist with much experience as research director of the National Bank of Egypt insisted in 1957, when pro-Soviet sentiment in the Arab world was very great, that Stalinist socialism was based on "Asiatic autocracy and ruthless exploitation of [the] illiterate peasantry." The suggestions that these Western socialists now offer to industrialize the underdeveloped areas, he went on, mean brutal exploitation of the workers and peasants. This type of socialism, he warned, has become "very common and influential in the Orient." In the West socialists cannot, he said, come to power with such a program because the workers and peasants can vote; so they relegate their theories and prescriptions to their books on imperialism, colonialism, and economic development.[43] In the Arab world, however, I would add in drawing the moral he did not explicitly state, the workers and peasants do not vote. Consequently the advocates of manipulative socialism can gain official support for their ideas without running the gauntlet of a free and articulate public opinion.[44] For a time these

[42] *Ibid.*, pp. 81–83.

[43] Koestner, p. 479.

[44] This economist, Nicolai Koestner, knew socialism in all its forms. A democratic socialist, he was a cabinet minister in Estonia when, after World War I, that small country regained independence of Russia, then already under Bolshevik rule. (The Soviets reincorporated Estonia in 1940 as an aftermath of the Stalin-Hitler agreement.) He later became a League of Nations economic expert and was stranded in Europe at the outbreak of World War II. He escaped the advancing Germans by going to Cairo with British help. There he joined the exchange section of

ideas seemed to appeal to certain Arab leaders bent upon rapid modernization. The disenchantment with Soviet promises not to meddle in internal Arab politics has stimulated some reconsideration of the Soviet model of economic growth as well. But the Arab world is too poor and too ambitious for change to be entirely immune to the temptation to squeeze the voiceless masses in order to pay for quick economic development.

Those countries following a plan of rapid economic growth must find a way to justify such a squeeze. Both the West and East agree that the "excess" labor force in certain poor but populous countries should be put to work in industries that need much labor rather than capital. Total consumption of good should, through new taxes, not be allowed to rise. The resultant forced savings would help pay the workers and create new industries. If a democratic regime tries this policy, the communists are the first to accuse it of exploitation, yet this is the policy Soviet-oriented regimes immediately adopt. A democratic regime, if it attempts such a policy, must allow consumption to rise too and must use political persuasion. But the non-democratic regimes do two other things instead: they destroy freedom of protest and develop a mass movement with endless exhortation and leftist rhetoric. The principle is

---

the National Bank, then became research director, a post he continued to hold after Egyptianization and nationalization of the Bank. For many years he edited the *Bulletin* of the Bank, which he made into the world's most reliable and authoritative source of information about economic affairs in the Near East. He also became an Egyptian citizen and served his country faithfully and well as an economic adviser. In 1955 the turning of the wheel began to reach full circle. The Bolshevism he had found repugnant when he fought it in Estonia as a democratic socialist even before it took power in Russia now came to Egypt itself in the grand trappings of a world power feared, respected and admired. When Nicolai Koestner spoke of the corruption of socialism both in the West and in Asia, he spoke from knowledge and experience in the inner circles. When he died in Cairo in February of 1959 he had already seen the beginning of a more realistic appraisal by Arabs of the Soviet system and international communism.

simple: only a "socialist" regime that speaks loudly in the name of the working class can so thoroughly exploit it.

Though socialism as a full-blown ideology has attracted many Arab intellectuals, its appeal for the leaders is less as an ideological system or as a cohesive economic program. For those who govern, socialism is a term that arouses a favorable response and stands for general social progress. They are not doctrinaire, as they never tire of pointing out, and want to adopt any plan that will help them industrialize and raise standards of living. These goals have now become as much a part of Arab nationalism as the goals of independence and unity. In the West we see Arab nationalism as a rush of newspaper headlines about riots, seizures, and revolutions. Within the Arab world it has a different face. There it is easier to see that Arab nationalism is, in each country, the effort to create a nation out of a mass. Against the advantage of the strong feeling of Arabism there is, in this effort, the handicap of poverty and disease, indifference to the world outside and absorption in private misery, lack of education or a sense of community to sustain hard work and new ways beyond the momentary exhilaration of a harangue in a public square. In the West, Arab nationalism is associated with "extremism," anti-Westernism, and chauvinism. In the Arab world it is connected with industrialization, health programs, land reform, civic improvement, expansion of education—the creation of a new world in symbol and fact. Outside, nationalism is "immoderate" and boastful. Inside, it is more modest and fearful. Nationalism looks best in its own habitat.

Part Three

SOCIAL CHANGE

CHAPTER 10

The Military Regimes

If we were willing to stretch the evidence a bit to
achieve order and symmetry, we could construct a con-
tinuum of the resort to military leadership in both the
economically advanced and the underdeveloped world. At
one end we should place those countries, in Africa for
example, which are achieving independence without benefit
of a native professional military elite. They are authoritarian in a traditional sense, but they have not yet been
able to build a modern military class because their defense
was until recently conducted by their European rulers.
Nearer to the middle of the scale we might place those
countries which have enjoyed independence for a longer
period. Several Near Eastern states, for example, with
more modernized institutions have reasserted their authoritarian tradition by becoming military republics, as
the European powers which built up their armies in the
first place have declined in influence. On the other side of
the center of the spectrum we should place those slightly
more developed countries, such as several in Latin America,
which have recently banished their military dictators. Farther along would come some Western countries which have
been guided by military father-figures, gentle or stern. And
at the end we should place those old-fashioned Western
nations which have kept the military elite in its traditional
place in a civil society.

In both economically advanced and underdeveloped
countries, the military elites assume increasing importance as wars and the preparation for them engage more
and more of a nation's resources, and as newly independent
states impatiently strive to achieve national power and a

higher standard of living. Though Western society has been profoundly affected by wars and their scientific-technological requirements, they have with few exceptions retained civilian control over military affairs; the military elites have not played an independent or major role in introducing social change. In the contemporary Arab world, however, the situation has been almost the reverse. There, technological backwardness has dulled the impact of war upon a loosely organized society whose social and geographical constituents have been somewhat isolated from one another. This backwardness has survived even the painful realization that political independence requires military strength, which in turn requires technological advance. Yet the military elites in the Near East, in Egypt, the Sudan, Iraq, Turkey, Iran, and Pakistan have been more important in introducing social change than their Western counterparts have been. One reason comes quickly to mind: in the effort to increase their national strength these countries have had to rely more upon their military than upon their native political and industrial elites, which have been weak and timid in an area that has known little democracy and technological-industrial growth but much subservience to local or foreign rulers. The impotence of other elites, like those that have reached dominance in the West, has placed the Near Eastern military elites in a strong position to introduce change.

The steady increase in the number of military regimes in the Near East world is impressive. Iraq became independent in 1932. Four years later the army officers became the pivot of political power, and in 1958 they stopped shuffling cabinets and began a social revolution. Syria became independent during World War II and by 1949 was ruled by army officers, then by politicians, until it joined the military regime of Egypt in 1958. Egypt became nominally independent in 1922 but was not effectively so until just after World War II; in 1952 its army assumed control. Pakistan was established in 1947, and its army took over in 1959. The Sudan became independent in 1955 and fell under military control in 1958. Turkey and Iran are two special cases. Turkey was under military control after World War I. Then the military regime invited back the civilians, and the country experienced a peaceful and democratic change of ruling party for a time until in 1960 the officers took control again. Iran had a military dictator in the 1920s who established a dynasty which now rules in alliance with the military elite.

There are important differences among the military elites of these countries. The officers in Egypt, Syria, and Iraq who took power had come to maturity in the period of imperial decline; many of them were trained within their own countries and had not been part of the machine by which England and France were able to rule. Unattached by economic interest or ideology to a ruling class, they were strong nationalists, easily won over to some form of political extremism. Hence the military elites of Egypt, Syria, and Iraq are statist in economic policy and anti-Western politically. In Pakistan, the Sudan and Turkey the situation has been different. There the military elites were attached to ruling groups—those of Pakistan and the Sudan to the British, that of Turkey to a native one. Thus, though they are moderately statist, they have not been ideologically receptive to the Soviet way. Not having been involved in nationalist struggles, the army in Pakistan and the Sudan is not anti-Western. The Turkish army went through its anti-Western phase in the 1920s.

The Arab military elites have in common a strong desire for rapid social change. It is this desire, rather than mere tradition, that impels them to become authoritarian, to stifle political opposition, and to organize the masses around the national goals which the elites have put forward. There is thus a vast gulf between the leaders and the led in attitudes and outlook as well as in background and education. This difference is far greater than the corresponding one in the Western democracies, where the high level of living, diffusion of education, and political freedom have narrowed the gap between rulers and ruled. The military elites intent upon social change—"modernization" in national terms—must prod, cajole, and push the masses. It is easy to induce people to demonstrate in the streets but it is far more difficult to get them to work hard for the unfamiliar goals the elites embrace in response to their own ambitions, their patriotism, and their new values learned in and from the West.

The native military elites have replaced the colonial or foreign governing elites not merely in the seats of power but also in certain political attitudes. The foreign elites were unwilling to share power (though they were forced to do so to an increasing extent) because it meant a loss of prestige and economic advantage. The native military elites, too, cannot abide democracy, for sharing power would not only weaken their own position but would make the social changes they favor more difficult to push through: with political freedom, those people who have to be jolted most abruptly would have greater control over those who want most to jolt them. The native elites, however, are in one sense different from those they replaced: they are far more radical. The foreign elites introduced economic, political, and educational changes which generally affected the lives of the ordinary people only indirectly. The native elites are less hesitant and seek to impose social change directly and swiftly. I am not arguing that the Arabs were better off under the French and British or that they prefer foreign to native rule. The evidence is overwhelming—in Africa and Asia as well as in the Near East—that the masses really believe in their inalienable right to be exploited by people of their own nationality and color.

To a certain extent the issue in the Near East—as in Africa—is: how much democratization is compatible with how much rapid modernization? Assuming for the moment (what may prove later to be unwarranted) that the military regimes want "ultimately" to establish political freedom and democracy, how much of it can they allow or encourage now while they stress industrialization and modernization? In this sense, too, the military elites echo their foreign predecessors, for both types of rulers insist that the "masses" are not "ready" for democracy because of their poverty, illiteracy, and so on. There is, of course, truth in all this, though I suspect it is so convenient a truth to a ruling group that they do not easily recognize other truths that might point in a different direction.

In defense of their emphasis on rapid modernization rather than political democracy, the military elites point to the need to reduce poverty. In the West we have heard the argument of the "revolution of rising expectations"—that the masses have come to expect such an improvement in their material well-being as to force their leaders to stress economic development at the expense of political development. I think too much is made of this argument in spite of the admittedly shocking poverty and the growing awareness that something can be done about it. The Arab masses, I think, are neither so stupid nor so optimistic as to expect that their leaders—military or civilian—can double their level of living in a few years or even decades. Undoubtedly they want a better material life but they have known poverty for so long that they are not likely to try to throw out their leaders if they fail to deliver on such rash promises.

What do the masses want? Though it may be presumptuous for an outside observer to offer a guess, I suspect that the leaders in the Near East, because of the wide gap between themselves and those they lead, may not be much better qualified to answer the question. I do not doubt that the masses consciously want a higher level of material welfare, better education and health, and to be part of a strong and respected nation—that is, all those goals their leaders announce and claim to be striving to achieve. But neither do I doubt that the masses also want something they cannot name—that degree of justice, stability, predictability, internal order, civil peace, and freedom from official arbitrary and whimsical domination that goes by the old-fashioned name of the rule of law. These aspirations are paid the honor of lip-service when a military regime takes over, but they are too quickly swept aside by the storm of propaganda and activity surrounding the goal of economic development. If a regime paid closer attention to these goals of fair play and efficient administration, it might find itself even more popular—and more enduringly so—than through the more obvious emphasis upon economic development.

The Western observer committed to both freedom and order is placed in a dilemma when he considers Near Eastern *coups d'etat* by military elites. On the one hand, democratic institutions there have not been successful; they have been accompanied by excesses, extremism, inefficiency, corruption, and public disorder. On the other hand, the military regimes are associated with efficiency and public order—a controlled extremism. These regimes do not shame democracy because they do not test it. The case of Turkey early in 1960 only emphasizes the need sometimes to choose between extremist, inefficient, bungling attempts at democracy, and efficient, neat, and orderly military rule without even the façade of democracy. There, a party that came to office in an experiment in democracy and peaceful transfer of power allowed extremism, inefficiency, and demagogy to go so far as to cause the return of rule by a military elite—enlightened, moderate, pro-Western, but not democratic.

Many Western observers have been favorable to the military regimes in the Near East. Those who are chiefly concerned to see the end of colonialism have praised these regimes because they are native and independent. Those who are worried about Soviet-Chinese power have praised them because they are anti-Communist, at least in domestic politics, and have been able to prevent internal chaos which would benefit Communists. Those who are favorable to the expansion of Soviet-Chinese power praise some military regimes for their "neutralism." None of these groups seems concerned about the prospects of freedom and democracy for the people of the Near East who live under these regimes. It is often pointed out that Europe, too, went through a stage of absolutism on the way to democracy. This kind of historical perspective can induce only political quietism. The "stages" of European history need not be repeated elsewhere and a particular "stage" is not overcome by affirming that it is inevitable. Many people in the Arab world who understand democracy and are "ready" for it are puzzled when Western observers, who are free to say what Arabs cannot say, choose to condone military rule in the belief that Arabs are not "ready" for democracy, or that efforts to achieve it may be safely postponed for a while, or that the route to democracy is through a stage of its opposite.

The Military Elite in Politics

In the West, military elites have been conservative or reactionary in outlook, especially in politics but even in economic and social policy. They have been interested in national strength, of course, but the impetus for economic development has come from the middle classes, and the impetus for widening democracy and social welfare from the liberal and working-class parties. Army officers have not been liberals or radicals in comparison with such classes and parties. In the Near East, however, the middle and working classes have been weak and, owing to the predominance of agriculture, not numerous. In that milieu, army officers interested in national strength through modernization of the economy have been as liberal and radical in their ideas on economic and political issues as any other elite or social group. This has been all the more the case in the Arab world where, as we saw in Chapter 9, it has not been possible thus far to build a viable liberalism. It became clear rather early that once the Western powers withdrew from direct control, any group, no matter what its program, would need the support of the military elite to achieve power. This was clearly seen in Iraq where since the *coup d'etat* of 1936 the army has retained a *de facto* veto power over internal politics, which it expanded into positive control in 1958. In Iraq the role of the military elite in the triumph of contemporary Arab nationalism also emerged most strongly just after World War I, when Arab officers trained by the Ottomans along Western lines played a leading role in the movement for Iraqi independence and pan-Arabism as well.[1] The need for army support has sent all groups in the Near East, of whatever political persuasion, to seek converts among the officers. This has had two effects. First, the armies became political schools. Second, liberalism, radicalism, nationalism, communism, socialism, religious fundamentalism have all attracted various sections of the military elite from time to time, so that conservatism alone has not prevailed among Near Eastern officers to the degree that it did among Western army leaders.[2]

Arab armies are embroiled in politics rather than insulated from it by institutional devices or tradition. The leader of the 1958 *coup d'etat* in Iraq, General Kassem, has stressed the "unity" of the army with the people and has described the army as "the only force which can be relied upon" in emergencies (the nature of which he did not specify). But once the army takes power, party politics becomes dangerous; so Kassem has also stressed that the army must retain its freedom of action by controlling the parties instead of allowing the parties to build their own support within the army. He told the officers a year after their *coup:* "I have never belonged to any particular party. . . . I advise you not to permit any specific party to get into the ranks of the Army. We serve the interests of parties on the condition that they remain outside the Army. . . . If once we permit one specific party to get into the ranks of the Army, then it is only fair that other parties should be allowed, too. But this will scatter us into groups and factions and our strength will become worthless."[3] This involvement of officers in the ideological ferment of Arab life is not a very recent development. As far back as the attempted revolution by the Egyptian

[1] See Khadduri, *Independent Iraq,* pp. 69–80, 126, and Kedourie, pp. 100–1.

[2] On this point see Khadduri, "The Role . . . ," pp. 517ff., and Sherman.

[3] Speeches of Prime Minister and Commander-in-Chief of Armed Forces, Abdel Karim Kassem, in *Principles of the 14th July Revolution,* The Times Press, Baghdad, n.d. (probably late 1959), pp. 12, 18, 22.

Colonel Arabi in 1881, Gibb points out, there has been a "close connection between the social policies sponsored by the army and the ideas current in the more advanced sections of their own people. The army, as it were, reflects these ideas in a Westernized mirror."[4]

In the Arab states, both the "revolutionary" character of the military elite and their accession to political power in Egypt, Syria, and Iraq stemmed from foreign rule and its recent decline. Drawn from the urban and peasant middle classes, the native officers felt no traditional loyalty to such conservative classes as the large landowners or the commercial interests—the former with strong Ottoman ties, the latter chiefly Western or Arab Christians. Western power, supplanting Ottoman rule, for a time firmly controlled the native military elite. The nationalist movement, in its political as well as violent phases, was led by absentee landowners, career politicians, lawyers, and journalists, not only by the military (except in Iraq). Army officers, whatever their sentiments, were too close to the means of violence to be permitted freedom of political action. But when the nationalists were victorious and the Western powers no longer controlled domestic politics, the inherent strength of the military could not be suppressed. Cohesive, relatively modern in outlook, not bound to conservative interests, and controlling the means of violence, officers were able to overcome the weak, confused, and inexperienced civilian regimes which succeeded foreign rule.

Social Policies

What do the Arab military elites do once they acquire power? Iraq has most recently displayed the trend clearly. Only a few weeks after the revolution of July 1958 the new military regime announced that Iraq was an integral part of one Arab nation; that its rulers would build na-

[4] Gibb, "Social Change . . . ," p. 46. On the background and policies of the Egyptian army leaders, see the recent account in Vatikiotis.

tionalism, socialism, and democracy and raise living standards through land distribution and industrialization; that such social reforms as the dissolution of tribal law would be pressed; and that political freedom would be withheld until the danger to the revolution was overcome.

These goals are even better seen in Egypt, which since 1952 has had more time to carry through some of the plans the officers had before they took power and others they acquired only later. Indeed, Egypt since Napoleon provides a good example of the introduction of social change under the impetus of military considerations designed to increase the nation's power in the international arena. It will be useful to consider briefly the sweep of change since that time.[5] We can distinguish two main periods and their "incubation" stages, so to speak.

The first era is that of Muhammad Ali, roughly the first half of the nineteenth century. Its preparatory period was the Napoleonic invasion and occupation of Egypt at the turn of that century. The second era, which we shall discuss in more detail, is the current one beginning in 1952 with the army officers' *coup d'etat* and continuing under Nasser's leadership. Its preparatory period was the previous British occupation. Between these two eras of change there was an abortive revolt of army officers led by Colonel Ahmad Arabi in 1881. Lasting only a few months, it nevertheless had an impact upon the national consciousness of Egyptians, although it did not in itself generate social change.

The Napoleonic adventure introduced some new ideas, techniques, and products, but these could hardly take hold in the short time the French army occupied Egypt. The main effect, in retrospect and from our viewpoint, was that it forced Egypt into renewed contact with the West. When, soon after the French were driven out, Muhammad Ali rose to power within the Ottoman social and political framework, there lay before him the vistas opened by Na-

[5] A fuller account may be found in Berger, *Military Elite and Social Change.*

poleon and by those Frenchmen who remained or came anew after the military expedition had failed. Muhammad Ali's goal was to make Cairo the center of an empire. Aiming at dynastic rather than national greatness, he nevertheless understood that he needed a modern army both to conquer other Ottoman territories and to defeat further European adventures in Egypt and the empire he sought to build. He clearly saw that to create a modern military force he had to introduce a range of techniques on several levels of society and touching many other institutions besides the military. He made the army his instrument for modernization, but this elite did not play an autonomous role in which it introduced social change deliberately.

Even before the death of Muhammad Ali in 1849 the pace of social change in Egypt had waned. Soon afterward, European power began to penetrate Egyptian society on European terms and not, as under Muhammad Ali, in ways determined and controlled by the rulers of Egypt. The dual process of Western exploitation and tutelage led to an early nationalist revolt, the high point of which was the movement led by Colonel Arabi in 1881, which culminated in the British occupation. This marked a new era in Western influence: it became steadier, more systematic, and wider-ranging, though perhaps less immediately shocking. Under British control, the Egyptian army was not an agency of social change but was itself an object of change. Since the British had contact with other Egyptian urban elites, the native army was only one of several that felt the Western impact. Because the Egyptian officers had intimate and enduring tutelage under the British both in Egypt and in England, and because they formed a disciplined, cohesive unit by the nature of their calling and professional education, they became the strongest and most solid native elite familiar with Western patterns of the rationalized application of violence.

As British power declined after World War I, the autonomous influence of the Egyptian military elite grew until a new group of officers was able, in 1952, to depose the government, dismiss the king, eradicate the monarchy, and embark upon a calculated course of change embracing all major aspects of Egyptian social life. In the current era, therefore, the army is a conscious independent agent of social change.

It is significant that in both preparatory periods foreign influences—Ottoman, French, British, and American—played upon Egyptian society, leading to the local military impetus to social change when the foreign controls were removed.

The Military Regime in Egypt Since 1952

In assessing the role of the army in the current period of social change, we are aided by the articulateness and public-relations sense of three important leaders, General Naguib, Colonel Nasser, and Colonel Sadat, all of whom have written revealing books about the army's relation to politics.

Sadat's book, *Revolt on the Nile,* is especially useful in its expression of the army's discontent with affairs before the 1952 *coup d'etat* and its consequent embroilment in various political and ideological movements. One of the "leading themes" of Egyptian developments in the last twenty years, Nasser says in an introduction to the book, has been "the Army's discontent at the decay of the state." Sadat asserts that the "squabbles" of the Egyptian political parties while the British "ruled by a hidden hand" gave the army "a right to intervene." According to Sadat, it was in early 1939 that several young officers, recent graduates of the Military Academy, formed a "secret revolutionary society dedicated to the task of liberation" of Egypt from its social and political ills. This group, he adds, "was the embryo of the Council of the Revolution which assumed power after the *coup d'etat* of July 23, 1952."[6]

Ideologically, the discontented officers had no firm roots except in the nationalistic passion to rid Egypt of British power and to make the nation strong. It would appear from

[6] El Sadat, pp. ix, 13–15.

Sadat's comments that they entered politics openly: "We organized lectures and public debates for the discussion of current problems. These meetings attracted a large number of young people anxious to learn and to make their own ideas known. Previously, the Army officer's life had been a daily routine of mathematics, military history, ballistics, theory of strategy, field exercises. The study of social reform gave their lives new meaning."[7]

Nationalism and political and social reform—in a word, modernization: this was the main preoccupation of many of the younger officers reared in a period of British imperial decline. Colonel Sadat's own criterion of the good officer is, at least inferentially, the degree of his familiarity with the West. Speaking favorably of the military capacities and the patriotism of the Egyptian chief of staff in World War II, Sadat adds as one of his good qualities: "He was receptive to modern ideas, having travelled in France, England and Germany."[8] For several years, therefore, the army included an active, influential core of young officers whose model of national political life was Western and who had justified to themselves their plans to seize power. Colonel Nasser remarks that the young officers saw it as their "duty" to turn against the regime: ". . . if we failed to discharge it, we would be failing in the sacred trust placed in us." And they were convinced that no other group would perform the necessary act. "If the army does not do the job," Nasser says the officers told themselves, "who will?"[9]

We are accustomed in Western European history to the army in politics playing a conservative role, upholding established social institutions even when it uses unorthodox political methods. But the Egyptian army, like others in the Near East, has not played a conservative or stabilizing role, for it is composed, as we have seen, of a different social class and acts in a different social situation from those we have been familiar with in European history. In

[7] *Ibid.*, p. 86.
[8] *Ibid.*, p. 31.
[9] Nasser, *Egypt's Liberation*, pp. 31–32.

the West, army officers have usually exercised a stable if not reactionary political influence, for they have been connected to the upper governing classes by ties of family, education, and common interests in political stability. As Naguib has himself pointed out, however, the social origin of Egyptian officers gave them little stake in existing social and political arrangements. "Except for the royal family," he wrote, "there was no aristocracy, and the landowners' and traders' sons who might have led the Armed Forces were too busy enjoying their wealth to be bothered with military service. The officers' corps in consequence was largely composed of the sons of civil servants and soldiers and the grandsons of peasants."[10] In their attitudes toward foreign rule and the influence of foreigners in Egypt, young Egyptian officers resembled other young men who went from the villages or from urban middle-class homes to fill the secondary schools and universities supported with public funds. The military school and the university alike were the avenue to social ascent: a secure post in the military or civilian service of the state.

Of all the native elite groups, the army has probably held the most rationally calculating, secular, and unromantic approach to the problems Egypt has faced. In this sense, it has been the most "Western" of the elites. Socially, however, the army officers have not transcended their conservative middle-class origins and upbringing. Their wives and families, for example, especially those of the few officers most prominent in the military regime, are seldom seen in public. Intense nationalism combines with social conventionalism to discourage Western patterns in their private lives. There is also among these leaders a certain tendency toward puritanical attitudes which is compounded of the sexual modesty enjoined by Islamic doctrine and their passion for work to transform their country.

The fact that Egyptian officers do not follow a native aristocratic military tradition has probably facilitated their

10 Naguib, p. 15.

integration into the civilian government since 1952. Most
of the officers who were members of the Revolution Command Council, which ruled Egypt in the early years of the
regime, became cabinet ministers. Several have remained
in such posts. Others who were less prominent hold important positions. Among those whom I have personally
seen at work, one was charged with revising the structure
of the civil service, another is Minister of Culture and
National Guidance and emphasizes the former as much
as the latter, a third is a novelist and secretary general of
the official Higher Council of Arts and Letters, a fourth
is in charge of cultural exchanges in the Ministry of Foreign Affairs. Other officers are ministers and ambassadors
to foreign countries, and still others are in important administrative posts in privately owned enterprises in which
the government holds shares. Indeed, some young officers
now think of their military careers as good training for
high administrative posts in governmental and private enterprises. Whatever the regime's political motive may be
in placing these dozens of officers in high posts, their performance of these civilian functions has not been "milita-
ristic" or unresponsive to non-military requirements. It is
entirely possible, moreover, that such power and responsibility has already made the upper reaches of this elite
much less responsive to adventurous policies in foreign or
domestic affairs. Professional tradition and present self-
interest can combine quickly to make them conservative
despite their own social origin.

The military elite's rationalistic, secular outlook and
temper are best revealed in its relationship to such a fundamentalist religious group as the Moslem Brotherhood.
Naguib summarized the attitude of the leaders of the military revolt when he said that though they sympathized
with the "desire to apply the teachings of Muhammad to
modern life," they also "were convinced that to do so
blindly would spell disaster." Intent upon increasing
Egypt's influence in the modern world, he added that:
"The rebirth of Egypt, in our opinion, depended on the

continued modernization of its social, political, and economic institutions."[11]

Colonel Sadat has provided some details of the relations between the army officers and the Moslem Brotherhood which reveal the attitude of the former irrespective of the reinterpretations the author may be presenting in the light of subsequent events. Pointing out that the Brotherhood "rose to a position of power with extraordinary rapidity," it seemed, he says, at least "in its early days," a "useful ally to our revolutionary movement." Sadat himself was the liaison between the officers and the Brotherhood's Supreme Guide, from whom he learned that "the dogmas of Islam must be inculcated in all branches of the Army." The officers "hoped to use our association with the Brotherhood as a lever to achieve our own ends," but, Sadat continues, "we were deceived in our calculations." In those ideologically confused times, many officers, Sadat states, were sympathetic to the Brotherhood. He himself believed that "great things" would follow their co-operation, but even before the officers had seized and were exercising state power, clashes between them and the Brotherhood were frequent. From Sadat's brief account, it is clear that the officers were secular and looked to a modernization of Egypt along Western technological lines, whereas the Brotherhood was, of course, fundamentalist before anything else. The mystery, the rough egalitarianism, the ignoring of civil-military status distinctions, the inconsistency and weakness of the program, the vagueness of the leaders as to the program, and the emphasis upon unquestioning faith in the Supreme Guide—all of these irrational, semi-charismatic and mysterious qualities of the Brotherhood repelled the army officers.[12]

It is not that the officers were ideologically consistent, but that they were a secularized group within the context of Egyptian social and political life. As individuals, the officers may have been no less superstitious or emo-

11 Naguib, p. 134.
12 El Sadat, pp. 28–30, 79–81.

tional or extremist than the members of other organizations then forming and dissolving and re-forming in Egypt. Yet their leadership had an image of the secular Egypt they wanted, and moved with as much directness as possible toward that goal, with no more secrecy, mystery, and conspiratorial ceremony than was necessary. General Naguib reveals an interesting difference between himself, as a leading officer, and his men. When he survived several wounds during the Palestine war, many of his troops believed it was the *"baraka* that I was supposed to possess—a special blessing that spared me for the accomplishment of some divine purpose." He hastens to add: "Although I don't really believe in my *baraka,* I have found it expedient to behave as if I did, as I think everyone in my position [of leadership], to be successful, must."[13]

As an advanced elite, the army has been aware of its own place in Egyptian life and can look back upon a tradition of nationalism and social change going back several generations. Nasser himself plainly expounded the role of the army in social change in a speech in 1954 celebrating the second anniversary of the revolution it led. The army, he said then, "is not merely barracks separated from the people by a high wall, but a university with open doors to all classes of the people, teaching them, strengthening their bodies and raising their morale . . . We assure our soldiers that armies can never gain a victory except by the aid of scientists behind their microscopes and test tubes and by the aid of every individual member of the nation."[14]

When the young officers took power they found it necessary, if they were to succeed in changing Egypt, to retain their hold rather than to share it for long with the older political elite. To protect both their goals and their new

[13] Naguib, p. 22. It is interesting, nevertheless, to see that Naguib does not say he disbelieves in "baraka" in general; he goes no farther than to say that he does not believe in *his* "baraka."

[14] Speech reprinted in *Goals of the Egyptian Revolution* (pamphlet distributed by Republic of Egypt in 1958 but indicating no date), p. 73.

position, they had to unfold a program, mobilize support
for their acts, and prevent the deposed forces from reas-
serting themselves. A few months after the 1954 internal
crisis as a result of which his leadership was consolidated
and made formal, Nasser described for an American audience the goals of the revolution: "to end the exploitation
of people, to realize national aspirations and to develop
the mature political consciousness that is an indispensable
preliminary for a sound democracy." In order to attain
these goals, he continued, "the standard of living of the
masses must be raised, education expanded and social
consciousness developed."[15]

In this deliberate attempt to introduce social change,
the officers have intensified two main tendencies begun
long before their advent: nationalism and industrialization. By a propaganda program that depends heavily upon
the media of mass communication, they seek to weld all
Egyptians into a conscious national unit and to make them
leaders among the Arabs, Moslems, and Africans who are
undergoing the same kind of transformation. They have
made reforms in education and encouraged certain types
of interpersonal relations to conform to the goals of nationalism and industrialization. Egypt has thus experienced increasing governmental direction of economic and
social life as well as of political affairs. This is a more serious
matter today than in previous eras in which Near Eastern
governments have made such claims, because today the
state apparatus, with its monopoly of new weapons and
of the means of mass communication, cannot be challenged as could a regime in the looser social structure of
the past. Many programs and acts are part of this trend:
abolition of political parties; reconstitution of an elected
parliament under the regime's own conditions; control of
press and radio and greater surveillance of all literary, artistic, and religious expression; encouragement of science
and technology; a shift of the acts of formerly somewhat
independent associations (trade unions and professional

[15] Nassar, "The Egyptian Revolution," pp. 208–9.

bodies) into closer alignment with the government's programs; more direct government role in economic life; mobilization of military forces and their equipment with more advanced weapons; heightening of national consciousness through acts in regional and world politics.

The officers display in their own service journals the sentiments, attitudes and intentions appropriate to the goals and policies just summarized. Some are technical journals for officers only. Others, more general and popular in tone, are apparently meant for enlisted men too. And one or two seem to be edited for the reading public at large. They contain articles on politics, nationalism, economic reform, culture, personal problems, and so on, as well as the more strictly military discussions. Though virtually all of the articles are written by officers, a few of the non-military ones are by civilians. An examination of some of these articles reveals the military elite's conception of its own role and of the nation it wants to build.

An article published in 1958 discusses "Military Education and Character Training."[16] Pointing out the place of military training in the development of nationalism and individual excellence, the author says: "Military life is the school of the people; it is an advanced school in public, social and national aspects of life, for the first lesson that a young soldier learns is self-denial and to exert all his efforts towards a noble cause. It is the repudiation of personal interests in favor of the public interest. Then the individual becomes a sound, ideal citizen."

The importance of creating a new type of individual to conform to the national goals is stressed in two other articles. One of them,[17] concerned with the fact that population is growing faster than food resources, warns that a powerful nation in peace or war needs healthy, properly-nourished citizens. The other[18] emphasizes that the individual human being is the basis of a strong economy, which in turn is needed to make a nation militarily power-

[16] Zabalawi, p. 50.
[17] Murad.
[18] Khuri, pp. 26–28.

ful. A sound military program is thus said to require the participation of the entire nation, direction by a central authority, equality of sacrifice, a high level of health and education especially among the youth, and an intimate relationship between the people and their military forces.

Some articles are designed to instruct the readers as to the new values the regime seeks to inculcate. Thus an officer writes[19] a general article on the nature of nationalism, defining such terms as nation and patriotism, because these concepts will be influential in the Arab world. In a more popular journal, an unsigned article[20] glorifies the industrial worker as intelligent and patriotic, sacrificing to contribute to his country's welfare. Describing the Egyptian workers in heavy industry, the writer asserts that they are well educated, endure great hardships, and are as skilled as foreigners. In the old days, the reader is told, a few years of formal education made a man aspire only to a clerical job, but now things have changed. "So," the reader is encouraged, "if you hold a general secondary school certificate, do not hesitate. You have a good job waiting for you and a secure future. But you must have the capacity for endurance to become one of the pioneers, the pioneers in the heavy industry of Egypt." An article in another magazine[21] reverts to the question of living standards and reviews the steps taken to increase industrial production so that the population may become healthy and well educated. An editorial in a more technical journal[22] summarizes not only these actions of the government but also praises the effort at land reform, improvement in water supply and roads, housing, sewage, and so on. In a naval magazine an officer discusses insurance schemes as a means of improving health standards.[23] He contends that "nationalization" of medical care, as in England, requires a high civic sense, an educated public with a high

[19] Ahmad.
[20] "This Worker . . ."
[21] Hudayb.
[22] "This Revolution."
[23] al-Shihabi.

standard of living, and a medical profession dedicated to service rather than its own interests. He therefore concludes that for Egypt it would be more appropriate to introduce health insurance based upon premiums.

The popular arts are covered now and then in one of the general military magazines. An article by a civilian[24] reports an interview with one of Egypt's most popular actresses and dancers. A famous photographer, the writer begins, has in the pages of this magazine presented pictures of such foreign beauties as Sophia Loren, Gina Lollabrigida, and Audrey Hepburn. Now he presents an Egyptian beauty whom the readers may compare to the others. The interview gives her views on art, politics, beauty, fashion, and her trip to the Venice Film Festival, in which Egypt participated. In Venice, the actress is reported as saying, she and other Egyptian delegates were able to show the rest of the world that Egypt is not just a "country of sand, veiled women and dirty children," that these things never existed, or have been eradicated by the new Egypt.

This is the image of the country the military elite would like to build—industrialized, militarily powerful, respected in the world community, and composed of educated, healthy citizens loyal to the nation-state. Because of the traditional weakness of civic spirit and the suspicion of government, it has been easier to use the state machine as the engine of movement and change. The regime has tried, nevertheless, to galvanize the nation into voluntary action as well, though always in strict accordance with official goals and without permitting the growth of competing centers of political power.

What is the relationship of the military regime to democracy and freedom? In common with elites in other societies undergoing modernization, the Egyptian military elite has looked upon democracy and freedom in national rather than individual terms. These goals are equated with self-government, that is, government by a native rather than a foreign elite. The freedom of the individual to chal-

[24] Abu Zikri.

lenge such native rule is not accepted as a mode of political life, though differences of opinion are expressed as
to the means by which the goals laid down by the regime
may be attained. The regime does not feel free to permit
an opposition in the traditional Western sense because it
fears that, given wide public apathy, such an arrangement
might enable deposed elites to return to power and reverse
the trend toward modernization. What the modernizers
want to do might thus be frustrated in a democratic system by those who oppose land reform, secularization, the
inculcation of political attitudes among the sections of
the population that lay outside the political community
until now, and the emphasis upon national power in the
world arena. Not bound to the past, as were the elites
they deposed and the masses they seek to arouse, the military elite feels it must impose change—and must therefore
retain control of the state machinery to help in this effort
and to prevent interference with it. For this reason it has
destroyed or transformed those political and professional
associations that have challenged its program or its
authority.

For all its suppression of political dissent, the military
regime has enlarged other kinds of freedom for the individual. Though it rejects Western parliamentary democracy (for the present only, it insists), it has not only permitted but even promoted liberalism in non-political
realms. It has broadened educational opportunity, supported efforts to overcome learning by rote, tried to develop education in science (traditionally neglected), and
encouraged methods of education that permit freer expression of individuality. In public administration it has tried
to encourage greater individual responsibility as part of a
broad program to increase efficiency as well as to develop a
spirit of public service. In family life it allows the growth
of liberal ideas of child rearing and above all the emancipation of women from seclusion through education and
employment outside the home. In art and literature, it
has encouraged new forms of expression and not interfered with the growth of various schools so long as imme-

diate political issues are avoided or, if touched at all, are treated in accordance with the official position.

All of these tendencies in education, position of women, and interpersonal relations, joined to the effects of a more politically alert population, urbanization, and the creation of articulate social groups of workers and executives in an industrializing economy may be setting up pressures for increased personal freedom in the political realm as well. The weakening of old authorities may prompt the questioning of new authorities too. Though perhaps not directly intending to promote democracy as a purely political arrangement, the military regime is, by its colossal effort to introduce social change, willy-nilly creating some of the socio-economic conditions, attitudes, and expectations that may one day be expressed in a greater demand for political democracy.[25]

In the next chapter I will draw a distinction between two types of Near Eastern regimes, the "pre-populist" and the "populist." The military regimes are clearly the latter. How are they to be compared with respect to the prospects for democracy? The "populist" regime, I should say, offers the more hope. Under the "pre-populist" regime it is not likely that the social and economic conditions conducive to freedom and democracy can be built. The rulers are interested in democratic forms mainly to use them and do little to awaken a demand for them in the masses. Under the "populist" regime political freedom is suppressed but at least the possibility of its growth remains because, as I have tried to show, such a regime may, however unintentionally, set in action certain processes that may create demands for greater democracy and freedom later on.

Social Change through Military Elites

This review of social change introduced through military needs or by a military elite raises two general questions

[25] On the socio-economic conditions associated with democracy and the degree to which they are found in the Arab countries, see Issawi, "Economic and Social Foundations ..."

concerning social change originating in this way. We can discuss each only briefly.

First, in what order is change diffused by borrowing or imposition? It is clear that generally a change in modes of transportation will be more easily diffused than a change in religious belief. Changes in military technique, too, will be readily adopted by a conquered people who want to resist further conquest. In Egypt, then, as perhaps elsewhere too, if the military elite becomes imbued with a will to change its ways in order to become more effective, other elites that are determined to preserve the nation's other values will not be likely to resist. Thus, no one in Egypt attacks military modernization as an undesirable imitation of the West, although many groups have resisted the introduction of Western political forms on two grounds: first, simply that they are Western and hence undesirable; and second, because such new political forms may threaten the power of established groups and classes or interfere with other goals sought by important and powerful elements of the society. Military change, or at least readiness for adoption of new military techniques, is a type of innovation that is not resisted very much. The implications of the desire for military change, however, such as improved technology, educational changes, industrial development, and so on may not be so welcome or may be difficult to impose upon a nation.

One of the oldest questions in the theory of cultural diffusion is whether material things are more quickly adopted than beliefs, ideas, tastes, and attitudes. In recent years it is coming to be realized that "ideas" and "things" are both involved in many instances of borrowing. Thus, diffusion of modern military weapons involves a capacity to use them, that is, a certain technological facility which in turn requires an attitude of mind receptive to a particular kind of rationalism. Generally, of course, a culture will borrow most readily those "things" that will permit it to realize its existing values and goals; this, too, makes it clear why Western military technology is attractive to nations already imbued with the goal of increasing their power in international relations. Indeed, it may be argued that "ideas" diffuse before "things," if we broadly interpret "ideas" to include tastes, desires, and attitudes. Thus, the modern Western idea of nationalism diffused to the Arab world long before Western technology. The desire for automobiles and radios, too, diffuses before the capacity to build them. So, too, Egypt's desire for tanks, planes and submarines is highly developed but not its capacity to produce them. Strictly speaking, the desire for a thing and the capacity to produce it are both complexes of non-material culture. Irrespective, then, of which diffuse first, those ideas *and* things that are most easily adapted to the existing institutions and goals are most readily borrowed.

Another facet of cultural diffusion is the agent through which change is introduced. Innovations may be the result chiefly of indigenous needs and inventions, as most of the communications media in modern Western society have been, or they may result from imitation of foreign models, as has happened with industrial and technological change in the contemporary Arab world. Military change in Egypt has been in the latter class, of course, but it leads to further changes of local origin, as we have seen in the sections on social change under Muhammad Ali and the present regime.

The second general question is: How enduring are the social changes introduced through military channels of any kind? This involves an even broader issue: How thoroughgoing can planned social change be, whatever its origin or motive power?

To help us understand planned social change in Egypt, especially in the present era, we can look at the experience of the Soviet Union and Turkey, where similar efforts have been made by a strong, authoritarian, centralized oligarchy. "In the Soviet case," Inkeles aptly points out, "we have the distinctive combination of planned social change instituted from above, centrally directed and executed by a body whose occupational role is that of effecting change, backed by the power and all the economic and

political force which a totalitarian regime can muster,
guided by a central theory or ideology, carried out at a
relatively unprecedented rate, and extending into every
dimension of social life."[26] Yet even in these surely unprecedented circumstances in modern history, Inkeles continues, there are many areas of social relations which the
Bolsheviks found they could not change directly and in
which, indeed, they had to retreat in their effort to remold
the nation.

"It appears," Inkeles concludes, "that despite the massive
destruction of the main formal elements of the old social
structure and the extensive elaboration of new social forms,
a large number of basic attitudes, values, and sentiments,
and of traditional modes of orientation, expression, and
reaction tend to be markedly persistent." He refers to the
popular attitudes toward authority, conceptions of private
property, kinship structure and interpersonal relations
within the family as features of Russian life resisting
change.[27]

Social change in the Turkey of Ataturk was in some
realms directly aimed at even more personal aspects of life
than in the Soviet Union. Thus, the equalization of
women's status, the reforms in dress, the alphabet change,
the secularization of law, education and personal relations,
and the weakening of the religious elite and the diminu-
tion of the place of religion were all probably meant to
upset traditional Turkish life more than the Bolshevik innovations did traditional Russian life. In other respects,
however, such as the distribution of political and economic
power, Turkish reform has not gone so far as the Soviet.
Yet the Turkey of Ataturk's successors has also had to retreat, especially in the area of religion.

The Russian and Turkish examples indicate the limitations of planned social change imposed by any means, for
some realms of life cannot be directly affected in an
enduring way through the machinery of government.

[26] Inkeles, p. 244.
[27] Ibid., p. 253.

Moreover, we could expect even less social change in a country like Egypt in the several periods we have reviewed because in none, including the present one, have the rulers enjoyed the degree of control and the explicit, detailed program and ideology of the Bolsheviks or the fierce intention to force rapid modernization that moved Ataturk. Yet Egyptian changes in education, encouragement of industry, development of a national spirit, and spread of the network of communications may encourage indirectly the changed family relations, the secular outlook, and the general complex of tastes and attitudes that we associate with an industrial, urban, technologically advanced society. Egypt has not decreed full equality for women, but if the primary and higher education of girls continues to grow, there will be a slower but perhaps irreversible trend toward equality in and outside the home. What is happening, therefore, is that the present regime is encouraging those developments in the economy that stimulate the growth of attitudes and tastes that cannot be directly induced by law or decree—that is, the change from a personality-type that is undisciplined, unaccustomed to the time-rhythm of an industrial society, oriented to local and family loyalties exclusively, and not anxious for self-advancement in modern terms, to a personality-type that displays wider loyalties, adjusts to the tempo of an industrial-urban society, is more oriented toward the future, strives for economic and educational advancement, and is an active part of the national community.

The "populist" Arab military regimes have already accomplished the easiest type of change; they have shifted political power from the combination of foreign interests, the monarchy, large landholders, and a small business and professional class, to the military elite and its mass organizations. The more fundamental economic changes have only been touched—land reform, redistribution of economic functions and wealth, quickening of industrialization, educational expansion, and changes in occupational distribution. The implicit goals of modernization of per-

sonality and interpersonal relations are only beginning to
appear—national orientation, new relations within the
family, loyalties appropriate to an industrial nation.

How enduring are the social changes imposed through
military channels of any kind? There have been few studies
of Western history designed to help answer this question,
perhaps none, and certainly none with respect to the Arab
experience. One hypothesis that suggests itself is that this
mode may be an effective way to introduce new ideas and
techniques which, left to other and less direct means of
diffusion, would spread less systematically and rapidly.
Social change through military considerations or by a military elite shocks a society into awareness of new things.
The deep penetration of this awareness, its transformation
into spontaneous, free desires and tastes and attitudes,
may require a longer process of consolidation through
means that are less arbitrary and authoritarian.

CHAPTER 11

Range and Cost of Social Change

The General Pattern

Consider the following specific changes that have swept over the Arab world in recent decades:

Entrance of large numbers of villagers into cities and factory labor.

Introduction of new methods and tools in farming.

Increase in communication, including the growth of education and literacy, the emergence of a new educated elite and an audience for the mass media.

Decline of religious authority.

Advent of national states backed by a nationalist feeling that spreads from the educated elite to the masses who until recently lay outside the political society.

New family relationships, including the growing equality of women and the loosening of not only male domination, but all parental authority.

Emergence of new political forms from constitutionalism to new kinds of military rule and the application of Western, secular legal codes.

Increasing use of science and technology in industry, agriculture and medical care.

We have touched on many of these changes in our discussion of particular institutions. Now we want to consider change itself. But how can we comprehend such a variety of changes as those just listed and many more (as general or more specific)? There are many ways of looking at social change. One might catalogue the innovations in familiar categories of behavior—political, economic, religious; in dress, cooking, housing; in technology, education, communication. Or one might inquire into the means by which changes are introduced—through conquest, education, growth of industry, and so on. A third way would be to consider the human agents of change—how do the innovators differ from the receivers in social class, nationality, religion, education, and occupation? Changes may be classified as deliberate and planned, or unintended and unplanned. Finally, one might study the varying rates of change—those elements of social life that change quickly and those that change more slowly.

All these general approaches lie beyond our purpose in discussing change in the Arab world. Our purpose is to: (1) look into two of the areas of most profound change, communications and modern industry, which are also among those potent forces leading to further change, (2) consider certain costs of change in the "dislocation" of elements of Arab life, and (3) see how the process of change and borrowing has affected the relations between the West and the Arab world.

For a method by which to comprehend all change in the Near East, broad summaries of change in other regions and other eras appear to be applicable enough to this one too. The sociologist R. M. MacIver has described the "broad pattern of social change" as an increasing specialization of institutions and associations, a decline in ritual, the advance of a utilitarian and secular approach to nature, the separation of cultural life from biophysical limitations through science and technology, and an increase in the "scale of community" or human interaction and interdependence.[1]

In a perceptive study of the modernization of the Near East, Lerner specifies certain changes that follow from these: "The underlying tensions are everywhere much the same—village *versus* town, land *versus* cash, illiteracy *versus* enlightenment, resignation *versus* ambition, piety *versus* excitement." Again: "The direction of change is the same . . . toward mobility—physical, social and psychic

[1] MacIver, *Society*, pp. 479–84, and Wilson, pp. 3–11.

mobility."[2] The old fusion of ends and means, as MacIver puts it, is loosening into separate strands in a process that began centuries ago in the West and is now beginning in Africa and Asia: "No ceremonies salute the time-clock and the steam whistle, no hierophants unveil the mysteries of the counting-house, no myths attend the tractor and the reaper-binder, no dragons breathe in the open hearth furnace. For multitudes the art of living is detached from the business of living, and must find what refuge it can in the now-lengthened interval between today's work and tomorrow's."[3]

One of the first things to change in the Arab world was the attitude toward change itself. When Europeans came to the Near East after the beginning of the transformation of Europe through exploration, growth of commerce, and the introduction of the modern factory system, they were struck by the difference between their own restlessness and the Moslem's acceptance of things as they were. One eighteenth-century British traveler among the Arabs saw the difference vividly but had a germ of doubt about Western "superiority": "Impatience, activity, and sanguine hope, are habits of an European. . . . The habits of the Oriental, on the contrary, are indolence, gravity, patience. His ideas are few in number; and his sentiments in course equally rare. They are, however, generally correct, springing from the objects around him, and for the most part limited to those objects."[4] But the Arabs have caught the spirit of change. The restlessness and impatience of the educated elite has impelled them to espouse, plan, and institute social changes more profound than those the Western powers ever dared to bring.

This enthusiasm for change has combined with nationalism to produce an ambivalence toward the past. On the one hand the educated Arab elite seeks continuity with a great tradition of Arab power and culture. On the other

[2] Lerner, pp. 44, 83.
[3] MacIver, "The Historical Pattern of Social Change," pp. 47–48.
[4] Browne, p. 426.

hand it wants to reject much of that tradition which it
regards as stagnant, ignominious, and a hindrance to progress as it is now defined. Nuseibeh, an Arab political scientist trained in the West, has put the matter plainly:
". . . historical traditions are in themselves a two-edged
weapon: they contribute to solidarity by keeping alive
memories of common historical antecedents and to dissipa-
tion by resuscitating unsavory episodes in which every
history abounds. When the theorists of nationalism, therefore, place historical traditions as the second most important factor in nationalism, they envisage a selective presentation, thoroughly cleansed of disruptive overtones."[5]

Much Arab historical writing, as one Arab historian comments, is little more than uncritical self-praise.[6] At the
other extreme are those who want to deny history in their
eagerness to overcome present Arab weakness and division
and the effects of recent subordination. Few writers on this
subject are as analytical as Nuseibeh who, while not denying the past and its influence on the present, insists upon
the differences between the Arabs of today and of earlier
eras: ". . . the thought and the beliefs of the contemporary Arabs are substantially at variance with those of their
predecessors in ages past . . ."[7] Seeking to free the Arabs
from the many limitations of history, he asks: ". . . why
should the theories or the practices of a thousand years
ago be regarded as more essential or innate . . . than
those of this century?"[8]

Uncritical veneration of the past comes from two attitudes toward the present: opposition to change for whatever reason, and a desire to stimulate revival through
change. The first attitude precludes scientific history, for
worship of the past does not permit objective study of it.
Those who imitate the past blindly do not really know it

[5] Nuseibeh, p. 80.
[6] Faris, pp. 156–57.
[7] Nuseibeh, p. vii.
[8] *Ibid.*, p. 107. In *Ourselves and History* (Ch. 1, 2), Zurayk discusses present Arab conceptions of history and their relation to nationalism.

because they cannot study it realistically; they know only the ways they have learned in their lifetimes, which they take to be the same as those in the eras before them. The second attitude is at least compatible with a serious and realistic effort to understand the past. A desire for change in the present may color one's approach to the study of the past but it does not prevent an evaluation of it. And once a critical attitude is adopted the way is open to discussion and hence to self-correction. A receptive attitude toward change, such as is now spreading among Arabs, affects every aspect of life including even the image of the past.

The "Old" Regimes and the "New"

It has become a truism by now to point out that Asia is going through at least two revolutions: one against Western domination and for national independence and self-direction; and one against social and economic tradition and for greater prosperity and social equality.[9] What are the specific features of these changes in the Arab world? We may distinguish two types of regime or emerging social order, the "pre-populist" and the "populist." They share three characteristics. First, they have all moved recently from some degree of foreign control to independence. Second, they are seeking to modernize by deliberately accelerating, through political means, certain underlying socio-economic processes that are to some extent independent of particular governments. Third, they are not ideologically committed on what I think of as the fundamental issue of freedom and control—that is, since their main goal is national strength through economic development, the question of political organization is secondary (except in Lebanon where, because of the balance of socio-religious groups, many leaders of all such groups hold political freedom to be a condition that may not be sacrificed to any other value, even Arab nationalism). The characteristics of each type appear in the following scheme.

[9] Ball, p. 1, and Nasser, *Egypt's Liberation*, pp. 39–40.

1. *Social Processes*

	PRE-POPULIST	POPULIST
COMMUNI-CATION	limited to elites and periphery	extended to whole society
VOLUNTARY ORGANIZA-TIONS	permits existence, makes some effort to control: few formal organizations, based either on religion or kinship	destroys or co-opts; creates mass organizations, substituting politics for kinship and religion; nationalizes loyalties, permits nothing between family and state unless controlled by latter
EDUCATION	emphasis mainly on higher education and on liberal professions; foreign schools permitted	greater emphasis on primary education and on science and technology; foreign schools nationalized
STATUS OF WOMEN	traditional subordination altered slightly	greater freedom through education and occupational mobility
SOCIAL STRUCTURE AND STANDARDS	loose, many differences; individual closely bound to family and other groups and to locale	greater individual freedom from family and all nonpolitical associations but deliberate effort to produce national uniformity of "acceptable" behavior

2. *Economic Processes and Policies*

	PRE-POPULIST	POPULIST
ORGANIZA-TION	loose controls, private enterprise dominant	extensive controls, claims of socialism
INDUSTRY	small but growing	great emphasis on industrialization
AGRICUL-TURE	large holdings	land reform, state-controlled co-operatives

OWNERSHIP	private, with considerable foreign interests	nationalization in two senses: transfer of foreign property to native control, and state's acquisition of private property and creation of new assets by state
TAXATION	burden falls on middle and upper classes; chiefly indirect	extension of direct taxation to lower-income groups; appeals for "voluntary" contribution of labor, wages, and salaries
PRICES	few controls	increasing control, mainly of food staples

3. Political Processes and Programs

	PRE-POPULIST	POPULIST
NATIONALISM OF DOMINANT ELITE	strong but mixed with older loyalties	intensified, less influenced by other loyalties
PARTICIPATION	masses left largely quiescent	goads, exhorts, draws in masses
FREEDOM: MEANING	Western sense: individual liberty	Synonymous with national independence
FREEDOM: INCIDENCE	some freedom resulting from competition for power among (1) foreign interests, (2) native elite in office, (3) new more nationalist native elite seeking power	no challenge to native ruling elite permitted
CLASS DISTINCTIONS	form basis of regime's policies	emphasis on "social" equality, "economic" democracy and appeal "beyond" classes

	PRE-POPULIST	POPULIST
PARTIES	several	one, or a mass political organization not called a party
LEGISLA-TION	by parliament, with strong executive	rule by decree of leader or cabinet; parliament, if existing, based on plebi-scite
REPRESENT-ATIVE CHAR-ACTER	not "representa-tive," in sense that rulers are traditional elite	more "representative" in sense that rulers' origin is middle or lower class
RULE OF LAW	slow, uncertain growth	reversal of direction
PUBLIC AD-MINISTRA-TION	civil service tends to be personal append-age to ruler; little effort at reform	efforts to introduce mod-ern bureaucratic structure

The United Arab Republic was clearly a populist re-gime and Egypt has remained one, along with Iraq. Leba-non cannot be classified so readily but on most criteria would be pre-populist. This immediately reveals the weak-ness of such classifications, useful though they may be, for Lebanon and Jordan have far less in common with each other than do Egypt, Syria, and Iraq. Another way to apply the classification is to point out that Egypt under the mon-archy, Syria before 1949, and Iraq before the revolution of 1958 were all pre-populist. Like all such schemes, this one exaggerates the differences between the two types. Indus-trialization, nationalism, state controls, land reform, and so on, are not pure populist innovations but have usually been begun under pre-populist regimes. This exaggeration, moreover, makes populism look more "progressive" and pre-populism more "reactionary" than either really is. Yet the scheme does, despite its limitations, bring out the dif-ferences between regimes in the Arab world and illuminate and summarize its myriad changes.

Let us apply the distinction to a particular issue. The Egypt of King Farouk and the Egypt of Colonel Nasser are in a sense opposite models of the political evolution of countries that seek to change from a traditional agricultural to a modern industrial society. Though Farouk's regime was not liberal, it allowed a certain amount of freedom and political dissent. Partly, this was the result of a balance of forces among the palace, the British, and the various Egyptian groups who opposed both; the hesitation or fear of each one to assume all power enabled the others to survive and express themselves. But it stemmed also from the nature of the monarchy as a pre-populist regime. Such a regime and social system does not rest on public opinion. It retains considerable latitude by ignoring the masses, by not drawing them into political life, by leaving them undisturbed in their private misery and political apathy. It can therefore allow greater freedom at the top to the articulate groups—the press, political parties, professionals, students. By leaving the masses dormant, it affords a modicum of freedom for the elites.

Nasser's populist Egypt is something else. Having destroyed the organizations (especially the political parties and the economic bases of the groups that supported them) which enjoyed that modicum of freedom under its predecessor, the populist regime cannot allow these erstwhile elites or their remnants the same degree of freedom in politics. Instead, it seeks mass support by drawing new classes into the political process. These are the peasants and urban workers, who are wooed to give the strength of numbers to the regime's support in the army and the upper levels of the civilian bureaucracy. The political process no longer embraces competing parties and relatively free parliaments but means (1) the single mass organization to arouse and channel political consciousness, (2) the professional associations, peasant co-operatives, trade unions, and religious groups harnessed to the regime's goals, and (3) plebiscites, and parliaments without parties.

Because the populist regime depends on the systematic cultivation of formerly isolated and ignored groups, it must rely on exhortation and propaganda to a greater extent than does the pre-populist regime. That is to say, it communicates with the masses more directly and more often, creates opinions in them, arouses their passions, stimulates their desires and tries to make them work harder for the elite's goal of modernization. In such a society, where mass opinion is stirred, the expression of any opinion becomes all the more significant because it is no longer confined to the homogeneous and articulate thin layer at the top. The populist regime suppresses freedom at the top because freedom may now penetrate the lower levels and have serious consequences. And precisely because opinion and communication may now move the masses being brought into the political spectrum, the populist regime seeks to control expression everywhere.

Revolution in Communications

Increased communication does not itself constitute democracy, though it enhances the role of classes formerly ignored. The American sociologist Charles Horton Cooley fifty years ago suggested that a "wider name" be given to this "modern movement," this "current of new life that is sweeping with augmenting force through the older structures of society . . ."[10] This quickening of life, this extended "scale of community,"[11] has been made possible by the remarkable growth of means of communication. Lerner has made this development the organizing principle of his useful analysis of social change in the Near East: "Central to this change is the shift in modes of communicating ideas and attitudes . . ."[12] And the Wilsons, British anthropologists, on the basis of study in Africa, have shown in detail the enlargement of "scale" in the process of modernization.[13]

The growth in communications is an educational as well

[10] Cooley, pp. 86–87.
[11] MacIver and Page, p. 633.
[12] Lerner, p. 45. See also pp. 55, 62, 185–86, 215.
[13] Wilson, Ch. II.

as a technological process. Through rapidly expanding education, Arab countries have reduced illiteracy, though (except in Lebanon) its proportions remain among the world's highest. Primary school enrollment has doubled for most countries since World War II (the increase has been especially great in state-supported institutions) until today a third to a half of the estimated total of children of primary school age are enrolled in Egypt, Iraq, and Jordan, and perhaps three quarters in Lebanon and Syria.[14] Secondary education, less widespread, has grown even more rapidly since World War II; in some countries the number of students has doubled; in others starting from a low point, the increase has been four- to eight-fold. Higher education has likewise grown enormously. The media of communication and their use have grown out of proportion to the population increase. Circulation of newspapers is now a quarter more to over double what it was a few years ago. Book production has increased too. But radio is the most widespread medium. Egypt has well over a million receivers, four times the number it had less than a decade ago. In 1950 Jordan had 2000; today it has about 50,000. Syria, Lebanon, and Iraq have more than doubled the number of receivers in less than a decade. Attendance at cinemas has risen too, both for Arab (largely Egyptian) productions and European and American films.[15] This expansion of communications is clearly at its beginning. The most explosive effect of widened educational opportunities will be felt in the coming years.

Little of this communication, as we have remarked, is politically free, but a great deal of it opens up new lines of thought and discussion, brings old patterns—even authorities—into question. Almost a century ago the British

[14] Unesco, Table 2, p. 28, and Table 3, p. 29.

[15] Statistics on communication are scanty, unreliable, and not always comparable; hence the avoidance of very precise statements in the text. The data given are computations from material in U.N. publications, mainly *Statistical Yearbook*, 1948, 1952, 1957, 1959, and the Unesco series *Basic Facts and Figures*, 1956, 1959.

publicist, Walter Bagehot, called ours the "age of discussion." He meant free discussion in the political realm but his remarks are relevant to the loosening of rigid structures which is taking place in the Arab world through increased communication. The "mere putting up of a subject to discussion," he said, "with the object of being guided by that discussion, is a clear admission that that subject is in no degree settled by established rules . . . It is an admission too that there is no sacred authority . . ."[16] So important have communication media become that they follow their own law of growth. In Egypt, for example, though the population rose by 25 per cent from 1920 to 1938 and the consumption of certain staple foods fell, yet the number of automobiles increased from 3500 to 33,500, private telephones from 16,300 to 48,900 and radios from none to 72,400.[17]

An American social scientist describes the extension of the idea of progress from the big urban centers of Iraq to a small village in the Southeast near the Iranian border: "Sitting in the guest houses and reed huts of Umm al-Nahr one hears talk about *taqaddum* (progress) . . . All are able, from time to time, to listen to the radio . . . a symbol in the village of prestige and status. Thus Umm al-Nahr includes itself in the plans of the Iraqi Government for the economic and social modernization of the country." Why, he asks, if the villagers are so eager for change, is it "so difficult" to bring it about? "One clue lies in the fact . . . that the villagers are waiting for government or some other outside agency to bring about this imperfectly understood 'progress.' "[18]

The rise of Arab nationalism is intimately connected with the growth of education and the consequent expansion of the press in the late nineteenth century. A British writer on Egypt has observed that during the increasing prosperity of the country under British rule a new and literate middle class was created, one with enough leisure

16 Bagehot, pp. 117–18.
17 Issawi, *Egypt at Midcentury*, p. 55.
18 Quint, pp. 372–74.

to enter politics and journalism. When nationalist agitation reached serious proportions, the British sought first to ignore it and then to offer it an outlet in relatively free journalism rather than in a free parliament.[19] The result was a heavy concentration of nationalist energy in the press, which took on the extremist character so familiar in the area. The British in Egypt, especially under Cromer, planned to create a contented rural middle class impervious to nationalism.[20] In the end this policy failed, of course. Freedom of the press became linked to political agitation very early and the relationship was intimate from about 1870 down to 1914; as a student of Egyptian parliamentary life points out: "The increase in the number of newspapers went hand in hand with an increase in the number of their readers, as education progressed in Egypt. A newspaper offered a connecting link between its readers. Thus, while in Europe groups and parties created their organs, in Egypt groups crystallized around already existing newspapers, and after a certain time grew into parties, the main interests and activity of which still continued to be centered in their organ."[21]

Language, says Nuseibeh, is the "principal factor" in contemporary Arab nationalism, the one generally given first place by Arab writers. "The nation-forming factor in the Arab world at present," he asserts, "is not a central organization in the political sense or a favorable geography. It is social communication. The modern press, radio and cinema are doing a more effective job in forming an Arab nation than all other factors put together. The Arab world does not have a recognized political or economic leadership, but it has an intellectual leadership whose authority recognizes no political boundaries. . . . In recognition of this fact the theorists of Arab nationalism have assigned to language the first place as a factor constituting the Arab nation."[22]

[19] Young, pp. 177–78, 182–83.
[20] Cromer, *Political and Literary Essays*, p. 253.
[21] Landau, p. 109.
[22] Nuseibeh, pp. 68, 76–77.

Though the extent of change is easy to exaggerate, this must not deter us from recognizing that the revolution in communications has begun to penetrate even the Arab village. Berque finds that politics are beginning to replace traditional rites, at least in the Egyptian village, as the occasion for emotional outbursts and even violence. In all this, he points out, the press and radio exert an influence beyond that indicated by figures of circulation and receiving sets. Indeed, he sees the birth of a new folklore, the joining of the political diatribe to the traditional song as both blare over the village radio.[23]

The Arab leaders are themselves quite aware of the power of the radio and use it to the full. For example, in an official history of the first year of the Iraqi revolution of 1958, the broadcasting service is mentioned in the same breath as the army for its heroic role. "If the Army and Ministry of Defense, were the mothers of the July 14 Revolution," says this account, "then the Ministry of Guidance and the Iraq Republic Radio were the guardians of that blessed revolution. From its microphone issued the first voice announcing to the Iraqi people . . . the birth of the popular republic. . . . Thus the Radio was the midwife by whose hands the republic came to life. . . . And from the first moment the radio and television have guarded the beloved republic and have gone hand in hand with it and step by step through the stages of its progress."[24]

Industrialization

We know a great deal about the social changes that attended industrialization in Europe and the United States, but we know very little about the same process in the Arab world. First, of course, it has not yet gone far there. Second, studies of the so-called "social aspects of industrialization" in the "underdeveloped" areas are very few, and most of them are not independent inquiries into

[23] Berque, *Histoire Sociale*, pp. 15–16, 42.
[24] Republic of Iraq, p. 255.

what actually happens in these areas but rather applications to them of what has been learned about the West. In the absence of a body of reliable accounts of changes wrought by industrialization in the Arab world itself, it may be more useful to discuss briefly some of the conditions which make industrialization possible in the first place, since it is by no means inevitable that the Arab world will become highly industrialized.

One condition is a stable political order upon a social and legal foundation that encourages a system of credit and investment over a wide area. Another is the development of an outlook that permits the mastery of natural forces and the application of such knowledge, through ambition and the creation of wants for material goods, to the production of such goods and services. These are far from appearing in the Arab world in sufficient strength to assure the success of the ruling elite's undoubted desire for industrial progress, especially in view of the Arab world's lack of the necessary raw materials as well.

One of the main issues is: who can carry through industrialization in the Arab world? The "middle class" is the common answer, but it does not tell us what this "middle class" is. Analogies to the West are deceptive in this respect. It is true that industrialization in Europe and America in the eighteenth and nineteenth centuries was intimately bound up with the rise of the middle classes and their prosperity. Inevitably, we ask whether the Near East can give birth to the same kind of dynamic middle class, the catalyst that stirs up a placid economy.

When we speak of a middle class in terms of its economic role, we are referring to two related but distinct elements within it: an entrepreneurial class that accumulates, organizes and allocates capital, and a technical-administrative bureaucracy that manages industrial enterprises. In an earlier era of Western industrial society, these two tasks were more likely to be fulfilled by the same persons than they are now. Especially in the last fifty years or so, the West has experienced too well-documented processes: first, the separation between entrepreneurship and management, and second, the relative decline of the individual entrepreneur and the concentration of the entrepreneurial function in management boards (in private or state enterprises).

If individual entrepreneurship in the West is becoming a rare commodity, can the Near East develop it in abundance? The Arab world, it appears, is not likely to become highly industrialized (if at all) through the efforts of a domestic entrepreneurial class of individuals acting in their private capacities. It is likely to be more successful in nurturing a "salariat" to manage industries set up by whatever combination of local or foreign and public or private capital proves to be feasible.

In order to industrialize, an economy needs to develop the two kinds of talent just mentioned: entrepreneurial (either based on public or private capital), and administrative-technological. Traditionally the middle class in the West supplied these abilities. Thus far the middle groups have failed to do so in the Near East; as we saw in Chapter 7, they have simply not engaged in that kind of activity. This failure is, in its turn, undoubtedly the result in part of an unfavorable economic environment, for there is certainly plenty of entrepreneurial talent there in a commercial sense and administrative talent as well. Religious and educational traditions, however, have combined with economic weakness and the lack of certain natural resources to discourage the talents needed specifically for industrial development: those entrepreneurial and technological skills associated with the machine process. In the past, but to a declining degree today, foreigners, non-Moslems and non-Arabs, performed these functions. More and more the Arab world will need, if it is going to industrialize, a new middle class of technicians and managers, engineers, skilled workers, and foremen—an industrial and not merely an administrative bureaucracy.

What will be the source of such a new middle class? Will the engineers and managers, the technicians and foremen, emerge from those middle groups from which the *administrative* bureaucracy in government and trade has been drawn? If so, there will have to be a change in the society's estimation of occupations, for the prejudice against technology and engineering is still intense and the attraction of clerical work, administration, and law very strong. It is entirely possible that the source for such a technological-managerial "salariat" may be not the present middle groups but the sons of the socio-economic layer just below them—the upper reaches of the peasantry and the urban industrial workers. For them the chance to rise to middle-class status through technical education and modern industrial employment is more likely to be welcomed as an unequivocal advance. For the sons of the middle groups as now constituted, however, such an opportunity would not be so eagerly seized.

The new regimes in the Arab countries may well find it in their interest to create other sources of support by encouraging the growth of a new social group. To draw these lower socio-economic elements into a different kind of middle class will require an even greater expansion of primary and secondary education and a greater emphasis on technical education. Public schools, beyond the primary grades especially, are still luxuries which a majority of the people in the Near East cannot afford for their children. But, as I have mentioned, compulsory elementary education is reaching an increasing proportion of the children of school age. Still the number receiving a technical education in the preparatory and secondary schools in Egypt, for example, actually declined in the early 1950s, although at the university level it increased somewhat.[25] The opportunities that would be created for such a new middle group by industrialization could be a stabilizing influence in the Near East. It would probably reduce the tendency of the educated elite to concentrate on politics, provide employment for many of them who cannot find useful work of a kind they have come to expect by virtue of their education, and in general open wider the door to social and personal advancement.

[25] National Bank of Egypt, *Economic Bulletin* (1957), 10:46.

Can the Near East breed the second middle-class component necessary for industrialization—the accumulators, organizers, and allocators of capital for industrial enterprises? Historically, Western entrepreneurs in private ventures emerged from the urban merchant class and the artisans rather than from the employed administrative bureaucracy or the independent professions. But the day seems to be past when a small merchant in the Arab world (such as constitutes about half of the Egyptian "middle class," for example) could accumulate enough capital or technical knowledge to go into industry on a scale that would make a real difference in the nature of the economy. For the same reasons that a firm starting out to manufacture a product today does not have to go through the stages of technological development that older firms did, an entrepreneur today, even in a non-industrial country, cannot establish an industrial enterprise with only the small amount of capital needed in an earlier era of modern capitalism. Studies indicate that the capital requirements for a modest rate of industrialization of essentially agricultural economies are so high that it is unlikely that a large proportion of either this capital or the talent needed to apply it will be obtained from private domestic sources. Capital and talent both are likely to be provided, if industrialization is to proceed substantially, by foreign sources (private, governmental or intergovernmental) and domestically by the state itself.

To be sure, various inducements, such as easy tax arrangements and compensated expropriations of large agricultural holdings, may divert domestic capital into industry, but this process will create investors rather than entrepreneurs. There is indeed a growing respect in the Arab world for the possibilities of personal and national benefit to be realized from modern industry, but there is also suspicion of certain features and effects of it.

The expansion of the oil industry in several Arab countries and the profit to others from shipments of oil to the Mediterranean area has led to the growth of some small ancillary private enterprise in the oil-producing countries and a desire in those countries and others for employment in the private, foreign firms (which produce and ship the oil) in which the conditions of work are so much more attractive than in government or domestic private firms. The high prestige traditionally associated with a government post has not yet declined much but there are signs, at least in Egypt, that it is beginning to lose its status in the eyes of the younger men and that it seems a less attractive career than formerly.[26] The careers that are gaining in prestige, however, are not private trade or manufacture but the independent professions and employment on the professional level in the large, well-established companies already engaged in manufacturing.

Private entrepreneurship is thus not growing much more attractive in the Arab world. Aside from the purely economic or traditional factors discouraging it, there is a political or ideological element worth mentioning. A socioeconomic class or a type of economy needs a rationale or an ideology to justify it. Western capitalism developed or found (depending on one's philosophy of history) its rationale in a certain kind of religious orientation, a secularization of social relationships, and in political liberalism. Its advocates and defenders (and even some of its most fervent enemies, such as Marx and Engels) could point not only to its productive power but also to its loosening of tradition, its role in scientific and technological progress, its relationship to political democracy and even to the arts. What sort of rationale can the Arab world develop for private entrepreneurship? I don't mean a rationale for industrialization itself—such a rationale comes easily because modern industry is associated with a higher standard of living and with national power. I mean a rationale for industrialization through domestic private capital and entrepreneurial talent.

The Near East has in this respect become a victim of its own ideology. For many years its leaders and its press have attacked the West as imperialist. In recent years, however,

[26] Berger, *Bureaucracy and Society in Modern Egypt*, Ch. 4–5.

they have identified imperialism with capitalism. Rightly or wrongly, and irrespective of the quasi-colonial background that impels them in this direction, they have identified private enterprise as the evil demon behind Western imperialism and expansion. And the foreign-owned oil companies stand even now as the kind of evidence of such claims that is widely accepted in the Arab world. The spokesmen for the articulate classes, who are themselves opposed to socialism at home, fully accept (though perhaps unaware of its source) the Leninist and Soviet Russian view of Western expansion. As Russian influence in the area has grown, this view has been further spread. With such a notion daily pounded into their minds, can the Arabs now, across the threshold of political independence at last, build up a rationale for private enterprise?

Our conclusion must be that if the Arab countries are to industrialize at all in the near future, it will be substantially through means other than private capital and private entrepreneurial talents. They will probably be able to produce the technological skills needed, and it is through this process that the middle groups are likely to play an important part in industrialization. Managerial and even entrepreneurial skills put to work by the state or through governmental stimulation in some other form are more likely to be the pattern of economic growth in the Arab world than the creation of a swarm of busy individual entrepreneurs acting for themselves in the image of the older Western pattern.

Yet to achieve even that form of growth the Arab countries face a severe test in finding suitable motives and incentives for the widely accepted goal of industrialization. The governments are seeking to impress upon the people the importance of material goals but are demanding material sacrifices at the same time. As de Jouvenel has pointed out (in an analysis already referred to in Chapter 9), it is one thing to share material goods equally when they are spurned, as in a small idealistic utopian or religious community, but it is quite another to demand unrestrained effort to increase material goods without rewarding such efforts with increased access to them.[27] The Arab countries that stress socialist goals face this dilemma acutely. The individual is asked to work hard but not to the point where he acquires too much for himself: first, because personal gain may retard social enrichment and thus interfere with nationalist goals; second, because personal gain is not always applied to industrialization; and third, because personal gain is probably the result of exploitation and hence a violation of socialism and Arab brotherhood. Emphasis on material values but social sacrifice is generally accompanied, as it has been in the U.S.S.R. and China and from time to time in Eastern Europe, by the severest form of repression and demagogy.

The problem here, as in other realms we shall mention in a moment, is that the Arab elites—and even more especially the masses—have adopted industrialization as a goal before they have developed the capacity, through ideological and scientific-technological experience, to achieve that goal. But there is another side. How can the capacity be developed if the desire or the want is not present? Not all countries need to go through every stage of the West, and it is true, in a rough, practical way, that the best way to industrialize is to go at it directly. I have tried here to indicate some of the barriers rather than to insist that industrialization is impossible in the Arab world.

Dislocations and Costs

A social problem arises when one kind of change is wanted but the things that it brings are not wanted. This is the cost of social change and everywhere in the Arab world it is mounting. Two realms in which these "dislocations" appear with especial force are religious belief and practice, and the ideas diffused through the mass media. Before considering these matters, however, let us examine the origins of the dislocations and some examples to indicate their range.

[27] De Jouvenel, pp. 11–12.

In a very revealing essay Gibb has pointed out that "all social changes in the Near East during the past century or so have arisen, directly or indirectly, from the impact of our Western society and the penetration of Western techniques and ideas into what used to be the Ottoman Empire as well as into Egypt and Iran."[28] Since this observation was made, two decades ago, its essential correctness has been further borne out, but now social change is occurring more on the basis of impulses within the Arab world, that is, motives and forces which are indirect rather than direct results of the Western impact. Gibb related the "uneven distribution of social changes" to two factors: (1) "variation in the force and duration of the external pressures" from the West; (2) differences in the desire of the people of the Near East to accept changes and in their capacity to do so.[29] The result, he added, is that such changes as do occur are more visible than even greater changes are in the West. This is because almost any change reveals the lack of homogeneity in Arab society, for some groups adopt it and others do not, and the contrast and clash between the old and new are quite obvious in everyday life.[30] Such is the case with traditional and modern dress for both men and women, secular and religious education, the donkey and the airplane, and so on.

Arabs are fond of saying that they want to borrow "the best" of Western life while retaining "the best" in their own tradition. This usually means a desire for Western science and technology without other Western values. But in recent years they are becoming aware that it is not easy to "borrow" a "technique" without first creating a "value" appropriate to it or at least developing such a value later in order to realize the technique's fruits in a reliable, stable manner. To say that they want industrialization, for example, means that Arabs must be ready to accept some of the things that go with it: greater incentives and creation of a new working class with an industrial discipline.

28 Gibb, "Social Change . . . ," p. 43.
29 Ibid., pp. 37–38.
30 Ibid., pp. 34–35.

Many Arab and Western observers who profess a concern for the preservation of tradition often complain that the West "offers" the Arabs the "solutions" that the West itself has adopted. This, it is held, is wrong, for the Near East should "work out" its own solutions. The question, left unasked, is simply: solutions to what? The leading spokesmen for the Arabs have been asking how to reduce poverty, illiteracy, and disease; improve material well-being; build industry; create national states; establish powerful armies with modern weapons. These are "Western" questions, and it should come as no surprise that the proposed solutions are also Western, for it was in Europe that these goals were first achieved. Some Arabs and Moslems, however, ask questions of a religious or spiritual nature and to these, it is true, the answers may not be Western. But these questions do not come from those who are shaping the Arab world today.

The attempt to borrow a finished Western product, so to speak—a radio, a political institution, a conception of family life—is often distorted because the cultural preparation for the institution or product is not adequate; it can also lead to the dislocations we have been discussing. Thus the Arabs have in several instances tried parliamentary democracy, but none of these efforts (except the highly modified one in Lebanon) has proved hardy enough to withstand the rigors of the new environment. Nor, to consider the question of education, has the economy of the Near East been able to absorb the large number of university-trained men and women it turns out each year, with the result that there is always a large, ambitious, articulate group that is frustrated and dissatisfied.

Some changes are deceptively easy to want. Few people in any society will object to the adoption of the goal of better education, health, and standards of living. In a nationalistic community, too, few will object to the goals of industrialization and the creation of modern military power. But despite the widespread agreement on such *goals*, there may be less agreement on the things they re-

quire in advance or on the consequences they bring in their
train. The father who wants his daughter to be educated
may be pleased that she is able to get a job in an office but
not so pleased when she wants greater freedom in deciding
whom she shall marry. The worker who likes the idea of a
powerful nation may not be willing to undertake the responsibility of hard and steady labor in a factory. The
religious man who wants to see a resurgent Islam may not
like the secular ideas and the attenuation of religious faith
and practice among the officers and soldiers exposed to
modern military-technological discipline. One writer of the
old generation, though a strong nationalist, understood the
difference between adopting goals and developing the
means to achieve them. The "contact of Easterners . . .
with the West," he wrote in 1948, exaggerating out of
disappointment, "has taught them nothing but extrava-
gance and ostentation. . . . We could have copied [from
the West] their painstaking perseverance, their industry,
and their care for the material and economic features of
life. We could have learned from them to be self-reliant
and dependent on personal effort and merit instead of on
ancestors and property."[31]

Very often dislocation is the result of rapid change in
one realm and slow change in another. The case of irrigation in Egypt provides a good example. For thousands of
years the Nile flood lasting six or seven weeks was the only
source of water. "Basins" connected to the river by canals
retained the water on the land, which supported one crop
each year. In the second quarter of the nineteenth century
the ruler of Egypt, Muhammad Ali, had "perennial" irrigation introduced on a limited scale, and the British expanded this system considerably. Under it, water from the
Nile was channeled and distributed all year round in such
a way as to permit a great expansion of cotton cultivation.
Cotton was the basis of the growth of prosperity in Egypt
and is still the economy's main source of foreign exchange.
But perennial irrigation did more than permit this expan-

31 Kurd Ali, pp. 182–83.

sion of wealth and growth of population. It also brought a great increase in the incidence of bilharziasis, a debilitating disease caused by a parasite, which has afflicted from half to three quarters of the men in the countryside. They work in the muddy water and become victims of intestinal attacks which kill so often that there has been a reduction in the male-female ratio.[32]

A prominent Egyptian geographer, Dr. Huzzayin, has argued that perennial irrigation has affected the very nature of the Egyptian village and the relations among its inhabitants. When the Nile at flood-time was the sole source of water, he says, the villagers had to build up a hill on which to place their settlement in order to keep it above the water level. They also worked together to build the dykes and basins, and in general engaged in a cooperative life based on their common needs. With perennial irrigation, villages did not have to be elevated and the work of maintaining the system was done through a central administration. "The real purpose and motive of solidarity, collaboration and cooperation had vanished . . . Thus Egypt had to face one of the most serious problems in its modern history, that of the decaying and somewhat disrupted large village system."[33]

Dislocations and costs pile up when adjustments to certain changes are not quick enough. If all change is coordinated so perfectly that each specific aspect is dovetailed with others, then dislocation can be minimized whether the rate of change as a whole is slow or rapid. But this is not possible even in countries like the U.S.S.R. and China, where controls have been exercised to the apparent limit of human capacity, if not beyond it. Moreover, if the rulers of a country are able to exercise such perfect control, they probably prefer to use it not to achieve balanced change and fewer dislocations but to move even more rapidly toward the goals they themselves set, and then take their chances on being able to "meet" the costs

[32] See, for example, Cleland, pp. 8off.
[33] Huzzayin, p. 271.

by suppressing the freedom to object and by offering enough incentives to make up for public dissatisfaction.

In the political realm, too, uneven change affects the basis of national loyalty today. The Arab world used to be ruled by emperors, kings, viceroys, and colonial agents. Now power is held by men who profess democracy and claim to represent the people. How can these new rulers insure obedience on such unfamiliar principles? The present leaders want to make the nation and the state coterminous, which is a new idea in an area accustomed for centuries to the accommodation of many nationalities and religions in one state. The quick rise of nationalist feeling is one prop to their leadership but obviously it is not enough, for all of them are seeking to speed up this transitional period by drawing new classes into the political system, as we have seen in Chapters 8 and 9. The locus of rule having been quickly changed by the advance of national independence, these new rulers must find new social bases for their regimes in other classes and groups. They seek, in a word, legitimacy, the recognized right to rule.

The Crisis of Religious Faith

To dramatize the secular challenge to religious faith, in the Arab world, Lerner once aptly referred to the issue of "Mecca *versus* mechanization."[34] Mechanization as a symbol of secular attitudes is so far ahead that it is even winning in Mecca itself, where the air age and the electronics revolution have already altered the setting, though not the procedure, of the ancient pilgrimage. Religious faith and Islamic loyalty remain very strong among the rural masses, but even there nationalism has come to challenge old loyalties. Among young people in both rural and urban areas religion is losing its hold in a world that emphasizes loyalty to state and nation, industrialization, modernization. It is not that atheism is in danger of sweeping the Near East, it is simply that religious values are weakened because they

[34] *The New Leader*, June 17, 1957, p. 25.

are not very relevant to the new goals. This is especially true among the urban educated classes. They defend Islam as a religion when it is under attack, and their attitudes, feelings, and ideas are still influenced by their Islamic upbringing. But for most of those who are shaping the Arab world today, religion is relegated to a special place. It no longer pervades the society, and it is no longer the source of social energy or the model of the future. And this is the hallmark of secularism.

Secularism is not a new challenge to Islam. In the past it has not, however, seemed to be a very serious threat. Because of the wide claims of Islam, its joining of "state" and "church" in a single community, and the identification of the Arab with the Islamic realm, von Grunebaum points out, the Arabs remained "immune to that movement of complete secularization which at one time seemed inseparable from Westernization" even when they adopted Western reforms.[35] As he has also remarked, Islam borrowed a great deal from the West and other societies, but always selectively. In its borrowing Islam "was careful to eliminate or neutralize any element endangering its religious foundation . . ."[36] In its relations with other societies before the modern era, the Moslem Arab world was faced mainly with rival religious systems which it feared and greatly resented. When the challenge of secularism came with the French Revolution, the Islamic world, as Lewis has astutely shown, was far from disturbed by the non-religious character of its ideology. Indeed, Moslems could accept the ideas of the French Revolution (which Lewis says "was the first great movement of ideas in western Christendom that had any real effect on the world of Islam") without fear that their own religion was the target of the Christian West. "The initial attraction of these ideas . . . is rather to be found in their secularism," Lewis remarks. As a secular, even anti-clerical movement, the French Revolution offered to Islam the hope of finding

[35] von Grunebaum, *Islam*, p. 60.
[36] von Grunebaum, *Medieval Islam*, pp. 320–21.

the "elusive secret of Western power without compromising its own religious beliefs and traditions."[37]

Today secularism is a real danger to traditional Islam because it is now an Arab, not a foreign, idea, and so threatens the Islamic community from within. Secularism finds expression chiefly through Arab nationalism and the strong desire to industrialize and become a powerful member of a secular world of nation-states.

There are two main responses to the secular challenge. The first is the "modernist" attempt, since the latter part of the nineteenth century, to interpret Islam liberally: to encourage science, more freedom for women, self-analysis, and an open attitude toward the new secular learning—in general, to change from slavish devotion to tradition. In the Arab world modernism seeks to base itself upon the traditional sources but to attach new and contemporary meanings to them. Modernists have been weak, timid, cautious and not very numerous. They have suffered the frequent fate of moderates in a period of rapid change. The secularists on one side have simply ignored religion and have gone ahead with their plans to modernize the Arab world without concern for religious tradition except to use Islamic loyalty as part of their nationalist appeal. On the other side, the "fundamentalists" have continued to insist upon the maintenance of Islam absolutely intact.

Fundamentalism has in its favor the weight of doctrinal purity and the conservatism of the mass of religious Moslems. The fundamentalists are quite aware that practice by no means hews to the line of doctrine, but that is to them no reason to alter doctrine. In addition to the inherent resistance of a doctrine to change, Islam has another impediment. "Change" means movement toward the Western pattern even when it is charitably called "modernization." But for many centuries Islam as a religion was under attack from the West. The character and motives of the Prophet were vilified, the beliefs of Moslems

[37] Lewis, "The Impact of the French Revolution on Turkey," pp. 105–6.

ridiculed. It is not easy, therefore, for staunch Moslems to alter their doctrine in the full light of day for the Western world to see.

So fundamentalism refuses to see any need for change and any good in it. Islam, in common with other religions and perhaps a bit more than most, inherently rejects change. The word for "innovation" in the religious sense is *bid'a*, meaning also heresy and something generally bad. It is the opposite of *sunna*, path, that is, the way of the Prophet or of his community of Moslems. Early in the development of Islam it became evident that some practices would have to be adopted for which there were no exact precedents in the Prophet's day. A distinction was made, therefore, between those innovations that contradicted the Koran and those that merely lacked precedent; among the latter, a good innovation became acceptable.[38]

But the major drift of Islamic thought has been to resist the new. This tendency went so far, in the judgment of one Orientalist, that for a long time the Moslem Arabs remained intellectually silent under the weight of the Koran. As a book that, by its own account, is an explanation of everything (Koran, ch. 12, verse 111), was sent down on a night when all things were made clear (ch. 44, verse 3), and overlooks nothing (ch. 6, verse 38), it seemed to make all other writing "superfluous or dangerous."[39] The teaching of the Moslem Brotherhood, perhaps the leading popular fundamentalist movement in the Arab world, stresses the completeness of Islam. An analyst of this movement says it claims to include "every principle and doctrine, whether found actually in religion or coming from outside." This strict fundamentalist group, claiming to adhere to Islam in all its purity, also insists that it includes the "best of the principles of the East and the West . . ." The Koran, its martyred leader is reported to have said, comprehends all the sciences in one verse. Fi-

[38] See article on "Bid'a," *E.I.* (*New*), Vol. I, p. 1199.
[39] Margoliuth, pp. 40–41.

nally, Islam is said to provide rules that combine all the good offered in any religious or secular idea on any subject.[40]

The ability to discover all modern principles in the Koran and the traditions of Islam is characteristic of both modernists and fundamentalists, though they seek different rationales, of course. One recent writer on economic affairs demonstrates one kind of modernist effort by finding that Islamic principles in ethics, politics, and economics have for their "ultimate object" the building of a "cooperative" society. (In common with other modernists and fundamentalists, he compares Islamic ideals with Western realities and finds the former superior, but that is not the point here.) The institution of private property in Islam is appraised as follows:

In Islam, the constitution is directed to the benefit of the owner of the property, thus maintaining the incentive of self-interest, an essential . . . of economic growth. At the same time, the institution, through its positive and negative obligations, based on the theory of trusteeship, is directed . . . to the service of the community. This harmonious balance of conflicting interests eliminates class hatred, affirms social cohesion, reduces the possibilities of accumulation of wealth in the hands of a limited group, and develops a more equitable distribution of national income.[41]

Fundamentalism resists reinterpretations and the implication that what was laid down by Allah through his Prophet needs to be elaborated or brought up to date. About a decade ago an Egyptian Moslem wrote a liberal interpretation of Islam. Arguing for the separation of church and state, he insisted that the task of religion is moral guidance, not power and rule. The Prophet, he claimed, exercised political power only because of the social circumstances of the day, which forced him to protect

[40] Husaini, pp. 40–41.
[41] El-Araby, pp. 1, 7.

his followers. Soon after its publication, this book was answered by a fundamentalist in a way that made clear that, since everything was divinely ordained in Islamic history, nothing can be "interpreted" anew in our day. "Is it true," he asked, "that local needs forced the Prophet to rule? . . . To answer in the affirmative would be a great error. It was God, not the so-called 'circumstances', that prescribed the Prophet's duty and made worldly rule an integral part thereof."[42] The extent of resistance to modernism, reinterpretation, even nationalism, all of which imply secularism from within, is revealed in the same writer. "Nationalism," he warns, "was our most important imitation of the West. . . . Every tiny Muslim state actively seeks its own independence . . . Nationalism has lost for us our Islamic unity . . . Even this is not all. The truth is that every growth of nationalism, racialism, and infidel patriotism is a loss of Islamic faith as well as a loss of Islamic rule. The revival of such evil fanaticism is a plot against God's religion . . ."[43]

Such extremism is stimulated by the secular drift. One of the surest signs of that drift is that religion is increasingly relegated to a special place, honored but restricted. This is especially so in education, where the secular public school system is rapidly displacing the old *kuttab*, or small religious school, even in the villages. Now that education is secular, a few hours a week are devoted to religious instructions.[44] As in the West, when religion is no longer so strong in the home and in the religious institutions themselves, it is introduced into the secular schools, where it fares no better for being imposed on a captive audience.

In Islam's travail as it confronts the modern world, the West has done little to help. It was the West, of course, that created the conditions in which Islam now finds it necessary somehow to comprehend what has happened in social thought and social life since the religion's principles

[42] al-Ghazzali, p. 40.
[43] *Ibid.*, p. 35.
[44] Unesco, Table 5, pp. 49–52.

were laid down from one thousand to thirteen hundred years ago. Western governments in the Near East have been concerned mainly with political and economic life. They adopted toward religion and ideas a self-righteous attitude, hardly consistent with their actions in general, that they must not interfere with indigenous customs and beliefs. Western thinkers, too, have been largely unsympathetic to Islam as a religious system.

There have been three kinds of Westerners concerned with Near Eastern thought. Missionaries have sought to convert Moslems. Some scholars have sought to show how their ideas came mainly from Judaism, Christianity, and ancient Greece. And romantics in flight from the modern West have sought refuge in Arab desert ways or in Islamic mysticism and have therefore bid Arabs and Moslems not to change. Moslem thinkers have thus had to reconstruct religious thought in an uncongenial environment, in which Western religion or rationalism put holes in its efforts at reform while Western romanticism's frantic embrace did not permit change to breathe and live. The West complained that Islam was static but greeted every sign of change as an abandonment of tradition or as an inadequate adjustment. This is true even of a recent sympathetic account of the "Islamic crisis" in Arab life. The author, a Western Orientalist, insists that Moslems must "bridge" the "gap" between their "faith" and the "modern" world. But he will not allow that anything they do or think can achieve this goal. Conservative Islam, he claims, "preserves a dignity and nobility . . . that cannot be lost without disaster to society." But it has a fundamental weakness, for it has failed "adequately to relate itself to modernity" and indeed does not "effectively grasp modern problems." Modernist Islam, on the other hand, loses "dignity" and "nobility" and lacks "intellectual and emotional integrity." Secularism is the answer, he feels, but where can an "Islamic" liberalism and humanism be found when both Arab and Islamic society rejected Greek and Christian humanism though they borrowed other features from those two systems of thought?

The author suggests two apparent possible sources, Islam itself (but reinterpreted), and the West. Yet it is just such sources that so many Western observers deny to Moslems. If they reinterpret and become modern, they lose touch with tradition. If they borrow from the West, they fail to preserve what is vaguely called the spirit of Islam. There seems to be no course that will satisfy the Western caretakers of Islamic purity, modern or traditional. As the same writer puts it, the problem is that "the degree to which those who in the fullest sense know the religion have largely lost contact with the modern world, and those genuinely oriented to modernity have largely lost contact with their religion."[45]

Just as Western governments in the Near East could find no genuinely liberal and democratic groups to encourage and support among the Arabs, so most Western students of Islam see no hope for a modernized Islam despite their frequent avowal of faith in Islam's creativity and vigor. And just as the Arabs resented the proconsuls who preferred the solid, decent peasants to the troublesome, unstable nationalists in the cities, so they suspect the motives and logic of those scholars who are distressed by "modernism" in Islam. One Arab writer anachronistically accuses most Western Orientalists of "promoting imperialist designs" when they study Eastern mysticism and spirituality. They intend by this, he says, "to emphasize the difference between Western and other peoples, encourage the latter to cling to their own traditions . . . and to dissuade them from adopting modern culture and thereby liberating themselves from Western domination."[46] The motive attributed is childish but the sentiment expressed is common in the Near East as the intellectual feels the restriction and frustration of the Western response to his effort to do what the West says he must do: "adjust" to the "world of today."

[45] Smith, pp. 92, 150–52, 160, 301–4.
[46] Ayyad, p. 466.

Modernism and Mass Media

The Arab writer just quoted tells a revealing story. An American came to the Syrian University to describe the cultural interests of the foundation he represented. "But," the author relates, "when some of the teachers urged the need of the university for laboratories and technical equipment, this American visitor immediately made excuses, pointing out a number of difficulties in the way of acquiring such things. As soon as the discussion turned towards the subject of Islamic mysticism, on the other hand, he pledged assistance to any institution set up for studies of such immense importance."[47]

The Arab writer's attitude is "modernism"—the desire for Western technology coupled with the somewhat patronizing attitude toward traditional Islamic thought. The Westerner tries to interest the Arab in his own past, but the Arab wants to fashion his future in the image of the West's present. The Arab author is himself quite aware of the possibility that such borrowing may also lead to the creation of a debased culture in which unguided masses will demand "new sensations . . . excitements which are of no permanence or value." But he is willing to face that problem and to try to solve it through proper leadership and "combined cultural and social planning."[48]

Having faced the problems of stagnation and weakness for so long, the Arabs would be very happy to have to face those of wealth and power and modernity. They are far from having to concern themselves with the first two, but the problems of modernity are already upon them. The expansion of education has made hundreds of thousands literate, creating a large market for newspapers, popular magazines, and sensational novels. Radio, motion pictures, and now television do not even require literacy to

[47] Ayyad, p. 467.
[48] Ibid., p. 473.

attract a mass audience. So the phenomenon of "mass culture," familiar in the West, begins to appear in the Near East, emerging from the growth of communications combined with two other developments. First, the advent of new ideologies like nationalism, socialism and democracy have given unprecedented importance to the tastes and demands of the ordinary man. Second, the availability of money has made it profitable to market cultural products aimed at an audience whose taste is uncultivated and therefore attracted to the lurid and the melodramatic. I do not mean by this that the level of living has advanced greatly, but merely that cash is now available to an increasing proportion of the society as urbanization grows and agriculture is shifted to a cash basis. The possession of cash confers the power of choice to some extent, and this choice is exercised more and more in the selection of the products of "mass culture": newspapers, picture and movie magazines, the movies themselves, radio, the gadgets and gewgaws of the West.

In this welter, the old folk culture is dying a quick death. Folk art yields place in three realms. First, the Arab cultural *avant-garde* borrows chiefly from the West in literature and art, rather than from folk sources. Second, on the popular level cultural products tend more and more to imitate Western models on the same mass level. Third, Arab traditional high culture is watered down in a process that has long been familiar in the West. Several decades ago the novelist John Dos Passos saw this process farther east in the Moslem world and put the matter succinctly: "Henry Ford's gospel of multiple production and interchangeable parts will win hearts that stood firm against Thales and Democritus, against Galileo and Faraday. There is no god strong enough to withstand the Universal Suburb."[49]

The media of mass communication play the leading part in acquainting the Arabs with the new ways of living that are deemed appropriate to a modern, progressive na-

[49] Dos Passos, p. 86.

tion. Thus as the Western rulers leave the Near East, the Near East becomes more Western. The Arab leaders face two ways: they push the West out politically and pull the masses Westward culturally. When Arabs now do the things that Westerners used to do in their countries, is that "Arabization" or is it "Westernization?" Perhaps the evasively neutral term "modernization" is better, since it avoids the question of imitation. The process, whatever it is called, goes on apace. There *dragomans*, tourist guides, who now wear coat-and-trousers instead of the *galabiya* or gown, and who can hardly be distinguished from European businessmen in the hotel lobbies.

There used to be three kinds of men's clothing in most Arab cities: the traditional *galabiya*, the Western suit, and the transitional striped pajamas chiefly worn by the youth. Now there are fewer and fewer pajama-clad boys; they make a clean jump from *galabiya* to coat-and-trousers. The fez and other Eastern headdresses have virtually disappeared. In Egypt the fez is still worn only by some older men of the lower socio-economic classes, a few sophisticated has-beens who live on their memories of the bygone nationalism of the Wafd party and the monarchy, and by servants and waiters. In more and more homes even the servants shed the *galabiya* for white jacket and black trousers, either on the insistence of their employers or on their own. In many homes, French period furniture, the customary sign of elegant taste among the elite, is fighting a losing battle against Chinese and lean Scandinavian "modern." Sometimes all three styles fill a room, with a few local trays and hassocks included as an uneasy nod to nationalism. Cairo and other cities have several shops selling "modern" furniture and *objets d'art* like those of the Left Bank in Paris, Soho in London and Greenwich Village in New York. This is the meaning of "modern" in everyday terms, and it is spreading, like most such innovations, from the upper-income and educated elite down to the middle groups who learn from the films and magazines that this is the way to live.

The movies are the most potent medium by which all

1

classes of people in the Arab world learn about the way other nations live and about the Arab style of modern living upon which most approval is placed by favorable portrayal. Egyptian films dominate the Arab market; no other Arab film industry approaches Egypt's in extent and popularity. A successful Egyptian film of 1958 illustrates the kind of themes and modes of living portrayed approvingly. Called *The Street of Love,* it tells the story of a young villager whose musical inclinations and talent are encouraged by an old man living in the same village—a great composer who has seen better days and now lives a simple rustic life. The hero goes to Cairo, where he teaches in an exclusive conservatory for girls. He becomes a famous composer. His life is complicated by two love affairs. Just before his masterpiece is to be performed at the Opera, the girl he has rejected schemes to prevent the conductor from appearing. At the last moment, the villagers arrive on the scene with the old man, who turns out to be the real composer of the great music. In a grand finale, the old man conducts a 100-piece orchestra playing a symphonic arrangement of a traditional Arab melody, as the hero and his fiancée sing and as a chorus does a modern dance. The ending is happy as the boy and girl are united, the old man vindicated, and the villagers pleased with their triumph.

The film shows the village as a place of refuge and solid virtues but the city exerts the stronger attractive force. When the hero is discouraged or perplexed, he returns to the village for understanding and compassion; but not only does he go back to the city, the other villagers go there too, one by one shedding their village dress for that of the city. Though the village is extolled, the city is not deprecated. The village people make good in the big city, but the lesson is not that the village conquers the city, it simply *becomes* the city. The extensive build-up for the grand finale puts in a favorable light the "modern" symphonic treatment of the traditional Arab melody, played by musicians in a concert-hall setting and wearing evening clothes. Finally, the old man from the village unexpectedly

appears at the Opera in white tie and tails and proceeds
to conduct the Western-style orchestra, singers, and dancers. Inasmuch as he had appeared only in a *galabiya* up
to that point, it took me a few moments to recognize him
and then to recover from the shock, but the audience in
the theater felt no such confusion and took it all gleefully
in stride. The film moved between modern urban scenes
and traditional rural ones, showing virtues in each but
making clear that the urban way is the approved one—approved by the characters in the film as well as by the audience, whose origin is rural but whose destiny is urban.

The mass media everywhere, seeking a large audience,
adopt conventional morality even while titillating their
consumers by showing violations of the code. Thus they
flatter the audience by vindicating its values while satisfying its appetite for the new and the sensational. In the
Arab world the mass media face a special problem, that
of censorship (or the threat of it) by the regimes. These
conditions make the mass media there guardians and pro-
moters of both political and cultural orthodoxy. Critical
and analytical tendencies are discouraged. The increase in
education has augmented the audience only for the mass
media, while the independent, thoughtful media for the
few do not gain support and indeed founder and sink for
lack of it. Under the weight of the orthodoxy of the mass
media and political controls, Arab intellectuals and artists
are seriously impeded in their attempt to understand and
portray Arab social life. Thus one writer says, in a book
published by the Institute of Higher Arab Studies of the
Arab League, that Arab society is filled with evils and im-
perfections, a legacy of imperialism and "feudalism" nourished by continuing ignorance and superstition and concealed by hypocrisy. The mass media do nothing to correct
or even to expose such conditions. The author insists that
the Arab artist must not abdicate the office of self-analysis,
and he calls upon Arab society to understand this critical
function. Society, he argues, must learn that the artist does
not really serve the public interest if he merely praises
what exists, affirms accepted morality, and glorifies tradi-

tion. He must be allowed the freedom to criticize, no matter how much his work may seem to be contrary to religious or national pride.[50] Such an independent position is seldom stated nowadays and usually in publications not intended for wide circulation. Yet it represents the point of view of an important section of the educated elite, both modern and conservative.

The view of the conservative older generation of intellectuals is expressed in an observation by a well-known Damascene writer: ". . . the more the Arab countries advance in knowledge, the worse they become in manners and character."[51] This is more than the common complaint of the older generations everywhere about the younger, for manners and morals are changing so rapidly that the governments have had to take notice of them. "Modernism" has quite visibly affected relations between men and women, and this is the most startling change of all. Islam is stricter than other Western religions in forbidding women to make themselves attractive in public, but this prohibition is increasingly violated in women's dress and their greater freedom and mobility. From time to time the authorities take some action, usually half-hearted and ineffective, to halt the trend. Public entertainments feel the stern glance of official prudery now and then. Several years ago Egypt required Oriental dancers to cover themselves from shoulder to ankle, however sheer the material might be. Egyptians are also forbidden to frequent public gambling places, but foreigners are admitted upon the presentation of their passports. Film censorship is concerned as much with sex and violence as with politics. Recently the government canceled a scheduled beauty contest and substituted one to select the most intelligent and athletic girl in Cairo. Often the West is blamed for this corruption of public taste but everyone knows the East has its own forms of loose morals and vice. Sometimes the campaign for public virtue is linked with

[50] al-Nuwayhi, pp. 85–86.
[51] Kurd Ali, p. 184.

the supreme effort to modernize the nation through industrialization, saving, hard work, and unswerving attention to national goals. But it seems unlikely that the general solemnity can be maintained for very long.

As in the West, the cry is now raised in the Arab world that even literary forms not previously intended for mass consumption have been debased. In a recent commentary on the Arab novel Mahmoud Taymur, a celebrated literary man, asserts that too many writers deal only with the surface and the trivia of modern life in the effort to excite and terrorize.[52] Such novels are to be found in all Arab cities, in bookshops, kiosks, held out by peddlers in the streets, and displayed on sidewalks—with garish covers usually showing women not fully dressed, or some violent scene. An American literary critic who traveled in several Arab countries calls this the result of a "series of explosions into a new illiteracy." He compares the process now going on there to one that has already advanced very far in the West: "to be 'literate' sometimes opens new avenues of corruption. That is what has happened throughout the Western world: *Corruptio optima pessima*. The current of the new literacy has followed the course of universal education . . . until now it has struck the Middle East . . ."[53]

A tendency toward cultural uniformity has appeared. There used to be two "Oriental" ways of life, one for the poor and one for the rich, each with its own style and isolated in its own way from that of the foreigner and the Westernized Arab. With the rush to modernism, these two ways are approaching each other as they move toward a dead center of what might be called "Arab modern." Upper-class Oriental elegance in stately homes and gardens behind imposing walls gives way to flashy and colorful villas which the owners are too proud of to hide. Lower-class simplicity gives way to easy sophistication and to boredom with old pastimes as the mass media reach farther and deeper into society. Western observers, having

[52] Taymur, p. 71.
[53] Blackmur, pp. 512, 514.

seen something like this process in their own cultures, may recoil in horror and "warn" the Arabs against debasement. But if this is corruption, the Arab is going to make the most of it. He has had enough of the spiritual joys of poverty and he is ready to be "spoiled" by materialism plain and simple.

The Confrontation of Westerner and Arab

No matter what facet of social life we consider—industry, the family, political organization, and so on—we are struck by the influence of the Westerner in the great changes the Arab is undergoing. This has been a psychological as well as a social process, an encounter of human beings as well as of institutions.

Western power and rule came to the Near East in the modern era after its cultural and religious influence had already been felt. Britain occupied Egypt in 1882 and, with France, succeeded the Ottoman Empire as the major power elsewhere in the area following World War I. This was after the heyday of imperialism, an Indian summer which was relatively mild and short-lived. By the time the West took power in the Arab world imperialism no longer was its own justification—it needed justification at home and before world opinion as "tutelage" or the "restoration of order." Subterfuges and euphemisms for rule were resorted to. For a quarter-century Lord Cromer ruled Egypt with the title of British Agent and Consul-General. After World War I Britain and France were merely "mandatory powers" to which the League of Nations entrusted certain functions in the Arab world. Formal independence had to be granted early under such conditions. Western influence sought to perpetuate itself in various guises, but whatever the form it was opposed by more and more articulate Arabs. The Arab elite did not consider itself in need of instruction. It had a vivid historical memory of Arab-Islamic conquest of large areas including Europe. It believed that it could run its own countries properly. It also resented Western political intervention as a betrayal of the West's own liberal, constitutional, and national ideals which Western-educated Arabs had already imbibed in Western schools before they had felt the power of Western armies. Slowly the Arab elite turned from these ideals, which it had first considered the "secret" of Western power and success, to a more extreme form of nationalism, and to a respect for economic and military power as the essence of that secret.

The West did not colonize the Near East as it did, say, Algeria and before that the New World. Westerners came to conquer and to rule, chiefly, which led to problems different from those created by the confrontation of a European "colony" with a "native" society, but no less personal. From the first, Westerners humiliated Arabs by the very fact of their coming and then by the way they acted in remaining. Their relationship with the Arabs is well expressed in the remark of a British education officer in Egypt. "The Egyptians," he says of the period in which British rule was at its zenith, "a friendly and hospitable people, were cut off from all social intercourse, and it was not considered *de rigueur* for British officials to consort with Egyptians in public."[54]

The capitulations system, under which European powers could try their subjects under their own legal codes, became a particularly flagrant abuse which exacerbated relations with the Arabs. A British police official in Egypt described one aspect of this situation—extreme but indicative—during the Italo-Turkish war in Tripoli in 1911. A Moslem mob in Alexandria demonstrated against the European power and moved toward a district "inhabited largely by low-class European prostitutes and their Greek bullies." He adds: "Within a few minutes bullets were ricochetting off the pavement with every other balcony holding a Greek or other Levantine letting off his revolver into the native crowd below. . . . It was a glaring example of the abuse of the Capitulations; one saw the Egyptian

54 Bowman, p. 40.

police trying to deal with this scum of the Levant, every man of them with a gun in his right hand and his *demotico* (nationality papers) in the other, ready to claim immunity from Egyptian police jurisdiction if interfered with."[55]

It is the fate of those who feel oppressed to imitate their oppressors in the effort to be free of them. The Arabs imitate the West in order to combat it, just as in medieval Spain the Christians adopted Islamic military and religious ideas in order to drive out the Moslems.[56] But it is awkward to admit that one is thus honoring the enemy. Von Grunebaum aptly points out that the triumphant Arab Moslems of the eighth century had little or no hesitation in borrowing from Hellenistic civilization, which was dead, or from India, which was not important to the future of the Islamic empire, or from Iran, which they had defeated. Borrowing in such situations was not an admission of inferiority. But in borrowing from the West in the last century and a half, Arab Moslems, von Grunebaum continues, sought not to perfect themselves as conquerors but rather to overcome the inferiority that made them subordinate to others. So they are now reluctant to admit that they borrow, or they insist that what they "borrow" is originally Arab anyway.[57] Only occasionally does an Arab writer face the issue directly, as Ayyad does when he insists upon the necessity to borrow from the West, points to Arab Moslem borrowing in earlier eras, and reminds us that the West itself owes much to what it borrowed from other civilizations, including the Arab.[58]

It was in their attitude toward the urban intellectuals that the British and French aroused most resentment. The French sought to weaken Arab leadership by making it as French as possible in feeling and taste, using force and outright purchase where loyalty was not otherwise assured. The British followed a different course, attempting simply to

[55] Russell Pasha, pp. 146–47.
[56] Castro, pp. 203–4, 219–20.
[57] von Grunebaum, "Problems of Muslim Nationalism," pp. 24–25, 29.
[58] Ayyad, pp. 468–69.

ignore the educated (as the British preferred to call them, the "half-educated") Arab elite in the cities. They claimed to prefer the solid peasant as a better human being. As a British official in Egypt wrote of Lord Kitchener, who became Consul-General in 1911: "He took up a policy like Lord Cromer's of favoring the peasants and constituted himself their protector and friend. He was quite civil to the intellectuals, and entered into any harmless schemes they put forward; but he was firmly convinced that they were of no importance from a political point of view."[59]

No assumption of the West has proved to be more mistaken than this one. Cromer himself saw that the contact between educated Egyptians and Europeans aroused great resentment among the former, not only because they were held to be inferior but also because they came to believe that there was no justification for the European sense of superiority. The result, Cromer added, was that the educated Egyptian rejected Europe: ". . . though he may himself become partially Europeanized, he will despise European civilization. In what respect, he says to himself, are we Egyptians morally inferior to our teachers? We may be deceitful, untruthful, and unchaste, but we are not one whit worse than those whom we are told to regard as the ultimate product of European civilization. The result is that the Europeanized Egyptian often returns to Egypt in order to become, both by precept and example, an apostle of anti-European ideas."[60] Since Cromer's day it has become clear that the Westernized Arab is not anti-European except in opposing European political influence in the Arab world. Indeed, whenever the Arabs gain independence they immediately adopt Western ways more rapidly than before.

The early Westernized generations of Arabs differ from later ones in several respects. The early ones, in the nineteenth century, learned Western ways in the West itself, where they spent years of study and travel. They went as

[59] Cecil, p. 196.
[60] Cromer, *Modern Egypt*, Vol. 2, p. 239.

already educated members of their own culture; and many of them were also religious. Yet they were greatly impressed by what they saw in the West, especially by parliamentary democracy, freedom of expression and the mastery of the environment through science and technology. They returned with an unashamed willingness to advocate change in their own society, but they were also further estranged from their own cultures by their experience in the West. In contrast, many of the Westernized Arabs in the present century did not go to the West at all but were transformed through contact with those who did, and by attending schools patterned after Western models. Those who did go to the West were less likely to be already established in their careers at home, were younger, and already familiar with Western ways which they could see in their own countries. Their interests turned more to practical politics because the possibility of Arab independence increased with the passage of time and the changing international scene. Therefore, though they were no less separated from the masses in tastes and attitudes than were their predecessors, they did not remain aloof but instead tried to influence the masses through newspapers and political parties. Ultimately, they competed successfully with the Western powers for the control of the Arab world. It was these despised intellectuals who spread nationalist ideas and stirred the imagination of the Arabs, and thus paved the way for the removal of Western political control.

By now many Western influences have been so far accepted in the Near East that it is often difficult to determine whether a man has or has not been in the West at all. Arabs become Westernized at home. Today, except in places like Saudi Arabia and Yemen, he can return from the West to a society of people like himself and live his life within it. He may find that the ideas on public administration or agronomy or elementary education that he learned in the West are not instantly accepted in the government agency where he is employed, but he can at least find a congenial community of others who have been in the West and are equally frustrated for the mo-

ment, or even of those who have become Western in the
Near East. This is the measure of how far social change has
gripped the Arab world: it is now the consequence of the
things Arabs do willingly or those that some Arabs impose
on others. The original impetus from the West has
created local generators of restlessness and aspiration. To a
greater extent than ever before in modern times, Arab
society will be what Arabs make it.

Sources

Wherever possible, the text refers to studies in English but there are a few in French and Arabic. The following list includes nearly all the works referred to in the text. (The main exceptions are publications of the United Nations and of some governments.) Arabic and other names with an article are alphabetized according to next name: e.g., El-Araby will be found under A, al-Munajjid under M.

An asterisk precedes those works in English which are especially useful as further reading on the contemporary Near East and its background.

ABDEL HAKIM, MUHAMMAD SUBHI, *The City of Alexandria* (in Arabic), Maktabat Misr, Cairo, 1958.

ABDEL-RAHMAN, I. H., "The Institute of National Planning. A General Review," U.A.R. Institute of National Planning, Documents and Occasional Notes, No. 2, Cairo, 1960.

ABU ZIKRI, Wajih, "Hind Rustum" (in Arabic), *Armed Forces* (1958), No. 332, pp. 24–26. (Pub. in Cairo by Dept. of Public Affairs, Egyptian Armed Forces.)

ADAMS, JOHN, "Communication and Change in an Egyptian Village," *Middle East Forum* (March 1957), Vol. 32, No. 3, pp. 15–17, 27–31.

AHMAD, CAPT. MUHAMMAD ANWAR ABDEL SALAM, "Nationalism" (in Arabic), *Artillery Magazine* (1958), No. 44, pp. 90–95. (Pub. in Cairo.)

ALDERSON, A. D., *The Structure of the Ottoman Dynasty*, Oxford University Press, London, 1956.

AMMAR, ABBAS M., *The People of Sharqiya*, 2 vols., Royal Geographical Society of Egypt, Cairo, 1944.

* AMMAR, HAMED, *Growing Up in an Egyptian Village*, Routledge and Kegan Paul, London, 1954.

* ANDERSON, J. N. D., *Islamic Law in the Modern World*, New York University Press, New York, 1959.

ANTONIUS, GEORGE, *The Arab Awakening*, Lippincott, Philadelphia, 1939.

EL-ARABY, MUHAMMAD ABDULLAH, "Economics in the Social Structure of Islam," paper delivered at Islamic Colloquium, Lahore, 1958.

ARMSTRONG, LINCOLN, and GORDON K. HIRABAYASHI, "Social Differentiation in Selected Lebanese Villages," *American Sociological Review* (1956), 21:425–34.

————, and RASHID BASHSHUR, "Ecological Patterns and Value Orientations in Lebanon," *Public Opinion Quarterly* (1958), 22:406–15.

* ARNOLD, THOMAS W., *The Caliphate*, Oxford University Press, London, 1924.

ASFOUR, EDMUND Y., *Syria: Development and Monetary Policy*, Harvard University Press, Cambridge, 1959.

AWAD, MOHAMED, "Settlement of Nomadic and Semi-Nomadic Tribal Groups in the Middle East," *International Labor Review* (1959), 79:25–56.

AYROUT, HENRY HABIB, *The Fellaheen*, tr. by Hilary Wayment, Schindler, Cairo, 1945.

AYYAD, MUHAMMAD KAMEL, "The Future of Culture in Arab Society," in Walter Z. Laqueur, ed., *The Middle East in Transition*, Praeger, New York, 1958, pp. 462–77.

BADRE, ALBERT Y., and SIKSEK, SIMON G., *Manpower and Oil in the Arab Countries*, Economic Research Institute, American University of Beirut, Beirut, 1960.

BAGEHOT, WALTER, *Physics and Politics* (1867), Beacon Press, Boston, 1956.

EL-BAHAY, MUHAMMAD, "The Attitude of Islam Towards Science," paper delivered at Islamic Colloquium, Lahore, 1958.

BALL, W. MACMAHON, *Nationalism and Communism in East Asia*, Melbourne University Press, Melbourne, 1952.

AL-BAZZAZ, ABD AR-RAHMAN, "Islam and Arab Nationalism," tr. by Sylvia G. Haim, *Die Welt des Islams* (n.s.) (1954), 3:201–18.

BELING, WILLARD A., *Pan-Arabism and Labor*, Harvard University Press, Cambridge, 1960.

BENNIGSEN, A., "Sultan Galiev: The U.S.S.R. and the Colonial Revolution," in Walter Z. Laqueur, ed., *The Middle East in Transition*, Praeger, New York, 1958, pp. 398–414.

BENNIGSEN, ALEXANDRE, and CHANTAL QUELQUEJAY, *Les Mouvements Nationaux chez les Musulmans de Russie*, Mouton, Paris and The Hague, 1960.

BERGER, MORROE, "Americans From the Arab World," in James Kritzeck and R. Bayly Winder, eds., *The World of Islam*, Macmillan, London, pp. 351–72.

———, *Bureaucracy and Society in Modern Egypt*, Princeton University Press, Princeton, 1957.

———, *Military Elite and Social Change. Egypt Since Napoleon*, Princeton University Center of International Studies, Princeton, 1960.

BERQUE, JACQUES, "Dans le Delta du Nil," *Annales de Géographie* (1955), 64:277–90.

———, *Histoire Sociale d'un Village Egyptien au XXème Siècle*, Mouton, Paris and The Hague, 1957.

———, *Leçon Inaugurale*, 1 December 1956, Collège de France, Paris.

———, "Sur la Structure Sociale de Quelques Villages Egyptiens," *Annales: Economies, Sociétés, Civilisations* (1955), Vol. 10, No. 2.

BLACKMAN, WINIFRED S., *The Fellahin of Upper Egypt*, Harrap, London, 1927.

BLACKMUR, RICHARD, "Toward a Modus Vivendi," *The Kenyon Review* (1954), 16:507–35.

BOURRIENNE, LOUIS ANTOINE FAUVELET DE, *Memoirs of Napoleon Bonaparte*, 1836 ed., ed. R. W. Phipps, 4 vols., Merrill and Baker, New York, n.d.

Bowman, Humphrey, *Middle-East Window*, Longmans, Green, London, 1942.

Browne, W. G., *Travels in Africa, Egypt, and Syria, from the Year 1792 to 1798*, Cadell, Davies, Longman and Rees, London, 1799.

Burckhardt, John Lewis, *Arabic Proverbs*, Quaritch, London, 1875.

Burton, Richard, *The Jew, the Gipsy, and El Islam*, Hutchinson, London, 1898.

Castro, Americo, *Structure of Spanish History*, tr. by Edmund L. King, Princeton University Press, Princeton, 1954.

Cecil, Edward Herbert (Lord), *The Leisure of an Egyptian Official*, Hodder and Stoughton, London, 1921.

Chejne, Anwar G., "Egyptian Attitudes Towards Pan-Arabism," *The Middle East Journal* (1957), 11:253–68.

Churchill, Charles W., *The City of Beirut*, Dar El-Kitab, Beirut, 1954.

Cleland, William Wendell, *The Population Problem in Egypt*, Science Press, Lancaster, Pa., 1936.

Clerget, Marcel, *Le Caire*, 2 vols., Schindler, Cairo, 1934.

Clot-Bey, A. B., *Aperçu Général sur l'Égypte*, 2 vols., Fortin, Masson, Paris, 1840.

Cooley, Charles Horton, *Social Organization* (1909), Scribner's, New York, 1925.

Coon, Carleton S., "Operation Bultiste—Promoting Industrial Development in Saudi Arabia," in H. M. Teaf and P. G. Franck, eds., *Hands Across Frontiers*, Cornell University Press, Ithaca, 1955, pp. 307–61.

Creswell, K. A. C., *A Short Account of Early Muslim Architecture*, Penguin Books, Harmondsworth, England, 1958.

Cromer, Lord, *Modern Egypt*, 2 vols., Macmillan, London, 1908.

———, *Political and Literary Essays, 1908–1913*, Macmillan, London, 1913.

DAGHESTANI, KAZEM, Étude Sociologique sur la Famille Musulmane Contemporaine en Syrie, Ernest Leroux, Paris, 1932.

————, "The Evolution of the Moslem Family in the Middle Eastern Countries," International Social Science Bulletin (1953), 5:681 91.

DAVIS, KINGSLEY, "Population Analysis," in Human Relations Area Files, The Republic of Lebanon, 2 vols., New Haven, 1956, Vol. I, pp. 54–77.

————, "Population Analysis," in Human Relations Area Files, The Republic of Syria, 2 vols., New Haven, Vol. I, pp. 49–77.

————, "Urbanization and the Development of Pre-Industrial Areas," Paul K. Halt and Albert J. Reiss, Jr., eds., Cities and Society, Free Press, Glencoe, Ill., 1957, pp. 120–40.

DICKSON, H. R. P., The Arab of the Desert, Allen, London, 1949.

DOS PASSOS, JOHN, Orient Express, Harper, New York, 1927.

DOUGHTY, CHARLES M., Travels in Arabia Deserta (1888), 3d ed. Random House, New York, 1936.

DOXIADIS ASSOCIATES, La Cité Gouvernementale, Athens, 1959.

————, The Future of the Cities of Nejef and Kufa, Preliminary Report, Athens, 1958.

DOXIADIS, C. A., "Standards of Housing Accommodation and Density," U.N. Department of Economic and Social Affairs, Housing, Building and Planning, No. 9, Sept. 1955, pp. 55–56.

EDDY, WILLIAM A., F.D.R. Meets Ibn Saud, American Friends of the Middle East, New York, 1954.

Egypt, Economic Organization, Annual Report of the Board of Directors, 1957 (in Arabic), Cairo, n.d. (1958).

* E.I.—Encyclopedia of Islam, 4 vols., Brill, Leiden, and Luzac, London, 1908–36.

E.I. (New)—Encyclopedia of Islam. New Edition, Brill, Leiden, and Luzac, Vol. I, London, 1954–60.

EUDIN, X. J., and R. C. NORTH, *Soviet Russia and the East, 1920–1927*, Stanford University Press, Stanford, 1957.

FARÈS, BICHR, "Des Difficultés d'Ordre Linguistique, Culturel et Social que Rencontre un Ecrivain Arabe Moderne Spécialement en Egypte," *Revue des Etudes Islamique* (1936), 3:221–42.

FARIS, NABIH, "The Arabs and Their History," *The Middle East Journal* (1954), 8:155–62.

FAWZY, SAAD EL-DIN, *Social Aspects of Low-Cost Housing in the Northern Sudan*, Sudan Survey Dep't., Khartoum, 1954.

FERRERO, GUGLIELMO, *The Principles of Power*, Putnam's, New York, 1942.

FINNIE, DAVID, "Recruitment and Training of Labor. The Middle East Oil Industry," *The Middle East Journal* (1958), 12:127–43.

FOLEY, DONALD, and others, *The Mediterranean Region and its Cities*, Bureau of Applied Social Research, Columbia University, New York, 1953.

FORSTER, E. M., *Alexandria: A History and a Guide* (1922), 2d ed., Whitehead Morris, Alexandria, 1938.

FRYE, RICHARD N., "Iran and the Unity of the Muslim World," in Richard N. Frye, ed., *Islam and the West*, Mouton, The Hague, 1956, pp. 179–93.

AL-GHAZZALI, MUHAMMAD, *Our Beginning in Wisdom* (1950), tr. by Ismail R. Faruqi, American Council of Learned Societies, Washington, D.C., 1953.

* GIBB, H. A. R., *Modern Trends in Islam*, University of Chicago Press, Chicago, 1947.

* ———, *Mohammedanism*, Oxford University Press, London, 1949.

———, "Social Change in the Near East," in Philip W. Ireland, ed., *The Near East. Problems and Prospects*, University of Chicago Press, Chicago, 1942.

———, and HAROLD BOWEN, *Islamic Society and the West*, Vol. I, Oxford University Press, London. Part I, 1950. Part II, 1957.

GILLESPIE, JAMES M., and GORDON W. ALLPORT, *Youth's Outlook on the Future*, Doubleday Papers in Psychology, No. 15, Doubleday, New York, 1955.

GOITEIN, S. D., "The Rise of the Near Eastern Bourgeoisie in Early Islamic Times," *Journal of World History* (1957), 3:583–604.

* GOLDZIHER, IGNAZ, *Mohammed and Islam*, tr. by Kate Chambers Seelye, Yale University Press, New Haven, 1917.

GOTTMANN, JEAN, *Megalopolis: The Urbanized Northeastern Seaboard of the United States*, Twentieth Century Fund, New York, 1961.

GRANQVIST, HILMA, *Birth and Childhood Among the Arabs*, Soderstrom, Helsinki, 1947.

————, *Marriage Conditions in a Palestinian Village*, Societas Scientiarum Fennica. Commentationes Humanarum Litterarum. III. 8, Helsinki, 1931.

GREENBERG, JOSEPH, *The Influence of Islam on a Sudanese Religion*, Monographs of the American Ethnological Society, No. 10, J. J. Augustin, New York, 1947.

EL-GRITLY, A. A. I., *The Structure of Modern Industry in Egypt*, Government Press, Cairo, 1948 (also in *L'Egypte Contemporaine*, 1947, Nos. 241–42).

* VON GRUNEBAUM, G. E., *Islam. Essays in the Nature and Growth of a Cultural Tradition*, American Anthropological Association, Menasha, Wis., 1955.

————, *Medieval Islam*, University of Chicago Press, Chicago, 1946.

————, "Problems of Muslim Nationalism," in Richard N. Frye, ed., *Islam and the West*, Mouton, The Hague, 1956, pp. 7–29.

HAIM, SYLVIA, "Arabic Antisemitic Literature," *Jewish Social Studies* (1955), 17:307–12.

* ————, "Islam and the Theory of Arab Nationalism," in Walter Z. Laqueur, ed., *The Middle East in Transition*, Praeger, New York, 1958, pp. 280–307.

EL-HAKIM, TEWFIK, *Maze of Justice*, tr. by A. S. Eban, Harvill Press, London, 1947.

HALLSWORTH, J. A., "Freedom of Association and Industrial Relations in the Countries of the Near and Middle East," *International Labor Review* (1954), 70:363–384, 526–541.

* HAMADY, SANIA, *Temperament and Character of the Arabs*, Twayne Publishers, New York, 1960.

HARBISON, FREDERICK, and IBRAHIM ABDELKADER IBRAHIM, *Human Resources for Egyptian Enterprise*, McGraw-Hill, New York, 1958.

HARVARD UNIVERSITY LAW SCHOOL, International Program in Taxation, *Papers and Proceedings of the Conference on Agricultural Taxation and Economic Development*, Cambridge, 1954.

HIRABAYASHI, GORDON K., and MAY ISHAQ, "Social Change in Jordan," *American Journal of Sociology* (1958), 64:36–40.

HIRABAYASHI, GORDON K., and M. FATHALLA EL KHATIB, "Communication and Political Awareness in the Villages of Egypt," *Public Opinion Quarterly* (1958), 22:357–63.

* HITTI, PHILIP K., *History of the Arabs* (1937), 5th ed. Macmillan, London, 1953.

HOSNY, A., "The Economic Structure of Egypt (A Summary Survey)" (mimeographed), Social Research Center of the American University at Cairo, Nov. 1959.

HOURANI, ALBERT H., *Minorities in the Arab World*, Oxford University Press, London, 1947.

―――, "Race and Related Ideas in the Near East," in *Race Relations in World Perspective*, ed. Andrew W. Lind, University of Hawaii Press, Honolulu, 1955, Ch. 6.

* ―――, *Syria and Lebanon*, Oxford University Press, London, 1946.

HUDAYB, COL. ABDEL TAWWAB, "Our Social Revolution" (in Arabic), *Army Magazine* (1956), No. 72, pp. 132–38. (Pub. in Cairo at al-Abbasiyah Barracks.)

HUSAINI, ISHAK MUSA, *The Moslem Brethren*, Khayat, Beirut, 1956.

HUSSEIN, AZIZA, "The Role of Women in Social Reform in Egypt," *The Middle East Journal* (1953), 7:440–50.

HUSSEIN, TAHA, *An Egyptian Childhood,* tr. by E. H. Paxton, Routledge, London, 1932.

HUZZAYIN, SULEIMAN, "Historical and Cultural Setting of Plans for Social Reform in the Arab East," in *Second Social Welfare Seminar for Arab States of the Middle East* (U.N., 1950), Government of Egypt, Ministry of Social Affairs, Cairo, 1950.

* IBN KHALDUN, *The Muqaddimah,* 3 vols., tr. by Franz Rosenthal, Bollingen Foundation, New York, 1958. *An Arab Philosophy of History,* tr. by Charles Issawi, John Murray, London, 1950.

I.B.R.D.—see International Bank for Reconstruction and Development.

INKELES, ALEX, "Social Change in Soviet Russia," in *Freedom and Control in Modern Society,* ed. Morroe Berger, Theodore Abel, and Charles H. Page, Van Nostrand, New York, 1954.

INTERNATIONAL BANK FOR RECONSTRUCTION AND DEVELOPMENT, *The Economic Development of Iraq,* The Johns Hopkins Press, Baltimore, 1952.

———, *The Economic Development of Jordan,* The Johns Hopkins Press, Baltimore, 1957.

———, *The Economic Development of Syria,* The Johns Hopkins Press, Baltimore, 1955.

IRELAND, PHILIP W., *Iraq: A Study in Political Development,* Cape, London, 1937.

ISSAWI, CHARLES, "Economic and Social Foundations of Democracy in the Middle East," in Walter Z. Laqueur, ed., *The Middle East in Transition,* Praeger, New York, 1958, pp. 33–51.

* ———, *Egypt at Midcentury,* Oxford University Press, London and New York, 1954.

IVERSEN, CARL, and others, *A Report on Monetary Policy in Iraq,* Baghdad, 1954.

IVERSON, KENNETH R., "The Importance of Rural Credit Expansion," in Harvey P. Hall, ed., *Middle East*

Resources, Middle East Institute, Washington, D.C., 1954, pp. 78–87.

JANE, CECIL, *Liberty and Despotism in Spanish America*, Oxford University Press, London, 1929.

JARGY, SIMON, "De Bandoeng au Caire: la Conférence de Solidarité des Peuples Afro-Asiatiques," *Orient* (1958), 2:59–71.

JARVIS, C. S., *Yesterday and Today in the Sinai*, Houghton, Boston, 1932.

DE JOUVENEL, BERTRAND, *The Ethics of Redistribution*, Cambridge University Press, Cambridge, 1952.

KEDOURIE, ELIE, "Pan-Arabism and British Policy," in Walter Z. Laqueur, ed., *The Middle East in Transition*, Praeger, New York, 1958, pp. 100–11.

KHADDURI, MAJID, *Independent Iraq*, Oxford University Press, London, 1951.

———, "The Role of the Military in Middle East Politics," *American Political Science Review* (1953), 47:511–24.

KHURI, MAJOR IBRAHIM, "Material and Moral Mobilization of Human Resources for War" (in Arabic), *Military Magazine* (1958), 8:26–34. (Pub. in Damascus by G.H.Q., 3d Div., Syrian Army.)

KINCH, E. A., "Social Effects of the Oil Industry in Iraq," *International Labor Review* (1957), 75:193–206.

KINSEY, ALFRED C., and others, *Sexual Behavior in the Human Female*, Saunders, Philadelphia, 1953.

KOESTNER, N., "A French Contribution to the Problem of 'Underdevelopment,'" *Kyklos* (1957), 10:473–79.

* *The Koran*, tr. by J. M. Rodwell, Everyman's Library, No. 380, Dutton, New York.

KOTB, SAYED, *Social Justice in Islam*, tr. by John B. Hardie, American Council of Learned Societies, Washington, D.C., 1953.

KURD ALI, MUHAMMAD, *Memoirs of Muhammad Kurd Ali. A Selection* (1948–49), tr. by Khalil Totah, American Council of Learned Societies, Washington, D.C., 1954.

LANDAU, JACOB M., *Parliaments and Parties in Egypt*, Praeger, New York, 1954.

LANE-POOLE, STANLEY, *The Story of Cairo*, 2d ed., Dent, London, 1906.

* LAQUEUR, WALTER Z., *Communism and Nationalism in the Middle East*, Praeger, New York, 1956.

————, *The Soviet Union and the Middle East*, Praeger, New York, 1959.

LEBKICHER, ROY, and others, *Aramco Handbook*, Arabian American Oil Co., New York, 1960.

* LERNER, DANIEL, *The Passing of Traditional Society*, The Free Press, Glencoe, Ill., 1958.

* LEVY, REUBEN, *The Social Structure of Islam*, Cambridge University Press, Cambridge, 1957.

* LEWIS, BERNARD, *The Arabs in History* (1950), Harper Torchbooks, New York, 1960.

————, "The Impact of the French Revolution on Turkey," *Cahiers d'Histoire Mondiale* (1953), 1:105–25.

————, "The Islamic Guilds," *Economic History Review* (1937), 8 (1st series):20–37.

LOCK, MAX, "Town Planning in the Middle East with Special Reference to Iraq and Jordan," Town and Country Planning Summer School, Bangor, 1958.

LOUTFY, ABDEL HAMID ALY, "Birth Control. A Sociological Study in the Population Problem of Egypt," unpublished thesis, Institute of Sociology and Social Science, Alexandria University, 1950.

MacIVER, ROBERT M., "The Historical Pattern of Social Change," *Journal of Social Philosophy* (1936), 2:35–54.

————, *Society: A Textbook of Sociology*, Rinehart, Holt, and Winston, New York, 1937.

————, and CHARLES H. PAGE, *Society—An Introductory Analysis*, Rinehart, New York, 1949.

McLEAN, W. H., *Regional and Town Planning*, Crosby Lockwood and Son, London, 1930.

* MAJDALANY, GEBRAN, "The Arab Socialist Movement," in Walter Z. Laqueur, ed., *The Middle East in Transition*, Praeger, New York, 1958, pp. 337–50.

MANDOUR, MUHAMMAD, *Journey in the Socialist World* (in Arabic), Dar al-Tab' al-Haditha, Cairo, 1957.

MARÇAIS, WILLIAM, "L'Islam et la Vie Urbaine," Académie des Inscriptions et Belle-Lettres, *Comptes Rendus des Séances de l'Année 1928*, Paris, 1928, pp. 86–100.

MAREI, SAYED, *Agrarian Reform in Egypt*, Imprimerie de l'Institut Français d'Archéologie Oriental, Cairo, 1957.

MARGOLIUTH, D. S., *The Early Development of Mahammedanism*, Constable, London, 1914.

MAROUF, MAROUF KHALIL I., "The Tendency to Marriage Postponement in the Middle Class," unpublished thesis, Institute of Sociology and Social Science, Alexandria University, 1951.

MELIKIAN, LEVON, "Some Correlates of Authoritarianism in Two Cultural Groups," unpublished Ph.D. thesis, Columbia University, New York, 1955.

————, and E. TERRY PROTHRO, "Goals Chosen by Arab Students in Response to Hypothetical Situations," *The Journal of Social Psychology* (1957), 46:3–9.

————, and E. TERRY PROTHRO, "Sexual Behavior of University Students in the Arab Near East," *The Journal of Abnormal and Social Psychology* (1954), 49:59–64.

MITO, MUHAMMAD ABD ELMONEIM S., "The Social Change of Daughters' Position in Egyptian Moslem Middle Class Families in Alexandria," unpublished thesis, Institute of Sociology and Social Science, Alexandria University, 1953.

AL-MUNAJJID, SALAH AL-DIN, *Sexual Life of the Arabs* (in Arabic), Dar El Kutub, Beirut, 1958.

MUNICIPALITY OF CAIRO, Planning Commission, *Master Plan of Cairo*, Cairo, 1957.

MURAD, COL. ALI MUNIR, "Agricultural and Food Resources and their Effect on the War Effort" (in Arabic), *Army Magazine* (1958), No. 68, pp. 30–35. (Pub. in Cairo at al-Abbasiyah Barracks.)

MURRAY, G. W., *Sons of Ishmael*, Routledge, London, 1935.

* MUSIL, ALOIS, *Manners and Customs of the Rwala Bedouins*, American Geographical Society, New York, 1928.

NAGUIB, MOHAMMED, *Egypt's Destiny*, Doubleday, New York, 1955.

* NASSER, GAMAL ABDEL, *Egypt's Liberation. The Philosophy of the Revolution*, Public Affairs Press, Washington, D.C., 1955.

————, "The Egyptian Revolution," *Foreign Affairs* (1955), 33:199–211.

NIAZI, MUSTAFA, *Cairo* (in Arabic), Anglo-Egyptian Bookshop, Cairo, n.d. (probably 1958 or 1959).

NUSEIBEH, HAZEM ZAKI, *The Ideas of Arab Nationalism*, Cornell University Press, Ithaca, New York, 1956.

AL-NUWAYHI, MUHAMMAD, *The Nature of Art and the Responsibility of the Artist* (in Arabic), Institute of Higher Arab Studies, Arab League, Cairo, 1958.

PAUTY, EDMOND, "La Défense de l'Ancienne Ville du Caire et de ses Monuments," *Bulletin de l'Institut Français d'Archéologie Orientale*, Cairo, 1931, Vol. XXXI, pp. 135–76.

PENROSE, STEPHEN B., *That They May Have Life: The Story of the American University of Beirut 1866–1941*, Trustees of the A.U.B., New York, 1941.

PIRENNE, HENRI, *Economic and Social History of Medieval Europe*, Harcourt, Brace, New York, n.d.

————, *A History of Europe*, Norton, New York, 1939.

————, *Medieval Cities*, Doubleday Anchor Books, New York, 1956.

PRESCOTT, MILES, "Rural Statistical Survey in Lebanon," *The Middle East Institute Newsletter* (Feb. 1953), Vol. 5, No. 5, pp. 6–8.

PROTHRO, E. TERRY, and LEVON H. MELIKIAN, "The California Public Opinion Scale in an Authoritarian Culture," *Public Opinion Quarterly* (1953), 17:353–62.

——, "Social Distance and Social Change in the Near East," *Sociology and Social Research* (1952), 37:3–11.

QUINT, MALCOLM, "The Idea of Progress in an Iraqi Village," *The Middle East Journal* (1958), 12:369–84.

RADWAN, ABU AL-FUTOUH AHMAD, *Old and New Forces in Egyptian Education*, Teachers College, Columbia University, New York, 1951.

REPUBLIC OF IRAQ, *The 14th July Revolution in Its First Year* (in Arabic), Baghdad, 1959.

RENGGREN, HELMER, *Islam, Aslama and Muslim* (Horae Soederblomiane, II), Gleerup, Uppsala, 1949.

RIZK, HANNA, "Fertility Patterns in Selected Areas of Egypt," unpublished Ph.D. thesis, Princeton University, 1959.

——, "The Individual and Society," in *Arab Society* (in Arabic), Institute of Arab Studies, American University of Beirut, 1953.

ROSE, S., "The Asian Socialist Conference of 1953," in G. F. Hudson, ed., *Far Eastern Affairs: One*, St. Antony's Papers, No. 2, Chatto and Windus, London, 1957, pp. 79–93.

ROSENTHAL, FRANZ, *A History of Muslim Historiography*, Brill, Leiden, 1952.

RUSSELL PASHA, SIR THOMAS, *Egyptian Service, 1902–1946*, John Murray, London, 1949.

EL SADAT, ANWAR, *Revolt on the Nile*, Wingate, London, 1957.

SALEM, ELIE, "Form and Substance: A Critical Examination of the Arabic Language," *Middle East Forum* (July 1958), Vol. 33, No. 7, pp. 17–19.

SALIBA, JAMIL, *Trends of Thought in Syria and Lebanon* (in Arabic), Institute of Higher Arab Studies, Arab League, Cairo, 1958.

SANTAYANA, GEORGE, *The Last Puritan*, Scribner's, New York, 1936.

* DE SANTILLANA, DAVID, "Law and Society," in Thomas
Arnold and Alfred Guillaume, eds., *The Legacy of
Islam*, Oxford University Press, London, 1931, pp.
284–310.

SARHAN, EL-DEMERDASH ABDEL-MEGUID, *Interests and
Culture*, Contributions to Education, No. 959, Teachers College, Columbia University, New York, 1950.

SARTON, GEORGE, *The Incubation of Western Culture in
the Middle East*, Library of Congress, Washington,
D.C., 1951.

————, "Islamic Science," in T. Cuyler Young, ed., *Near
Eastern Culture and Society*, Princeton University
Press, Princeton, 1951, Ch. 5.

SAYIGH, YUSIF A., "Lebanon: Special Economic Problems
Arising from a Special Structure," *Middle East Economic Papers 1957*, Economic Research Institute,
American University of Beirut, 1958, pp. 60–88.

————, "Management-Labor Relations in Selected Arab
Countries: Major Aspects and Determinants," *International Labor Review* (1958), 77:519–37.

* SCHACHT, JOSEPH, "The Law," in Gustave von Grunebaum, ed., *Unity and Variety in Muslim Civilization*,
University of Chicago Press, Chicago, 1955, pp. 65–
86.

————, "Pre-Islamic Background and Early Development
of Jurisprudence," in Majid Khadduri and Herbert
J. Liebesny, eds., *Law in the Middle East*, The Middle East Institute, Washington, D.C., 1955, Vol. I,
Ch. II.

SEDKY, MONA, "Groups in Alexandria, Egypt," *Social Research* (1955), 22:441–50.

SENIOR, NASSAU WILLIAM, *Conversations and Journals in
Egypt and Malta*, ed. M. C. M. Simpson, 2 vols.,
Sampson Low, Marston, Searle, and Rivington, London, 1882.

SHAFIK, DORIA RAGAI, *La Femme et le Droit Religieux
de l'Egypte Contemporaine*, Paul Guethner, Paris,
1940.

SHERMAN, A. V., "Intellectual Ferment in the Middle East," *Soviet Survey* (June–July 1957), No. 16–17, pp. 22–26.

AL-SHIHABI, MAJOR ABDEL SHAKUR SALIH, "Health Insurance" (in Arabic), *Fleet Magazine* (1955), 3:29–32. (Pub. in Cairo by Naval Forces of Egypt.)

SIMMONS, JAMES S., and others, *Global Epidemiology*, 3 vols., Lippincott, Philadelphia, 1944–55.

SMITH, WILFRED CANTWELL, *Islam in Modern History*, Princeton University Press, Princeton, 1957.

SOCONY-VACUUM Co., Cairo, Industrial Relations Department, "Survey of Laborers' Living Conditions," unpublished study, 1953.

SPECTOR, IVAR, *The Soviet Union and the Muslim World 1917–1956*, University of Washington, Seattle, 1956.

STRAUSS, E., "The Social Isolation of Ahl Adh-Dhimma," in O. Komlos, ed., *Etudes Orientales à la Mémoire de Paul Hirschler*, Allamositott Kertesz-Nyomda, Karcag, Budapest, 1950, pp. 73–94.

TAYMUR, MAHMUD, *Fiction in the Literature of the Arab* (in Arabic), Institute of Higher Arab Studies, Arab League, Cairo, 1958.

"This Revolution" (in Arabic), unsigned editorial, *The Military Engineers*, Jan. 1956, pp. 3–6. (Pub. in Cairo.)

"This Worker Lives Under 165° of Heat" (in Arabic), unsigned, *Armed Forces* (1958), No. 332, pp. 22–3. (Pub. in Cairo by Dep't. of Public Affairs, Egyptian Armed Forces.)

TYAN, EMILE, *Histoire de l'Organisation Judiciare en Pays d'Islam*, 2 vols., Recueil Sirey, Paris, 1938, 1943.

———, *Institutions du Droit Public Musulman*, 2 vols., Recueil Sirey, Paris, 1954, 1956.

U.K., Board of Trade, *Report of the United Kingdom Trade Mission to the Egyptian Region of the United Arab Republic* (March 1960), H.M.S.O., London, 1960.

UNESCO, *Compulsory Education in the Arab States* (Studies on Compulsory Education, No. 16) Paris, 1956.

UNWIN, GEORGE, report of a paper on "Eastern Factors in the Growth of Modern Cities: Baghdad and St. Nicholas," *Journal of the Manchester Egyptian and Oriental Society* (1916), 5:13–17.

————, *Studies in Economic History. The Collected Papers of George Unwin*, ed. R. H. Tawney, Macmillan, London, 1927.

VATIKIOTIS, P. J., *The Egyptian Army in Politics*, University of Indiana Press, Bloomington, 1961.

VESEY-FITZGERALD, S. G., "Nature and Sources of the Shari'a," in Majid Khadduri and Herbert J. Liebesny, eds., *Law in the Middle East*, The Middle East Institute, Washington, D.C., 1955, Vol. I, Ch. IV.

* WARRINER, DOREEN, *Land Reform and Development in the Middle East*, Royal Institute of International Affairs, London and New York, 1957.

WATT, W. MONTGOMERY, *Free Will and Predestination in Early Islam*, Luzac, London, 1948.

————, *Muhammad at Mecca*, Oxford University Press, London, 1953.

WEIR, JOHN M., and others, "An Evaluation of Health and Sanitation in Egyptian Villages," *Journal of the Egyptian Public Health Association* (1952), 27:55–122.

WENSINCK, A. J., *The Muslim Creed*, Cambridge University Press, Cambridge, 1932.

WESTERMARCK, EDWARD, *Pagan Survivals in Mohammedan Civilization*, Macmillan, London, 1933.

————, *Wit and Wisdom in Morocco*, Routledge, London, 1930.

WEULERSSE, JACQUES, *Paysans de Syrie et du Proche-Oriént*, Gallimard, Paris, 1946.

WILMINGTON, MARTIN W., "Aspects of Moneylending in the Northern Sudan," *Middle East Journal* (1955), 9:139–46.

WILSON, GODFREY and MONICA, *The Analysis of Social Change*, Cambridge University Press, Cambridge, 1954.

YAUKEY, DAVID, *Fertility Differences in a Modernizing Country: A Survey of Lebanese Couples*, Princeton University Press, Princeton, 1961.

YOUNG, GEORGE, *Egypt*, Scribner's, New York, 1927.

ZABALAWI, CAPT. SHARAF AL-DIN, "Military Education and Character Training" (in Arabic), *Military Magazine* (1958), 8:49–54. (Pub. in Damascus by G.H.Q., 3d Div., Syrian Army.)

ZIADEH, FARHAT J., "Equality (*Kafa'ah*) in the Muslim Law of Marriage," *The American Journal of Comparative Law* (1957), 6:503–17.

ZIADEH, NICOLA, *Syria and Lebanon*, Benn, London, 1957.

ZURAYK, CONSTANTINE K., *The Meaning of the Disaster* (1948), tr. by R. Bayly Winder, Khayat, Beirut, 1956.

———, *Ourselves and History* (in Arabic), Dar al-Ilm li al-Malayin, Beirut, 1959.

ZWEMER, SAMUEL, *Heirs of the Prophets*, Moody Press, Chicago, 1946.

———, *Studies in Popular Islam*, Macmillan, New York, 1939.

Index

ANCHOR BOOKS